THE HISTORY OF RUSSIA

The Twentieth-Century

Professors Alexander A. Danilov,
Michael M. Gorinov, Sergei V. Leonov,
Ekaterina P. Lugovskaya, Alexander S. Senyavski,
and Alexander P. Naumov

Translated by
Galina Ustinova

Translated and Edited by
Vincent E. Hammond

The Heron Press
1996

Library of Congress Cataloging-in-Publication Data

The history of Russia : the twentieth-century / Alexander A. Danilov
. . . [et al.] ; translated by Galina Ustinova ; translated and edited
by Vincent E. Hammond.
    416p. 23cm.
  Includes bibliographical references and index.
  ISBN 0-9649764-0-4 (pbk.)
  1. Soviet Union—History. I. Danilov, A. A. (Alexander A.)
II. Hammond, V. E. (Vincent E.)
DK266.H439 1996
947—dc20   96-25266
                                      CIP

© 1996 by Heron Press
All rights reserved
Manufactured in the United States of America

ISBN 0-9649764-0-4

Contents

Introduction 1
CHAPTER 1—THE OCTOBER REVOLUTION 25
Europe in 1917 25
Perspectives on Social Development and the Balance of Forces 28
The Growth of Revolutionary Elements 37
The July Uprising and Further Political Polarization 43
The Kornilovshchina 49
The Course of the Bolsheviks to an Armed Uprising 53
The October Coup in Petrograd 58

CHAPTER 2—THE CIVIL WAR AND THE FORMATION OF THE BOLSHEVIK REGIME 69
Europe at the End of the Period between 1917 and 1920 69
The Formation of the Soviet State 76
The Treaty of Brest-Litovsk 86
The Turning Point in the Spring of 1918 90
The Civil War in Russia 96

CHAPTER 3—RUSSIA DURING NEP 102
The USSR and International Relations in the 1920s 102
Russia at the End of the Civil War: The Kronstadt Revolt 109
The NEP Concept: Its Origins and Its Basic Features 114
The Economy 117
Politics 122
Culture 135
The Contradictions of the NEP Social Model 140

CHAPTER 4—THE CONSTRUCTION OF SOCIALISM BY COERCION 144
The World and the USSR in the 1930s 144
Developing Society in the Late 1920s and Early 1930s 152
The Anatomy of Stalinist Modernization 158
The Formation of the Totalitarian Regime in the USSR 166
Culture in the 1930s 182

**CHAPTER 5—THE SOVIET UNION
IN THE SECOND WORLD WAR (1939-1945)** 193
The Sources of the World Conflict 193
The Beginning of the Second World War 202
The Beginning of the Great Patriotic War 210
The Turning Point in the War 219
The Victory over Fascism 226
The Defeat of Japan 228

**CHAPTER 6—THE CLIMAX OF TOTALITARIANISM:
THE USSR (1945-53)** 231
From the Anti-Hitler Coalition to the Cold War 231
The Choice of an Economic Development Model 241
The Time of Unrealized Hopes 248

CHAPTER 7—THE USSR DURING THE THAW 262
The Collective Leadership and the Rise of Khrushchev (1953-58) 262
    The Death of Stalin and the Beria Plot 262
    The Twentieth Party Congress 273
    The Liberalization of the Political Regime 278
    The Power Struggle 281
The Premiership of N.S. Khrushchev (1958-64) 283
Economic and Social Development 284
The Development of Culture 290
Foreign Policy 292
Politics and Society in the 1960s and Khrushchev's Dismissal 295

**CHAPTER 8—THE PATH TO GLOBAL CRISIS:
THE USSR UNDER BREZHNEV (1964-82)** 302
New Reform Attempts 302
Authority and Society from the Mid-Sixties to the Early Eighties 307
The USSR and the World in the Brezhnev Era 316

**Chapter 9—"PERESTROIKA"
THE NEW RUSSIA (1985-1994)** 323
The Pre-History of Perestroika 323
The Search for Ways to Perfect Socialism 326
Perestroika in Crisis 329
Glasnost and the "Revolution of Minds" 337

New Political Thinking 342
The August Coup and the End of Perestroika 345
The New Russia 348

CHAPTER 10—RUSSIA AND THE WEST 359
Roots of the Originality of the Motherland's History 365
The October Revolution 367
Russian Reform: Characteristics and Landmarks 370

BIBLIOGRAPHY 376
The October Revolution 376
The Civil War and the Formation of the Bolshevik Regime 377
Russia during NEP 377
The USSR on the Road to the Construction of Socialism 378
The Soviet Union in the Second World War 379
The Climax of Totalitarianism: The Soviet Union (1945-1953) 380
The "Thaw" 381
On the Road to Global Crisis: The USSR (1964-1985) 382

A SHORT CHRONOLOGY 383

INDEX 391

PREFACE

The Twentieth Century is the first volume to appear in English of the two volume *History of Russia* originally written in Russian by an authors' collective headed by Dr. Alexander A. Danilov and edited by Dr. Sergei Leonov, Professors of History at the Moscow State Pedagogical University. *The History,* which is being published in the Russian Federation by VLADOS under the title of *Istoriia otechestva* (*History of the Motherland*), is the first non-Marxist synthesis of Russian history written by Russia's leading historians since Sergei M. Soloviev's *History of Russia since Earliest Times* in the later half of the nineteenth century.

The events of the 1980s convinced Russia's leading historians of the need to reinterpret her historical development in light of communism's failure and the success of democracy and free enterprise. The History faculty of Russia's premier teacher training institution, Moscow State Pedagogical University, decided to present the results of the reassessment of Russia's past in a college text that would introduce students to the "new thinking" in the historical profession.

The authors of *The Twentieth Century* summarized the results of their research and analyzed Russia's recent past in *Essays on the Motherland*, a series of interpretative essays on the nation's development from the Great Reforms of the 1860s to the present. As the events of the late 1980s and early 1990s unfolded the authors saw communism as a failed "Slavophile" ideology which had to be replaced by western democracy and free enterprise for Russia to take her rightful place among the modern democratic states of the world. They maintained that Lenin's incorporation of the conspiratorial legacy of earlier Russian revolutionaries (Nicholas Chernyshevsky, Sergei Nechaev, and Peter Tkachev) into Bolshevism, his utilization of the revolutionary potential of the peasants (long recognized by Russia's Social Revolutionaries), and Stalin's creation of "socialism in one country" through the administrative-command economy resemble Slavophilism by adapting Marxism to Russian conditions.

The History of Russia is a comprehensive survey of the political, economic, social, and cultural history of Russia. The volume on the twentieth century focuses on the October Revolution and the birth of the Bolshevik state, the partial retreat to capitalism during NEP, the strengthening of the party's control of the Soviet state, and the creation, practice, and failure of the left totalitarian model known as the administrative-command system under Joseph Stalin, Nikita Khrushchev, and Leonid Brezhnev. The volume concludes with an analysis of perestroika and an assessment of Russia's future.

The authors attribute the Bolshevik victory to the failure of the other political parties to cooperate with one another within the power vacuum created by the fall of tsarism in February 1917. Unlike their western counterparts, the liberals (Kadets and Progressives) did not attract the support of workers or peasants and were unwilling to cooperate with the socialist parties (Social Revolutionaries and Mensheviks) who did have mass appeal. Although liberals served with socialists in several coalition governments, neither the liberal Prime Minister Prince George Lvov nor his socialist (Trudovik) successor Aleksandr Kerensky was willing to make a separate peace with Germany and distribute the land to the peasants. Lacking a program with mass appeal, the Provisional Government was actually its own worst enemy. It survived the July demonstrations in Petrograd, which nearly brought the Bolsheviks to power, only to rely on them to defeat the Kornilovshchina, General Lavr Kornilov's abortive attempt to restore order through a military dictatorship with himself as dictator.

The Bolsheviks' role in Kornilov's defeat was the catalyst which led to the successful October Revolution. The stigma of collaboration with the Germans stemming from Lenin's return to Russia in a sealed railway car provided by the Germans, which Kerensky had used to defeat the Bolsheviks in July, was removed and the Bolsheviks emerged as heroes of the revolution. While the Bolsheviks were winning over the local soviets and the Petrograd garrison, the Kadets, Mensheviks, and Social Revolutionaries who supported the Provisional Government were unable to agree on a common program. Instead of extricating Russia from the war and implementing a land reform program, the Provisional Government waited until the peasants took matters into their own hands in the late summer by seizing the landlords' land, by withholding grain, and by bringing the cities to the edge of starvation. The deteriorating economic situation and the weakness of the state power contributed to the radicalization of the masses which, as the authors observe, turned democracy into anarchy.

Convinced that the time was ripe, Lenin persuaded a reluctant Central Committee to launch the October Revolution despite the initial opposition of Grigory Zinoviev and Lev Kamenev, two distinguished Old Bolsheviks. Working through the Military Revolutionary Committee established by the Bolshevik-dominated Petrograd Soviet, the Bolsheviks were easily able to take power on October 25 and 26, 1917 (November 7 and 8). The flexibility and unity of the Bolsheviks had triumphed over the rigidity and disunity of the other parties.

The authors' discussion of Lenin's New Economic Policy (NEP) contributes to our understanding of one of the most important issues in the historiography of the Soviet period. The traditional view presented in Nicholas Riasanovsky's *History of Russia,* 5th. edition, was that NEP "proved a great economic success" by restoring industry to the 1913 level of productivity and bringing slightly more land under cultivation than before the war. The party's fear of the restoration of capitalism by the growing number of urban Nepmen and rural kulaks rather than economy's performance caused the party to replace NEP with a command economy. The revisionist view discussed in John Thompson's *A Vision Unfulfilled: Russia and the Soviet Union in the Twentieth Century* emphasizes NEP's limitations while conceding its significance in Russia's economic recovery during the 1920s. Although industrial output was close to the prewar level by 1927, the state could not provide the funds to modernize Russia's technologically backward prewar plants and machinery. The workers "abandoned by their unions, ignored by the proletarian state, toiling under their old bosses, lacking job security, and paid poorly . . . lamented the loss of their revolution." Agrarian output neared the prewar level by 1928, but the number of returning soldiers and unemployed urban workers swelled the ranks of the peasants who demanded land.

The evidence presented by the authors supports the revisionist view. Industrial productivity grew rapidly enough (especially heavy industry) to almost reach the prewar level by the late 1920s, but the economy was less efficient. Recent research by Russian scholars has found that industrial output was 12-15% and per capita national income was 17-20% lower in 1928 than in 1913. The restoration effect was responsible for most of the gains as the prewar plants and machinery which had stood idle during the revolution and civil war resumed their operations. Since Russia's technology was already behind western Europe and the United States before the war, the need to finance modernization caused the Bolshevik government to extract more and more private capital from the industrial and consumer sectors through high taxes and rents.

The restoration effect also explains the recovery of agriculture during the 1920s. NEP was able to bring almost all of the land cultivated before the revolution under cultivation by 1923 by planting the old arable land seized by the peasants during the civil war. Although the 1925 harvest was actually 20.7% above the prewar level, the increase in industrial crops in the later 1920s reduced the grain harvest while the breakup of the larger and more efficient farms leased by the kulaks (who were trying to escape high taxes) lowered agrarian productivity. This reduced the size of the grain exports which provided foreign capital for modernization.

The authors attribute the demise of the New Economic Policy to the "inconsistencies in the NEP model" which became more pronounced during the last years of reconstruction. Although the state required a large influx of capital to modernize industry, foreign capital was cut off by the Bolsheviks' refusal to repay the old regime's debts and to compensate foreigners for the nationalization of their factories. The party's fear of restoring capitalism prevented it from allowing the accumulation and utilization of private capital. The party was also afraid of the growing demands of the private sector for political guarantees to preserve its economic position while the workers in the cities and the poor peasants in the countryside, who filled the ranks of the party and state apparatus, hated Nepmen and kulaks and wanted to create a genuinely socialist economy.

The abandonment of NEP and the adoption of the left model of building socialism in one country through rapid industrialization and collectivized agriculture, first proposed by Evgeny Preobrazhensky, led to the creation of the administrative-command system (left totalitarianism). The decision to attain industrial self-sufficiency or autarky by emphasizing the development of capital-intensive heavy industry greatly expanded the scope of central planning and the size of the bureaucracy. The collectivization of agriculture, which ensured the uninterrupted delivery of grain to the cities and provided the government with the capital needed to finance industrialization, required coercion to suppress the peasants' resistance, resulting in perhaps five to eight million deaths and the imprisonment of two million in state labor camps under the GULAG.

The need for a "chief engineer" to lead the construction of socialism in one country in a hostile world inevitably caused the concentration of power in the hands of the general secretary, who stood at the top of the administrative-command system. Stalin's personal ambition and his ability to manipulate the party apparatus determined the scope of that authority. Stalin's control of the party after the demise of the Right Deviation in 1929 failed to eliminate all of the opposition within the party since Sergei Kirov, the Leningrad party boss, was more popular than the general secretary. Kirov's assassination on December 1, 1934, which Stalin either ordered or organized, began the Great Purges of the 1930s. Almost all of Lenin's former comrades, the Old Guard, and all actual or potential opposition were eliminated.

The authors conclude that the mass repression and periodic purges were inherent in the administrative-command system required by the rapid industrialization model. The expanded scope of planning and the potential for social unrest caused by the excessive concentration of resources in some, to the neglect of other, sectors of the economy required firm control by the center. During the period the shift in authority from the old bureaucracy to the extraordinary party organizations (the political departments of the Machine Tractor Stations, collective farms, and factories) and the secret police confirmed the role of the party as the "leading instrument" in the administrative-command system. The "total ideological mobilization" of the workers, who were given the illusion of being the masters of their own country, was needed to keep the workers "in a state of mass preparedness resembling mobilization." Fear for their lives, families, or careers stimulated productivity and prevented them from accepting any information contrary to the party line. The higher standard of living and the new educational opportunities which enabled "millions of ordinary people" to improve their social status during the later 1930s made workers receptive to the massive propaganda campaigns and the cult of the working man characterized by the Stakhanovite movement.

The textbook's importance as the first non-Marxist synthesis of Russian history justifies the translation project undertaken by Professors Galina Ustinova of Moscow State Pedagogical University and Vincent Hammond of the University of Central Arkansas. The recently released archival materials used by the authors contribute to our understanding of modern Russian history. Their analysis of Beria's fall, for example, benefits from his private notebooks which have never before been available to scholars. They show that he intended many of the reforms later sponsored by Malenkov and Khrushchev but could not overcome the burden of his bloody past as the head of Stalin's secret police. The authors' discussions on such important topics as the causes of the revolution, the significance of NEP, the Great Transformation, and the purges provide a useful introduction to modern Russian historiography for instructors and students alike. The detailed bibliography of Russian monographs, most of which are not available in the West, is an invaluable guide for scholars who want to become familiar with the recent historical research being conducted in the Russian Federation.

The authors who contributed to the text include several internationally known specialists in Russian history. Dr. Alexander A. Danilov, the head of the authors' collective serves as Chair of the History Faculty at Moscow State Pedagogical University and is an international authority on Russian political parties. Mikhail M. Gorinov, who is affiliated with the Institute of Russian History at the Academy of Sciences and edits the journal *Russia XXI* is a specialist on the Khrushchev and Brezhnev years.

The Russian historical profession has recognized the scholarly importance of the Danilov collective's work. The text was reviewed by Dr. E.I. Pivovor, Professor and Head of the Department of Modern Russian History of the Russian State Committee for State Universities and Dr. G.Z. Ioffe, Professor of History at the Institute of History of the Academy of Sciences, which restricts its membership to Russia's leading scholars, those who have attained the rank of Candidate member or Academician. The State Committee for Higher Education, which supervises undergraduate and graduate instruction in the Russian Federation, officially recommended the Russian edition of the textbook.

    The translators and editor have used a modified form of the Library of Congress system to transliterate Russian names and terms from the Cyrillic to the Latin alphabets. Diacritical marks and ligatures are omitted while the initial "ia" and "iu" are given as "ya" and "yu" ("Yury," eg.). The suffix "ii" is rendered "y" ("Leon Trotsky," not "Leon Trotskii") while the form "oi" has been replaced by "oy" ("Tolstoy," not "Tolstoi"). The hard sign, which is represented by a single set of quotation marks ("), has been replaced by "i" in most cases. The soft sign, which is indicated by an apostrophe in some transliteration systems, has been dropped altogether. Thus "Sokolínikov" is rendered "Sokolnikov."

V. E. Hammond

INTRODUCTION

RUSSIA IN THE AGE OF REFORM AND REVOLUTION (1894-1917)

Russia and the World at the Turn of the Century

The so-called ladder (echelon) theory of the development of capitalism gives us an approximate representation of Russia's historic place in the world community at the turn of the century. According to this theory the rise of capitalism in the countries on the first rung of the ladder (England, France, the United States, and others) was a natural historical phenomenon influenced by internal factors. The strength of their economies, the few surviving features of traditional society (the result of successful revolutions), parliamentary democracy, and strong liberal traditions facilitated the consistent and relatively peaceful development of these countries at the turn of the century.

Russia belonged on the second rung of capitalism together with Germany, Japan, Italy, Central, and Southeastern Europe. The "catching up" type of development, in which some stages are replaced or omitted altogether, characterized these countries because of their relatively late development of capitalism. In one important respect, Russia was unique among these countries. Generally speaking one can say that bourgeois revolutions in the West as a rule paved the way for an agricultural revolution, while the industrial revolution followed later. In Russia the industrial revolution of the 1890s preceded the bourgeois revolution of the early twentieth century, while the agricultural revolution was not completed at all.

Outside influence played an important but not a decisive role in the development of Russia, and the state more actively promoted capitalism to compensate for the weak stimulus provided by the domestic market. The rapid pace and the uneven development of these countries under conditions where major features of feudalism survived (a consequence of the nonrevolutionary and reformist nature of the transition to capitalism) conditioned the "painful" and contradictory nature of their social development. In addition, being deprived of economic and political spheres of influence (despite the rapid growth of their economic and military potentials), many of these countries, especially Germany and Japan, strove for the repartition of the world.

The market system already was operating in Russia, although not everywhere, surpassing the average level of the west in its dynamics. The volume of Russian production grew seven times between 1861 and 1900 (5 times in Germany, 2.5 in France, 2 in Britain). At the beginning of the twentieth century, Russia occupied the fifth place in the world in the size of industrial production, approaching France, but in some branches (in machine construction, for example) surpassing it. Russia provided one fifth of the world's grain harvest and up to 40% of the world's wheat export. But its industrialization was not completed. The leading sector of Russia's economy continued to be agriculture, in which the traditional mode of production with its primitive technology and precapitalist relations was integrated weakly with the progressive sectors. Russia was far behind the great powers in per capita industrial production and in the standard of living of its citizens. As much as 73.3% of the population was illiterate.

The originality of Russia was shown in the lateness of the formation of the typical class structure for an industrial society, in the preservation of obsolete social classes, in the enormous social and cultural estrangement between upper and lower classes, and the phenomenon of the Russian intelligentsia. The intelligentsia, or the *raznochintsy*, which arose in the middle of the nineteenth century, did not belong to the ruling class. Access to power was closed to it; it was especially sensitive to the arbitrariness of the bureaucratic autocracy. Its appearance was by no means directly connected with the formation of capitalism. All these traits contributed to the nonbourgeois character of the group, to their perception of new ideas, to their stable moral values, and in general to a certain opposition between the intelligentsia and the regime.

The absolute monarchy, with its absence of political rights and freedoms, transformed Russia at the beginning of the twentieth century into a unique phenomenon among the relatively developed countries. (A constitution actually had been accepted in Japan in 1889.) The contradiction between the rules of the autocracy and the modernizing economy, the new social relations, and the awakening national movement reached an unprecedented level of tension at the beginning of the twentieth century.

All of these factors determined the specific conditions for the formation of political parties. The parties were forming not so much from "below," growing out of the existing social relations, but from "above" with the help of the intelligentsia, who were called the "yeast" of Russian history in the beginning of the twentieth century. The process of forming Russia's political parties was reversed—from the provinces to the center and from the left to the right. The nationalist and socialist parties were the first to appear. They were Gnchak (1887), Dashnaktsutiun (1890), the Social Democrats of the Kingdom of Poland (1893), Bund (1897), RSDRP (1898-1903)—the Russian Social Democratic Workers—founded by George Plekhanov, the Social Revolutionary Party (1901), and so forth. The liberal and traditional monarchist parties were only created in 1905-1906. The formation and structure of the Russian party system (with the considerable influence of the revolutionary socialists) was not very conducive to smooth evolutionary development.

The difficulties of Russian modernization and the internal social tension conditioned the relative cautiousness of the foreign policy of the country in Europe without in any way destroying its annexationist designs. The desire to avoid a military-political conflict in Europe where the growing conflicts between England, France, and

Germany were shaping international relations and the simultaneous search for a new sphere of economic influence increased Russia's presence in the Far East. But the war with Russia unleashed by Japan (behind which Britain and the United States were standing) not only exposed the foreign policy mistakes connected with the miscalculation of the strength and aggressiveness of Japan, but the military and political weakness of the tsarist regime. Russia's casualties in the war of 1904-1905, including wounded and prisoners, were around 400,000 persons. The war not only exercised a revolutionizing influence on Russian society and weakened the country's international position, but also, in the words of the Minister of Foreign Affairs (since 1906) A.P. Izvolsky, "shook the whole foundation of European policy."

As a result Russia's ties with England were strengthened (her ties with France had been strengthened some time earlier). For Russia, the beginning of this rapprochement for the most part was conditioned by the need for a breathing space in foreign policy to restore her internal stability and military strength. The Anglo-Russian Treaty concluded in August 1907 completed the formation of the Entente.

The division of Europe into two military and political blocs, however, did not prevent the deterioration to a world war. The number of colonial crises, the Bosnian crisis of 1908-09, the Balkan wars of 1912-1913, and so forth were evidence of the world war's approach.

As the relations with Germany and Austria-Hungary grew tense, P.A. Stolypin's cautious foreign policy with its motto "peace at any price" was slowly changed into a preparation for a major war. But this course, which the leaders of the Octobrists, the Kadets, and the Progressives supported, was not realized. Stolypin could neither safely stabilize the country's social and political situation (which Stolypin dreamed of doing), nor could he complete the massive program for the armed forces' development. It is not surprising that the tsarist regime sought to delay the onset of war.

Nevertheless the country was drawn into a conflict in which, according to P.N. Miliukov, Russia's national interests gave way to the confrontation of the interests of the European democracies with the Weltpolitik (world policy) of William II (German Emperor, 1888-

THE AGE OF REFORM AND REVOLUTION

1918). In the struggle with Germany, France and Britain counted on the considerable military strength of Russia, whose army was the largest in peacetime and had excellent military training. Taking advantage of the alliance with Britain and France, Russia in turn not only was trying to remove the threat of German hegemony in Europe (this was the common goal of the Entente), but was also trying to realize her own goals in the war: to acquire the lands in the lower part of the Neman River and Eastern Galicia, to force Austria out of the Balkans, and to establish its own dominance over the region—to capture the straits of the Bosporus and Dardanelles or at least to guarantee the free passage through them for Russian vessels. The trigger for the war was the assassination of the heir Archduke Francis Ferdinand to the Austria-Hungarian throne on June 28, 1914. Thirty-eight states with a total population of 1.5 billion people participated in the war, three-quarters of the globe.

The western front became the main theater of war. The Russian army more than once drew the opponent's forces to itself in the moments which were critical for the English and French troops. In August-September of 1914 the Russian offensive in East Prussia helped to save Paris and provided for the success of French and English troops on the Marne River even though the offensive was prepared in a hurry and cost Russia a great many lives. The German plan for the rapid, consecutive defeat of first France and then Russia failed. Despite all expectations it was the Russian army which turned out to be the Triple Entente's main striking force in 1914. The losses of Austrian and German troops on the Eastern front significantly exceeded those on the western front.

The year 1915 proved to be even more difficult for the Entente and most of all for Russia. The German and Austrian troops launched their main attack on the eastern front. At the same time, the armies of France and Great Britain did not provide timely support for their own ally. The acute shortage of armaments (a consequence of the lack of preparedness for war and the tsarist bureaucracy's slowness in mobilizing the economy for military needs) caused major losses in the Russian army. Russian troops had to evacuate Poland, Lithuania, parts of Belorussia, and the Baltic region. But despite the heavy defeats, the Russian front held all the same. Great Britain and

France managed to use 1914-1915 for a dramatic increase in their armaments production.

The broad enlistment of the middle class and the work of social organizations to secure the necessities of war accelerated the conversion of the Russian economy to a wartime footing. In 1916 the volume of steel production tripled, the production of ordnance grew 2.5 times, of rifles 11 times. As a result of the celebrated Brusilov offensive the Russian army occupied almost all of Bukovina province, which created the threat of an invasion into Hungary. The Austro-Hungarian army was on the verge of defeat. The breakthrough helped the other Entente countries to stop the Germans at Verdun and to strengthen their positions. But by the end of 1916 and the beginning of 1917 Russia was the most vulnerable among the Triple Entente countries. In two and a half years of war Russia lost 6.5 million people, more than Great Britain and France taken together, and more than 1.5 times Germany's losses.

This explains how bloody historical events stimulated the economic, social, and political development of Russia. The growing world conflict gave Russia little time to get ready for the war, while the slowness of social and political reform in Russia did not allow the country to make good use of the short time it had. The ruling class wanted "extensive" development without serious reform (e.g., by economic and political expansion in Manchuria and in the Balkans). Russia was drawn into wars for which it was not prepared and which brought the country into crisis.

The Struggle of the Liberals for and the Traditionalists against Reform

After the death of Alexander III the liberal public organizations, which were made up mostly of noble landlords, expected the renewal of the reforms interrupted in the 1880s. But Nicholas II, who ascended the throne in 1894, was against the reformists' ideas and tried to follow his father's will as closely as possible. The need to modernize industry compelled the tsar to consider the reformist frame of mind of his officials, especially S.Yu. Witte (Minister of Finance,

1892-1903; president of the Council of Ministers, 1905-1906). The tsar saw his support in the traditionalists (the Interior Minister V.K. Pleve and others), who stood for the stability of the autocratic order and social classes. At the beginning of the century Witte himself was a supporter of the autocracy. His efforts were concentrated mainly on the industrialization of the country (whose sources were the peasants' redemption payments, the state liquor monopoly, indirect taxes, protectionism, and foreign capital), and hence on the monetary reform of 1897, a limited reform for the benefit of the workers. But these measures (and especially his growing plans for the reformation of the commune, *obshchina*) aroused the opposition of the conservatives and served as the cause of Witte's resignation from the post of Finance Minister. The retreat from the policy of reforms drove the unsolved problems inside.

The liberal movement, which was rather leftist (because of the intelligentsia) and was taking shape organizationally, was the basic force that pressured tsarism to conduct a reform policy. In 1903 such liberal groups appeared as the "The Union of Zemstvo Constitutionalists" (P.A. Geiden, S.N. Trubetskoi, D.N. Shipov) and "The Union of Liberation" (P.N. Miliukov, V.D. Nabokov, I.I. Petrunkevich, P.B. Struve). The leftist "free" liberalism, in contrast to liberals active in the land assemblies (*zemstvos*), unconditionally denied the necessity of autocracy, persistently put forward social and economic demands on behalf of "the working people," and used tactics involving illegal actions.

The fall of 1904 was the "spring" of the liberal movement. It was closely connected with the political course of a new Interior Minister, P.D. Sviatopolk-Mirsky (who replaced Pleve following his assassination by the SRs, Social Revolutionaries) and the "banquet" campaign in honor of the 40th anniversary of the judicial reform. Nicholas II's decree on December 12, 1904, proclaiming the uncompromising character of the autocratic regime put an end to the rather moderate demands of the liberal opposition. The absence of serious political and agrarian reforms inevitably led to a revolutionary explosion. Essentially, the liberal movement stimulated the growth of an oppositional and revolutionary frame of mind in Russian society.

The revolution of 1905 forced tsarism to return to the problems of social and political reforms which were coming to a head. On August 6, 1905, the tsar announced the establishment of a new constitutional body—the State Duma (which was named the Bulygin Duma after the interior minister, A.G. Bulygin). But the tsar's concession proved insufficient: the Bulygin Duma was boycotted. Under the conditions of the rising wave of revolution (All-Russian October strike) Nicholas II signed the Manifesto "On Perfecting the State Regime" on October 17, 1905, which was prepared by Witte. The Manifesto proclaimed some political freedoms (speech, press, religion, assembly, associations, and so forth); the Duma received legislative rights; and strata of the population who had lost their electoral rights under the Bulygin constitutional project received the right to participate in elections.

The temporary compromise reached by the tsar with the Liberals on October 17 secured the preservation of the monarchy after the first Russian revolution. The governmental reforms at the end of 1905 and the beginning of 1906 represented the maximum granted by tsarism in that revolutionary time (the extension of electoral rights to the workers, the reorganization of the State Council, and the formation of a unified Council of Ministers).

During this period the liberal camp found a place for itself and established political parties. "The Union of October 17" represented its right, the conservative-liberal wing (whose leaders were P.A. Geiden, A.I. Guchkov, M.A. Stakhovich, M.V. Rodzianko, and D.N. Shipov). The total membership ranged from 65,000 to 70,000 members. The social composition of the members included the industrial and financial bourgeoisie, liberal landholders, and the well-to-do intelligentsia. The Union's program involved cooperation with the government, "following along the path of safe reform," the modernization of the country, the defense of the principle of constitutional monarchy, a single and indivisible Russian state, the resolution of the peasant question with as little alienation of the landlord as possible, the restriction of the right to strike, and the eight-hour working day.

The left, radical-liberal wing comprised the Constitutional Democratic Party (whose leaders were the brothers Dolgorukov, A.A. Kizewetter, A.A. Kornilov, S.A. Kotliarevski, V.A. Maklakov, P.N. Miliukov, I.I. Petrunkevich, and P.B. Struve). The total membership

THE AGE OF REFORM AND REVOLUTION

ranged from 50,000 to 55,000; the social composition consisted primarily of the intelligentsia, the liberal bourgeoisie, and landlords; the membership of workers and peasants did not exceed 15%. The Kadets (from KD, the Russian abbreviation for the party) represented the Russian left variant of European liberalism. Their program consisted of a legitimate government in the form of a constitutional monarchy; equal rights for all national, social, and cultural groups; the settlement of the agrarian question through the compulsory expropriation of some of the landowners' estates; recognition of the workers' right to strike; and the eight-hour working day.

The traditionalist camp of the nobility was an obstacle to the realization of reform: The Russian Monarchist Party (V.A. Gringmut and I.I. Vostorgov), the Union of the Russian People (the Sheremetevs and F. Golitsyn), and the All-Russian Union of Landowners (V.N. Osnobishin and A.A. Chemodurov). The Union of the Russian People (A.I. Dubrovin, V.M. Purishkevich, and A.I. Trishatni), whose total membership reached 410,000 in 1907, was the leading force among them. They were united around the ideas of "Russian patriotism," the protection of Orthodoxy, the unity and indivisibility of the Russian Empire and autocracy, and their opposition to the "native bourgeoisie," who were infected by the corruption of the West. Combat squads and sedition appeared in 1905; The Black Hundreds organized pogroms in 150 cities of the country.

The attempt to realize radical liberal alternatives was connected with the activities of the First State Duma, which opened on April 27, 1906, in opposition to tsarism. The Duma comprised 161 Kadets, 70 Autonomists, 97 Trudoviks (representing the interests of radical peasant democracy), 17 Social Democrats, and 103 independents. The Kadet S.A. Muromtsev served as the Duma's chairman. The tsar repudiated the Kadets' Duma address which was sent to him and refused to permit a discussion of the problem of land reform provided for in the projects of both the Kadet and Trudovik deputies. The tsar's manifesto of July 9, 1906, dismissed the Duma, "the main position, captured by the revolution." The Kadets, who signed the Vyborg Appeal calling on the population to wage passive resistance, were arrested and convicted. At the same time the seriousness of the situation forced the regime to maintain a moderate policy and agree to some compromising reforms.

An attempt to stabilize the political situation by searching for a balance between the interests of the declining nobility and rising bourgeoisie characterized the work of Petr Stolypin, who was appointed Prime Minister (chairman of the Council of Ministers) on the day of the Duma's dismissal. The extreme conditions and the distribution of political forces caused P.A. Stolypin's policy of rightist or liberal-conservative reforms to combine the harsh measures of the reaction with the gradual renewal of the old regime.

The Stolypin course proposed the implementation of a series of reforms: agrarian peasant reform, local government reform, judicial and educational reforms, and introduction of workingmen's insurance. The reforms were supposed to strengthen the state in every possible way, by modernizing the society, by creating a new social pillar for the regime (a conservative class of small landowners, the so-called "filthy landlords"), and by strengthening their political influence.

The most important decree concerning Stolypin's agrarian reform was issued on November 9, 1906. It gave every head of household in a commune (*obshchina*) the right to use part of the land due him as private property. The reform also included cooperation in establishing individual farms, the beginning of the activities of the Peasant Bank, and the transmigration of peasants to the lands behind the Urals. The reform was an attempt to settle the peasant question without encroaching on the landlord's holdings. The results of the reform were as follows: the withdrawal of around 27% of peasant households from their communes by 1915; the creation of 1,265,000 small farms representing 10.3% of all peasant farms; the departure of four million communal residents from the villages to the towns after the sale of their own lands; and the resettlement of more than three million people beyond the Urals. The implementation of the reforms slowed considerably around 1911.

In 1906 and 1907 Stolypin tried to rely upon the Council of United Nobility, the Octobrists, and the Independent Nationalists' party (P.N. Balashov, V.A. Bobrinski, and V.V. Shulgin) which came together between 1908 and 1910. Stolypin tried to direct the Second State Duma which opened on February 20, 1907, along the course determined by the tsar's government. The major factions in the Second State Duma were Kadets—98; Trudoviks—104; Autonomists—76; Social Democrats—65; Octobrists—54 and "The Black Hundreds" members—10. The Kadet F.A. Golovin was chairman of the Duma. The intractable second Duma was dissolved on June 3, 1907, on the pretext that fifty-five members of the Social Democratic faction were preparing an armed uprising. The electoral law under which the duma was elected was changed in violation of the Manifesto of October 17 (and the Fundamental State Laws). This political coup was the end of the first Russian revolution.

The new Electoral Law of June 3, 1907, provided for the reduction in the number of peasant electors for deputies to the Duma by 56%, the election of deputies from the workers only in the provinces, the reduction of the representation of the non-Russian nationalities, and an increase in the number of electors from the landlords by 33%. The monarchy of June 3 relied on the nobles, landlords, upper and middle commercial-industrial bourgeoisie, and on the population's attitude toward Russia as a great power.

In the fall of 1912 new elections returned the more conservative Third Duma which, in contrast to the previous two, championed the projects developed in Stolypin's government. The majority of right Octobrists (283 members) and left Octobrists and Kadets (225 members) predetermined the Duma's decisions. The Octobrists N.A. Homiakov, A.I. Guchkov, and M.V. Rodzianko served as successive chairmen of the duma. The nobles and monarchists who dominated the State Council, however, rejected a significant part of the Stolypin reforms earlier passed by the Duma. The bills on the expansion of the Duma's budget rights, the introduction of zemstvos into the western provinces, local government, the communities of Old Believers, and the improvement of the court system were rejected.

By 1911 Stolypin's policy of "Bonaparte maneuvering" was no longer able to satisfy the traditional nobility who opposed his "extreme" reforms. The nobility also opposed the pacification policy whose failure was revealed by the noticeable revival of the revolutionary movement. At the same time the liberals were greatly dissatisfied by the delay in reform; the Kadets could not forgive Stolypin for his "undemocratic" behavior and for the coercive methods used to introduce his program. On September 1, 1911, Stolypin was assassinated in the Kiev City Theater by D. Bogrov who was known to be a double agent of the revolutionaries and the tsar's Secret Service (*Okhrana*). This combination in itself was quite symbolic.

The period between 1911 and 1914 witnessed the slow decay of the June 3 system, when some unsuccessful attempts to restore the old order were made. The State Council finally became "the cemetery of reforms," and the key post of Interior Minister was given to N.A. Maklakov who was planning the dissolution of the Duma. Having finally chained itself to the traditionalist nobles, the tsarist regime was in a state of decay, abandoning its reform policy without developing a clear political program.

The political reaction after the suppression of the revolution of 1905-1907 and the gradual exhaustion of Stolypin's reforming course had a negative influence on the liberal parties. By 1912 the Kadets' membership had fallen to 10,000. The crisis in "The Union of October 17" split its Duma caucus into the Zemstvo Octobrists (M.V. Rodzianko and N.V. Savich), the rightists (who left the party—N.P. Shubinski and G.V. Skoropadski), and the leftists (A.I. Guchkov), breaking up the party's organization.

The growing progressive movement among the bourgeoisie was a prospective political force. The movement embraced a liberal nationalist ideology with the idea of a Great Russia as its foundation, a "positive militarism," an active foreign policy, and Russia's economic revival through the activity of the commercial-industrial class. The Progressives wanted the rule of law and refused to share the Kadets' idealistic views on democracy. Their publications were the magazines *Great Russia* (1910), *Russian Thought*, and *Moscow Weekly* as well as the newspapers *Word*, *Russian Morning*, and *Russian News*. The Progressives were the party of the commercial and industrial bourgeoisie founded by the young Moscow capitalists A.C. Vishniakov, A.I. Konovalov, V.P and P.P. Riabushinski, S.N. Tretiakov, and S.I. Chetverikov in November 1912. The most important demands of the Progressives' congress were the abolition of the reinforced and extraordinary position of the Okhrana; the extension of the Duma's rights; the reform of the State Council; freedom of speech, press, assembly, and unions; and a constitutional monarchy with a minis-

THE AGE OF REFORM AND REVOLUTION

try responsible to the Duma. The Progressives' movement was a potential alternative to the revolutionary movement and a natural outgrowth of the country's social development.

World War I considerably changed the social and political situation in the country. The great wave of patriotism dampened interparty disputes. Most political parties, with the exception of the Social Democrats, voiced their confidence in the government and refused to engage in opposition activity. Strong social organizations sprang to life helping the war effort and bringing the bourgeois liberals who participated in them closer to power. The All-Russian Union of Zemstovs and the All-Russian Union of Towns were founded in July-August 1914 and united in 1915; the Military-Industrial Committee was set up in 1915 under the chairmanship of N.S. Avdakov and A.I. Guchkov "to assist industrial enterprises in the business of the supply of the army and fleet."

The defeats of 1915, which exposed the government's incompetence, and fear of new social upheavals again drove the liberals into opposition to the tsarist regime. The Fourth State Duma (December 15, 1912-February 25, 1917) included 185 Rightists, 98 Octobrists, 97 Progressives and Kadets, 10 Trudoviks, and 14 Social Democrats and was chaired by Mikhail V. Rodzianko. It became the center for the liberal opposition after 1915. A Progressive Bloc was formed in August uniting 236 of the 422 Duma deputies: the Kadets and Progressives, the two factions of Octobrists, and the center and left wings of the nationalists. The actual leader of the bloc was P.N. Miliukov, who called the bloc "the last attempt to find a peaceful way out of the situation, which is becoming more and more threatening each day." The establishment of a "ministry of public confidence" was the bloc's main demand. The opposition came together when tsarism was in a condition of advanced decay: the "Rasputin phenomenon," the rapid ministerial changes (the replacement of four prime ministers and six interior ministers during the war—"ministerial leapfrog"), and the appointment of unpopular and discredited statesmen to the highest positions.

Even the tsar's inner circle was displeased with his policies. Many grand dukes advised Nicholas II to send away Rasputin and yield to the Duma's demands. Rasputin's assassination on the night of December 17, 1916, had the appearance of an open protest by "an upper class Fronde." The assassination was carried out by Prince F.F. Yusupov, V.M. Purishkevich, and the Grand Duke Dmitri Pavlovich.

The opposition of the Progressive Bloc, which vehemently criticized the government, went beyond the limits of a movement inside the Duma. It significantly contributed to the further discrediting of the regime and helped the people realize the need for rapid change, thereby accelerating the revolutionary explosion "from below."

The Road to the Climax of the Revolutionary Process

After the great reforms between 1860 and 1880, the period of the counterreforms of the 1880s and 1890s, and the quasi-reforms at the turn of the century (excluding the reform of 1897), an age of revolution came to Russia. In an international context it was a continuation of the Great French Revolution of 1789-1795, the European revolutions of 1847-1849, and the Paris Commune of 1871. The age of revolution came late to Russia in comparison to the West. It is mostly for this reason that the revolution acquired new features and a new social "engine." The revolution was driven by the Russian proletariat, which was not numerous but had been hardened in strikes, and the Russian peasantry, which comprised three-fourths of the country's population. The communal peasants, who held a traditional outlook, had supported the autocracy for a long time. But the painful period after the reforms, the acute hunger for land, the redemption payments, and the beginning of the social stratification led to the accumulation of a significant degree of social unrest within the ranks of the peasantry, which was directed against the autocratic regime. At the same time the small bourgeoisie (who had arisen from the landowners and bureaucracy, in contrast to the European bourgeoisie of the age of revolution) could not and did not want to struggle openly against absolutism, feeling its weakness and fearing the growing proletariat.

The spiraling growth of lower class activity compensated for the relative weakness of the bourgeoisie between 1900 and 1917. The distinctiveness of the working class movement in Russia was determined in the early years of the twentieth century through political activity and demonstrations (the Obukhov strike of May 1901, the Rostov strike of November 1902, and the general strike engaged in by southern Russian workers in 1903). At the beginning of the century, for the first time since the Great Reforms of the 1860s and 1870s, the peasant movement acquired a mass character (670 incidents between 1900 and 1904). The lower class movement was characterized by the growing fusion of the intelligentsia's socialist tradition with popular actions, having the character of a spontaneous revolt. The powerful socialist parties played an important role in that fusion.

The Social Revolutionaries (SRs) followed a neo-Populist ideology (with some elements of Marxism) and acted in the name of a "united working people"—of all "exploited working people" from the proletariat to the laboring peasants. Its leaders were E.K. Breshko-Breshkovskaia ("the grandmother of the Russian Revolution"), G.A. Gershuni, V.M. Chernov, and others. Their main goal was the world struggle of labor against the exploitation of the human person and the realization in the long run of the "socialist state" ("a state where everyone's organized labor is used for everyone's benefit"). SRs considered social revolution to be the proper course of development. Their program's most important demands were the socialist ownership of land, distribution of the land to communes and equitable allocation by the latter among the peasants, and the development of cooperation and self-government among the workers. Their main political demands were a democratic republic, communal autonomy, and civil rights. In connection with the special role assigned to terrorism, the SRs created a combat organization in 1901.

Developing under the influence of Marxism, the Social Democratic movement brought into existence the Russian Social-Democratic Workers Party (RSDRP). Its leaders were G.V. Plekhanov, V.I. Lenin, Yu.O. Martov, and others. At the beginning of 1905 its total membership was 26,500. Its social composition included workers (61%), employees and intelligentsia (33%), and peasants (4%). Their program, which was adopted at the II RSDRP Congress in Brussels and London (1903), proclaimed the transformation of capitalist economic relations into socialist ones by means of a social revolution and the dictatorship of the proletariat as their main goal. They saw the class struggle as the main force for progress. Together with their political demands—the overthrow of the autocracy, the establishment of political liberties, and so forth—they demanded better working and living conditions for the working class and peasants.

The unique feature of Russian social democracy was its clear division into two factions—the Bolsheviks ("people of the majority") and Mensheviks ("people of the minority")—who not only were organizationally independent but also began to disagree more and more, first on tactics and later on the strategy of the revolutionary movement. The Mensheviks found more similarity between the revolutionary process in Russia and Europe, taking western democracy as their model and emphasizing the reformist and economic side of Marxism. Mensheviks preferred agreements with liberals to the search for an alliance with peasants.

The Bolsheviks relied on the traditions of Russian revolutionary movement and concentrated on the revolutionary and political side of Marxism, trying to accelerate the revolutionary process with the help of the so-called "subjective factor," a powerful centralized organization. They saw the peasantry, especially the poor and extremely poor peasants, as the proletariat's natural ally, unconditionally disassociating and isolating themselves from the liberal bourgeoisie.

The unusual character of the Russian revolution of 1905-1907 was conditioned by the uniqueness of its capitalism. The combination of feudal, autocratic, and capitalist social structures gave rise to the antifeudal, antiautocratic, and anticapitalist movements. The active participation of the workers in strikes, which grew during 1905 from 440,000 in January to two million in October, became the core of the revolutionary movement. The tsarist regime, which had ignored the demands of the liberals, was forced to agree to social and political changes under the pressure of revolution. Citizens were granted limited political rights (representation in the Duma and the right to assemble, to form trade unions, and to strike). This was accompanied by a considerable rise in the workers' living standards (the average annual wage grew from 205 rubles in 1905 to 241 rubles in 1907, fines were reduced, and a shorter working day was introduced).

The revolution changed the workers' way of thinking. The attempts of Gapon and Zubatov failed to integrate the working class into the political structure of the autocracy. The workers became aware of the success of united collective actions against the monarchy. The soviets, a new organ of working class power, appeared and in a number of cases (55) included soldiers and peasants along with the workers' deputies. The Soviets demonstrated their competence and became popular.

Many workers attributed the failure of the revolution of 1905 to lack of weapons and the absence of an effective organization (the December armed uprising is an example). These ideas formed the psychological basis for the later realization of the lessons learned during the course of 1905.

The peasants were beginning to participate actively in political life. The All-Russian Peasants' Union, which was formed on the crest of the peasant movement in the summer of 1905, brought together as many as 200,000 peasants by the end of the year. The peasants began to lose their faith in the tsar because they had not received an answer to their radical democratic demands. The peasants began to act openly, forcing the landlords to abandon their villages.

The revolutionary mood spread to the army and navy. The revolutionary activity included the mutiny on the battleship "Potemkin" in June 1905, the uprising on the cruiser "Ochakov," the revolt of the soldiers and sailors of Sevaspotol in November 1905, and the mutiny on the military bases at Sveaborg and Kronstadt in the summer of 1906.

The national liberation movements appear during the general course of the revolutionary liberation movement in 1906. Neo-Populist parties like the Armenian Dashnaktsutiun, the Georgian Revolutionary Party of Socialist Federalists, and the Belorussian Socialist Gromada ("The Masses") demanded national autonomy. The Bund, the Ukrainian Social Democratic Party, and the Lithuanian Social Democrats pursued cultural and national autonomy.

As K. Tarnovski observed, "The objective prerequisites for a new type of revolutionary movement, which was characterized by the fusion of three revolutionary forces—the working class movement, the peasant agrarian revolution, and the national liberation movement—appeared for the first time in world history in early twentieth-century Russia."

The Social Democrats and SRs played an important role in revolutionizing the masses. During the revolution the nucleus of the parties, which had been formed by the intelligentsia, was surrounded by workers and peasants. The membership of the RSDRP, for example, grew from 26,500 in the spring of 1905 to 167,000 (including the national organizations) in the spring of 1907. Of those who joined the party during the years of revolution 71% were workers. After the spring of 1906 the Bolsheviks (30,800) outnumbered the Mensheviks (24,500).

With 65,000 members the Social Revolutionaries became a mass party during the years of revolution. It relied for its support on the communal peasantry and workers who experienced the peasants' hunger for land. More than 88% of the SRs were workers and peasants. The Russian socialist parties ranked immediately after the Union of Russian People and surpassed the major liberal parties in membership and number of local organizations. This characteristic feature of the Russian political system reflected the predominance of the social revolutionary ideology and its preference for mass actions over the liberal and reformist paths, which could not help but show in the results of social development.

The development of the revolutionary process could not be absolutely consistent and abstractly objective. It was followed by some elementary and anarchic events and also by the appearance of a new sort of terrorism (P.B. Struve's definition). According to official statistics 9700 officials were killed and wounded in 1906 and 1907 as a result of terrorist acts and revolutionary developments. Prime Minister Stolypin survived ten attempts on his life.

The first Russian revolution turned the workers and peasants toward revolutionary activities while the following decade saw the formation of revolutionary political parties and prepared a generation of leaders for the revolutionary year of 1917—Lenin, Spiridonova, Trotsky, Chernov, and others.

The revolutionary movement was on the decline between 1907 and 1910, but it was only a valley between the two peaks of the revolutionary process. The number of strikers between June 1907 and December 1910 was twice the number between 1901 and 1904

THE AGE OF REFORM AND REVOLUTION

(1901-1904: 530,000; 1907-1910: 100,000).

The reaction was critical for the revolutionary parties. The declining membership and disintegration of the revolutionary parties was accompanied by internal factionalism and the search for new policies. The RSDRP factions were the Bolsheviks, Menshevik-Liquidators, pro-party Mensheviks, and Recallers. The PSR factions were the rightists, who were led by N.D. Avksentiev and I.I. Fundaminski and published the magazine *Initiative*, and the centrists, who published the newspaper *Labor Banner* and were led by V.V. Lunkevich, M.A. Natanson, N.A. Ustinov, and others.

As the ruling elite's "resources" for reform became more and more exhausted, the revolutionary movement, which was characterized by a number of newly acquired features, began to rise again in 1910 and 1911. The unresolved conflict between the peasants and landlords in the villages was supplemented by a new conflict between the communes and private farmers. The new activities of the peasant movement included actions against land reform and the so-called *kulaks*, the wealthier peasants who owned small farms. The shooting of workers at the Lena gold mines (April 1912) raised the level of participation in the workers movement to 1,092,000 by May 1913. By summer 1914, the number of workers participating in strikes exceeded the 1905 level when official statistics recorded 1,291,000 strikers for the whole year compared to 1,500,000 strikers for the first six months of 1914.

Some socialists tried to work out reformist tactics which reflected their search for more civilized ways of conducting the political struggle; they included the Liquidators and the "working groups" operating in the military-industrial committees during the First World War. These socialists relied on a small group of the workers' intelligentsia (trade union leaders like F.A. Bulkin and K.A. Gvozdev), engineers and other technical intelligentsia, as well as state officials and cooperative institutions. These attempts generally remained mere sprouts in the wild forest of the revolutionary atmosphere.

Serious defeats in the First World War speeded up the revolution. Peasants made up the bulk of the army (80-90% of the 15,798,000-man army). Years of unsuccessful bloody war transformed the soldiers into a powerful revolutionary force, as a significant degree of antitsarism was added to their feelings against the landlords. The strike movement, which had been growing since the spring of 1915, was purely economic at first, but in 1916 it took on a more political character, embracing a million people.

Food riots became very typical. In 1916 grain supplies were only 170,000,000 puds rather than the anticipated figure of 500,000,000 puds (the pud was a measure of weight equal to 16.38 kilograms and 36.113 pounds); at the end of 1916 the people of Petrograd were receiving only a third of the necessary bread.

The socialist camp was divided on the basis of attitudes toward the war: the defenders were G.V. Plekhanov, V.I. Zasulich, and the right wing SRs—I. Bunakov, N.D. Avksentiev; the center of neutralists and pacifists were *Reveille*, N.A. Potresov, N.E. Cherevani, and the SRV.M. Chernov; the internationalists were *Our Word, The Beginning*, Yu.O. Martov, L.D. Trotsky, and the left SRs, headed by M.A. Natanson. Lenin's Bolsheviks took an uncompromising position, calling for the transformation of the imperialist war into a civil one.

The competition between the revolutionary and reformist variants, which was taking place within the socialist parties and could be seen in the changing political course of the SRs and the organizational splits in the Social Democrats, reflected the general situation—the gradual narrowing of the possibilities for peaceful reform in the country. The revolutionary actions of the parties of the radical left were closer to the political experience of the people than the reforms.

February 1917

The February Revolution of 1917 logically completed the cycle in Russia's historical development that began at the turn of the century. The country was trying to accomplish the traditional tasks of the Western European (bourgeois) revolutions: the introduction of a constitution, political freedom, and the opening of a clear path for the development of capitalism in the industrial and agricultural sectors.

In contrast to the first Russian revolution of 1905-1907, which first demanded political changes and then a solution to the agrarian problem, the February Revolution developed on the wave of a social and economic crisis connected with the First World War (the disorganization of railway transportation, the severance of economic ties, and the closing of businesses—fifty in Petrograd alone). In January and February 1917 the population received less than 25% of its food necessities and "a wild wave of stealing, high prices, and undue gains" (A.I. Denikin) occurred, discrediting the authorities to an unprecedented degree.

The liberals played the role of critics of the decaying tsarist regime, repeating the so-called "liberal spring" of 1905 in the fall of 1916. Before February 1917 the opposition was distinguished by fear of the "anarchy" of 1905 which one could feel within its ranks. But in both cases the liberal democratic movement only indirectly pushed the country toward revolution.

Instead of the painful and long revolution of 1905, which weighed the opportunities for the rebirth of the monarchy on the scales of history, February 1917 caused the fall of the monarchy in a few days. The workers and soldiers mostly carried out the revolution, which sprang naturally from massive dissatisfaction with the war and its consequences. The delay in the food supply provided the dynamics of the Petrograd revolutionary movement. On February 23, 128,000 people were on strike; 214,000 on February 24, and 305,000 on February 25. The principal change occurred during the night of February 26, when the soldiers of the Petrograd garrison joined the workers. By the evening of February 27 the number of revolutionary soldiers had reached 67,000 (one fourth of the garrison); by the next evening—50%, by March 1—almost all the garrison.

The spontaneous revolutionary explosion surprised the socialist parties who had been weakened by acts of repression and deprived of many leaders through exile and emigration. But the Bolsheviks, Mensheviks, SRs, and those in between quickly entered the revolutionary movement, accompanied by their organizational elements. The experience which they gained in 1905 helped them to organize the Petrograd soviet on the initiative of the Mensheviks on February 27. Around six hundred Soviets of Workers, Soldiers, and

Peasants' Deputies began to function in March, playing a significant role in the consolidation of the revolutionary masses. The Petrograd soviet was headed by the Menshevik N.S. Chkheidze, assisted by his first deputies, the Trudovik (since March an SR) A.F. Kerensky and the Menshevik M.I. Skobelev.

The Petrograd Soviet of Workers' and Soldiers' Deputies did not require supreme power since it was influenced by the Menshevik and SR mottoes "to be the center for the consolidation of revolutionary democracy." But at first it was the soviet that concentrated real power into its hands. The soviet focused its attention on the city's food supply problem and the organization of a workers' militia. Order Number One, which initiated the radical democratization of the army, was the soviet's most important act. On March 2 the soviet supported (under certain conditions) the establishment of a provisional government by the Temporary Committee of Members of the State Duma, which had appeared on February 27 under the leadership of Duma Chairman Mikhail V. Rodzianko. On February 28 the Temporary Committee announced that it would take upon itself the functions of "restoring the state and public order" and creating a liberal provisional government. The Provisional Government included G.E. Lvov (the Prime Minister), P.N. Miliukov (the Foreign Minister), A.I. Guchkov, A.I. Konovalov, A.F. Kerensky, and other well-known officials. This event exposed the characteristic feature of the February Revolution: the lower class's concession of power (although far from complete power) to the liberals and bourgeoisie who had opposed the autocracy earlier.

During the first weeks of its existence the Provisional Government was extremely popular and enjoyed wide support among the people. Far-reaching democratic reforms were proclaimed: the people were given political rights and freedoms, national and religious restrictions were lifted, and executions were suspended, amnesty was granted, and the repressive bodies of the tsarist regime were liquidated. Popular pressure sanctioned the arrest of the tsar and a number of his close associates. An extraordinary commission was organized to investigate the legality of their actions.

The February Revolution in Russia became a moment of national unification, temporarily consolidating the divided society and combining the revolutionary and reformist traditions. But, of course, the diversity of social and political forces united by the February Revolution did not fade. The complete change in the country's internal situation only modified the "accents" in the activities of political parties. The liberals were turning into a conservative force while the socialist parties (first the Mensheviks and SRs) captured the banner of reform, gradually abandoning revolutionary activities.

CHAPTER 1

THE OCTOBER REVOLUTION

Europe in 1917

International relations and the internal political situations of the European powers in 1917 were mostly conditioned by the world war. Germany's dominance, which was connected with the best preparedness for the war, by this time had disappeared. After the entry of the United States into the war on April 6, 1917, the superiority of the military and economic potential of the Entente became overwhelming but the realization of that potential would take some time. Meanwhile, the countries of the Entente, who in 1916 had seized the strategic initiative from the four-power alliance [Central Powers],[1] were unable to build upon their success and attain the decisive breakthrough in the war. Germany and her allies, straining their strength to its limits and taking advantage of their enemy's mistakes, successfully defended themselves and struck back. In April the Anglo-French offensive in the region of Arras and Rheims failed, as did the Russian army's offensive in July. At the beginning of September the Germans seized Riga and in October the strategically important Moonzund Islands. In October the Austro-Hungarian army routed the Italians at Caporetto. In November the offensive of the

Anglo-French troops in the region of Ypres was inconclusive.

Meanwhile, the gigantic grinder of the war continued to pulverize the best of human and material resources. More than seventy million men, who were active and capable of work, were separated from their homes and jobs and dragged into the bloody meat grinder. By the end of 1916 the belligerents had lost six million dead and around ten million wounded and mutilated. The long bloody war overburdened the economy, reduced the population's standard of living, and significantly expanded the scope of governmental intervention into social life, militarizing it and restricting democratic freedoms.

Germany was a remarkable example of this process. The militarization of labor was accomplished in 1915-16: compulsory labor was introduced for men between 17 and 60 years. The state grain monopoly was introduced in 1915. In 1916 the government took over the distribution of necessary provisions and even attempted to regulate the production of agrarian products. In 1916 ration cards were introduced for bread and in the following year for all of the most important products. In 1917 the value of the grain collected represented only 55% of the prewar level and the daily distribution of grain was reduced to 170 grams.[2]

In France, where the situation was somewhat less serious, more than 60% of the male population had been mobilized, some of whom were detached for duty in war factories. Already in 1915 workers' real wages were 5% lower than in 1900. In 1917 ration cards were introduced in the developed agrarian sector and in major settlements.

The prospect of an indefinite war and the growth of domestic political instability pushed the representatives of the ruling elite of the belligerents to explore the possibilities for peace while at the same time searching for the resources to continue military operations. Under the influence of wartime losses and burdens, the patriotic attitudes of the masses swiftly disappeared and an antiwar strike movement grew which often assumed an antigovernmental character. According to the available evidence, between 1915 and 1916 the number of strikes in France increased from 98 to 314, in Germany from 137 to 240, and in Russia from 928 to 1410. And so by 1917 the war had been transformed into a major factor, revolutionizing the masses and complicating the internal political situation in the European states. Ultimately the destabilizing influence of the war appeared in those countries where the "hardships of war" greatly affected their economic potential, and also complicated the inveterate and relatively complex social and political conflicts, thus discrediting ruling regimes. The countries on the second rung of the ladder of capitalism, and especially Russia, reacted in this fashion. It is enough to observe that the number of strikers (1,086,000) in Russia in 1916 exceeded Germany (129,000) by 8.4 times, and France (41,000) by 26.5 times.³

The February Revolution, which at the time relieved the political tension in the country, at the same time accelerated the scope of the antiwar, revolutionary actions in all of Europe. In April 1917, 300,000 Berlin metal workers, supporting the workers of other countries, went on strike. The strikers demanded peace without annexations, cancellation of the state of war, and the restoration of democratic rights and freedoms. In August mutinies took place in the German fleet where one of the sailors' organizations attempted to create soviets on the Russian model. In April 1917 the Independent Social Democratic Party, led by K. Kautsky and H. Haas, was created. The party disassociated itself from the defensive position of the German Social Democratic Party and promoted a "just peace." In July the Reichstag accepted a resolution to strive for a peace through agreement. In Italy the slogan "Do as they do in Russia!" was adopted by the workers. The strikes, which spread throughout the country in 1917, culminated in the uprising at Turin, during which the workers of the suburbs and the factories were temporarily under the control of the insurgents. In the various regions the peasants began to seize the landlords' estates. In May and June a wave of strikes and demonstrations spread throughout France. Unrest began in the army. Upon learning of the shooting of Parisian strikers in May 1917, two regiments proceeded from the front to the capital on their own initiative but were stopped by artillery fire. In 1916 a mutiny flared in some of the Russian expeditionary forces operating in France; by 1917 a similar eruption involved nearly 45,000.⁴ Even in the comparatively "unrevolutionary" Great Britain, which suffered rather less from the war, 250,000 machine workers went on strike in

April and May. After a series of strikes and news of the collapse of the offensive on the front in June, an antiwar conference was created at Leeds which welcomed the revolution in Russia and called for the formation of soviets of workers' deputies on the Russian model. After his journey to Russia, the Laborite Minister Henderson called for as swift a peace as possible and left the ministry in August.

The wave of revolutionary unrest spreading through Europe did not lead to the ruin of the existing political regimes and did not even pose an immediate threat in most countries. The wave gradually began to recede. But the revolutionary splash in Europe encouraged the Russian socialists to have faith in the international strength of the working class in the struggle for peace and even in the proximity of a world revolution, which further accelerated the radicalization of the forces of the left. Lenin's faith in the growing prospects of a world proletarian revolution was one of his most important arguments for a socialist revolution in Russia. "We only began our task counting on a world revolution," Lenin admitted in 1920.[5]

Russia after February: Perspectives on Social Development and the Balance of Forces

Although the February Revolution was the most important, it was only the initial, predominantly destructive stage in the country's democratic transformation. Russia still had to form stable and unified state structures by selecting and constitutionally confirming the form of government. She had not resolved the intensifying conflicts among the nationalities, defined her attitude toward the war, or solved the agrarian problem. It was necessary to organize food and fuel supplies, to secure elementary order, and to stabilize the country's economic situation without delay. The harsh wartime conditions, the incomplete development of civil society (which caused extreme social and political instability in the absence of a strong authority), and the 57% adult illiteracy rate complicated the solution of these problems.

The direction of Russia's further development depended on

the resolution of these urgent problems. And the path of the country's social development depended in the final analysis on the forces unleashed by the struggle between the basic interest groups in society.⁶ In fact the choice depended on the balance of political forces: the complex interaction of parties, governmental and public organizations, and their leaders who tried to express—through the prism of their ideologies—the interests of society while simultaneously influencing them in the necessary direction.

The vacuum of legitimate authority which had taken shape after the liquidation of the autocracy (the tsar had played the key integrating role in the Russian state system for more than four centuries) and after the demise of the State Duma* (the only organ of national representation) immediately expanded the scope of the political struggle while greatly strengthening the role of political parties, social organizations, and the broad masses who were unstable and oriented toward nonparliamentary, violent methods of struggle. All this, against the background of a schism within the new power structures (the so-called "dualism") reflecting the deep social chasm between the lower and upper classes and the delay in convening the Constituent Assembly, caused a lengthy crisis of authority, which continued with its own peaks and valleys throughout 1917 and, in the broad context, until 1922.

After the February Revolution the Russian party system that included more than fifty parties shifted to the left. The February Revolution destroyed the traditionalist-monarchist parties of the right wing. The political center became weak also. The liberal parties of the Progressives and Octobrists gradually withdrew from the political arena. In fact the Kadets remained the only major liberal party in Russia. Their membership increased after the February Revolution to 100,000. But the party was still much smaller than the major socialist parties.

Under the influence of the revolutionary changes, the Kadets moved to the left. They abandoned their traditional orientation toward constitutional monarchy at their Seventh Party Congress at the end of March and advocated a republic at their Eighth Congress in May. Having embraced the tactics of "a left block," the Kadets adopted the course of cooperation with socialist parties. They retained their support for the war until victory, opposed the immediate introduction of an eight-hour working-day, and tried to postpone major reform (e.g., agriculture) until the formation of the Constituent Assembly. They dragged out the convocation of the latter because of their fear of the revolutionary elements and the desire to secure the most democratic type of elections. The Kadets, many of whom were prominent jurists, paid great attention to constitutional problems; they advocated the rule of law but opposed national self-determination for the borderlands. The social expectations of the revolutionary masses, who did not want to carry the burden of the war, far exceeded the Kadets' proposals. The Kadets' position was complicated by the fact that, in contrast to Western Europe and the USA, the Russian liberals had failed to create a firm base among the workers and peasants. By March and April of 1917 most of the Petrograd and Moscow workers favored the socialist parties (most of them were leaning toward the moderate socialists).[7] The unprecedented strengthening of the socialist parties and their domination of the party system was brought on by the abolition of the autocracy and the traditional monarchist parties which had restrained and counterbalanced the powerful socialist parties, by the involvement of the broad masses in politics, while the upper and lower classes were culturally and to some extent politically estranged, and because society was caught up in the revolutionary excitement.

The growth of the Social Revolutionary Party (the SRs) was especially rapid. Whole villages and army units joined it. The SRs membership ranged from 400,000 to 1,200,000 according to different sources. The SRs attracted the peasants with their radical agrarian program, their demand for a federal republic (which the SRs were the first Russian party to propose), their somewhat vague but traditional Russian ideology (which implied Russia's ability to follow her own unique path to socialism), and the heroic halo of their courageous fighters against tsarism, for "Land and Liberty." Although the party had its own views on the development of the revolutionary process after February, the SRs privately recognized the "ideological hegemony" of the Mensheviks on many of the important problems. The SR leaders were V.M. Chernov and N.D. Avksentiev. The left wing of the party (B.D. Kamkov, P.P. Proshyan, and M.A.

Spiridonova), which demanded concrete measures to end the war and the immediate expropriation of the landowners' land, became quite strong and opposed an alliance with the liberals.

The number of Mensheviks grew rapidly from around 100,000 in April and May to 200,000 in the fall. After the February revolution the Menshevik groups remained autonomous, lacking a central committee. An Organizational Committee headed by I.G. Tsereteli and F.I. Dan partially performed those functions. Although at the unification congress in August 1917 the Mensheviks managed to elect a Central Committee and party Chairman (P.B. Akselrod), the split into two relatively independent factions continued: The Menshevik-Internationalists' faction was headed by Yu.O. Martov, and the Menshevik-Defenders faction was divided into a right wing headed by A.N. Potresov and a left wing of "revolutionaries" headed by Tsereteli and Dan. In addition, Plekhanov's right wing Social Democratic group "Unity" and the leftist "New Life" (non-faction Social Democrats) broke their ties with Mensheviks; the part of the Menshevik-Internationalists headed by Yu. Larin joined the Bolsheviks.

The core of the Menshevik and SR ideology in 1917 was their belief that Russia was not ready for socialism. They considered premature socialist experiments harmful, advocated cooperation and compromise with the liberal, middle class bourgeoisie, and gave conditional support to the Provisional Government. Because of their desire for reforms on behalf of the working people, the moderate socialists were afraid to break their ties with bourgeoisie which threatened a restoration and eventual civil war. So they reluctantly agreed to delay the most important social reforms until the Constituent Assembly, but tried to realize separate, compromise reforms. The Mensheviks and SRs compromised on their attitude toward the war, which was for them a rather complicated issue. Not seeing a realistic way for Russia to withdraw from the war, most of them denied expansionist aims and called themselves "revolutionary defenders" of the motherland.

A small (4,000) but influential group in Petrograd known as the Intermediates (*Mezhraiontsy*) occupied the middle ground between the Bolsheviks and Mensheviks. L.D. Trotsky became their leader after his return from emigration.

After the February revolution the major differences which separated Trotsky's theory of permanent revolution from Lenin's views disappeared. Following his theory of permanent revolution independently of Lenin, Trotsky spoke on March 6, 1917, in favor of a proletarian revolution in Russia that was to rest upon the soviets of workers, soldiers, and peasants deputies.[8] The growing closeness to the Bolsheviks resulted in the Intermediates joining the Bolsheviks at the Sixth Party Congress. Trotsky became the second leader after Lenin.

The relative parity in membership between the Mensheviks and Bolsheviks was preserved during the spring and summer of 1917. The Bolsheviks had 100,000 members in the spring and summer of 1917 and by August 200,000 to 215,000 members (the traditional figure is 240,000).[9]

After February the Bolshevik leadership took some time to work out new strategy and tactics. In early March the Russian Central Committee Bureau declared the Provisional Government counterrevolutionary and tried to form a new revolutionary-democratic government, but it was not supported by either the rank-and-file Bolsheviks or the workers. The Bolshevik party was influenced greatly by the Petrograd committee's moderate position and especially by prominent Bolsheviks like L.B. Kamenev (who practically headed the Bolsheviks in Russia in 1912 and 1913), J.V. Stalin (a central committee member), and M.K. Muranov (a member of the Bolshevik faction in the Fourth Duma who returned from exile on March 12). Under their influence the Russian Bolsheviks veered toward the right, taking the Menshevik and SR position on many issues. They combined the formula of conditional support for the Provisional Government with pressure to conclude peace and develop the revolution. The tendency toward an organizational alliance with the Mensheviks appeared at both the grass roots level—in the mass creation of unified (Bolshevik-Menshevik) party organizations—and at the top—in the negotiations for unification. But Lenin's arrival to Petrograd on April 3, 1917, put an end to those tendencies.

In Switzerland, after the receipt of news about the victory of the February Revolution, Lenin proposed to establish a dictatorship

THE OCTOBER REVOLUTION

of the proletariat and the poorest peasants, which he considered the prologue to ripening world revolution. Considering the confidence of the masses in the Provisional Government, Lenin advocated a peaceful transition to the "second stage of the revolution" during which the slogan of "All Power to the Soviets," the broad indoctrination of the people on the "imperialist nature" of the Provisional Government and the continuing war would play key roles. The economic program envisioned the confiscation of the landowners' land as well as nationalization and the introduction of soviet control over production and distribution. Lenin was not bothered by the fact that he, in contrast to the other politicians, was proposing a course to split rather than consolidate the social and political forces of society, to separate the proletariat and "proletarian" party from the rest of society and seize power. It is not surprising that he was immediately blamed for stirring up a civil war. G.V. Plekhanov called Lenin's thesis nonsense.

There was no confidence in Lenin's strategy; it was not even supported by the Bolshevik leadership (L.B. Kamenev, A.I. Rykov, V.P. Nogin, and J.V. Stalin) who thought that the bourgeois democratic revolution in Russia was not finished.[10] Struggling against the "old Bolsheviks" who, according to Trotsky, comprised the party's "general staff," Lenin managed to rely upon "the noncommissioned officers" of the party who were closer to the revolutionary masses. They were gradually becoming disillusioned with the Provisional Government, but they did not have a broad political outlook. The support of G.E. Zinoviev and Ya.M. Sverdlov and Stalin's rapid switch to Lenin's side, which secured a place for him in the new party leadership, played an important role in the victory of Lenin's course. The victory, although incomplete, was won in April at the Seventh All-Russian Conference of the Russian Social Democratic Workers' Party of Bolsheviks, the RSDRP(b), which after sharp debate approved most of the items of Lenin's strategy.

The conduct of the Provisional Government was the most important factor which influenced events in Russia. In the first weeks of its existence it had the advantage of extraordinary popularity and the people's support. The Provisional Government implemented extensive democratic reforms: it proclaimed political rights and free-

34 CHAPTER ONE

Vladimir Ilich Lenin
Library of Congress, Prints & Photographs Div, LC-USZ62-98685

doms, it abolished the death penalty, it canceled the restrictions suffered by national and religious minorities, and it eliminated police powers of incarceration and censorship. The structure and hierarchy of many state bodies were reorganized. Political amnesty was announced. At the same time the arrest of Nicholas II, his ministers, and a number of representatives of the old regime was sanctioned. An Extraordinary Commission was set up to investigate their illegal actions (almost none were later tried, and their penalty was limited to moral condemnation).

The pressure of the soviets caused the Provisional Government to radically democratize the Army to protect itself from counter-revolutionary riots. The Petrograd soviet's well-known Order Number One and the government's special commission played a significant role in this. A purge of the high command was carried out, the courts martial in the field were suspended, and political commissars were introduced to check on the loyalty of the officers. The real levers of power passed from the officers to the soldiers' committees. The radical democratization of the army (which in terms of function and structure is the most undemocratic state institution) accelerated the rapid deterioration of discipline and combat effectiveness in the units. The inconsistent and delayed attempts to save the army from demoralization were a failure.

Although the Provisional Government did its best to postpone the problem of autonomy for the nationalities until the Constituent Assembly, on March 17 it had to announce its agreement to create an independent Poland in the future, on condition of its military alliance with Russia. Later it had to concede wide autonomy to Ukraine and Finland.

THE OCTOBER REVOLUTION **35**

Tsar Nicholas II and Family

The Provisional Government embarked on the path of social and economic reform far more cautiously. In March it acquired the cabinet (formerly imperial) and appanage lands. In April, land committees were set up to prepare an agrarian reform. Since the realization of reform was postponed until the Constituent Assembly, special acts were issued to prevent the unauthorized seizure of landowners' lands. The state bread monopoly was introduced on March 25 to overcome food difficulties, committees were set up to handle provisions, and a Ministry of Provisions was created on May 5. The Economic Council and Chief Economic Committee were established in June to strengthen the state's regulation of the economy.

On April 23 the government sanctioned the plant committees that had appeared at the enterprises. A Ministry of Labor, chambers of conciliation, and a labor exchange were created to attain "class peace." Greater attention to social problems was displayed when the Charity Ministry, which assumed the functions of the former charitable organizations, appeared. But the eight-hour working day introduced at many enterprises without preliminary permission was not sanctioned.

The possibilities for reform were limited by the continuing war, the difficult economic situation, and the effort of the moderate Socialists and Kadets to keep a balance between the interests of major social and political forces which were essential to the country's stability. The weakness of its actual authority and the absence of support at the local level sharply reduced the effectiveness of the Provisional Government's policy.

Immediately after February power at the local level belonged to the community executive committees—broad democratic organizations which had appeared spontaneously and had united different social and political forces. But soon those bodies, which personified the national character of the February Revolution, were being attacked both from the right and left.[11]

On March 5 Prince Lvov, the Prime Minister, issued an order to replace the governors and other tsarist administrators with provincial and district commissioners from the Provisional Government. The chairmen of corresponding zemstvo councils took the seats. The Provisional Government tried to make zemstvos but not pubic executive councils the bearer of its policy on the local level. The zemstvo reform which was undertaken in May and June caused a network of zemstvos to spread all over Russia. Their electoral system became more democratic while volosts zemstvos were created at the same time as the old class-dominated administrative organizations were being disbanded and regional town urban councils (*dumy*) were being set up. But the zemstvos, which in the eyes of the working people were connected with the old tsarist regime, were gradually superseded by the authority of the soviets. At the same time the influence of radical elements was becoming quite pronounced in some zemstvos.

The workers and soldiers supported the soviets that were in close contact with them; the soviets had spread throughout Russia shortly after February. From March to October 1917 the number of soviets grew from 600 to 1429. Soldiers' committees, analogous to the soviets, united up to 300,000 servicemen at the front.

Because of their program's appeal to the masses, the SRs and Mensheviks dominated the composition of the soviets until the fall of 1917. There were only sixty-five Bolsheviks (2.3%) out of the

2,800 deputies in the Petrograd soviet, which actually headed the country's soviets in the spring of 1917. The Bolsheviks were only strong in the Kronshtadt (31.8%) and Ekaterinburg (40%) soviets. The first All-Russian Congress of Soviets (June 1917) elected 320 people to the Central Executive Committee: 242 Mensheviks and SRs and only 58 Bolsheviks (slightly over 18%).

Although the soviets did not want to take power, their support for the Provisional Government was far from unconditional. They exerted powerful pressure over the government from the left and undertook a number of independent activities that ran further than—and sometimes counter to—governmental policy. Besides Order Number One, the agreement signed by the Petrograd soviet on March 10 with the Petrograd Association of Factory and Plant Owners proclaimed the eight-hour working day and the manifesto "To the Peoples of the World" (issued on March 14) repudiating the expansionist goals of the war, annexations and reparations, and only recognized a revolutionary war against Germany which greatly influenced the internal situation. On the whole the masses were satisfied, but not the Kadets and the Russian bourgeoisie.

The Growth of Revolutionary Elements

The problem of the attitude toward the war was the remaining burning issue of the revolution; it served as the catalyst for the soldiers' and workers' dissatisfaction with the Provisional Government and became the cause of the first political crisis in Russia after the February Revolution which shattered the relative unity and cohesion of society. On April 18, when Russia for the first time openly celebrated International Proletarian Solidarity Day, Foreign Minister Miliukov sent a government note to the allies confirming Russia's obligation to continue the war until victory. The publication of the information in the Petrograd newspapers on April 20 caused a spontaneous antiwar demonstration of armed soldiers. The demonstration ended in a meeting at the Marinsky Palace, the headquarters of the Provisional Government. Some 100,000 workers came out into Petrograd streets on the following day. Demonstrations also took place in Moscow and other cities. The demonstrators' demands were

"Down with Miliukov!" and "Long live peace without annexation and reparations!" The first clashes with the supporters of the Provisional Government took place. On April 21 the Kadet Central Committee called on people to support the government. General Kornilov, the commandant of the Petrograd Military District, ordered troops and artillery to prepare to disperse the antigovernmental demonstrations.

An emergency meeting of the Bolshevik Central Committee on April 20 resolved that personnel changes could not change the "imperialist character" of the Provisional Government and that a democratic peace could only be secured after the transference of power to the revolutionary proletariat and soldiers, represented by the soviets. On April 21 the Bolsheviks openly called for massive protests.[12] Some Bolsheviks called for the overthrow of the Provisional Government, having considered the resolution a decision for a open struggle. Only in the evening of April 21 did the Bolshevik Central Committee announce that it was necessary to stick to peaceful demonstrations and rallies.

In this dangerous situation the Menshevik and SR leaders of the Petrograd soviet were able on April 20 to persuade the soldiers to discontinue their meetings, and later averted the use of General Kornilov's forces. Having obtained a concession from the Provisional Government in the form of an explanation that "final victory" meant "lasting peace," which in many respects disavowed Miliukov's note, the Petrograd soviet called the incident closed.

The April crisis revealed the weakness of the Provisional Government's social and political support and caused the formation of a new coalition government. Guchkov and Miliukov left the government while six socialist commissars took office after much hesitation and discussion. In March the socialists had refused to enter the government with the single exception of A.F. Kerensky, who acted at his own risk. The six socialist commissars were A.F. Kerensky (War and Naval Affairs), the Trudovik P.N. Pereverzev (Justice), the SR V.M. Chernov (Agriculture), the Menshevik I.G. Tsereteli (Post and Telegraphs) and the Populist socialist A.V. Poshekhonov (Provisions). The representatives of the liberals retained ten seats in the government. On May 6 the Provisional Government issued a Declaration to conclude a democratic peace without annexations or reparations as soon as possible. To deal with the collapse of the economy, the government decided to implement general state control and regulation. Measures were planned to protect labor, to prepare an agrarian reform, and to further democratize and simultaneously raise the combat effectiveness of the army. But since the possibilities for reform were limited by the coalition with Kadets, joining a government which was losing popularity only increased people's expectations and made the Socialists responsible for the government's policy, thereby diminishing their image as "defenders of the interests of the working people."

Despite the Provisional Government's efforts, the situation in the country was not stabilized. On the contrary, the economic situation began to deteriorate again: in May labor productivity fell, in June the growth in the workers' real wages stopped.[13] The separatist tendencies on the part of the nationalities along the border grew more intense. In Russia the contradictory demands of the various social groups became clearly delineated. On the one hand the bourgeoisie, part of the urban middle class, demanded the restoration of order in the country and war until victory; on the other hand the soldiers, especially those in the rear who did not want to go to the front, demanded the immediate end of the war; the workers repeatedly demanded a sharp increase in wages; and peasants wanted the rapid division of the landowners' estates. The slogan of "All Power to the Soviets!" was becoming more and more popular because it united the people of the lower class. The strike movement which had been sharply curtailed after the February Revolution gradually began to grow again. Between March and June 2944 peasant uprisings occurred.

The very atmosphere in society was changing sharply as the euphoria of the February victory finally evaporated. Moreover, the tremendous psychological change caused by the fall of the monarchy, the break with old traditions, and the lack of strong state power caused an explosion of dissatisfaction and resentment, causing the masses to feel their own strength and to become revolutionized. I.A. Bunin remembered: "All Russia stopped working . . . there was a frenzy and acute madness. A soldier at Arbat square almost killed me at the end of March because I permitted myself a certain "freedom of speech," cursing the newspaper *Social Democrat* that was forced on me by a newsboy. . . . The crowd immediately took his side."[14] During the February Revolution criminals were set free from prisons which, together with the government's weakness, caused crime to rise. In March and April of 1917, in Moscow the number of burglaries grew by 800%, murders by 500%.[15] In May even the revolutionary "bard" Maksim Gorky was alarmed about the growth of intolerance, cruelty, and antisemitism. Pointing out the "pogroms in Samara, Minsk, and Iuriev, the wild actions of soldiers at railway stations, and other evidence of disorderly conduct, debauchery, and boorishness," Gorky warned, "Culture is in danger!"[16]

In this situation the popularity of the Bolsheviks sharply increased with their simple ultraradical slogans pointing to the "bourgeois" as the source of evil and promising the immediate satisfaction of all of the workers', soldiers', and peasants' demands. In June the Petrograd plant committees supported their position. The Bolsheviks obtained sixteen of the thirty-five seats in the temporary All-Russian Central Trade Union executive committee elected at the All-Russian Trade Union Conference on June 20-28. The number of Bolsheviks also grew in the new soviets which were elected in May and June, although they remained in the minority.[17]

The demagogic appeals of their propaganda also contributed greatly to the Bolsheviks' success. Desperately gambling on the growing demands of the masses for peace, the Bolsheviks furiously condemned the "vicious slander that we approve of separate peace with Germany"[18] and saw a world revolution as the only way out. And so while spreading the illusory possibility of a rapid peace with Germany, the Bolsheviks were actually proposing to change the world war into a civil war. Advocating the confiscation of the landowner's estates, they failed to discuss the most important question for the peasants, the principles upon which the land distribution would be based because in reality they did not intend to distribute the land to the peasants, but to form "a large model farm collectively managed by the soviets out of each landowner's estate. . . ."[19]

As soon as the people became radicalized and the influence of the Bolsheviks and Anarchists in the Kronstadt soviet grew, the Provisional Government's commissar in the city was dismissed on May 16 and the soviet assumed power. The news shocked the country. Newspapers were full of sensational articles about the "Kronstadt secession" and the proclamation of "the Kronstadt republic." The conflict was settled with great difficulty. But the "Kronstadt incident" which rang throughout Russia was clear evidence of the fact that the Provisional Government was losing its authority and the slogan "All power to the Soviets!" was becoming more and more popular.

The rise of the revolutionary elements was clearly displayed in the activism of the anarchists. After February their organizations were operating in seven cities, while groups from seventeen cities attended the July Conference of Russian Anarchists. Soon after the February Revolution the Anarchists expropriated the country seat (*dacha*) of the former Interior Minister P.N. Durnovo in the Vyborg region of Petrograd and transformed it into their headquarters. They held two armed demonstrations in May. And on June 5 a detachment led by the Anarcho-Communist I.S. Bleikhman captured the printing house of the right wing newspaper *Russian Freedom*. The action exasperated the authorities. But after liberating the printing house, the authorities were prevented from taking the Durnovo dacha by the Anarchists' powerful support among the Vyborg workers and Kronstadt sailors. The Anarchists took advantage of the situation and created a "Provisional Revolutionary Committee," including even the Bolsheviks at first, which became one of the centers of revolution in Petrograd, openly defying the Provisional Government.[20]

The continuation of the war destabilized the situation and undermined the prestige of the Provisional Government. Considering the over extension of Germany's forces and the irrepressible growth of the revolutionary mood in Russia, the authorities prepared an offensive which would deal a decisive blow to Germany and at the same time save Russia from the impending catastrophe, or at least arouse patriotism in the country. The Bolshevik Central Committee military group decided to hold a massive soldiers' demonstration demanding the cancellation of the offensive, the end of the war, and the transfer of all power to the soviets. The Bolshevik leadership supported the idea despite the protests of Kamenev and Nogin. At the same time at least some Bolshevik leaders were ready to use the demonstration to seize key objectives in Petrograd.

On June 9 the first All-Russian Congress of Soviets prohibited all demonstrations in the city for three days. In order to avoid political isolation, the Bolshevik Central Committee decided to cancel the demonstration. The resignations sent by the protesting Central Committee members I.T. Smilga and J.V. Stalin were not accepted.

Trying to utilize conditions which seemed favorable for victory, the Congress of Soviets on the proposal of the Mensheviks designated June 18 for their own demonstration in support of the Provisional Government and the Congress's decisions. The Bolsheviks agreed to hold the previously planned antigovernment demonstration that day to take advantage of this situation. As a result the Bolshevik slogans "Down with the war!" "Down with the ten capitalist ministers!" and "All power to the Soviets!" prevailed in the demonstrations in Petrograd where half a million people participated and in Riga, Helsingfors (Helsinki), Ivanovo-Voznesensk, and some other cities. During the Petrograd demonstrations Anarchists attacked the "Kresti" prison and liberated seven convicts. The next day, June 19, after armed clashes the government troops stormed the Durnovo dacha and arrested fifty-nine Anarchists. Four plants on the Vyborg side of the city immediately responded by going on strike.[21]

The June event demonstrated that the crisis of authority and the dissatisfaction of the masses with the Provisional Government were growing stronger. The mood of the people had changed noticeably. At the meeting of the Central Committee, the Petrograd committee, and the Military Organization held on June 22, the Bolshevik leaders said that the masses demanded action, that "it was often impossible to decide where a Bolshevik finished and an Anarchist began," and that "it was necessary to restrain fiery minds from all excesses."[22] The government was able to stand because of the new offensive and because of support of the First All-Russian Congress of Soviets that took place in Petrograd from June 3 to June 24.

Out of the 777 deputies to the Congress who claimed a party affiliation there were 290 Mensheviks, 285 SRs, and 105 Bolsheviks. After discussing the attitude of revolutionary democracy toward the government, the war, preparations for the Constituent Assembly, the nationalities, and land questions, the Congress adopted Menshevik and SR positions on all of the items, including the question of confidence in the Provisional Government and support for the offensive at the front. The Bolsheviks and Intermediates (Mezhraiontsy) who joined them were in the minority.

Still answering the Congress's call for the consolidation of democratic forces and parties, Lenin for the first time declared publicly that the Bolsheviks were ready to assume power in the country on their own. Lenin presented the Bolshevik program, citing economic stabilization as the most important task. Kerensky, who spoke after him, pointed out that Lenin's prescriptions for handling the economy—the publication of military profits and the arrest of fifty or 100 of the largest millionaires—were primitive and that his program had nothing to do with Marxism; it was simply naive and brutal. But Lenin's words were listened to attentively and were accompanied not only by laughter, but also applause in the hall. The Bolshevik's slogans, which were easily understood and full of promises, found an ear among some of the workers' and soldiers' deputies.[23]

The July Uprising and Further Political Polarization

The political breathing space for the Provisional Government was short. On July 2 a number of Kadet commissars resigned following actions by the central committee of the "People's Freedom" party and as a protest against a compromise agreement with the Central Rada on broad autonomy for the Ukraine prepared by the Socialist commissars. The purpose was also to pressure the government into taking a firm position on the struggle against the Bolsheviks and revolutionary elements.

The governmental crisis coincided with, and possibly accelerated, an explosion of dissatisfaction among the mass of soldiers and workers who were falling under the influence of Bolshevik agitation.[24] The whole city of Petrograd was involved in demonstrations and meetings on July 3. The initiator of the action, the First Machine Gun Regiment—ready for an insurrection long before July

3—and other units, demanded the transfer of power to the soviets and called for an armed uprising. It was the beginning. Armed people with red banners drove the streets in confiscated cars frightening the city residents. The Central Executive Committee of the Soviet of Workers' and Soldiers' Deputies and the Bureau of the Executive Council of the Soviet of All-Russian Peasants' Deputies announced that everyone who joined the demonstration would be considered a traitor to the revolution. At night on July 4 the Bolshevik leadership, including Trotsky, tried to prevent an armed uprising and give the demonstrations a peaceful character, sensing an unfavorable alignment of forces. Lenin, who came to Petrograd on July 4 from Bonch-Bruevich's dacha, participated in the decision. Although the initial position of the Bolshevik leadership on an armed uprising is not clear, there is no doubt that many, especially the military organizations and many rank-and-file Bolsheviks, prepared for and participated in the uprising. Later at the Ninth Bolshevik Party Conference Trotsky and Lenin compared the events with "an attempt to perceive with a bayonet whether Poland was ready for a social revolution in 1920." They called the April, June, and July actions "half demonstrations and half uprisings." [25]

A half million people came into the Petrograd streets on July 4. Some armed demonstrators rushed into the Tauride Palace, where the Central Executive Committee was in session, and demanded the immediate surrender of power. At the same time members of counterrevolutionary organizations, such as "the Union for the Defense of the Motherland and Order," "the Military League," and "the League of the Struggle against the Bolsheviks," shot at demonstrators in the streets. Armed demonstrators fired back. Kerensky issued an order to disperse the demonstration and to bring the guilty to trial. Army units were sent from the front to Petrograd.

An extended session of the Bolshevik Central Committee took place on the evening of July 4 and discussed the situation in Petrograd. Smilga, M.I. Latsis, other Central Committee members, the Petrograd Committee, and especially the leaders of the Military Organization—V.I. Nevsky and N.I. Podvoisky—insisted on an armed uprising against the Provisional Government, relying on the mood of the masses. After sharp discussions Nogin, Kamenev,

Zinoviev, and the other Bolsheviks who realized the country was not ready to support the uprising argued for stopping the demonstrations. The Bolshevik Central Committee started negotiations with the Central Executive Committee. But this time the SR-Menshevik Central Executive Committee took the side of the government, an action which it believed "corresponded to the interests of the revolution."

In all about 700 people were killed and wounded in Petrograd. The news about the demonstrations in Petrograd incited demonstrations and meetings in Moscow, Orekhovo-Zuevo, Ivanovo-Voznesensk, and other cities. But the provinces and the front did not support revolutionary Petrograd. This gave confidence to the Provisional Government and it went on the offensive.

The following day the editorial office of *Pravda* (Truth) and the *Trud* (Labor) printing house were smashed while the luxurious Kshesinskaya mansion where the Bolshevik headquarters were located was captured. The sailors, soldiers, and workers who participated in antigovernmental actions were disarmed. Thanks to the position of the socialist parties, there were few bloody incidents. The Provisional Government ordered the arrest of Lenin, Trotsky, Kamenev, Zinoviev, and some other Bolsheviks.

To discredit the Bolsheviks they used documents about the cooperation between Lenin and the other leaders with German intelligence and the German General Staff to demoralize the Russian home front. They remembered the sealed carriage used by the Bolsheviks to pass through Germany while she was at war with Russia. Lenin and some other prominent Bolsheviks were accused of state treason. But at that time they had not succeeded in collecting direct evidence. Now the proof has been found in the documentary evidence.[26] The campaign struck a terrible blow to the Bolsheviks' prestige which many people thought irreversible. Lenin and Zinoviev refused to come to the court and went underground. Trotsky, Kamenev, F.F. Raskolnikov, A.M. Kolontay, and some other Bolsheviks were arrested—some of them surrendered voluntarily. (Between August and October they were, eventually, freed.)

In an attempt to strengthen the position of the "revolutionary democracy" and to react to the growing dissatisfaction of the masses, the socialist commissars published the Provisional Government's Declaration of July 8. The declaration proclaimed Russia a republic, it dismissed the Temporary Committee of the State Duma, it prohibited land deals, and other measures. Prince Lvov resigned as Prime Minister in protest. On July 8 A.F. Kerensky was appointed Prime Minister and War Commissar of the Provisional Government. To preserve the army he undertook the measures suggested by the Kadets. An order to suppress all opposition to the government in the army was issued on July 9. The death penalty at the front was reintroduced on July 12. The military courts were also restored. On July 18 "liberal" Commander-in-Chief A.A. Brusilov was replaced by L.G. Kornilov, who was ready for a decisive struggle against the revolutionary element.

On July 13 negotiations were undertaken with the Kadets to form a new coalition government. In contrast to the views of Miliukov and some other Kadet leaders, the Central Committee of the "People's Freedom" party agreed to a new coalition with the socialists after proposing a number of conditions. Among them were the commissars' responsibility to their consciences, which in practice meant their independence from the soviets, the delay of all social reforms and the form of Russia's government until the convening of the Constituent Assembly, the observance of the principle of complete unity with the allies, and the termination of the "multiple authorities," which meant the removal of the soviets from power. After dramatic negotiations the conditions were accepted at a joint meeting of the Social Revolutionaries, Mensheviks, and liberal parties on July 22, 1917. The formation of the second coalition government was completed on July 24. Seven socialists, four Kadets, and two radical democrats were included; Kerensky became premier and commissar of war with N.V. Nekrasov as deputy premier and commissar of finance.

The new situation forced Lenin to rethink the Bolsheviks' tactics. He concluded after July that the "counterrevolution had won" and the period of dual power was over. The soviets supported the Provisional Government. It was therefore necessary to abandon the slogan of "All Power to the Soviets!" and consider the peaceful development of the revolutionary process. Somewhat later Lenin

THE OCTOBER REVOLUTION

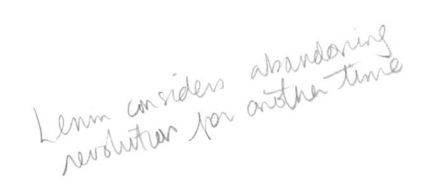

claimed to have only spoken about the temporary abandonment of the slogan. But for a short time he favored using the factory committees as revolutionary centers.

Lenin's conclusions, which meant a sharp turn in policy, were not favorably received by the Bolshevik membership. There were an especially large number of objections to the abandonment of the slogan of "All power to the Soviets!" and to the transfer of power to the counterrevolutionaries. There were sharp discussions at an expanded meeting of the Central Committee (July 13-14), the Second Petrograd Party Conference, and the Sixth Bolshevik Party Congress that took place surreptitiously in different buildings from July 26 to August 3.

After discussion, the congress spoke against Lenin's appearance in court (Lenin at one time favored turning himself in to the authorities). But the congress gave most of its attention to the political situation and Lenin's new tactics. One of the most important moments involved the political report of the Central Committee delivered by J.V. Stalin. Some Bolsheviks (E.A. Preobrazhensky, I.S. Angarsky) opposed a socialist revolution in Russia without the support of a proletarian revolution in the West. Most of the active delegates spoke against the abandonment of the slogan "All power to the Soviets!" As a result the congress resolved to underscore the temporary nature of the slogan's abandonment on the grounds that it was necessary to clear the counterrevolutionaries out of the soviets and then concentrate the party's main forces on them. With these corrections the congress approved Lenin's course on the change in the rather vague prospect for a socialist revolution.

Two days before the Sixth Bolshevik Party Congress, on July 23 the Ninth Congress of the People's Freedom Party opened in Moscow and later continued its work in Petrograd. In contrast to the two preceding congresses, the ninth marked the movement of the Kadet party to the right. Most delegates supported the course proposed by Miliukov for strengthening the state's authority, the maintenance of order, the liquidation of the political influence of the soviets, and conditional support for the coalition government if it seemed capable of becoming a "strong and independent authority." The congress finally rejected the principle of political self-determination for the nationalities and canceled their earlier acceptance of the demand for the separation of church and state.

While the right (Kadets) and the left (Bolsheviks) wings were becoming more and more radical and inclined to take concrete action, the center (Mensheviks and SRs) experienced growing ideological and organizational disunity. The majority of the Mensheviks, who were headed by Tsereteli, generally approved of the actions of the Provisional Government in the July crisis and stood for further cooperation with the liberal bourgeoisie and for the unity of all forces in their struggle against counterrevolution and "anarchy." At the same time Martov spoke in favor of a uniformly socialist government. But despite the internationalists' considerable and still growing influence (more than one-third of the deputies voted for their resolutions at the unification congress), they were still a minority.

The Social Revolutionary leaders' support of the Provisional Government's actions in July failed to provoke a unanimous reaction and accelerated the polarization of the party's forces. Its leadership tried to separate itself from the party's right wing which had rallied around Kerensky and the newspaper *People's Will,* but that could not prevent the further growth and organization of the SRs left wing. The left SRs became stronger in the provinces where they frequently formed blocs with the Bolsheviks and demanded the immediate seizure of the pomeshchik's lands, the dissolution of the coalition with the Kadets, and the transfer of power to the soviets.

In August the decisions of the left SRs began to be officially published in the party publications along with those of the majority. During this period there was a noticeable decline in the popularity of the Mensheviks and SRs. Their adherence to democratic principles and cooperation with the bourgeoisie required compromise and class consolidation. While the situation in the country deteriorated, their policy lost more and more ground and was criticized as "rightist" and "leftist," since it could not fully satisfy the interests of either social force. The growth in the Menshevik's membership fell off in the fall of 1917.

The Provisional Government, trying to consolidate its supporters and avoid a civil war, held a State Conference of representatives in Moscow between August 12 and 15. Around 2500 delegates from the commercial and industrial bourgeoisie, the Army, soviets, zemstvos, cooperatives, intelligentsia, clergy, and all of the State Dumas participated. At the call of the Bolsheviks a great strike of 400,000 workers was held on the opening day of the conference, paralyzing the city.

At the conference the socialists who supported the platform of the All-Russian Central Executive Committee favored strengthening the government's authority and making a number of concessions to the demands of the liberals and bourgeoisie. But they still supported reform and opposed removing the soviets from politics. Most of the conference's participants supported tougher measures to maintain order and accepted the liquidation (or significant curtailment) of the soviets and the soldiers' committees, the introduction of the death penalty even on the home front, the mobilization of transport and industry, and war until victory. The conference's participants warmly welcomed General Kornilov who was considered among the potential dictators.

The Kornilovshchina

The conference did not bring the consolidation of bourgeois and socialist forces but it contributed to their shift to the right. It pushed Kornilov and Kerensky to work out measures to limit political freedoms and set up a dictatorship. But the disharmony between them became more evident as the conference continued. Each one wanted to use the other for his own purposes and each saw himself as the future dictator.

On August 26 when General Krimov's Third Cavalry Corps was ready for the march to Petrograd, Kornilov sent Kerensky a demand to transfer military and civil power to him, impose marshal law in Petrograd, and come to the General Headquarters for security reasons. Fearing that Kornilov could do without him, Kerensky tried to dismiss him and, when that failed, accused him of treason.

The Kadets decided against openly supporting Kornilov. The soviets and all of the socialist parties including the Bolsheviks acted decisively against the Kornilovshchina. Some 60,000 Red Guards, soldiers, and sailors took up the defense of Petrograd. Railway workers disassembled tracks and routed the trains with Kornilov's troops onto sidings. Propagandists actively worked in the units coming to Petrograd trying to demoralize the soldiers. Kornilov's troops were stopped practically without a shot. General Krimov shot himself, and Kornilov was arrested on September 1.

Kornilov's defeat sharply transformed the balance of forces. The most active counterrevolutionary forces were crushed. More than that, it dealt a powerful blow to the Kadets' prestige, since they were connected with the Kornilovshchina in the eyes of the masses. The workers and soldiers were rapidly becoming radicalized. Because of these events the Menshevik and SR Central Committee spoke against the participation in the government of the Kadets and the other groups who were involved in the Kornilovshchina. But the majority of the leaders of these parties still opposed an exclusively socialist government and advocated a coalition with well-to-do "zenz" elements.

The radical change in the situation changed the mass perception of the Bolsheviks. Their active participation in the defeat of the Kornilovshchina removed the label of "collaborators with the German General Staff" from the Bolsheviks. They began to enjoy an extraordinary rise in popularity. Between August and October the membership of the party grew 1.5 times and reached (according to the traditional figures) 350,000. Moreover, in contrast to the Mensheviks and SRs, the Bolsheviks preserved a flexible but unified organization.

Striving to resolve the government crisis which had originated with the Kornilov mutiny, on September 1, after negotiations with the All-Russian Central Executive Committee, Kerensky created a new organ of power, the Council of Five or the Directory, without the Kadets' participation. Acceding to the demands of the leftist forces, Kerensky declared Russia a republic. Nevertheless, the position of the Directory, created in place of a full-fledged government, remained precarious.

The Bolshevization of the local soviets began after Kornilov's defeat. On August 31 the Petrograd soviet supported the Bolshevik resolution on authority. Prepared by Kamenev, the resolution repudiated the idea of a coalition with the Kadets and well-to-do and supported the transfer of power to the representatives of the revolutionary workers and peasants. Soon L.D. Trotsky, who had recently been released from prison, became chairman of the soviet. The Moscow Soviets of Workers' and Soldiers' Deputies supported the declaration on September 5. The Bolshevik faction was victorious during the reelection of the executive committee of the Moscow Soviet of Workers' Deputies on September 19, and V.P. Nogin became chairman of the soviet. In general eighty soviets of large and medium size cities supported the Bolshevik resolution in the first half of September.

Lenin, who was hiding underground, saw in these events an opportunity to restore the peaceful development of the revolution. At the beginning of September he suggested an agreement with the Mensheviks and SRs to form the government that would be responsible to soviets, while the Bolsheviks "would refrain from immediately pressing their demand for the transfer of power to the working class and poorest peasants and would not pursue revolutionary methods of struggle for their demand."[27] The Bolsheviks, who only recently under Lenin's influence had adopted the course of an armed struggle and repudiated the slogan "All Power to the Soviets!" were puzzled with the new shift in policy. Only after long arguments on September 13 did the Central Committee decide to include Lenin's ideas in the Bolsheviks' declaration at the Democratic Conference.

The All-Russian Democratic Conference that took place in Petrograd on September 14-22 was convened on the decision of the All-Russian Executive Committee and the Executive Committee of the Soviet of Peasants' Deputies to strengthen the unstable government's authority and to form a new coalition government during the period before the Second Congress of Soviets, which had originally been called for September and then postponed. Present at the conference were 1582 delegates from the soviets, trade unions, cooperatives, and the Army. Among the delegates who stated their party affiliation were 134 Bolsheviks, 172 Mensheviks (including 56 Internationalists), and 582 SRs (including seventy-one left SRs). After endless discussions on September 19 a small majority of conference delegates approved in principle a coalition with the liberals. Thanks to the efforts of the Bolsheviks, Menshevik-Internationalists, and Left SRs, amendments repudiating the idea of a bloc with the Kadets and other groups who had supported the Kornilovshchina were adopted, ending the real possibility of a coalition. But the resolution as amended was defeated at its final reading. To find a way out of the stalemate, it was decided on September 20 to elect a new representative body out of the composition of the factions—the All-Russian Democratic Council (later Preparliament), which would have the function of settling the question of power. On September 23 the Democratic Council approved the idea to form a coalition government with the Kadets.

The third coalition government included ten socialists and six liberals (four of whom were Kadets). Kerensky became premier and commander-in-chief, A.I. Konovalov deputy premier and trade commissar. The renewed coalition with the Kadets and the Preparliament's support of the government helped to overcome governmental crisis but could neither stabilize the country's political situation nor correct the sharply growing economic dislocation.

The paralysis of the Russian economy was caused by the excessive burden of the continuing war, the decline in labor discipline and productivity, and the escalation of the social demands of the masses. Industrial output fell by 36.4% in 1917 in comparison with 1916. Railway transportation collapsed. In 1917 the war consumed 86% of budgetary expenditures. The eight-hour working day, introduced without permission, reduced the working time in industry by about an hour. The workers demanded a 100% rise in wages and more. In the first half of 1917 alone 799 enterprises were shut down—most due to the lack of raw materials and fuel. Inflation grew rapidly. From March to September the quantity of paper money in circulation increased from 9.9 to 15.4 billion rubles, 1.6 times more than during the period from the beginning of the First World War to February 1917.[28]

The workers' real wages fell rapidly after July. The keen dissatisfaction of the masses caused food supply difficulties. Having despaired of its efforts to restore the disorganized trade in commodities between the town and countryside by significantly raising the price of grain, the Provisional Government tried to correct the situation with administrative and organizational measures: the introduction of a grain monopoly, card rationing (May-June), and even

THE OCTOBER REVOLUTION

attempts to requisition grain by force (autumn). But the government's weakness prevented these measures from having the desired results. There was bread in the countryside, but the cities, especially the large ones, were on the verge of starvation in the fall of 1917. At the end of August the bread ration in Moscow and Petrograd was reduced to half a pound a day. On October 5 the men at the front only had a six-to-fifteen-day reserve of flour; on October 14 Petrograd had seven-to-eight days of flour reserves.

The deterioration of the situation and the essential demise of the Provisional Government accelerated the economic and political struggle of the lower classes. The total number of strikers in September and October 1917, in comparison to the spring, grew 770%, reaching around 2.5 million workers. The peasant revolts of the summer and especially the autumn, as several historians have observed, were becoming a real agrarian revolution. They embraced about 90% of the districts of European Russia: the peasants seized the landlords' estates, wrecked their farms, and disobeyed authority. According to certain estimates the pomeshchiks' lands in 15% of the volosts were registered by the peasants before the October revolution.[29]

The Course of the Bolsheviks to an Armed Uprising

The rapid radicalization of the masses, which was clearly apparent in the Bolshevization of the soviets, and the unwillingness of the overwhelming majority of the Menshevik and SR leaders to form a bloc with the Bolsheviks (because of their lack of confidence in the latter and their fear of counterrevolution) forced Lenin to back away from the proposed compromise. The Bolshevik Central Committee had scarcely approved of Lenin's proposals when a day later, on September 15, Lenin's letters on "The Necessity for the Bolsheviks to Seize Power" and "Marxism and the Revolt" were received, in which he demanded the immediate adoption of a program to seize power by force of arms without waiting for the completion of the work of the Democratic Conference (at which the Bolsheviks were also planning to propose their own compromise). The Central committee rejected Lenin's suggestions and decided to burn all but one copy of his letters so they would not fall into the hands of the workers and cause a schism in the ranks of the Bolsheviks.³⁰

On September 21, the Bolshevik Central Committee agreed to stay at the Democratic Conference but boycott the Preparliament. But the Bolshevik faction of the Preparliament, taking advantage of the fact that the final decision on this question had been left to them, disagreed with the Central Committee. Only on October 5 did Lenin's and Trotsky's point of view prevail. They favored a boycott of the Preparliament and the concentration of their forces on work in the soviets to overcome the opposition's resistance.

Trotsky and the other Bolsheviks who were promoting a proletarian revolution hoped that the coming Second Congress of Soviets would peacefully take the power and that the overthrow of the Provisional Government would not only be approved, but would become a simple technical operation. At the same time the "right wing" Bolsheviks (Kamenev, Rykov, Nogin, and others), who supported the friendly position of the Menshevik-Internationalists and left SRs and who were not oriented toward a proletarian revolution and a dictatorship of the proletariat, not only formed the base of the soviets, but their other organizations as well. These moderates wanted the creation of revolutionary, democratic authorities, represented by a coalition of the socialist parties,

Lenin, who thought that Europe was "on the eve of a world proletariat revolution" and that the balance of forces in the country was extremely favorable for the armed seizure of power by the Bolsheviks, persistently demanded preparations for the immediate overthrow of the Provisional Government. He believed that under these circumstances it was impossible to wait for the Second All-Russian Congress of Soviets, while the counterrevolutionaries gained strength and the favorable opportunity passed. The Congress could fail to introduce the expected Bolshevik resolutions and one could not expect it to approve of a clearly Bolshevik government. Lenin called the charge of unleashing a civil war a propaganda trick, "scare tactics," believing that "no stream of blood" in an internal civil war could be compared with the "seas of blood," which the Russian imperialists shed during the offensive of June 19, 1917.³¹ As a matter of fact the total losses of the Russian army caused by the unsuccessful offensive amounted to 150,000 men, while the total loss of popu-

THE OCTOBER REVOLUTION

lation suffered by Russia during the civil war reached 15,000,000!

Still even the most radical Central Committee members continued to believe that the conditions for an uprising were not ripe and that only the Congress of Soviets could give the new government legitimacy, authority, and broad support in the country. Lenin answered that with an ultimatum on September 29. He threatened to resign from the Central Committee but "leave the freedom for himself to agitate among the rank-and-file party members and at the party congress." [32]

Lenin's tough position and the dissatisfaction of the Moscow and Petrograd Bolsheviks when they learned that his letters had been kept secret caused the Bolshevik leaders to reconsider their position. On October 7, after Trotsky's statement on the counterrevolutionary nature of Preparliament and the Provisional Government and on the need to transfer power to the soviets, the Bolsheviks left the Preparliament. From the following day until October 25 most of Petrograd was talking about the uprising which was being planned by the Bolsheviks.

In fact the question of the armed uprising was settled on October 10. That evening a meeting of the Bolshevik Central Committee attended by Lenin was held in the apartment of the prominent Menshevik N.N. Sukhanov, at the invitation of his wife, who was a Bolshevik. Sukhanov was absent and knew nothing about the meeting. Despite Kamenev and Zinoviev's opposition, the majority decided to begin preparing an armed uprising.

On October 12, despite the resistance of the Mensheviks and SRs, the Petrograd soviet began the creation of the Military Revolutionary Committee (*Voenno-revoliutsionnyi komitet* or VRK). The committee was originally named the Revolutionary Staff for the Defense of the City, but in fact it turned itself into the staff preparing for an armed uprising. The left SR P. Lazimir, the leader of the Soldiers Section in the Petrograd soviet, was chairman. Three Bolsheviks—V.A. Antonov-Ovseenko, N.I. Podvoisky, A.D. Sadovsky, and another left SR, Sukharkov—were also in the committee bureau.

The decision of the Central Committee on October 10 did not end the disagreements among Bolsheviks. The preparation of the uprising was difficult. The Bolsheviks were worried about people's passivity and apathy and that the broad mass of workers and soldiers would participate in the uprising only on the summons of the soviet, not the Bolshevik party. The left SRs, who were the closest group to the Bolsheviks among the socialists, were against an armed uprising before the Congress of Soviets. A secret meeting of the Bolshevik Central Committee took place on October 16 in which some of the leaders of the Petrograd Committee, the military organization, the Petrograd soviet, and the trade unions and plant committees participated. In his speech Lenin argued for an immediate armed uprising. He pointed out that one could not be guided by the changing moods of the masses and that they expected decisive action from the Bolsheviks. Having affirmed that "we will have the proletariat of Europe on our side," he again expressed his concern that the bourgeoisie wanted to surrender Petrograd to the Germans, so the uprising could not be delayed.[33]

Kamenev and Zinoviev, and those among the Bolsheviks who sympathized with them, once more affirmed that there was no support for the Bolsheviks among the majority of the population. Contrary to Lenin's statement, they argued, and the elections to the Constant Assembly later confirmed this conclusion, the working class could not carry the revolution through to its conclusion given the dominance of the petty bourgeoisie in the country, and furthermore assistance from the European proletariat was very problematic. After the sharp debates, nineteen voted for Lenin's resolution, two were against, and four abstained. There were six votes for Zinoviev's resolution, fifteen were against, and three abstained.[34] Sure of the burdensome consequences of the seizure of power, Kamenev and Zinoviev demanded a Central Committee plenum. Kamenev announced his departure from the Central Committee. When it was clear that the publication of his views on the future uprising was impossible in the Bolshevik press, he published his own article (co-written by Zinoviev) in *New Life*. An angry Lenin called Kamenev and Zinoviev "strikebreakers" and demanded their expulsion from the party. The Central committee did not agree but accepted Kamenev's resignation and forbade him to oppose the decisions of the Central Committee in public.

THE OCTOBER REVOLUTION

The Provisional Government, the All-Russian Executive Committee, and the leadership of the various parties were continually meeting, trying to stop the preparations for the uprising. But they could not overcome the existing disagreements. The Kadets, as it became clear at their Tenth Party Congress (October 14-15), were even more inclined toward harsh measures. Even before the Congress they were actively at work in the army and promoting the work of the zemstvos, city councils, and various bourgeois organizations to form a "Green Guard" to oppose the workers' "Red Guard." But their weak formations were clearly inferior to the Red Guards who were created in the spring of 1917 and numbered nearly 100,000 people by October.

The Menshevik-Internationalists and left SRs, who were trying to prevent a Bolshevik uprising and avert a possible counter-revolution at the same time, adopted the resolution proposed by Dan at the October 24 session of the Preparliament, which demanded that the Provisional Government immediately begin peace negotiations and distribute the land to the peasants. But Kerensky refused.

The Provisional Government unsuccessfully tried to neutralize the revolutionary troops in the capital. In connection with the Germans' seizure of the strategically significant Moonzund Islands, Kerensky gave the order to send part of Petrograd's revolutionary garrison to the front. The soldiers, who did not want to fight, refused to obey the Provisional Government and declared their support for the soviets. The sailors of the Baltic fleet had already broken their allegiance to the Provisional Government at the end of September. The Bolsheviks predominated in the Central Committee of the Baltic Fleet (*Tsentrobalt*) elected by the sailors. The Bolshevik P.E. Dibenko headed Tsentrobalt.

In an attempt to forestall a Bolshevik coup, Kerensky started moving loyal units to Petrograd. In response, on September 20 the Military Revolutionary Committee decided to send their commissars to all the units. Orders not signed by them were considered invalid. The control of most of the garrison finally passed into the hands of the Bolsheviks.

Having lost his last support, Kerensky, who had clearly overestimated the strength of the Kadets, Cossacks, and others loyal to him, decided to occupy Smolny during the night of October 24, to close the Bolsheviks' *Workers' Path* (*Rabochii put*) and *Soldier* (Soldat), and to arrest the members of the Military Revolutionary Committee. On the 23rd, he unsuccessfully tried to secure the support of the Preparliament.

The October Coup in Petrograd

On the morning of October 24 in response to the junior officers' looting of the printing house where the *Workers' Path* was printed, the Bolshevik Central Committee and Military Revolutionary Committee took defensive measures to neutralize the Provisional Government's units. In the afternoon the troops of the Military Revolutionary Committee began to press their opponents, who offered practically no resistance, and seized the telegraph office, bridges, and some other strategic places. Their active defense had plainly developed into an offensive.

On the evening of October 24, Lenin sent a letter to the Bolshevik leaders demanding the immediate overthrow of Kerensky and proceeded from his secret apartment to Smolny. During the night and in the morning of October 25 the revolutionaries took the railways, the telephone exchange, and the majority of other key points in Petrograd. In the daytime the VRK troops surrounded the Marinsky Palace and expelled the Preparliament which was in session there.

Most of the people of Petrograd were unaware of the events taking place in the city. All of the plants, theaters, and restaurants were open and for the most part life in the city was normal. At ten in the morning Lenin wrote a VRK declaration "To the citizens of Russia" in which he announced the deposition of the Provisional Government and the transfer of power to the Military Revolutionary Committee. The majority of the deputies of the Petrograd soviet approved the resolution. They welcomed the deposition of the Provisional Government and assured the committee that the Western European proletariat would assist in the attainment of the complete victory of socialism.

But despite all of the efforts of Lenin, who urged its rapid seizure, the storming of the Winter Palace was delayed. The movement

THE OCTOBER REVOLUTION

of the revolutionary units was slow. The leaders of the military operation—Antonov-Ovseenko and G.I. Chudnovsky—who did not want excessive bloodshed, waited and watched the number of the government troops melt. They were clearly unwilling to defend the commissars of the Provisional Government in the palace. Kerensky left in the afternoon for reinforcements.

At seven in the evening an ultimatum of surrender was sent to the Provisional Government. After it was declined, at 8:40 p.m. blank artillery shorts were fired from the Petropavlovsk fortress and then from the cruiser Aurora. Afterwards the Winter Palace was under rifle and machine gun fire for ten or fifteen minutes. After this some of the Cossacks, officer cadets, and half a squadron of the women's battalion surrendered. Those who remained in the Winter Palace received a new ultimatum. When they refused to surrender, the artillery shelling began which finally demoralized the defenders of the Provisional Government. In fact they did not render any organized resistance. Around 2:00 a.m. detachments from the Military Revolutionary Committee infiltrated the Palace and arrested the commissars of the Provisional Government. The insurgents lost six people.

The same night at 10:45, in the name of the Central Executive Committee, Dan opened the Second All-Russian Congress of Soviets of Workers' and Soldiers' Deputies. The exact party composition of the delegates is unknown. However it seems obvious that the Bolsheviks and Left SRs had a small majority. The work of the Congress was dramatic. Although mostly Bolsheviks and Left SRs were elected to the Presidium, the Congress almost unanimously supported Martov's proposal for a peaceful settlement of the political crisis and the beginning of negotiations to form a democratic coalition government.

After that the Right SRs and Mensheviks sharply condemned the Bolsheviks, but meeting no support they left the Congress. Martov, who wanted "to stop the development of a civil war" and obtain an agreement between the socialist parties, suggested a resolution which condemned the Bolsheviks for carrying out a coup before the opening of the Congress and insisted on the formation of a completely democratic government. But, after an ovation at the arrival of Bolshevik members of the City Duma and Trotsky's impassioned speech, in which he sharply ridiculed Martov's proposal, the Menshevik-Internationalists left the congress. At 2:40 in the morning Left SRs who tried to support Martov's point of view demanded a break.

When the break was over, Kamenev announced the occupation of the Winter Palace and the arrest of the commissars of the Provisional Government. That finally changed the mood of hesitant delegates in favor of the Bolsheviks. In the morning the Congress listened to and unanimously adopted an appeal "To the workers, soldiers, and peasants" written by Lenin, in which the transfer of power to the Second Congress of Soviets and in the provinces to Soviets of Workers', Soldiers', and Peasants' Deputies was announced.

On the evening of the 26th, after Lenin's report, the Congress adopted a decree on peace suggesting that "all belligerents and their governments should immediately start negotiations about a just democratic peace" without annexations or reparations. The appeal was directly made to the peoples of the belligerents without reference to their government, mainly for propaganda effect.

The Congress adopted a decree on land. The decree in many respects repeated the SRs agrarian program and was a serious step back from the Bolshevik program. The decree provided for the transfer of the pomeshchiks' and other lands to the control of peasant committees and district peasant soviets before the final resolution of all land questions by the Constituent Assembly. For practical guidance regarding "the great land reforms," the Order concerning Land prepared in August 1917 by the editorial office of *Izvestiia* from 242 peasant orders were included. According to the order private land ownership was canceled, the land was decreed to be "property of all the people," and with the exception of certain model farms it was to be divided equally between the peasants according to a labor or consumption norm.

Lenin's firm position, as well as that of the left SRs, resolved the Bolshevik debates on whether the new government should be a socialist coalition or a purely Bolshevik commissariat. Finally the Congress agreed to a Bolshevik Provisional Government of workers and peasants, the Council of People's Commissars (*Sovnarkom*), which was only supposed to last until the Constituent Assembly. It was difficult for Bolsheviks to form that government. Many prominent Bolsheviks refused to take governmental posts, trying to place the burden of the completely unfamiliar administrative functions on somebody else.

At last the Second Congress of Soviets approved a government with the following members: Chairman (Prime Minister)—V.I. Lenin (Ulianov); People's commissars (narkoms): internal affairs—A.I. Rykov, agriculture—V.P. Miliutin, labor—A.G. Shliapnikov, trade and industry—V.P. Nogin, foreign affairs—L.D. Trotsky (Bronshtein), finance—I.I. Skvortsov, education—A.V. Lunocharsky, justice—G.I. Oppokov (Lomov), food—I.A. Teodorovich, post and telegraph—N.P. Avilov (Glebov), nationality affairs—J.V. Stalin (Dzhugashvili), and the army and admiralty board—V.A. Antonov (Ovseenko), N.V. Krylenko, and P.E. Dybenko. The post of railway transportation narkom remained vacant.

The Congress elected a new All-Russian Central Executive Committee (VTSIK). Its 101 members included sixty-two Bolsheviks, twenty-nine left SRs, and six Menshevik-Internationalists. L.B. Kamenev was elected its Chairman. On November 8 (after his resignation) Ia.M. Sverdlov replaced him.

The Bolshevik government was unstable. The results of armed conflict in Moscow were not clear. Kerensky was unable to collect enough troops. But the units of the Third Corps under the command of General Krasnov, who supported Kerensky, occupied Gatchina on October 27, Tsarskoe Selo on the 28th, and were coming to Petrograd. The anti-Bolshevik forces were consolidating in the capital: on October 24 a committee of public safety was set up by the city's mayor, G.I. Shreider; on October 26 the SRs, Mensheviks, city council members, the former members of the All-Russian Executive Committee, the Executive Committee of the All-Russian Soviet of Peasants' Deputies, and the members of the factions of the various socialist parties who had left the Second Congress of Soviets established the Committee for the Salvation of the Motherland and the Revolution. The committee planned to start an uprising against the Bolsheviks as soon as General Krasnov's troops entered Petrograd. But they had to begin their actions earlier. The mutiny, whose major force was officer cadets, flared on October 29. The mutiny was accompanied by cruel murders on both sides and was relatively easy to suppress.

The left wing of the Mensheviks and SRs, who did not support the armed uprising against the Bolsheviks, still blamed the Bolsheviks for the bloodshed. On October 29 the All-Russian Executive Committee of the Railway Workers' Trade Union (*Vikshel*), which was threatening a general strike, demanded the cessation of military operations and the beginning of negotiations to form a unified socialist government. During the course of the negotiations the Bolsheviks agreed to expand the "base of the government" and to change its composition and were even inclined to drop Lenin and Trotsky which the Mensheviks and SRs were pressing for. They nevertheless tried to support the other decisions of the Second Congress of Soviets. At the same time Kamenev, Riazanov, and many other Bolsheviks were ready to go much farther in meeting the tough demands of the Mensheviks and SRs. In particular, they agreed to the creation of a "People's Soviet" instead of the All-Russian Central Executive Committee (VTsIK) chosen at the Second Congress of Soviets and the advancement of V.M. Chernov or even the more right wing N.D. Avksentiev to the position of head of the new government. But after the defeat of Krasnov's troops on October 30 and 31, Lenin acted to end the negotiations. His position prevailed after long and sharp debates. The talks were canceled after the Bolshevik Central Committee adopted an ultimatum on the night of November 2. Kamenev, Rykov, Miliutin, and Nogin left the Central Committee in protest. A number of people's commissars and high officials (Nogin, Rykov, Milutin, Teodorovich, Riazanov, Derbyshev, Arbuzov, Yurenev, and Larin) resigned. They were supported by Shliapnikov. That first acute intraparty crisis among the Bolsheviks after October 25 reflected the vague disagreements on the prospects of the revolutionary process in Russia since the spring of 1917. The governmental crisis was overcome only in December 1917 when after long hesitation the left SRs entered the Soviet of People's Commissars.

Why did the Bolsheviks win after the collapse of democracy in February? Among the factors was the weakness of the Russian bourgeoisie in both economic and political power. Because of the major role played by foreign capital in Russian industrial development and the role of the state in all economic matters, there was no strong middle-class tradition from which a liberal power-base could emerge. At the same time, the rapid spread of socialist ideas, which resembled the radicalism and collectivist spirit of the masses themselves, contributed to the tremendous growth of the socialist parties. The factors which contributed to this growth were the absence of a broad layer of private property owners in the village, the survival of the traditional communal leveling consciousness, and the masses' deep distrust of the "barons" (the upper class and the educated layers of society). The huge "left wave" made the formation of a stable political regime extremely difficult. The most important destabilizing factors were the continuing world war (the conclusion of a separate peace, which would have been unanimously denounced by all political forces, was the only way out), the unsolved agrarian question, the complicated economic situation, and, finally, the most serious power crisis in Russian history, which was caused by both the fall of the autocracy and the dual authority of the Provisional Government and the soviets. Even the coalition of Kadets with the Mensheviks and the SRs could not fill in the power vacuum because their conflicts did not allow them either to reform the country rapidly or to defeat the revolutionary elements. As a result of the rapid radicalization of the masses and the absence of firm state power, the democracy which was taking shape soon turned into an anarchy and ochlocracy (mob government). In these circumstances the Bolsheviks fully utilized their advantages: the will to act firmly in politics, the desire for power, a flexible but unified party structure, and ultrapopulist propaganda which had a wide appeal. They managed to bridle the revolutionary-anarchic element (to whom they had given every possible encouragement) and to take advantage of the Provisional Government's weakness. The huge reservoir of social hatred and impatience and the hunger of the masses for just equality allowed the Bolsheviks to take power under the Soviet flag and implement their own ideological doctrines.

Notes

[1] On the western front the French and English troops successfully repulsed the Germans' general offensive at Verdun. In the course of the attack at the Somme River, during which tanks were used for the first time, the French and English succeeded in pressing the Germans and capturing more than 100,000 prisoners. On the eastern front as a result of the remarkable Brusilov breakthrough, Russian troops captured 25,000 square kilometers and more than 400,000 prisoners. Only the transfer of German troops saved the Austro-Hungarian army from catastrophe.

[2] Z.K. Eggert, *Borba klassov i partii v Germanii v period pervoi mirovoi voiny* [*The Class and Party Struggle in Germany during the First World War*], Moscow, 1957, pp. 80-86, 373.

[3] *Mirovaia voina v tsifrakh* [*The World War in Statistics*], Moscow-Leningrad, 1934, p. 88.

[4] Two special Russian brigades were sent from France to Greece, to the Salonika front.

[5] V.I. Lenin, *Poln. sobr. soch.* [*Complete Collected Works*], vol. 42, p. 1.

[6] Among the forces one can distinguish first, the bourgeoisie (around three million persons), the landowners who were close to them (700,000 to 800,000 people) and a considerable part of intelligentsia. The role of this group was determined by its economic strength and high European culture. Second, the rather small but well-organized and literate (up to 64%) industrial working class which had become conscious of its own strength (3.4 million in the cities and nearly fifteen million people counting the village workers). But the majority of the population included 120 million peasants, the more than 6.5 million soldiers serving in the army, and the urban middle class. These rather less organized and politicized forces in the event of their involvement in the political struggle could determine the outcome through the strength of their numbers and the presence of armed soldiers.

[7] See *Piterskie rabochie i Velikii Oktiabr* [*Petrograd Workers and Great October*], Leningrad, 1987, p. 87.

[8] L. Trotsky, *Soch.* [*Works*], vol.3, part 1, Moscow 1925, p.13.

[9] V.I. Miller, "K voprosu o sravnitelnoi chislennosti partii bolshevikov i menshevikov v 1917 g." in *Voprosy istorii KPSS* ["On the Problem of the Comparative Number of Bolsheviks and Mensheviks in 1917" in *CPSU Problems of History*], 1988, no. 12, pp. 115-118.

[10] See *Pervyi legalnyi Peterburgskii komitet bolshevikov v 1917 g.*

[*The First Legal Petersburg Committee of Bolsheviks in 1917*], Moscow-Leningrad, 1927, pp. 86-89; V.N. Zalezhsky, *Iz vospominanii podpolshchika* [*From the Memory of a Member of the Underground*], Kharkov, 1931, pp. 178-80; and A.G. Shliapnikov, *Semnadtsatyi god* (The Year 17), Book 3, Moscow-Leningrad, 1927, pp. 260-63.

[11] See G.A. Gerasimenko, *Pervyi akt narodnovlastiia v Rossii: obshchestvennye ispolnitelnye komitety*, 1917 [*The First Act of People's Power in Russia: Community Executive Committees*], Moscow, 1992.

[12] V.I. Lenin, *Poln. sobr. soch.* [*Complete Collected Works*], vol.31, pp.291-292, 309-311.

[13] P.V. Volobuev, *Proletariat i burzhuaziia v 1917 g.* [*The Proletariat and Bourgeoisie in 1917*], Moscow, 1964, pp. 138,157.

[14] I.A. Bunin, *Okaiannye dni* [*Cursed Days*], Moscow, 1990, pp.44, 45.

[15] V.P. Portnov and M.M. Slavin, *Stanovlenie pravosudiia Sovetskoi Rossii (1917-1922)* [*Soviet Russian Justice in the Making (1917-1922)*], Moscow 1990, p.10.

[16] *Novaia zhizn* [*New Life*], 1917, May 9.

[17] Occasionally the Bolsheviks encountered strong opposition from the soviets, other political parties and the masses. From time to time the Bolsheviks could not speak at meetings because of loud whistles. Lenin remarked with pessimism at a session of the Petrograd Bolshevik Committee (May 30, 1917): "The execution of our party by a firing squad is always a possibility. We are on the eve of the June shootings." See the *Central State Archive of Historic Party Documents*, St. Petersburg (TsGAIPD s-Pb) f.1, op.1, d.1-a, l.54-65.

[18] *Sedmaia (Aprelskaia) Vserossiiskaia konferentiia RSDRP(b). Protokoly* [Seventh (April) All-Russian Conference of the Russian Social Democratic Workers' Party (Bolsheviks). Protocols], Moscow 1958, p. 243.

[19] See above. p. 247.

[20] S.N. Kanev, *Revoliutsiia i anarkhizm* [*Revolution and Anarchism*], Moscow, 1987, pp. 262, 263, 274, 275.

[21] Kanev, pp. 278-79.

[22] TsGAIPD, f.1, op. 1, d. 5, l. 3-6.

[23] *Pervyi Vserossiiskii sezd Sovetov rabochikh, soldatskikh i krest'ianskikh deputatov. Stenogr. otchet.* [I All-Russian Congress of Workers', Soldiers' and Peasants' Deputies. A Stenographic Account.] Moscow-Leningrad, 1930, vol. 1, pp. 65, 70-77.

[24] The most fundamental and accurate research about the July crisis is the work by A. Rabinovich *Krovavye dni. Iiul'skoe vosstanie 1917 g. v*

Petrograde [*Bloody Days. The July Uprising of 1917 in Petrograd*], Moscow, 1992. (For the American edition see *Prelude to Revolution.* Bloomington and London, 1968). The author believes that the governmental crisis had secondary importance in the actions of the masses (see page 10 of the Russian edition).

[25] Istoricheskii arkhiv [History Archive], 1992 No. 1, p.28.

[26] See R. Pipes. *The Russian Revolution.* vol. 2, Moscow 1994, p. 84-86. Also see Iu. Felshtinsky, *Krushenie mirovoi revoliutsii. Brestskii mir. Oktiabr 1917-Noiabr 1918* [*The Downfall of the World Revolution. The Peace of Brest. October 1917-November 1918*], Moscow, 1992, pp. 29-67. One must observe that the Bolsheviks were not German agents. The receipt of assistance from Germany while she was fighting Russia was considered in Lenin's tactics "the utilization of the internal contradictions within imperialism."

[27] V.I. Lenin, *Poln. sobr. soch.*, vol. 34, pp. 135, 222.

[28] *Istoriia SSSR s drevneishikh vremen do nashikh dnei* [*The History of the USSR from Ancient Times until Our Days*], vol. 40, Moscow, 1967, pp. 36, 39.

[29] V.V. Kabanov, "Agrarnaia revoliutsiia v Rossii" in *Voprosy istorii* ["The Agrarian Revolution in Russia" in *Problems of History*], 1989, No. II, p. 29.

[30] *Proletarskaia revoliutsiia* [*Proletarian Revolution*], 1922, No. 10, p. 319.

[31] V.I. Lenin, *Poln. sobr. soch.*, vol. 34, p. 226.

[32] Lenin, vol. 34, p. 282.

[33] Lenin, vol. 34, pp. 394-95.

[34] *Protokoly TsK RSDRP(b), Avgust 1917-Fevral 1918* (Protocols of the Central Committee of the RSDRP(b), August 1917-February 1918), Moscow, 1958.

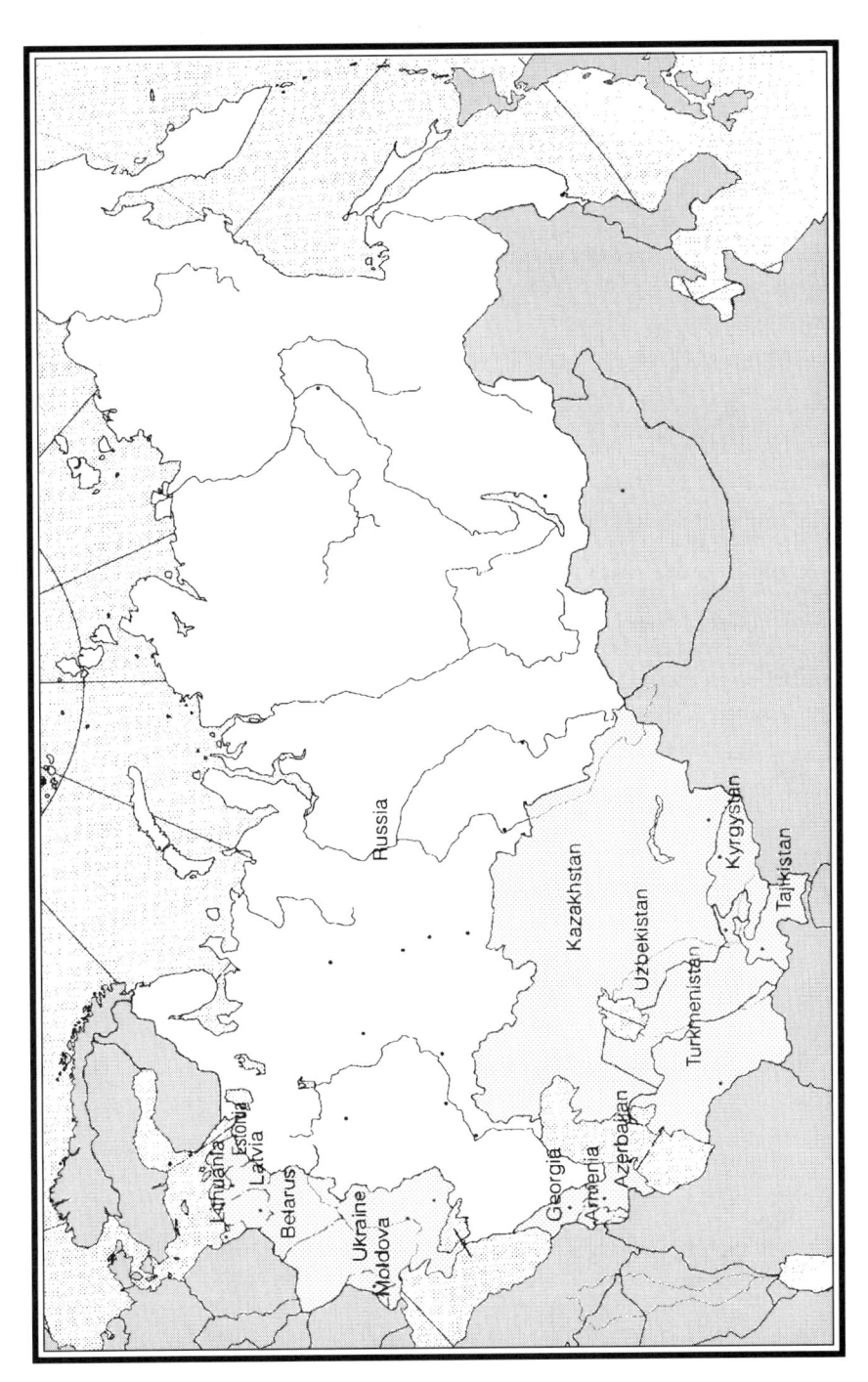

THE OCTOBER REVOLUTION **67**

RUSSIAN REPUBLIC 1917-Present

68 CHAPTER ONE

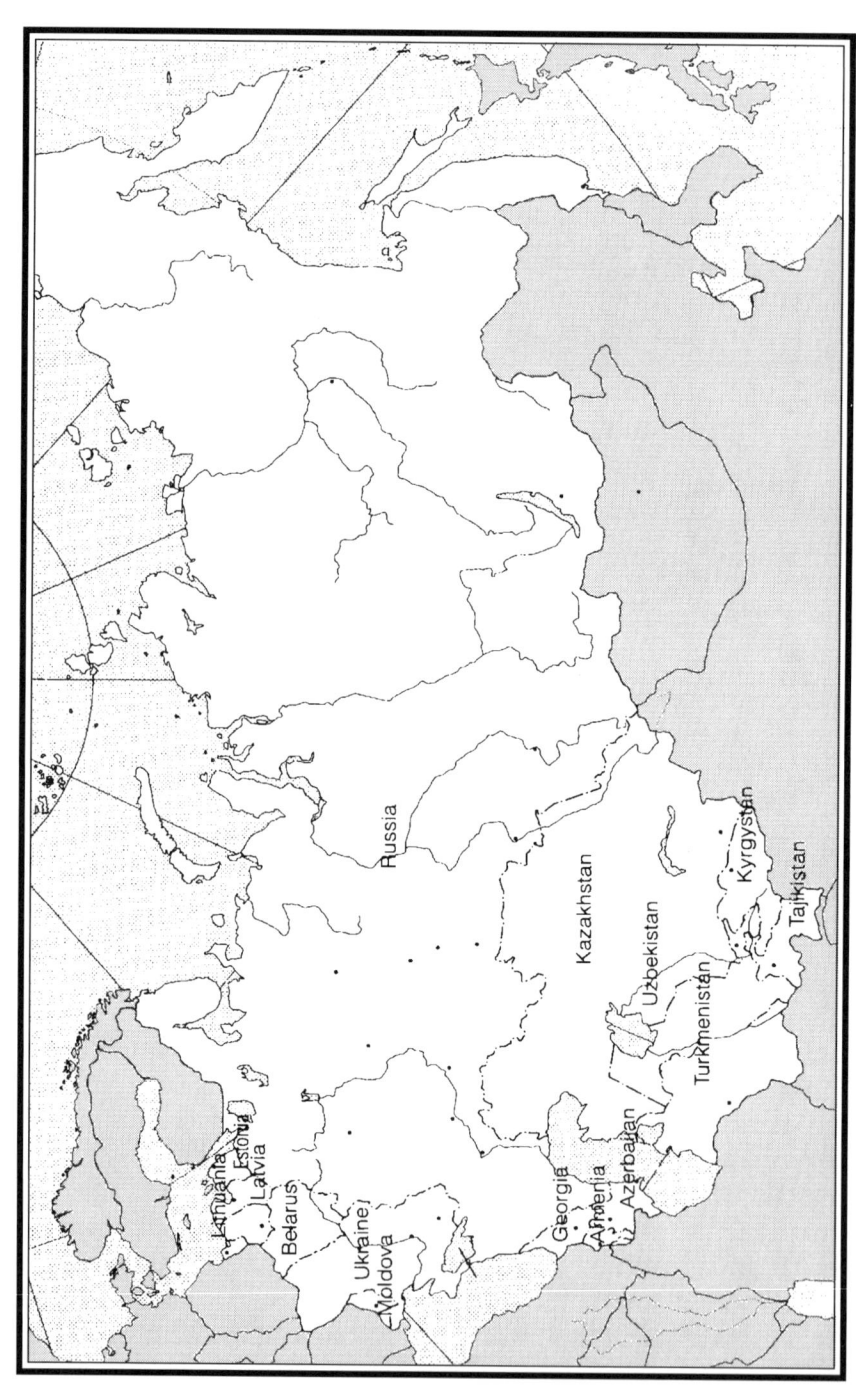

USSR 1923-1991

CHAPTER 2

THE CIVIL WAR AND THE FORMATION OF THE BOLSHEVIK REGIME

Europe at the End of the Period between 1917 and 1920

The European crisis caused by the First World War was aggravated even more by the October Revolution and the armistice with Germany signed by the Bolshevik government on December 2, 1917. Since American troops had only just begun to arrive on the continent, Russia's withdrawal from the world war threatened the Entente with the very real possibility of defeat. The growth of antiwar and revolutionary sentiments, stimulated by the "Russian example" and the Decree on Peace, destabilized the situation even more. The American president, W. Wilson, was concerned about the growing influence of Bolshevik propaganda in European politics.[1] Accepting the challenge and at the same time trying to strengthen the position of the United States in the competition with Great Britain and France for world leadership, Wilson proposed his own peace program, the "Fourteen Points," on January 8, 1918, which envisioned the end of the war on the condition of Germany's withdrawal from the occupied territories and the fundamental restructuring of inter-

Russia in World War I
1914 to the Revolution of 1917
Fartherest Russian Advance in Germany and Austria, 1914
Major Battle Sites
Principal Russian Railways
White Sea
Archangel
N. Dvina
L. Onega
Kotlas
L. Ladoga
Viborg
Helsingfors
Viatka
Reval
Petrograd
Vologda
SWEDEN
Baltic Sea
Pskov
Iaroslav
Volga
Nizhnii Novgorod
Libau
Riga
Tver
Dvinsk
W. Dvina
Moscow
Smolensk
Riazan
Danzig
Vilna
Oka
Tula
Sept. 1914 Masurian Lakes
Tannenberg Aug. 1914
Minsk
RUSSIA
Penza
GERMANY
Orel
Gomel
Bug
Pinsk
Warsaw
Brest Litovsk
Voronezh
POLAND
FRONT LINE AT THE TIME OF THE OCTOBER REVOLUTION, 1917
Vistula
Rovno
Don
Kiev
Kharkov
Cracow
GALICIA
BRUSILOV OFFENSIVE 1916
Tsaritsya
Donets
AUSTRIA
Ekaterinoslav
Dniester
UKRAINE
Budapest
Prut
Rostov-on-Don
HUNGARY
Odessa
Dnieper
RUMANIAN AND RUSSIAN FORCES 1916
Kersh
Kuban
Belgrade
CRIMEA
RUMANIA
Sarajevo
Sevastopol
Terek
Bucharest
CAUCASUS
MONTE-NEGRO
SERBIA
Danube
BULGARIA
Varna
Black Sea
Sofia
ALBANIA
Sinope
Batum
Kura
Kars
Bosporus
Salonika
Constantinople
Gallipoli
Dardanelles
Fartherest Russian Advance 1916
GREECE
TURKEY
Allies, 1915-16
Athens
1914 boundries
0 Miles 300
Kevin Trezise GEO. DEPT. UCA

THE CIVIL WAR

national relations.² The Fourteen Points recognized Russia's right to select her own political development. Some ideas of the program were obsolete, but despite the popular reception of the Fourteen Points, they were coolly received by the governments of England, France, and the Four-Power alliance.

Meanwhile, having taken advantage of the separate peace treaty with Russia concluded on March 3, 1918, Germany transferred part of its army to the Western front and on March 21 opened an offensive there. The Germans managed to approach the Marne river, 70 kilometers from the French capital, and started long-distance artillery shelling of Paris. But Germany was not strong enough to do more. Fifty to sixty thousand American soldiers were arriving in Europe weekly and by the fall of 1918 their total number would reach one million. The Entente started an offensive along the whole front early in August. One by one Germany's allies left the war. On November 3, 1918, the German sailors and workers initiated a riot at Kiel that developed into a revolution. It reached Berlin on November 9. On November 11, 1918, the Compiegne armistice was signed. The First World War had ended.

But the Versailles peace treaty, concluded in Paris in June 1919, did not eliminate the existing international disagreements and it exposed a sharp difference of opinion within the Entente. Great Britain and France managed to ward off the establishment of American hegemony in Europe. Italy clearly felt deprived of its proper share of power. And a whole series of new national states were built on the ruins of the Russian and Austro-Hungarian Empires (Finland, Estonia, Latvia, Lithuania, Poland, Hungary, Czechoslovakia, Austria, and the Kingdom of Serbs, Croats, and Slovenes which was later renamed Yugoslavia) complicated the situation.

In Germany, Austria, and Hungary military defeat and the Russian Revolution of October 1917 created social tension in the form of the democratic revolutions of 1918-1919, during the course of which socialist tendencies appeared. In the first half of 1919, soviet republics emerged in Bremen, Bavaria, and Slovakia but only lasted, on average, for three weeks. However, the Hungarian Soviet Republic that was set up peacefully on March 21, 1919, survived for more than four months. There was revolutionary turmoil in other countries as well. Influenced by Russian events, a revolution broke out in Finland in January 1918. Soviets involving 60,000 to 70,000 workers also were set up in "peaceful" Norway in 1918. In response to the intervention in Russia, a movement of solidarity with the Soviet state developed in the Entente countries. In September 1920 Italian workers began seizing entire plants.

The war, the destruction of the established world order, and internal instability, exacerbated by the economic crisis at the end of 1920, led to political polarization and the appearance of masses of radical workers on the political scene. In 1918-1919, leftist radical communist parties and groups emerged outside of Soviet Russia. At their first congress, which took place in Moscow on March 2-6, 1919, representatives of thirty-five leftist socialist and communist organizations from twenty-one countries of Europe, Asia, and America formed the Third Communist International or Comintern. The primary task of the Comintern was to overthrow capitalism and establish socialism by means of proletarian revolutions and the creation of soviets as the new seats of political power. The revolutionary activity of the Comintern, headed by the Executive Committee (chairman—G.V. Zinoviev), relied on certain layers of working people and ultraleft intelligentsia.

A radical right wing fascist movement, another of the twentieth century's mass uprisings, appeared in Italy and Germany at practically the same time as the Communist movement. The fascist movement also denounced the bourgeois world order and appealed to the lower classes through social rhetoric. But in contrast to communism, in the center of which was the idea of a class struggle and internationalism, fascism was based on the idea of nationalism, carried to its logical completion. Fascism rapidly gained strength. On March 23, 1919, the former socialist Benito Mussolini set up an organization known as the *"fascisti di combattimento"* ("Union for the Struggle"). In 1921 the fascist movement in Italy had 300,000 members, mostly from the lower classes. Of the Italian fascists 40% were agrarian and urban workers, 13% students, 12% farmers, 10% private company employees, 9% traders and craftsmen, and 2.6% industrialists.[3] In the autumn of 1919 a demobilized noncommissioned officer, later one of the Reichswehr's political informers, Adolf

Hitler, unexpectedly found himself in the ranks of the small "German Workers' Party." In 1920 the party grew from 100 to 3,000 members and after being officially recognized changed its name to the National Socialist German Workers' Party. Hitler became its leader.

The European ruling elite resorted to political maneuvers and social concessions to the masses more and more often. Coalition governments with socialist participation were already becoming common in the war. After the war socialists headed governments in Austria, Germany, and Sweden. A tendency toward authoritarian rule was simultaneously gaining force. Dictatorships, semifascist, and fascist regimes were established in 1920 in Hungary and later in other eastern and southern European states.

The revolution in Russia was a manifestation of the general European crisis and at the same time its catalyst. But the length of the world war and the tendency to underrate the Bolsheviks' victory, which Kerensky considered an "affair" or in any event a relatively short episode, delayed the great powers' direct interference in "Russian affairs," while the disagreements between them reduced the effectiveness of their operations all the more.

The Quadruple Alliance's offensive which began on February 18 resulted in occupation of vast territories: the Baltic coast, Belorussia, Ukraine, the Crimea, the Caucasus, and the Don region. This considerably reduced the territory under Soviet control and contributed to the appearance of counterrevolutionary bridgeheads in Russia. The White Army of the Don, armed by the Germans, grew rapidly. Nevertheless, the conclusion of the Brest peace, which was advantageous for a Germany exhausted from the war, more or less stabilized the position of the Soviet Republic although it did not halt Germany's expansion on the former territory of the Russian Empire. Germany's policy was not directed toward the suffocation of the Bolshevik state, but toward the maximum utilization, or rather the theft, of the nation's resources[4] and opposition to the Entente. On the whole Germany tried to prevent any alliances (revolutionary or counterrevolutionary) that could threaten it. After its defeat in the World War and the November Revolution (1918), the German troops were evacuated and Germany's influence rapidly declined, disappearing altogether in 1919.

The Entente states did not recall their representatives from Russia despite their nonrecognition of the Soviet regime and their secret support for some anti-Bolshevik forces. The desperate situation on the western front prevented the Entente's intervention in Russia and also pushed it into attempts to preserve an eastern front even under the Soviet flag, since the eastern front had tied down a third of the German forces (1.7 million men) in the autumn of 1917. Only after the conclusion of the peace of Brest did the London conference (March 15, 1918) reach a decision on the Entente's intervention into Russia. G.V. Chicherin, who became People's Commissar for Foreign Affairs in March 1918, originally considered it an attempt to restore the Russo-German front.[5]

From March 6, 1918, relying on an agreement with the executive committee of the Murmansk soviet on joint operations against the German threat, Great Britain and then France and the United States started landing their first small units at Murmansk. On April 5, 1918, Japan started landing its troops in the port of Vladivostok on the pretext of an attack by several unknown persons on a branch of a Japanese firm in the city. The American government decided to intervene in the Far East on July 6. But there remained serious differences in the positions of the great powers. Great Britain and the United States were inclined to divide Russia, while France on the contrary wanted to keep a unified and strong Russian state as a counterweight to Germany. The struggle against the Bolsheviks was not the main goal of Japan and the United States; both wanted to establish their influence in the Far East and Siberia and develop the territory economically. America was also interested in counteracting Japanese activity. But in general, before 1918 the Entente actions were neither decisive nor offensive. The situation changed after the mutiny of the Czechoslovak Legion on May 25, 1918. The legion had been formed by the Provisional Government, the Czechoslovak National Council, and the Entente with Austro-Hungarian POWs in January 1918. The legion declared itself a constituent part of the French army and tried to leave Russia via the Far East. The attempts of the Bolsheviks to disarm it and, in part, the activities of the Entente provoked the Czech mutiny which served as a turning point in the civil war in Russia.

The Entente did not begin to intervene in Russia on a relatively large scale until the end of the world war. The intervention took place under the guise of liberating the country from the "Bolshevik usurpers." At the end of November French, British, Greek, and Rumanian troops began landing in the Ukraine, the Crimea, and the port of Novorossiisk. The British started intervening in the Caucasus and Caspian sea regions as early as August. By February 1919 more than 202,000 servicemen were participating in the intervention against Russia, among them 45,000 British, around 14,000 French and American, 80,000 Japanese, 42,000 Czech, 3,000 Italian, 3,000 Greek, and 2,500 Serb soldiers.

At first France and Great Britain played the leading role in organizing the intervention. But the complex internal political situation and revolutionary ferment in the army and navy in the spring of 1919[6] forced the French to withdraw from direct armed intervention into Russia. The defeat of Udenich and Denikin in autumn 1919 compelled Britain to reconsider its policy. Lenin proudly stated: "We deprived the Allies of their troops by means of canvassing and propaganda."[7] Great Britain and France tried to set the buffer states which appeared after the fall of the Russian Empire (Poland, Finland, Lithuania, Latvia, and Estonia) against the Soviets. But the threat to their sovereignty posed by the victory of the Whites, struggling for a "united and indivisible Russia," caused these buffer states to abstain from the war with the Soviet Republic. The war with Poland was the only really dangerous consequence of that policy for Soviet Russia. Having set up a 730,000-man army with Allied assistance, Poland began an offensive in the Ukraine on April 25, 1920. Yet after some dramatic engagements, Polish military actions terminated in October 1920. Although Japanese intervention in the Far East continued until 1922, the attitude of the leading European states to Soviet Russia had changed. Great Britain started to trade with it in March 1920. Gradually the West had to extend de facto recognition to the RSFSR.

Thus, although the European crisis did not develop into a "world revolution," much to the Bolsheviks' disappointment, it was still one of the basic factors that made the Bolshevik victory in Russia possible. The Entente's actions were neither coordinated nor consistent, and despite their significant assistance to the White Army[8] and their delayed military intervention, the great powers did not decisively influence the outcome of the Civil War in Russia. Ironically the number of internationalists—foreign citizens who fought with the Reds—reached 250,000 to 300,000 people and was roughly comparable to the number of interventionist troops. The Bolshevik victory split Europe and the world and challenged western civilization. The latter was not ready for this challenge. But the Bolsheviks, who had hoped for a world revolution from the beginning, were not ready either.

Aleksandr Kerensky

The Formation of the Soviet State

The consolidation of their own power and the destruction of the former social structures were the primary tasks of the Bolsheviks after the October coup in Petrograd. Believing that they were on the eve of the world revolution, they placed their hopes on the revolutionary masses' hatred for the "rich" and the old order. Their action and "class consciousness," in Lenin's opinion, permitted the rapid suppression of the "exploiting" classes and the creation of the new communal soviet state, "the most advanced type of democracy." That state was to give the broadest possible rights to "the majority"—the working people—and only maintain a dictatorship over the minority—"the exploiters." According to Marxist theory, which Lenin adapted to Russian conditions, the regular army was to be replaced by arming all of the people, and the role of officialdom was to be reduced to a minimum and given completely to elected officials who would not receive more pay than the average qualified worker; since it was unnecessary under socialism, the separation of powers was to be eliminated and the legislative and executive authority were to be placed in the hands of the soviets.⁹ Lenin believed that the broad participation of the masses in the administration was the most important condition for the implementation of far-reaching social reform and the satisfactory resolution of the existing social and economic problems. Trying all the more to encourage the "revolutionary-expropriatory" zeal, Lenin on a number of occasions had successfully used the slogan "steal what has been stolen,"¹⁰ which was so dear to the masses.

The wager on the masses seemed correct at first. Through the land committees and the volost soviets, the peasants divided the pomeshchiks' lands among themselves, liquidating the pomestia, monastic, and crown lands by the spring and summer of 1918. This secured the peasants' loyalty to the Soviet regime and removed one of the economic bases for a potential counterrevolution. But in truth, contrary to the peasants' expectations, the hunger for land in the village was not fully eliminated. As a result of the confiscation of the pomestia, monastic, and state lands by 1919, the peasants only received 17.2 million desiatins. The figure of 150 million desiatins common to Soviet historiography is a myth.¹¹ In addition, large numbers of urban residents who had not lost their rural ties migrated to the village. As a result, according to several estimates, the original landholders in the majority of provinces only gained on the average about half a desiatin of additional land.¹²

Political considerations also dominated the Bolsheviks' economic policy in the towns. Soon after coming to power they undertook steps to establish control over industry and finances. At first Bolsheviks did not stress nationalization but emphasized "workers' control" over industry, which was considered a temporary stage necessary to suppress bourgeois sabotage and to give the masses time to learn management skills. Factory and plant committees and trade unions had begun to assume control over the production cycle even before the October coup just as the peasants had begun to seize the pomeshchiks' lands; the process took on a mass character immediately after the coup. The control of many enterprises had actually passed into the hands of managers from the working class. In mid-

November, partially as a result of the employers' secret opposition to workers' control, a wave of nationalization rose. The Bolsheviks immediately tried to nationalize the State Bank, but they only succeeded in getting or, in truth, purloining the first sums for the Council of People's Commissars (*Sovnarkom* or SNK) on October 17, and took control of the bank some time later. Private banks were nationalized in December and January. In the process of these changes the Soviet system for managing the economy was gradually taking shape. The Supreme Economic Council was set up on December 2, 1917, first headed by N. Osinsky and after April 1918 by A.I. Rykov. In Lenin's opinion it was the "instrument of war" in the economic struggle against the bourgeoisie; it depended on the economic departments of the soviets and, at the end of 1917, on the People's Economic Councils created in the provinces. Nevertheless, the Bolsheviks failed to create an effective management system. The workers, who thought that they were the owners of their own enterprises (even when they were not officially nationalized) and trade unions competed with the state bodies in their management. But still for the Bolsheviks, who were carried away with the "Red Guard's" attack on the capital, this was not important.

Some democratic measures were introduced immediately after October: the estates (*soslovie*) and former ranks were abolished while "citizen of the Russian Republic" became the sole title for everyone; the Church was separated from the State and religious instruction in schools was terminated; a decree on civil marriages was adopted. The Bolsheviks tried to improve the life of workers who were their main social base. They issued several decrees on an eight-hour working day and on unemployment and medical insurance; temporary regulations about vacations were introduced. But the growing economic crisis brought all of these measures to no account, and the eight-hour day had actually been introduced before the October Revolution. The decisions on the housing problem, which permitted workers to occupy abandoned apartments and reside in the homes and apartments of the bourgeoisie, intelligentsia, and employees, were the only exception. The reduction of the amount of living space formerly enjoyed by the bourgeoisie created a phenomenon characteristic of all Soviet history, the "communal apartment."[13]

On November 2, 1917, the "Declaration of the Rights of the Peoples of Russia" proclaimed the equality of the nationalities and their right to self-determination, including the formation of independent states. This had great political and propaganda value for the country, 57% of whose population belonged to non-Russian nationalities. In fact, the free and sovereign development of the various nationalities did not concern the Bolsheviks who were interested only in tactical considerations; the objective was to secure the support of the non-Russian nationalities and facilitate the development of the revolutionary process. The commissar for nationalities, J.V. Stalin, as usual, yearning for a stratagem from Lenin's ideas, tried to make the delegates of one of the delegations at the nationalities conference in May 1918 understand that the Soviet regime could not grant autonomy since all of the power inside the nationality belonged to its bourgeoisie. There could only be "such autonomy, where all power is in the hands of the workers and peasants, where the bourgeoisie of all nationalities have been removed not only from power, but from participation in the election of the organs of government."[14] Moreover, no one could doubt the future union of the nationalities and their relatively rapid pacification after the world revolution, and the latter apparently was approaching. It is not surprising that the rapid disintegration of the Russian Empire at the end of 1917 and beginning of 1918, although provoked by the October Revolution,[15] only proceeded in the areas where the Bolsheviks did not have power. As early as December 1917 the Bolsheviks had to recognize the independence of Finland and Ukraine (although a number of harsh conditions, which resembled an ultimatum, were proposed to the Central Rada). Moreover, in the winter of 1917 and spring of 1918, Lithuania, Latvia, Estonia, and Belorussia—territories occupied by the Germans—proclaimed their independence and in April the Transcaucasian Democratic Federal Republic arose, which soon broke up into Georgia, Azerbaijan, and Armenia.

For the radical Bolsheviks, the moderate internal policy during the first months after October and their dependence on the "creative revolutionary work" of the masses was the result of their weak power and the undeveloped new state apparatus. There was no one to rely on except the masses of workers and soldiers revolutionized by the

Bolsheviks. The new state was gradually being created. But authority was extremely decentralized.

Although the former organs of self-government, the urban dumas and rural zemstvos, were preserved until the spring and summer of 1918, the Soviets took power in the provinces. Some provincial and even district soviets declared their territories republics and created their own councils of people's commissars and decided local questions independently, without any regard whatsoever for the central government. At the center the executive and legislative functions were concentrated in the Council of People's Commissars. The All-Russian Central Executive Committee (VTsIK) played somewhat less of a role from the very beginning and with the consolidation of party membership was finally transformed into a ceremonial institution. Although the continually sitting Sovnarkom overwhelmed the country with a pile of decrees which represented, with some exceptions, the fruit of hasty improvisation, it could not get control of the staff until the end of 1917 and the beginning of 1918. Contrary to the Bolsheviks' expectations, taking possession of the state administration was extremely difficult and without the assistance of the old bureaucracy totally impossible. Meanwhile the general strike of the state and financial officials together with some members of the intelligentsia, which had paralyzed the state apparatus since its beginning on October 26, continued to unfold. According to the smallest estimate, there were 44,000 banking, postal, and telegraph office workers, and bureaucrats on strike in St. Petersburg alone. But with the assistance of arrests, the confiscation of property, and intimidation—strikers were called "enemies of the people"—the "sabotage" conducted by the civil servants was basically overcome in early 1918. Not having, as a rule, any other stable means of subsistence besides the civil service, the old bureaucracy and civil servants had to give their services to the Soviet state. This was a major victory for the Bolsheviks, although it was obtained at the expense of the rapid bureaucratization of the state structures, a retreat from the principles of a "state-commune."

Attempts were made to replace the demoralized and demobilized old army with the voluntary Red Guard and with squadrons of soldiers and sailors. The formation on December 7, 1917, of the All-

THE CIVIL WAR

Russian Extraordinary Commission for the struggle with the counterrevolutionaries and saboteurs (the VChK or Cheka) under the leadership of F.E. Dzerzhinsky greatly strengthened the Bolsheviks' authority. In contrast to the All-Russian Revolutionary Committee (the VRK), which had carried out some of these functions earlier, the Cheka was intended to be a "party weapon" rather than a organ of the soviets (although during the coalition with the left SRs, some of its representatives were included in it).

The struggle against political opposition immediately became the Soviet government's most important activity. On October 27, on Lenin's initiative, the Decree of the Press was approved, which marked the beginning of the suppression of the opposition press, first the "bourgeois" and later the socialist press. In the first two months alone 150 newspapers were closed. On November 28, the Sovnarkom declared the Kadets to be "the party of the people's enemies" and demanded the arrest of their leaders as the "bosses of the civil war." The soldiers and sailors who were armed but had lost all semblance of discipline and the revolutionary workers who considered themselves the masters of the situation and zealously searched for the "enemies of the revolutionary people" created an atmosphere of psychological and sometimes physical terror against the bourgeois and intellectuals whom they hated. In Soviet Russia this was said to be a kind of "trench-barracks socialism" based "on the detailed interrogation of all life, not on the cult against the 'callous' kulak, but against any kulak, that considered anyone cultured guilty of being bourgeois,"[16] wrote Yu. O. Martov. The attitude of the majority of the intelligentsia, which had sparkled in the spring of the revolution, became nearly apocalyptic in the autumn. "Servitude will return to us, only in a strange distorted form and in the mask of terror," wrote Z. Hippius in November 1917.[17]

But the power of the Bolsheviks was still weak in the autumn and winter of 1917. They did not have at hand a strong apparatus for repression. Their position on the periphery and especially in the village was very tentative. Among 130 million peasants there were only 203 Bolshevik cells, including 4100 peasants. The villages were under the influence of the SRs. Essentially, the power of the Bolsheviks was only based on the unstable support of the revolutionized masses of workers and soldiers, the benevolent neutrality of the peasantry (secured by the decrees of the Second Congress of Soviets) and the absence of any kind of strong, cohesive counterrevolutionary force. The convocation of the Constituent Assembly which lay in the future hung like a sword of Damocles over the Bolshevik government.

All of these circumstances forced the Bolshevik leadership not only to struggle with the socialist parties, but to maneuver around, searching for allies among them. Probably, such a "natural" ally, valuable to the Bolsheviks because of their leftist nature and especially for their influence in the village, was clearly found during the October Revolution in the Left SRs. But they were supporters of a broad socialist coalition government. Moreover the mood in favor of a homogenous socialist government was widespread in the masses and in the Bolshevik party itself. The collapse of the negotiations for the creation of a coalition government at the end of November 1917 by no means removed the problem from the agenda.

The left SRs, in the process of forming their own organization whose membership was drawn from the Socialist Revolutionary Party, were interested in an alliance with the Bolsheviks. Therefore, despite some differences with the Bolsheviks over their program and tactics, the Left SRs agreed in principle to entering into the Bolsheviks' Council of People's Commissars on November 17. They were not supporters of nationalization but of the socialization of land, and they condemned the decree on the press and the dissolution of the Petrograd town duma, where the SRs predominated, Seven representatives of the left SRs entered the Sovnarkom on December 9, including A.L. Kolegaev (agriculture), I.Z. Shteinberg (justice), and V.E. Trutovsky (local government) but only with the approval of the First Congress of the Party and the attainment of a majority in the provisional and Second All-Russian Congress of Peasants' Deputies (November 11 to December 10, 1917).[18]

The joint work of the Bolsheviks and left SRs in the government was far from harmonious. In December 1917 and January 1918 alone the Sovnarkom twice considered the complaints of Shteinberg about the Cheka, which did not burden itself with legality and failed to respect the People's Commissariat of Justice. Nevertheless, before the Peace of Brest, both sides succeeded in making compromises. On the whole this first and last governmental coalition in Soviet Russia played an indispensable role in the preservation of Bolshevik power by ending the governmental crisis of November and securing a base for it among the peasantry while helping it deal with the basic problem of the Constituent Assembly.

In the nineteenth century, in the eyes of the liberals, the socialists, and after the February revolution in the eyes of the broad masses, the Constituent Assembly had been transformed into a cherished, semilegendary entity through which the hope for the radical democratization of society and the just resolution of the fundamental political and socioeconomic problems was connected. These expectations were also reflected in the Second Congress of Soviets which recognized the Constituent Assembly's full authority to finally resolve the questions on authority and landholding. Under these conditions the Bolsheviks decided not to postpone elections, as Lenin had suggested immediately after the October Revolution.

Before coming to power Lenin officially did not oppose the convocation of the Constituent Assembly but understood that it would not be Bolshevik.[19] Chosen by universal and equal suffrage in "petit-bourgeois" Russia, the Constituent Assembly would not be compatible with the "dictatorship of the proletariat," precluding the possibility of securing the priorities of the workers (as they had been able to do in the soviets) and even more so of the "proletarian party" which the Bolsheviks considered to be themselves.

Taking power, and together with it the unique possibility of realizing socialism, Lenin was not in any way prepared to carry out the promise given on October 26 to the Second Congress of Soviets to yield to the will of the people in the event of his party's defeat in the elections.[20] When after the elections, which had proceeded as planned on November 12 (later in some regions), it became clear that the Bolsheviks and Left SRs actually were in the minority, Lenin raised the question of the possible dispersion of the Constituent Assembly. But the Bolsheviks and especially the Left SRs did not rule out the possibility of a relatively brief symbiosis of the soviets with the Constituent Assembly, obtained by changing the composition and planetary power of the latter. The distribution of the land to the peasants, the demobilization of the army, and the later conclusion of an armistice with the Germans somewhat reduced the value of the Constituent Assembly in the eyes of some of the peasants', workers', and soldiers' masses and raised the "prestige" of the soviets and the Bolsheviks who had implemented these measures. Lenin also considered the possibility of having another election, with the members of the Constituent Assembly being elected by the working class. As a result the government went on the offensive. It pushed through a decree on the removal of the deputies who did not warrant confidence through the All-Russian Central Executive Committee, it disbanded the All-Russian Commission on Elections to the Constituent Assembly, and after arresting some of their members, it set the quorum for the Constituent Assembly. On November 28 it began the arrest of the Kadet deputies. Nevertheless the Bolsheviks did not succeed in changing the situation. There was even strong sentiment among the Bolshevik faction for considering the Constituent Assembly as the highest authority.

As a result of the first universal and equal elections in Russian history, based on accurate data, the votes were distributed in the following manner: SRs—40.6%, Mensheviks—2.8%, other socialist parties (mostly of the nationalities)—15%, the non-socialist parties of the nationalities—8%, the Kadets—4.6%, the confessional parties, cooperatives, Cossacks, and rightwingers—6.1%, and the Bolsheviks—22.9%.[21] At key points—Petrograd, Moscow, the army, and provincial towns—the share of the vote given to the Bolsheviks exceeded the average by 1.5 to two times. In both capitals and in many large towns it was double (for the Bolsheviks or SRs), while now and then the Kadets occupied the first place among the votes. On the whole the results of the voting clearly reflected the specific political development of Russia, which was connected with the liberals' weak base among the masses outside of the major cities, the masses' strong "socialist instincts" and relative radicalism, which for the first time in world history gave 81.3% of the vote to the socialists. For the Bolsheviks, who received, according to the available evidence, 175 seats out of 715, and the Left SRs, who had 40 seats, the results were far from satisfactory.

The Constituent Assembly which opened on January 5, 1918,

THE CIVIL WAR   85

proceeded under extraordinary conditions. The Tauride Palace, where it sat, was not only completely surrounded by troops but was packed with sailors and soldiers who did not conceal their own Bolshevik sympathies, aiming their rifles at speakers whom they disliked. Lenin, leaving for the Constituent Assembly, carried his own pistol which later was taken from his overcoat by sailors of the guard.[22]

In the final analysis, the Bolsheviks did not fear the deputies, who were prepared for the worst, but an armed uprising in support of the Constituent Assembly. But the introduction of martial law in Petrograd, the clear preponderance of force, and the indecisiveness of the SRs—the only party at the time which was able to lead the opposition—enabled them to ward off the danger. The shooting of peaceful demonstrators marching under the slogan "For the Constituent Assembly" during the afternoon of January 5 gave the Bolsheviks confidence.

After the opening of the Constituent Assembly Ya.M. Sverdlov on behalf of the All-Russian Central Executive Committee proposed the adoption of the "declaration of the Rights of Workers and Exploited People" prepared by Lenin on a take-it-or-leave-it basis. The Mensheviks and SRs attempted several times to moderate the radicalism of the Bolsheviks and redirect the discussion onto another path. "It was unnecessary to prove to the Constituent Assembly, which sang the International, that socialism was better than capitalism," I.G. Tsereteli observed, but "I have not heard from the Bolsheviks 'one affirmative argument that the immediate implementation of socialism will have positive results.'"[23] The Bolsheviks did not intend to engage in discussions for a long period or to search for compromises. Having taken advantage of the refusal of the Constituent Assembly to promulgate their own declaration, they, and later the Left SRs, deserted the Tauride Palace. The delegates who remained were dispersed by armed guards in the morning. Even so, the Constituent Assembly had succeeded in passing a law on land and declaring itself the supreme authority.

Although the dispersal of the Constituent Assembly did not cause mass uprisings of protest in the country, it was a major step toward a general civil war. The political conflict had not in fact been resolved and all of the illusions about the peaceful development of events had finally disappeared while the anti-Bolshevik forces had received a powerful motive for consolidation. The victims of the shooting at the demonstration in Petrograd[24] became the first instance of the Bolsheviks' armed repression against the broad masses.

The Third Congress of the Soviets of Workers' and Soldiers' Deputies, which opened on January 10, 1918, approved the dismissal of the Constituent Assembly and accepted the Declaration of the Rights of the Workers and Exploited People. After the Third Congress of Peasants' Soviets became part of the Congress (and accepted its decisions), Russia had a single system of Soviets of Workers', Soldiers', and Peasants' Deputies. The All-Russian Central Executive Committee chosen by the Congress included 160 Bolsheviks (52.3%), 125 Left SRs (40.8%), and seven Maximalists and SRs, three Anarcho-Communists, and four Mensheviks. In this way the peasant soviets also fell under Bolshevik control.

The creation of the Soviet state and the possession by the Bolsheviks of the key mechanisms of power were the major results of the first "clearly political" stage of the post-October history. Their authority was still not stable and the Bolsheviks had to share power with the Left SRs and the soviets who were relatively independent (although they supported the Bolsheviks) as well as the trade unions and other social organizations of "workers."

The Treaty of Brest-Litovsk

Until 1918 Bolsheviks linked Russian withdrawal from the war with the expected world revolution and with the transformation of the "imperialist" war into a civil war and the overthrow of "the entire capitalist order." Two principal components formed the basis of the Bolsheviks' strategy in foreign affairs: (1) a peace offer to all of the belligerent states on the condition of liberation for the colonies and all oppressed peoples,[25] and (2) in case of refusal—the development of a revolutionary war. The first component was actually a propaganda ploy calculated to enhance the revolutionary movements in other countries. But the Bolsheviks were unable to realize the second, key point without the support of the European revolutions. Therefore, when the Entente ignored the proposals of the Bolshevik government on peace, it concluded an armistice with the Germans. The Bolsheviks dragged out the peace negotiations which began on December 9 as long as possible, using them for propaganda purposes and waiting for revolutions in the countries of Europe, especially in Germany. The concessions of the Germans, who agreed to recognize the formula of a general democratic peace in the event of its recognition by the Entente, were regarded by the Bolsheviks to be a sign of the Germans' inability to attack.

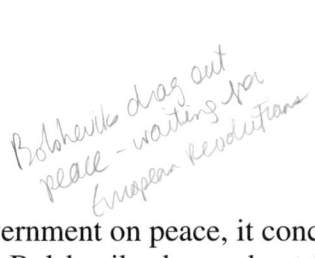

Taking advantage of the fact that the Entente had again ignored their peace proposals, the delegation of the Quadruple Alliance advanced their own draft of the peace treaty. With reference to the principle of national self-determination proclaimed by the Bolsheviks and the corresponding desire of the peoples of Poland, Lithuania, and Latvia, the draft provided for the seizure of these territories from Russia and their transfer to German control. So the Soviet delegation's attempts to delay the talks failed.

It seems that under the circumstances, Lenin for the first time came to the conclusion that a separate peace with Germany was a vital necessity. Some authors, however, think the separate peace treaty was predetermined earlier by secret agreements between the Bolsheviks and Germany.[26] "If the birth of the European revolution is delayed," Lenin affirmed, "we can expect the heaviest losses because we have neither an army nor an organization.... If you are unable to adjust and do not want to creep along, crawling on your belly, you are not a revolutionary but just a chatterbox...."[27] Trotsky agreed with Lenin that Russia was incapable of continuing the war but he was against concluding a peace treaty. He hoped Germany would not be able to attack; but if it could, then the thing for Russia to do would be to sign the peace treaty under direct military pressure. He hoped that would save the moral purity of the revolutionary banner (loyalty to the general democratic peace that had been proposed) and avoid the Entente's accusations of violating the obligations of an ally. Trotsky was impatiently waiting for revolutions in Europe and was afraid to frighten them by signing a separate peace treaty. Trotsky underlined the fact that "All our previous talks with Germans and our propaganda had revolutionary meaning only to the extent that they were taken at their face value."[28] The so-called "left communists," namely N.I. Bukharin, N. Osinsky, E.A. Preobrazhensky, and A.M. Kolontay, strongly opposed a separate peace treaty. Most of the Bolshevik leaders and the largest party organizations supported this point of view. Believing that only a world revolution could save the Russian revolution and that the conclusion of a separate peace would not give a sufficient breathing space to Soviet Russia, they saw a revolutionary war against Germany as the only way out. In their opinion the war could be carried on with small detachments using partisan methods, which would not only prevent them from throwing the Ukrainian, Belorussian, and Baltic workers "under the boots of German soldiers," but would incite the world revolution.

The conclusion of a separate peace was not only opposed by a majority of the Bolsheviks but by all of the other socialist, liberal, and right-wing parties and organizations. In this way, the war with Germany consolidated the various political forces which had been in opposition and at the same time made an agreement with the Entente possible. The beginning of the revolutionary war with Germany created the conditions for the establishment of a broad coalition government of socialists. Perhaps that was why Lenin fought for a separate peace treaty so desperately, not sparing himself even when it seemed that he was practically alone. And again, as in 1917, Lenin's will and the masses' attitude (the vast majority of whom clearly did not want to resume the fight) turned the wheel of Russian history. And, as before, the turn was dramatic.

On January 28, 1918, Trotsky, who headed the Soviet delegation to the negotiations, under German pressure announced his refusal to sign the peace but at the same time announced the end of the war on the part of Russia. The All-Russian Central Executive Committee approved this decision on February 14, representing the centrist, intermediate position between Lenin's position and the left Communists. On February 16, the Germans announced the end of the armistice and began an attack on February 18, almost without resistance. Only under the influence of Lenin's threat to resign from the Central Committee and the German attack did a majority of the members of the Bolshevik Central Committee, after sharp debate during the evening of February 18, agree to the signing of the peace.

However the Germans did not answer the radiogram and continued to advance. They did not ask for a confirmation until February 20, while on February 23 the Bolsheviks received new, even harsher conditions for peace. They were accepted after a dramatic discussion. The peace was concluded at Brest-Litovsk on March 3, 1918. Despite the resistance of Left Communists and Left SRs, it was approved by the Seventh Extraordinary Congress of the Bolshevik Party and by the Fourth Extraordinary Congress of Soviets, which sat in Moscow from March 14 to 16. At the same time they began to call the party the Russian Communist Party of Bolsheviks.

In accordance with the peace, which amounted to open thievery, Poland, the Baltic, part of Belorussia, Ardagan, Kars, and Batum were taken from Russia. The Ukraine, through an agreement with the Central Rada, was actually occupied while Finland was recognized as independent. The lost territory amounted to 780,000 kilometers. Fifty-six million people, a third of the Russian Empire's population, lived on it and it comprised a quarter of all arable lands; 70% of the iron and up to 90% of the coal and sugar industries were found there. The loss of 40% of the industrial workers was especially serious for the Bolsheviks. Soviet Russia also had to demobilize its army and navy and pay huge reparations (six billion marks).

The political consequences of the Brest peace treaty turned out to be no less significant. The Left SRs resigned from the Sovnarkom in protest against the peace. There was no point in even discussing the possibility of agreements with the other socialist parties. The Entente, as has already been observed, decided to begin the intervention in Russia. At the same time the Bolsheviks kept power and were fully occupied in consolidating their own regime. For a time they stopped considering the October Revolution a direct stimulus for a revolution in Europe. The Brest peace treaty represented a serious tactical retreat by the Bolsheviks to play for time and to wait for the world revolution which had been "delayed." Lenin underscored this: "Given all possible, conceivable scenarios, we will perish if the German revolution does not come." Nevertheless even this inconsequential and brief change nearly set off an explosion among the Bolsheviks, some of whom could not be reconciled to the suspension of the "cavalry attack against capitalism."

The Turning Point in the Spring of 1918

The change from "revolutionary romanticism" to a serious struggle for existence was reflected in domestic policy. The boundary between the two periods of Soviet history was clearly defined when the Sovnarkom moved to Moscow in March 1918. The change of capital was caused not only by the relative remoteness of "the city of the first throne" from the borders but also by a calmer political atmosphere in the city, and the latter—in its turn—was a sign of the time.

In spring 1918, the Bolsheviks encountered a severe economic, political, organizational, and to some extent ideological crisis. Their banking on the revolutionary masses began to turn against them. The masses handled the destructive function brilliantly but were incapable of a constructive function. This was demonstrated first in the economy.

The management and control of enterprises by workers failed: labor productivity fell, payment by time was introduced instead of payment by piece, and with the abolition of worker searches thefts spiraled. Some workers' collectives officially announced the conversion of the enterprises into their own property and decided to sell the factory's assets.[29] The situation was aggravated by the consequences of the Brest peace treaty and the disorderly demobilization of industry.[30] By the end of 1917 industrial production had fallen by 36%. In 1918 the reduced industrial output represented a third of the previous year's level. By mid-1918 unemployment in Soviet Russia had risen to 600,000 persons. Workers' real wages had declined to 20% of the 1913 level.

But hunger became the major problem. In February and March of 1918 the country's main consuming regions only received 12.3% of the planned amount of bread. The daily ration in industrial centers was reduced to 50-100 grams, but sometimes even that was unavailable. Hunger revolts began.

The loss of the principal grain producing regions—the Ukraine and later southern Russia—was not the only cause of the hunger. The reduction in the market value of farm produce was a result of the destruction of the pomeshchiks' landholding and the growth of peasant consumption. But the main cause was the peasants' disinterest in selling grain to the state at fixed, low prices. Because of inflation the value of the grain was considerably higher than the state's fixed price, and payment in the form of suitable consumer goods was a failure as a result of the disorganization of industrial production and the disruption of trade connections. The Bolsheviks continued the state grain monopoly introduced by the Provisional Government; the detachments of workers or Red Guards who traded and sometimes just requisitioned grain in the villages could not solve the supply problem. "On the one hand the villages gave the cities fewer and fewer necessities, but on the other hand cities have less and less left to buy them," N. Osinsky observed at the All-Russian Congress of People's Economic Councils (Sovnarkhozy).[31]

Hunger, growing unemployment, and the exhaustion of the workers, who unlike the peasants got nothing from the revolution but a certain moral and political satisfaction, caused the rapid spread of anti-Bolshevik feelings. Despite the obstacles created by the Bolsheviks at the time of the reelection of the soviets, the Mensheviks and SRs strengthened their position in some cities. "Assemblies of factory and plant representatives," who were trying to become the organs of workers' representation in opposition to the Bolshevik-dominated soviets, were established at enterprises in Petrograd, Moscow, Tula, Kharkov, and other cities. From October 1917 to the summer 1918 Bolshevik party membership dropped from 350,000 (the traditional figure cited in Russian historiography) to 150,000. Except for some specific issues such as the migration to the village and the growth of unemployment which sometimes caused a rupture between the Bolsheviks and their party organizations, such a sharp decline in the membership of the Bolshevik party was an alarming symptom. In total membership, the Bolsheviks were not significantly ahead of the Left SRs (80,000) or Mensheviks (who had at least 60,000 members).

It seems that many of the characteristic features of the pre-October period were reproduced in the spring of 1918: a growing crisis and massive dissatisfaction with the government, the relative weakness of central power, opposition inside the Bolshevik party and the ruling coalition (the coalition ended in the government but continued in the soviets), and the absence of a realistic program by the government to resolve the crisis. In fact, activities of the Bolsheviks failed to meet the expectations of the party members and the masses; there was a growing suspicion that this was a blind alley. But a strong political will and tactical flexibility along with contempt for "purity" and "formality" were the important trump cards of the Bolsheviks.

In answer to the challenges of the time Lenin quickly changed emphasis. Instead of calling the weakened bourgeoisie the "chief enemy of socialism," he applied the term to the "petit-bourgeois element"—the peasant farm and private trade were its essential elements—which undermined the bread monopoly; the black market and the so called "bagmen" (*meshochniki*) supplied the vast majority of the grain and provisions for the towns. Lenin called for the suspension of the "Red Guards' attack on capital" in the cities and encouraged so-called "state capitalism." Lenin understood it as the introduction of standardization, "inventory and control" at enterprises, the adoption of progressive methods of organizing labor borrowed from capitalism (Taylor and Ford), and some productivity incentives. He underscored the need for the active involvement of "bourgeois specialists" and some of the capitalists who were ready to cooperate with Soviet power. To strengthen workers' discipline and responsibility he suggested, among other measures, the need to use extremely harsh methods, including the "shooting on the spot of one out of every ten people guilty of parasitism." Instead of the democratic management of enterprises by the workers, rigid centralization and the concentration of the "unlimited power of dictators" in the hands of some officials was introduced. Lenin was affirming that the "dictatorship of a few individuals has very often been the mouthpiece, exponent, and bearer of the dictatorship of the revolutionary classes."[32]

Such a management model was entirely incompatible with a communal state governed by the masses themselves. From that time the idea of a communal state was only remembered every now and then and only in official speeches. The failure of attempts "to arm the people" caused the Bolsheviks to issue a decree on January 15, 1918, on the introduction of a permanent Red Army; compulsory conscription replaced voluntary conscription on May 29. On April

29, 1918, the specialists' and managers' salaries were increased. The number of former clerks working in the People's Commissariat of Finance by the autumn of 1918 was 97.5%, in the Railway Commissariat—88.1%, and in the State Control Commissariat—80%.³³ Naturally, the election of officials or their accountability to the workers was out of the question. The only thing left of the idea of a "communal state" was the integration of the legislative, executive, and, for all practical purposes, the judicial functions which was very convenient for the Bolsheviks.

The attempt to bring Lenin's "state capitalism" to life was on the whole a failure. The Russian bourgeoisie could not agree to cooperate with the Bolsheviks because of the existing economic situation (the nationalization of the banks, the prohibition against paying dividends for shares, the tax burden, and the innumerable requisitions) and especially because of the lack of political rights, resulting in the arbitrary arrests of plant managers as well as threats and physical violence against their persons. Workers' management was discrediting itself more and more. As a result 836 enterprises were nationalized by March 1918, and 1222 between March and the end of June.

At the same time a "crusade" against the village was launched. In order to overcome the food crisis, in the spring of 1918 the socialist parties did not insist on an unrestricted free market in grain because of the catastrophic consequences for the hungry and partially employed proletariat. They supported "mild" state control and the regulation of the exchange of commodities with the village. Many Bolsheviks preferred this variant, too. But the seriousness of the situation, the bias against the market, and the desire to approach nonmarket socialism pushed Bolshevik leadership into tightening the grain monopoly and introducing food rationing in May 1918. The peasants had to turn over all of their "surplus" grain above the established minimal norms to the state at fixed—and extremely low—prices. In other words, now they could be deprived of anything. The commissariat of food supplies received extraordinary authority to seize grain from the peasants; it even had its own food supply army. In order to gain political support for the forced requisition of grain from the peasantry and at the same time to liquidate the "exploiters—the kulaks," the regime decided to split the peasantry by organizing the poor and starting a class war in the village. The committees of the poor (*kombedy*) which were established by the All-Russian Central Executive Committee's decree of June 11, 1918, not only helped to take the grain from the prosperous peasants but also implemented a new redistribution of the land, taking almost fifty million desiatins of land from the "kulaks"—almost three times more land than was taken from the pomeshchiks after October. On the average, less than two-thirds of the members of the committees were peasants, while up to 28% of the chairmen and nearly 60% of the treasurers were workers. The "socialist reform in the village" was accompanied by mass lawlessness and tyranny. The military and political pressure on the village, which introduced the schism within the peasantry, provoked widespread dissatisfaction and created a massive base for counterrevolution.

The centralization of power, the abolition of democracy for the workers, and even more for the peasants reduced the importance of the soviets. In March 1918, the Seventh Congress of the Russian Communist Party (the Bolsheviks) issued an official regulation shifting functions from soviets to the Bolsheviks' party. Some of the soviets, which were controlled by the Mensheviks and SRs, were dissolved by force. The soviets of workers' representatives were suppressed also. The extraordinary administrative methods became widespread in March 1918, following the so-called "railroad decree." The growing centralization and use of repression not only against the "exploiters" but also against the "workers" was for the Bolsheviks a natural way to compensate for the contraction of their social base and to maintain power.

This tendency in the Bolsheviks' policy and especially their attitude toward the village finally broke their coalition with the Left SRs. The latter, having left the government after the Peace of Brest, had remained in the soviets and cooperated with the Bolsheviks on some questions. The Bolsheviks were burdened with their partners more and more. In this situation on June 6, 1918, the Left SRs Ya.G. Bliumkin and N.A. Andreev penetrated the German Embassy with the assistance of their Cheka credentials and assassinated the German Ambassador, Count Wilhelm von Mirbach. After that both disappeared in the headquarters of the Cheka group commanded by the Left SR D.I. Popov. Dzerzhinsky, who came into the headquarters and demanded the terrorists' expulsion, was arrested. In response the Left SR faction at the Fifth Congress of Soviets headed by M.A. Spiridonova was arrested on the evening of July 6. That act, in due course, caused the Left SRs (about 1,800) to begin hostilities. Their disorganized and generally passive actions allowed Bolsheviks to suppress their "mutiny" relatively quickly with the help of two Latvian regiments and other units who were two-and-a-half to three times larger than the mutineers. There is no doubt that the mutiny of some of the Left SRs did not intend to overthrow the Bolsheviks, but to destroy the Peace of Brest and launch a revolutionary war which would immediately change the situation in Soviet Russia.

Although only a narrow circle of the Left SRs' leadership knew about the attempt upon Mirbach's life, the Bolsheviks used the events of June 6 to crush the Left Social Revolutionaries' party and form a one-party regime. Most of the Left SRs who did not dissociate themselves from the position of their central committee were immediately expelled from the soviets. The control of the "bourgeois and non-Soviet" press was tightened.[34] Actually this meant all non-Bolshevik publications, since by that time there were no other major socialist parties in the soviets. On June 14, 1918, the Mensheviks and SRs were removed from the soviets. Around five hundred anarchists had been arrested earlier in Moscow, on the nights of April 11/12, 1918, which had significantly weakened their movement. Later, because of the changed situation and the attitude of the moderate socialists toward the Bolsheviks, who found themselves sandwiched between the "Reds" and the "Whites," those decisions were canceled (on November 30, 1918 with regard to the Mensheviks and on February 26, 1919 with regard to the SRs). But this did not lead to any major changes in the essentially one-party regime that already had taken shape. The Bolsheviks were even harsher on their own former allies, the Left SRs. On March 14, 1919, after Dzerzhinsky's report, the Bolshevik Central Committee adopted the following resolution: "Propose to the press to intensify the harassment of the Left SRs. All former Left SRs should be under surveillance, and Left SRs should only be permitted to occupy important and responsible posts on the personal responsibility of the commissars."³⁵ The formation and violence of the one-party Bolshevik regime was partially responsible for the bitter Civil War.

The Civil War in Russia

The October coup started a Civil War in Russia. However, until spring 1918 military engagements on Russian territory (excluding the nationalities' regions) were sharp but mostly local: in the vicinity of Petrograd (Gen. P.G. Krasnov), in the southern Urals (Gen. A.I. Dutov), and on the Don (Gen. A.M. Kaledin). At first neither the workers nor the peasants and soldiers had any sympathy for the Provisional Government that had been overthrown and the other counterrevolutionary forces that had arisen, and even the officers did not display a great deal of interest. Only 3% of the 250,000-strong officer corps were involved in the armed struggle against the Soviet power in the first months of its existence.

Nevertheless General M.V. Alekseev began to organize a volunteer army in the city of Novocherkassk from the small groups of anti-Bolshevik officers who had found their way to the Don. General L.G. Kornilov became the head of it on December 25. In January 1918, under attack by an overwhelming number of Reds, the volunteer army had to retreat through the steppe to Kuban suffering from cold, a lack of munitions, and the hostility of the population ³⁶ (the so-called "Ice March"). After Kornilov's death in the battle of Ekaterinodar on March 31, 1918, the White Army was headed by A.I. Denikin.

By this time the harsh policies of the Bolsheviks were slowly changing the situation in the country. In April after the uprising of the Don Cossacks in the region of Novocherkassk, the Don Army was formed under the command of Gen. Krasnov. The army's strength reached 17,000 men by May, 40,000 by June. On May 25 the Czech Legion of 45,000 men, which was stretched out on trains between Penza and Vladivostok, revolted. The SRs and the officer corps supported it and by the summer of 1918, the authority of the soviets had been overthrown from the Volga to the Pacific Ocean.

General Anton Denikin

Library of Congress, Prints & Photographs Div, Am. Nat'l. Red Cross Coll., LC-USZ62-97997

The Bolsheviks only controlled the territory of the central provinces of Russia with a total population of only sixty million people. In the autumn of 1917 the population of Russia inside the borders established in 1920/1921 comprised 147,600,000 people.

The absence of strong political organizations which could take advantage of their influence with the masses retarded the formation of the anti-Bolshevik military forces. The rightists had no significant support in the nation. The February Revolution finally destroyed the traditional monarchist parties. The Kadets were an incomparably stronger political force and contributed greatly to the "political platform" of the White movement. However, by their own admission, the decision of the Kadet party conference in May 1918 to send their leaders to different regions of the country where struggle with Bolsheviks was going on diffused their effectiveness. Moreover, their leaders had conflicting orientations: Miliukov insisted on a pro-German orientation and others supported the pro-Entente Volunteer Army. These differences as well as the differences between Kadets and the White generals seriously undermined their abilities to form a unified whole. In addition the popularity of the party among the broad masses of the people was not very great.[37] After the dissolution of the Constituent Assembly and the conclusion of the Peace of Brest, the SRs played the leading role in the consolidation of the anti-Bolshevik political forces.

Notes

[1] See A.E. Utkin, *Diplomatiia Vudro Vilsona* [*Diplomacy of Woodrow Wilson*], Moscow, 1989, pp.167-179.

[2] The program denounced secret diplomacy (a blow to the allies' secret treaties), proclaimed "freedom of the seas" and trade, and underlined the need for disarmament and the open and impartial settlement of colonial claims, autonomy for the peoples of the Austro-Hungarian and Ottoman Empires and independence for Poland. The creation of an international organization embracing the entire world, the League of Nations, was proposed "for the purpose of securing general guarantees for the political independence and territorial integrity of large and small countries alike."

[3] Calculated in accordance with the data in *Istoriia Italii* [*History of Italy*], vol.3. Moscow, 1971, p. 36.

[4] Only from the Ukraine the states of the Quadruple Alliance carried off two million puds (a pud is equal to thirty-six pounds) of sugar, 31,300 wagons with food supplies, 201,500 horses and cattle, and two billion rubles worth of the Black Sea fleet and ports' property.

[5] T.E. O'Connor, G. *Chicerin i sovetskaia vneshniaia politika 1918-1930 gg.* [*G. Chicherin and Soviet Foreign Policy in 1918-1930*], Moscow, 1989, p.98.

[6] The Foreign Collegium established by the Bolsheviks in Odessa managed to get in touch with almost all of the interventionist units and vessels situated in Odessa. Their propaganda added to the fatigue of the soldiers and sailors which was growing from the war rapidly yielded results. Some French units were refusing to fight as early as March 1918. Red banners were raised at the French Navy vessels in Sebastopol on April 20. The French commander-in-chief, General D'Anselm admitted that half of his army had been demoralized by Bolshevik propaganda. See *Istoriia KPSS* [*The History of the Communist Party of the Soviet Union*], vol. 3, Moscow, 1968, pp. 182-186.

[7] V.I. Lenin, *Polnoe sobranie sochineniia*, vol. 40, p.125.

[8] For example, Great Britain and the United States gave no less than 350,000 rifles, 130 tanks, 200 artillery units and other weapons to General Denikin.

[9] For more details see S.V. Leonov, Sovetskaia gosudarstvennost: zamysly vi deistvitelnost' (1917-1920) ["Soviet Statehood: Plans and Reality (1917-1920)"], in *Voprosy istorii* [*Problems of History*], 1990, No. 12.

[10] V.I. Lenin, *Poln. sobr. soch.*, v. 35.

[11] The desiatin is measure of land equal to 2.7 acres. By 1917 landowners only had forty-four million desiatins, twenty million of which were leased by peasants who for all practical purposes considered the land their own. See V. Kabanov, "Agrarnaia revoliutsiia v Rossii (The Agrarian Revolution in Russia)" in *Voprosy istorii* [*Problems of History*], 1989, No. 11, pp.28,29.

[12] See B. Knipovich. *Ocherki deiatelnost Narkomata zemledeliia za tri goda 1917-1920* [*Essays on the Activities of the Peoples' Commisariat of Agriculture for Three Years (1017-1920)*], Moscow, 1920, p. 9.

[13] "Kommunalki" in workers quarters existed in pre-revolutionary Russia as well. Their expansion everywhere in the cities during the Soviet period can be explained by the deepest economic shocks and later by inceasing economic deprivation. They originally fully conformed to the spirit of socialism. It is typical that the official head of the Soviet state (the Chairman of the Central Executive Committee of the Peoples' Congress of Soviets, Ya. M. Sverdlov) resided at the Tauride Palace where he shared a communal apartment with other Bolsheviks. They lived as a "commune." K.T. Sverdlova remembered, "All of the simple property of each of us, which consisted of glasses and cups . . . was shared in common. *Utro strany sovetov. Vospominaniia uchastnikov i ochevidtsev revoliutsionnykh sobytii v Petrograde 25 oktiabria 1917 - 10 marta 1918* [*The Dawn of the Soviet State: Memoirs of the Participants and Eyewitnesses of the Revolution in Petrograd from October 25, 1917 to March 10, 1918*], Leningrad, 1988, p. 350.

Yet in 1918 and 1919 the privileges of the Bolshevik leaders were increasing so rapidly (against the background of people's impoverishment) that the problem became the subject of serious intraparty discussion and leaflets were made at home. The Politburo and the IX All-Russian Conference of the Communist Party (the Bolsheviks) took it upon themselves to resolve the problem and created a special commission. But in fact the matter was allowed to drop. See *Neizvestnaia Rossiia, XX vek* [*Unknown Russia. The Twentieth Century*], Moscow, 1992, pp.261-270.

[14] J.V. Stalin, *Sochineniia* [*Works*], vol. 4, p. 87.

[15] The February Revolution gave the first stimulus to this process.

[16] *Martov i ego blizkie* [*Martov and His Colleagues*], New York, 1957, p. 49.

[17] Z. Hippius, *Chernye tetradi* [*Rough Notebooks*]; *Zvenia. Istoricheskii almanakh* [*Historical Almanacs*], 2nd. ed., Moscow-St Petersburg, 1992, p. 21.

[18] Furthermore, a schism developed at the II Peasant Congress and its SR component proclaimed itself the All-Russian Congress of Peasant Deputies.

[19] V.I. Lenin, *Poln. sobr. soch.*, vol. 34, p. 393. Trotsky explained it in this fashion: "If we did not formally deny the Constituent Assembly earlier, that is only because it did not oppose the authority of the Soviets, but the power of Kerensky himself. . . . " See L. Trotsky, *Terrorizm I kommunizm* [*Terrorism and Communism*], Petrograd, 1920, p. 43.

[20] *Vtoroi Vserossiiskii sezd rabochikh i soldatskikh deputatov* [*II All-Russian Congress of Workers' and Soldiers' Deputies*], Moscow-Leningrad, 1928, p. 57.

[21] L.G. Protasov, Sudby politicheskikh partii v Rossii v svete itogov vyborov v Uchreditelnoe sobranie ("The Fortunes of the Political Parties in Russia in Light of the Results of the Elections to the Constituent Assembly") and 1917 god v istoricheskikh sudbakh Rossii ("The Year 1917 and the Historic Fate of Russia") in *Problemy oktiabrskoi revoliutsii* [*Problems of the October Revolution*], Moscow, 1993, p. 126.

[22] N.K. Krupskaia, *Vospominaniia o Lenine* [*Memories of Lenin*], Moscow, 1989, pp. 351-352.

[23] *Vserossiiskoi Uchreditelnoe sobranie* [*The All-Russian Constituent Assembly*], Moscow-Leningrad, 1930, pp. 42,43.

[24] According to different estimates the comprised from eight to twenty-one people.

[25] See V.I. Lenin *Poln. sobr. soch.*, vol.35, p.20 and vol.27, p.56.

[26] See Yu. Felshtinsky, *Krushenie imperii. Brestskii mir* [*The Fall of the Empire. The Brest Peace*]. Moscow, 1992.

[27] V.I. Lenin. *Poln. sobr. soch.* , vol. 36 p.18.

[28] *Sedmoi ekstrennyi sezd RKP(B). Stenogr. otchet.* [*The Seventh Extraordinary Congress of the Russian Communist Party (Bolsheviks). The Stenographic Account*], Moscow, 1962, p.62.

[29] A.F. Kiselev, *Profsoiuzy Sovetskoi gosudarstva (Diskussii 1917-1920)* [*Trade Unions and the Soviet State (Discussions of 1917-1920).*] Moscow, 1991 p.30.

[30] The number of workers at the twelve largest military plants of Petrograd fell 80% between January and September 1918.

[31] *Trudy I Vserossiiskogo sezda Sovetov narodnogo khoziaistva, 25 maia - 4 iiulia 1918 g. Stenogr. otchet.* [*Proceedings of the First All-Russian Congress of People's Industrial Councils, May 24- July 4, 1918. Stenographic Accoun*t], Moscow, 1918, p.57.

[32] V.I. Lenin, *Poln. sobr. soch.*, vol. 36, p.199.

[33] *Problemy gosudarstvennogo stroitel'stva v pervye gody sovetskoi vlasti* [*Problems of State Building in the First Years of Soviet Power*], Leningrad, 1973, p.54.

[34] *Tsentralnyi gosudarstvennyi arkhiv istoriko-partiinykh dokumentov* [*Central State Archive of Historical and Party Documents*], (TsGAIPD, St Petersburg) f. 1, op. 1, d. 64., l. 28.

[35] Rossiiskii tsentr khraneniia i izucheniia dokumentov poveishei istorii (Russian Center for the Preservation and Study of Contemporary Historical Documents) (RTsKhIDNI), f. 17, op. 2, d. 10, l.2.

[36] Fearing to restore the Cossacks, Kornilov forbid any requisition. But soon hungry and poorly clothed volunteers had to supply themselves all the same. The introduction of "purchased requisitions" also could not finally liquidate this phenomenon, which was gradually becoming a genuine scourge in the White Army, turning the population against it and destroying discipline. See A.I. Denikin, *Ocherki russkoi smuty. Borba generala Kornilova* [*Essays on the Russian Troubles. General Kornilov's Struggle*], Moscow, 1991, p. 232. The problem existed in the Red Army as well, the First Cavalry being especially notorious in this regard.

[37] See *Istoricheskii Arkhiv* [*Historical Archive*], 1992. No. 1, pp.92-94, and Denikin, p. 232.

CHAPTER 3

RUSSIA DURING NEP

The USSR and International Relations in the 1920s

As a result of the First World War and the Civil War, a completely new geopolitical situation emerged in Europe which destroyed the traditional eighteenth- and nineteenth-century "two plus one" balance of power during which Great Britain played the role of arbitrator, preventing either of the two continental centers of power from becoming too strong.[1]

The ruin of the Quadruple Treaty bridled German expansion and seemed to return Europe and the world to a situation that closely resembled the prewar balance of power. But that was only a surface impression. President Woodrow Wilson's Secretary of State, Robert Lansing, commented in his diary on May 5, 1919, that the provisions of the Treaty of Versailles "will undoubtedly cause new wars and new social upheavals."[2]

The victory of Bolshevism in Russia also destabilized the balance of power in the world because the Bolsheviks favored world revolution. So the "two plus one" system of two continental powers and Great Britain was replaced by a system of "two (France against Germany) plus one (Great Britain) plus one (the USSR, which stood outside the system of civilized states)." This, in due course, influenced the foreign policies of the leading powers.

Britain's foreign policy was the most consistent. Its support of the European balance of power by manipulating the interests of its continental neighbors left its hands relatively free, preventing the appearance of any alignment in Europe with the potential to surpass the power of the British Empire and her allies. Soviet Russia was included in the list of potential adversaries along with Germany. Prime Minister David Lloyd George remarked in 1919 that "the future of the British Empire may depend on how the situation in Russia will develop" and that he had difficulty thinking calmly about a unified Russia with a population of 130,000,000 people.[3] France was Britain's strategic ally and to some extent its rival as far as influence on European affairs was concerned.

France found itself in a precarious situation. It still had a defeated but not destroyed Germany as its potentially powerful adversary while Russia, France's natural continental partner in an anti-German alliance, no longer seemed part of the system of international relations. Russia's repudiation of the tsarist regime's debts after the conclusion of the separate peace of Brest-Litovsk with Germany in 1918 seriously injured French economic interests because French financiers were the tsar's major creditors. Thus French public opinion was set against Russia. France was concerned about the rapprochement between Soviet Russia and Germany.

France's attempt to establish a system of alliances (the *cordon sanitaire*) with the small Eastern European states (Poland, Czechoslovakia, Yugoslavia, and Rumania) in the 1920s could not compensate for Russia's withdrawal from the system. Great Britain was far more sympathetic to Germany because she opposed French dominance on the continent. The disagreements within the Anglo-French alliance prevented France from achieving the main objective of its foreign policy, the preservation of the general status quo in Europe. On the whole the extent of the French government's pro-Russian sympathy depended on German strength.

The Treaty of Versailles made the situation for Germany, which was exhausted by the war, extremely difficult. The treaty required Germany to pay huge reparations to Britain and France and practically liquidate its armed forces, restricting the size of the army (the Reichswehr) to a 100,000 men and the fleet to a few ships and forbidding Germany's acquisition of military aircraft, tanks, big battleships, submarines, and other kinds of modern military weapons.

German diplomacy was very flexible in its attempts to come out of international isolation. On the one hand German national consciousness never parted with the idea of the "movement toward the East" (*Drang nach Osten*), which could only mean economic and territorial expansion at Russia's expense. On the other hand the arrogance of the victorious powers and Germany's inferior position in the European community caused her leaders to conclude the Treaty of Rappalo with Russia in 1922 and to cooperate rather closely with the USSR on economic and military affairs in the 1920s and early 1930s. Germany's rapprochement with the Soviets, which was heading toward the establishment of a German-Soviet center of power although the Soviet Union's offer of a military alliance was rejected, forced the victors to adopt a more flexible policy. The United States, Great Britain, and France were interested in the growth of German finance since Germany could not pay her reparations without the restoration of her economy.

The withdrawal of French troops from the Ruhr in 1923, the reparations plan of 1924, the Locarno agreements of 1925 guaranteeing the inviolability of Germany's western (but not eastern!) borders, and Germany's acceptance into the League of Nations were clear evidence of the beginning of its adaptation to the new international system. But a full adaptation had not been made.

In this situation the United States, which became stronger during and after the war, began to play an important role in Europe. While Europe was going through destructive wars and revolutions, America consolidated its economic superiority and transformed herself from a debtor into Europe's largest creditor. The end of the war left "Uncle Sam" with a difficult task: how to obtain payment of its debts (around ten billion dollars) from the impoverished Europeans?

Under the solution adopted in August 1924, the Dawes Plan, America gave considerable assistance to Germany to rebuild its economy so the Germans could pay reparations to Great Britain and

France, enabling the latter to pay their war debts to the United States. A committee of financial experts headed by Owen D. Young reconsidered the plan in 1929 and after 1931, in accordance with an announced moratorium, Germany stopped paying reparations altogether. A hidden purpose of the Dawes and Young Plans was to restore Germany's military potential through the revitalization of German industry because it was seen as a "natural" counterweight to the Soviet Union.

Germany received around 32 billion marks in the form of loans and investments (mostly from Great Britain and the United States) between 1924 and 1932 while paying 19.2 billion marks in reparations and interest. The remaining 12.5 billion marks, which stayed in the country, helped Germany to restore its industrial capacity by 1930. The rapid restoration and renovation of heavy industry financed with the help of American and British loans was the most important "material" prerequisite for Germany's economic recovery.

One of the most important factors in the destabilization of international relations in the Far East was the growing strength of Japan, the only state in the region that managed to avoid colonial or semicolonial dependence. After the "Meiji" restoration of 1867-68 Japan embarked on a path of rapid capitalist development. The average rate of growth of Japan's gross national product after 1874 was 4.8%, more than Europe's and more than the American figures during some periods. Japan created a modern industry in the shortest amount of time. Government investment in Japanese industry doubled or tripled every dozen years or so.

Still technologically lagging behind the western states in the 1920s, Japan needed extensive colonies on her periphery where competition with higher quality western goods was absent. Economic considerations and the nationalist and military spirit which was restored after the successful wars with China (1895-96), Russia (1904-1905), and World War I (when Japan was allied to Great Britain) pushed Japan, which lacked colonies, into territorial expansion, beginning in China.

Despite the hostility to the USSR, opposing geopolitical interests prevented the formation of an anti-Soviet coalition to say nothing of military intervention in the USSR. This created favorable conditions for Soviet diplomacy.

The attempt to bring a world revolution to Europe "with the revolutionary bayonet" during the Soviet-Polish war failed. The revolutionary wave in the West subsided and hopes for a world proletarian revolution expired (especially after 1923 when the revolts in Germany and Bulgaria, which were incited to some extent by Moscow, were suppressed). As a result the Soviet leaders put forward a relatively flexible model of development for "a socialist state surrounded by capitalist powers." The model rested on two contradictory assumptions: the ideological principle of proletarian internationalism and a pragmatic belief in the peaceful coexistence of states with different social systems. Following the first assumption always caused the USSR to support world communist and national-liberation movements (hoping for the world revolution which was inevitable, from their perspective). The latter implied the normalization of interstate relations with the very countries whose stability the Comintern was supposed to undermine. In general the Soviet foreign policy in the 20s slowly subordinated ideological imperatives to a more pragmatic course.

The normalization of Soviet relations with the West was definitely outlined in the spring of 1921 when trade agreements were signed with Great Britain and Germany and later with other countries. The question of the repayment of old Russian debts was raised at the Brussels International Conference in October 1921. The conference recommended that the participating governments extend credit to Russia to overcome hunger, subject to its recognition of the debts of the tsarist regime and Provisional Government, and acceptance of a food commission to control the distribution of provisions. On January 28, 1921, the Soviet government issued its "Declaration Admitting Debts" which stated its readiness to conduct negotiations on mutual demands and prewar debts if diplomatic recognition was extended to the Russian Soviet Federated Socialist Republic (RSFSR) and the actions which threatened the security of the Soviet republics were terminated. An international economic conference was suggested to discuss the problems; the Supreme Soviet of the RSFSR adopted a resolution to convene the conference.

The conference on the international economic situation and financial problems was held in Genoa, Italy, from April 10 to May 19, 1922. Representatives of twenty-nine states including Soviet Russia and all of the great powers participated (the American ambassador to Italy was present as an observer). The Soviet delegation's attempt to discuss the problem of disarmament was not supported. The western states demanded the complete payment of all of the debts of the tsarist regime and the Provisional Government, either the return of, or compensation for, the foreign property nationalized by the Bolshevik regime (the latter was a stumbling block at the conference), and a ban on foreign trade monopolies. In turn the Soviets demanded compensation for the damage caused by the Allied intervention and blockade. A mutual agreement was not reached. The fruitless negotiations continued at the Hague conference of experts (June 26 - July 19, 1922). The Moscow conference on reducing armaments (December 2-12, 1922), in which Latvia, Poland, the RSFSR, Finland, and Estonia participated, failed as well. The USSR did not ratify the convention of the Lausanne Conference (November 20, 1922 - June 24, 1923) on the straits question, which provided free passage to the Black Sea for any country's ships. As a result the Soviet Union failed to become a full and equal partner in the system of international relations in the 1920s.

The Soviet government's bilateral relations had better results. The Soviet rapprochement with Germany in 1919-1920 has already been observed. During the Genoa conference (1922) Soviet Russia and Germany signed a bilateral treaty at Rapallo, a Genoa suburb, which provided for the restoration of diplomatic relations and the mutual renunciation of all reparations for the damages incurred and losses suffered during the war. In fact Germany refused to honor all financial claims because Soviet Russia had repudiated the old tsarist debts and had nationalized foreign property. On October 12, 1925, a Soviet-German treaty on nonaggression and neutrality was signed. The economic ties between the Soviet Russian and Weimar German Republics grew rapidly since they enabled the latter to evade some of the articles of the Versailles Treaty and modernize their army.

Relations with Great Britain were more complicated. On May 8, 1923, Britain accused the USSR for having broken the trade agreement of 1921 and for anti-British propaganda in Asia (the "Curzon's ultimatum"). Even so, the conflict was settled and after the Labour Party came to power Great Britain officially recognized the USSR in February 1924, an action that encouraged other states to do the same. On August 8, 1924, the Anglo-Soviet General Treaty on Trade and Navigation was signed. On October 10, however, British intelligence published the so-called "Zinoviev letter."[4] The letter, in which the Comintern head Grigory Zinoviev had recommended subversive operations in the British Isles, which contributed to the Labour Party's defeat in the general election. During the British coal miners' strike, which began on May 1, 1926, and the general strike which lasted from May 3 to May 12, 1926, the Comintern gave material assistance to the British Miners Federation through the Soviet trade unions. From May 1926 to March 1927 16 million rubles came to the Assistance Fund. The British government blamed Moscow for interfering in British domestic affairs in violation of the Anglo-Soviet trade treaty. On May 1927 the British government broke off diplomatic relations with the USSR and revoked the trade agreement of 1921.

In the mid-1920s the USSR obtained diplomatic recognition from most of the developed capitalist countries. By the end of the decade the United States was the only major capitalist power which had not recognized the Soviet Union.

Soviet policy in the East, mostly in neighboring states, became more active. In March 1923, as a favor to the Chinese leader Sun Yat-sen a group of military and political experts (P.A. Pavlov, V.K. Bliukher, M.M. Borodin) was sent to South China. In May 1923, diplomatic and consular relations were set up between the USSR and the central government at Beijing. All treaties, agreements, and other acts between the former tsarist regime and any other party touching upon Chinese sovereign rights and interests were revoked. Between 1924 and 1928 new friendship and neutrality treaties with China were concluded along with various economic agreements with Turkey, Afghanistan, Iran, and Yemen. As a result during the 1920s the Soviet Union managed to overcome its diplomatic isolation by the world community which continued to consider it a strange and hostile entity.

Foreign affairs significantly influenced the internal policies of the Bolshevik party. The crash of hopes for a rapid world revolution and assistance to the Soviet state from the western proletariat caused the Bolshevik leaders to investigate the possibility of using domestic policy to consolidate the Bolshevik regime, which in the final analysis resulted in a more flexible policy toward the Russian peasantry and the transition from war communism to NEP. At the same time the severance of diplomatic ties with Great Britain was used to justify a harsher domestic political policy.

Russia at the End of the Civil War: The Kronstadt Revolt

By the end of the Civil War Russia lay in ruins. Industrial production was one-seventh and the gross agricultural product was two-thirds of the prewar level.[5] The resolutions of the Eleventh Communist Party Congress, which was held in March and April 1920, and the Eighth All-Russian Congress of Soviets, which took place in December 1920, show that the first Bolshevik plans for the reconstruction of the economy proceeded from the concept of war communism, which mostly involved direct compulsion by the state.[6]

The strategy of continuing war communism encountered growing popular resistance. As the threat of the restoration of the prerevolutionary agrarian relations receded, the peasants did not see any reason to continue to deliver grain to the government for free according to the surplus appropriation system. A peasant riot headed by A.S. Antonov blazed in Tambov and Voronezh provinces in August 1920. The struggle against the peasant rebels was assigned to one of the best Red Army commanders, M.N. Tukhachevky, under whose command were brought together more than 50,000 soldiers, three armored tank battalions, three armored squadrons, and seventy guns. Yet they failed to suppress the revolt. The authorities resorted to the harshest measures, including arrests and the shooting of hostages (sometimes even children), summary executions (for hiding rebels, for keeping weapons), and even used poison gases to smoke peasants out of the woods. But, extinguishing the Tambov revolt with blood, the Bolsheviks were unable to suppress Antonov's resistance before the summer of 1922.

Powerful peasant groups were operating in the Ukraine where N. Makhno continued the struggle. Disturbances occurred in the middle Volga, Don, and Kuban regions. Bands of Basmakhs became active in Turkistan. In February and March 1921 the rebels in Western Siberia formed armed units of several thousand people, capturing practically the entire territory of the Tumen province, Petropavlovsk, and Kokchetav, stopping railway transportation between Siberia and the central region of the country for three weeks. Toward the spring of 1921 the peasant uprisings enveloped almost the whole country. The Red Army's losses during the suppressing of the uprising in 1921 exceeded 171,000 men. And this does not include the losses of the Cheka units, the militia, and the special Communist squads.

The situation was critical in the major industrial centers, where there were not enough provisions, the factories were closed from the lack of raw materials and fuel, and the workers were on the street. The dissatisfaction of the workers in the "cradle of the revolution"—Petrograd—grew quickly. The closing of ninety-three Petrograd businesses until March 1 was announced on February 11, 1921. Such giants as the Putilov, Sestroretsk and the "Triangle" [*Treygolnik*] were among those named. The authorities had to use some of the Petrograd students still loyal to them to disperse the demonstrators. Martial law was introduced in the city.

The uprising reached Kronstadt, the naval fortress on the Gulf of Finland twenty-nine kilometers from Petrograd. The sailors of Kronstadt, who had supported the Bolsheviks during the October days of 1917, understood that the authority of the soviets had been replaced by the authority of the party, and the ideals, for which they had fought, had been betrayed.

On February 28, 1921, the sailors of the battleships "Petropavlovsk" and "Sevastopol" called a meeting and passed a resolution in which they demanded the reelection of the soviets by a secret vote, freedom of speech and the press "for the workers and peasants, anarchists and left socialist parties," the release of political prisoners (the socialists and all of the participants in the Red Army, naval, workers' and peasants' demonstrations), the equalization of the bread-rationing for everyone, except the "working people of the sweatshops," and the abolition of forced requisitioning. Demands were made for free labor for craftsmen who did not use hired workers; for the peasants—full freedom of action "over all the land as they have wished, and also to have cattle which they have to support and manage by themselves, without using hired labor."

The resolution of the Kronstadt sailors was essentially only a call to observe the rights and freedoms proclaimed during the revolution. It did not demand the overthrow of the government.

In connection with the disturbances at Kronstadt, the chairman of the Central Executive Committee, Kalinin, was sent there, but he did not succeed in persuading them to withdraw their demands.

On March 2 the Kronstadt sailors organized a Provisional Revolutionary Committee including sailors of working class and peasant origin. The secretary of the battleship "Petropavlovsk," S.M. Petrichenko, became chairman of the committee.

The Bolshevik leadership hurried to label the Kronstadt sailors. Their action was denounced as a counterrevolutionary plot, instigated by the imperialist Entente. An extensive propaganda campaign was begun in the press, deliberately distorting the meaning of the events and representing the Kronstadt sailors as a "group of bandits," while their address was the work of the hands of tsarist generals and the Black Hundreds.

The Kronstadt men strove for open, public negotiations with the authorities; but the latter's position was simple: no negotiations of any kind, no compromises, the rebels had to have severe punishment. The truce envoys sent by the men of Kronstadt to Petrograd were arrested. Martial law was declared in Petrograd and Petrograd province on March 3. Measures were undertaken to isolate Kronstadt completely from the outside world. In connection with the direct threats of the official authorities to punish the Kronstadt sailors by force of arms, the Provisional Revolutionary Committee turned to the military experts found in Kronstadt to ask for assistance in organizing the defense of the fortress. The experts proposed, without waiting for an attack, to go over to decisive offensive operations. But the Provisional Revolutionary Committee refused to attack: "Our uprising," its members later said, "was based on the fact that we did not want bloodshed. Why bloodshed, when everyone without exception understands that our cause is just."

The task of suppressing the uprising so dangerous to the Bolsheviks was entrusted to Tukhachevsky and the Seventh Army. It was decided to begin the storming of the fortress at seven in the evening on March 8. After several changes in the date, the opening of the Tenth Congress of the Russian Communist Party (the Bolsheviks) was scheduled for March 8. The military leaders wanted to report to the delegates the seizure of the fortress on the first working day of the congress.

The opening of the congress was also anticipated in Kronstadt. Even when the bombardment of the fortress began, some of the Kronstadt rebels hoped that their demands would be heard and that at the congress Lenin would finally make the correct decision.

But the Kremlin did not desire a peaceful resolution of the conflict. Deciding to change internal policy under enormous pressure, the Bolshevik leadership considered it necessary to proceed with punitive actions against people who dared to openly express their pressing demands to the government. It understood that changing economic policy required definite political reforms. The punishment of the Kronstadt men would show the limits of the retreat, in that any political changes would not affect the Bolsheviks' fundamental monopoly of power. Several months later Lenin frankly declared: "It is necessary to teach the public a lesson so they will be unable even to conceive of any opposition for several decades." And that related not only to the church.

The hopes of crushing the mutineers in one blow on the opening day of the Tenth Party Congress were in vain. Taking a great loss, the army retreated. One of the basic reasons for the lack of success was the political attitude of the Red Army soldiers who were sympathetic to Kronstadt. The situation escalated to direct disobedience to the commanders and even demonstrations in support of the Kronstadt sailors. In response repression followed. The unreliable units were disarmed and sent to the rear, but those who were considered the instigators were shot. The sentences to death by firing squad, passed by the field assizes of the revolutionary military tribunals, the extraordinary three-man panels, "for refusing to fulfill military duties" and "for desertion" followed one after the other. They were carried out immediately.

New units were raised which were considered more reliable, including the 27th Omsk infantry division. But upon its arrival unrest began in the regiments of the 79th brigade. The authorities responded with arrests and executions.

To strengthen the combat readiness of the units it was decided to introduce party mobilization. Near Kronstadt around 1000 Communists were mobilized, and also a fourth of the delegates of the Tenth Party Congress.

During the night of March 17 after intensive artillery bombardment a new assault on the fortress began. During the second half of the day, when it became clear that further resistance was useless, the men of Kronstadt decided to retreat to Finland. Around 8000 people, including almost all of the members of the Kronstadt revolutionary committee, succeeded in leaving across the ice of the Gulf of Finland.

The fortress was taken toward the morning of March 18. The authorities did not tally the number of dead, missing, or wounded Red Army soldiers. But it is known that in individual units that advanced on Kronstadt casualties exceeded fifty percent.

After the seizure of the fortress massive repression began not only with respect to its defenders, but also the civilians who resided in Kronstadt. The fates of thousands of people were decided in the sessions of the extraordinary three-man and two-man tribunals. With the aid of massive terror the authorities intended once and for all to end the possibility of a repeat of the anti-Bolshevik demonstrations in the fortress. Toward the summer of 1921 2,100 people were sentenced to the firing squad while up to 6,500 people were given terms of various length. Around 1,500 of the people arrested for being "Kronstadt rebels" were freed, but the charges were not dismissed.

In the winter of 1922 the mass resettlement of the residents of Kronstadt began, in the first instance, of families in which someone had been shot, condemned, or was missing. Between February 1922 and April 1923 alone 2,514 persons had been resettled. The purge was introduced in Petrograd following Kronstadt.

Lenin having declared the transition from a civil war to civil peace at the beginning of 1921, the Bolsheviks in the example of Kronstadt visibly demonstrated how they understood this peace, how they would ruthlessly suppress any activities against the absolute authority of the Bolsheviks.

The NEP Concept: Its Origins and Its Basic Features

The most severe crisis of early 1921 forced Lenin to conclude: "Only an agreement with the peasants can save the socialist revolution in Russia until the revolution comes to other countries."[7]

In March 1921 the Tenth Congress of the Russian Communist Party (the Bolsheviks) decided to replace the requisitioning of farm produce with a tax in kind, the first step toward a New Economic Policy (NEP). Instead of taking all of the peasant's "surplus" grain, depriving him of the incentive to produce, a fixed tax—a percentage of the harvest—was introduced. Material interests replaced naked force. At first the peasants were only allowed to sell their "surplus" product (the percentage of the crop remaining after taxes) in the local market near their place of residence. The direct exchange of consumer goods for agrarian commodities through the apparatus of the People's Commissariat of Food and the cooperative, which bypassed the market, was supposed to be the main link (*smychka*) between industry and the farm.

Experience showed the utopian character of the concept. The shortage of consumer goods, the weakness of the cooperatives' apparatus, and the incidence of famine, which devastated entire provinces (starvation and illness reduced the population by five million in 1921 and 1922) forced the Soviet leadership to permit free trade in grain in August and September 1921.

The Bolsheviks' plans for building socialism in the fall of 1921 were different than those of the spring of 1918 because they recognized the need for the extensive use of the market system during the transition period from capitalism to socialism. Lenin characterized the New Economic Policy model as "state capitalism in a proletarian state."[8]

In general contemporaries saw NEP as a transition stage in the history of Russia during the 20s. There were different opinions on what the transition was leading to. Some thought that, despite the utopian character of their ideas, the Bolsheviks were opening the door to capitalism through NEP. The adjustment of the political system to the requirements of the economic system would follow with the establishment of a democratic republic. That position was represented by the so called "Smenovekhovtsy," the ideological spokesmen of the intelligentsia who got their name from the collection of pro-Kadet essays "Signposts" (*Smena Vekh*) published in Prague in 1921.

The Mensheviks and SRs had been talking about the need for a mixed economy and some democratization since 1918. The Menshevik leader L. Martov remarked that Bolshevik rule represented "the partisan dictatorship of a minority" and that "its logical result—systematic terror" had been invented by its creators to pressure society into overcoming its "historical inertia" and "to create socialism in a country in which nine-tenths of the population dreams of becoming petty bourgeois." With the transition to NEP the Bolshevik dictatorship had lost "its own natural justification." The complexity of the market system did not permit the resolution of social conflicts "by the methods of police surveillance." This meant that the Bolsheviks had to restore full democracy.⁹

The Bolshevik theoreticians (V.I. Lenin, E.A. Preobrazhensky, and L.D. Trotsky) had different ideas. They considered the turn to NEP as a tactical maneuver, a temporary retreat caused by the unfavorable alignment of forces. Then in the fall of 1921 the Bolshevik leaders gradually began to consider NEP as one of the possible routes to socialism (conceiving socialism to be a socioeconomic system without a market—the very antithesis of the market economy). NEP was not the direct route to socialism, which involved a struggle against nonsocialist structures and a rapid transition from a market to a planned economy (after the failure of war communism the direct route was only considered acceptable for developed capitalist countries); it was the indirect route—through a rather long period of coexistence between the socialist and nonsocialist structures and the gradual replacement (with a foothold in the "commanding heights" of politics, economics, and ideology) of nonsocialist with socialist forms. Some Bolsheviks did not accept NEP, considering it a capitalist economic plan.

Unlike his opponents on the right, who believed that Russia should return to capitalism if her productive capacity had not reached the level where socialism was possible, Lenin believed that socialism could be slowly built by relying on the dictatorship of the proletariat. Besides, Russia's technical and economic backwardness did not permit the immediate introduction of socialism.[10]

That thesis did not imply the softening, but the strengthening of the proletarian state, which in reality was a Bolshevik dictatorship. Terror was used to compensate for the immaturity of the social, economic, and cultural prerequisites of socialism (as in the period of war communism). Lenin did not agree with the measures for political liberalization even being proposed by some Bolsheviks: allowing socialist parties to operate, freedom of the press, and the creation of a peasants' union. On the contrary, Lenin was thinking about "expanding the use of shooting (or foreign exile) . . . against all sorts of Mensheviks or SRs. . . ."[11] The remnants of the multiparty system in the USSR were forcibly liquidated, the church was persecuted, and the internal party regime became more severe.

And so, the NEP model of social organization worked out by the Bolshevik leadership, mostly Lenin, in the early 1920s had the following basic components:

— in the political and ideological sphere, a harsh authoritarian regime;
— in the economy, an administrative market system, including a minimal connection with the world economy (conducting foreign trade on the basis of a state monopoly), state ownership of the large-scale (and a significant part of the medium-scale) industry and trade, as well as rail transportation; economic planning, which operated to a limited degree only on the level of the trusts, not in businesses or shops; the nonequivalent exchange with the village (the uncompensated assignment of some of the produce in the form of a tax in kind); the curtailment of the growth of the large-scale peasant (kulak) farm in the village.

How did Russian society develop within the boundaries of the (NEP) social organization in the 1920s?

The Economy

Between 1921 and 1924 administrative reforms were implemented in industry, marketing, the cooperatives, and credit financing. The State Planning Commission (*Gosplan*) was set up in February 1921. The denationalization of small and some medium-size industries at the end of 1922 only left a third of the previously nationalized firms in the state's possession. The big and well-equipped plants and factories were combined into trusts: Southsteel (*Yugostal*), Chemcoal (*Khimugol*), Doncoal (*Donugol*), the State Machine-Building Plant Trust (*Gomza*), Northern Timber (*Severoles*), and Sugartrust (*Sakharotrust*). The Supreme Economic Council (VSNKh) exercised general supervision over the trusts and redistributed their profits. Equal wages were replaced by a new pay-scale that considered workers' qualifications and the number and quality of goods produced. Universal labor conscription and mobilization were canceled.

The development of commercial and monetary relations restored the All-Russian domestic market. The large fairs were reborn in Nizhni Novgorod, Baku, Irbit, and Kiev. Stock exchanges were opened. Some freedom to invest private capital in industry and trade was permitted. The creation of a small number of private businesses (with no more than twenty workers), concessions, leasing and joint stock companies was allowed. As far as credit, taxes, and supplies were concerned, the consumer, agricultural, and artisan cooperatives enjoyed more favorable conditions than private capital.[12]

A two-tier banking system was set up between 1921 and 1924. There was the State Bank, a network of cooperative banks, the Trade and Industry Bank, the Foreign Trade Bank, and a network of local communal banks. The issuance of banknotes, which used to be the main source of state revenue, was replaced by a system of direct and indirect taxes (the profits earned in commercial activities and incomes were directly taxed; excise taxes were levied on agricultural produce and manufactured goods).[13] Charges for transportation, communication, and communal services were introduced.

The instability of the monetary system and inflation slowed the NEP reforms. In 1922 the government began a monetary reform. At the end of the year a stable currency, the chervonets (literally, "the Red note"), was issued. The chervonets, which was equal to ten prerevolutionary rubles, was backed by gold and other easily sold valuables and commodities. The reform was completed by 1924: the new banknotes and copper and silver coins replaced the worthless Soviet banknotes issued after the October Revolution. The budget deficit was liquidated, and after October 1924 the issuance of banknotes to cover the budget deficit was prohibited by law. But the chervonets did not remain convertible for very long. By 1926 the demand for foreign currency in the private market exceeded the supply to such a degree that the State Bank and the Finance Commissariat concluded it was necessary to stop the practice.

Industrial productivity rapidly grew during the 1920s: in 1921—42.1%, 1922—30.7%, 1923—52.9%, 1924—14.6%, 1925—66.1%, 1926—43.2% and in 1927—14.2%. Heavy industry grew faster than light. At the end of the 1920s the Soviet economy on the whole had reached the prewar level.

The pace of industrial reconstruction was remarkable, but was lower than the official statistics. The problem was that in their accounts the industrial trusts exaggerated their results. They were not the only ones. According to official data, the national income of the USSR in 1928 was 19% higher than in prerevolutionary times. According to the calculations of contemporary scholars, it was 12-15% lower than the 1913 level while per capital national income was 17-20% lower.

The efficiency of NEP was lower than the prerevolutionary economy. The output of industry and transport was 25% lower in 1928 than 1913. The profits generated in industry were 20% and in railway transportation 400% lower than before the war; the combined profits of both branches were 200% lower than before the war. This was connected with the high degree of nationalization of the NEP economy, since workers in private industry produced twice as much as those in state enterprises. The following table characterizes the composition of the manufacturing industry of the USSR for 1925/26 (in percents):

Manufacturing in the USSR 1925 / 1926(%)			
Sector	No. in Operation	Avg Gross Prod.	No. of Workers
State	64.4	93.1	89.6
Cooperatives	18.3	4.3	6.4
Private	16.9	1.9	3.6
Concessions	0.4	0.7	0.4
Total:	100	100	100

Whether the indices of development attained in the 1920s could be maintained was questionable. The high growth-rate of the NEP years was mostly explained by the "restoration effect": the equipment which they already had but was standing idle was assigned work. The old arable lands seized during the civil war were returned to cultivation. When these reserves were exhausted at the end of the 1920s, the country had to invest capital in industry to rebuild the old factories whose equipment was worn out and create new branches of industry.

Meanwhile the legal restrictions (private capital was not allowed in large and, to a significant degree, in medium-sized industry) and the high tax rate levied on private businessmen—both in the city and village—extremely limited the level of nonstate investment. As the emigre economist A. Yugov observed, "the Soviet government did not even have a modest amount of spare cash in the country at its disposal since the population struggled to promote its own prosperity and kept its savings in secret places or engaged in speculation instead of putting them in savings banks or lending institutions."

The Soviet government failed to attract a significant amount of foreign capital. As S.N. Prokopovich (the economist and former Provisional Government minister exiled from Soviet Russia in 1922) noted, foreign countries "would not give capital funds to an industry in which Communists played the role of the capitalists, and engineers were put in the category of suspicious persons on whom one had to keep a constant eye. Russian industry was backward even before the war. While the Communists were implanting Communism after the October Revolution, and later weeding it out during NEP, a serious gap between the technology of Russia and Europe, without mentioning America, was taking shape. No one would give money to shore up firms incapable of survival."

Encountering a shortage of capital to develop industry and being unable (or, to be more exact, not wanting) to use native and foreign private capital for this purpose, the Bolsheviks finally brought more and more of the available financial resources under central control and extracted private capital from industry and commerce through taxation and rent increases.

A typical anecdote of the times: two Nepmen meet, one asks the other: "How is life?"—"I am living like a potato!"—"Is there a potato here?"—"It is very simple. If they are not eaten, they are planted, but if not planted, then they are eaten." Here are the cold facts of the statistical calculations. Private and concessionaire industry in 1923-1924 produced a gross product of 1,467 million rubles, and in 1925-1926 2,478 million rubles. But later production began to decline and by 1928-1929 had fallen to 1,975 million rubles. The proportional weight of private industry (including small and handicraft) in 1924-1925 was 27.3%, in 1925-1926—23.9% and in 1928—17.6%.

Unlike industry the output of agriculture did not rise immediately. In 1921 the agrarian economy of Soviet Russia suffered from severe drought, the consequences of which were present in 1922. The area under cultivation was reduced to 77.7 million hectors. The rise of industry and the introduction of a hard currency stimulated the restoration of the agrarian economy. The area under cultivation gradually increased: in 1923 it reached 91.7 million hectors, which comprised 99.3% of the 1913 level. In 1925 the total grain harvest exceeded the average annual harvest for the five-year-period between 1909 and 1913 by 20.7%. But in later years the production of grain gradually declined on account of the growth of industrial crops. In 1927 the prewar level was almost reached in animal husbandry.

Tax policy restrained the growth of the large commercial peasant farm. In 1922/23—3%, in 1923/24—14%, in 1925/26—25%, and in 1927—35% of the poorest peasants were exempt from the rural farm tax. The prosperous peasants and kulaks making up 9.6% of the peasant households paid 29.2% of the taxes. Later the proportional weight of this group in the tax structure grew larger. The tax policy in the 1920s caused the peasant farms to break up twice as fast as before the revolution, with all of the negative consequences derived from this for the development of production and especially its marketability. The prosperous layer of the village tried to slip out from under the oppressive taxation by dividing their farms.

The low percentage of the gross agrarian product (*tovarnost*) represented by the individual peasant farm reduced the volume of export commodities, and, consequently the volume of imports so necessary for the modernization of the country's equipment. The volume of agricultural commodities exported in 1925 and 1926 represented 21.7% and 27.1% of the 1909-1913 level. In 1928 the small volume of exports only allowed the USSR to import half of the equipment of prerevolutionary Russia (the import of consumer goods, which was ten times lower than 1913, had to be given up).

The decline in the Russian economy's efficiency since prerevolutionary times had other causes besides the bureaucratization connected with the growth of nationalization. The state authorities could not deal with the workers' and peasants' active demands for a better life after the civil war.

The reconstruction of industry created the conditions for a relative improvement in the workers' standard of living (in comparison to the early 1920s). In 1925/26 the average length of the working day for industrial workers was 7.4 hours. The proportional weight of those working overtime fell from 23.1% in 1923 and 18% in 1928. All manual and service workers had the right to a regular annual vacation of no less than two weeks. The workers' real wages had increased. In 1925/26 the average in industry represented 93.7% of the prewar level.

Inflation and the consumer goods shortage, which rose again in 1924 and continued throughout the following years, slowed the restoration of the standard of living. Despite the rapid rise in the number of workers in industry, construction, and transportation, unemployment not only existed but even grew larger during NEP. Unemployment stood at 160,000 in 1922, 980,000 in 1924, and

1,478,000 in 1926. On the eve of the first five-year-plan unemployment comprised 12% of the manual and service workers in the national economy.

In the towns of the 1920s housing was the major social problem for working people. Here is how L. Reisner described the workers' quarters in the Don Basin (Donbas). "Long dilapidated huts—barracks of rotten wood. The windows were boarded up or filled with rags. Dirt was everywhere, garbage was thrown out on the porch. There were no chairs, a table of significant size, or shelves. There are not books to speak of. Only the oldest workers have tiny private quarters. Lice and hunger are in abundance. Dozens of seasonal workers do not even have their own plank bed. The successors take the place of their departed comrades. Only twenty houses and four common dwellings were constructed for the 20,000 Donbas workers."

The peasants were nourished better than before the revolution. The peasants per capita grain consumption rose to 250 kilograms in 1928 (from 217 kilograms in 1921), meat consumption rose to twenty-five kilograms (from twelve kilograms before 1917). But the growing consumer goods shortage caused severe unrest here.

Politics

In 1918 the search began for a way to unify the Soviet republics on the basis of the nation-states, but the vagueness of the corresponding ideological and theoretical views of the Bolsheviks, and the civil war, prevented its completion. At the end of the civil war the territory of the republics connected by the so-called "military and political alliance" (the Russian Federation, which included the Far Eastern Republic after November 1922, the Ukrainian, Belorussian, Azerbaijan, Armenian, and Georgian Soviet Socialist Republics and also Bukhara and Khorezm) was stabilized and the unification processes sharply accelerated. In 1920-1921 in the Central Executive Committee of the Russian Federation the representatives of Ukraine, Belorussia, and Transcaucasia began to unify some people's commissariats. In the spring of 1921, in response to Lenin's instructions on the economic unification of Georgia, Armenia, and Azerbaijan, the creation of the Transcaucasian Federation began. It was created despite the opposition of some of the Transcaucasians, especially the Georgian Communists, in March 1922. The formation of the Transcaucasian Federation sharpened the disagreements among the Bolshevik leadership on the principles and methods of unification. As the result of a sharp struggle the Stalinist project for "autonomy," which presumed the admission of the soviet republics into the Russian Federation with the rights of autonomy, was rejected. In every case Lenin's idea of a union of sovereign republics ceding a number of their sovereign rights to the All-Union organs on the principles of equality was victorious. In December 1922 at the First Congress of Soviets of the USSR, the Russian Federation, Belorussia, Ukraine, and the Transcaucasian Federation signed the union treaty and formed the Union of Soviet Socialist Republics. In September 1924 the republics of Khorezm and Bukhara were admitted to it. The Constitution of the USSR, accepted on January 31, 1924, guaranteed the right of secession to each republic; the territories of the republics could not be changed without their consent.

As far as the complete fulfillment of Lenin's plan (in fact the Soviet Union was more centralized than the leader wanted), the union republic's sovereignty was nominal. The real power was concentrated in the hands of the committees of the Russian Communist Party (the Bolsheviks), which were formed on the basis of the principles of "democratic centralism." The key political and economic decisions were made by the central organs of the party, which were responsible for all party organizations, including the republics'.

The Soviet Union, which was created through the use of administrative and political pressure (that was especially apparent during the formation of the Transcaucasian Republic), was essentially a unitary, nonfederal state from the very beginning. The national territorial units (autonomous republics, national territorial districts, and national regions existed along with the union republics) were only supposed to have cultural autonomy. Nevertheless this seemed somewhat progressive in comparison to tsarist times. In the 1920s schools, theaters, and newspapers were established for the nationalities and literature was widely disseminated in the vernacular. For the first time some nationalities received literature written by their own scholars.

The plenitude of political power in the country formally belonged to the soviets. But they were actually powerless. In the city the soviets were deprived of any real authority by the party committees; in the village, where the agrarian cells of the party were relatively few and smaller than the rural soviets, the traditional organ of the communal organization, the communal assembly (*mirskoi skhod*) held the power. Only 20.4% of the electorate voted in the 1922 elections to the village and district soviets. This forced the leadership of the party and state to undertake "political" work (the dispatch of agitators, the creation of different types of sections and commissions within the soviets, and after 1925 groups of the poor and so forth). In the 1926 elections to the soviets the percent of voters grew to 50.8%. But the coming to life of the soviets was an illusion. In 1927 the percentage of voters fell somewhat. The number of people deprived of voting rights had risen sharply: in 1926—4.5%, in 1927—7.7%, while in rural areas the figures were 1.1% and 3.3% respectively. The chief reason for this was that the soviets could no longer possess any political power or even serious economic functions.

The creation of the Soviet administrative and legal apparatus was completed in the early 1920s. In 1922 the criminal and civil codes were prepared and accepted, a judicial reform was introduced (the revolutionary tribunals and administrative judicial proceedings were abolished; prosecutors and lawyers was established and regulated), censorship was institutionally strengthened while the functions of the Cheka were restricted somewhat. In 1922 the Cheka was transformed into the State Political Administration (GPU) at the People's Commissariat of Internal Affairs (NKVD), which became the Main State Political Administration (OGPU) within the Council of People's Commissars of the USSR in 1923. The rights of the GPU were expanded quickly. Moreover, the state security apparatus began to interfere in the internal affairs of the party, transforming itself into an instrument for the creation of Stalin's regime of personal power.

Most of all the Bolsheviks were afraid that "state capitalism in a proletarian state" would exceed the limits "defined for it by the proletariat," in reality by the party. The strategy of the Bolshevik party and state leadership was based on the premise that in order to compensate for the retreat in economics, one had to intensify the struggle against other ideas, against all of the party's political opponents, since the transition to NEP objectively opened up favorable prospects for their activities. "If the peasants need free enterprise under the present conditions and within definite limits, we should give it to them, . . ." Lenin remarked. "That does not mean that we permit the sale of political literature, which calls itself Menshevik or SR and which keeps the capitalists of the whole world in money. . . . And whoever holds the opposite view, to that man we say that we would all rather die to the last man than yield to you! And our courts should not abolish terror" but justify and "legalize" it.

In March 1921 the Bolshevik Central Committee opposed the legalization of peasant unions. In December of that year the legalization of some of the Socialist Revolutionaries was forbidden and the political influence of the Mensheviks was "eliminated." The arrests of the members of the other socialist parties in the country began. Some of the Mensheviks were exiled. By truth or falsehood OGPU helped the Bolsheviks to discredit their opponents and force other parties to "dissolve themselves." In the summer of 1922 falsified proceedings were held against thirty-four prominent Social Revolutionaries accused of counterrevolutionary terrorist activities. At the "congress" of the SRs called in March 1923 fifty SRs announced the dissolution of the party and called on its members to join the Bolsheviks. In 1923-1924 a number of Menshevik organizations met the same fate, although the Bolsheviks failed to obtain an official announcement of the dissolution of the whole party. And so toward the middle of the 1920s the remnants of the multiparty system in the USSR had been violently eliminated. The Bolsheviks' monopoly on political power in the country was complete. The few remaining organized Russian political parties only continued to operate in the emigre world.

In June 1922 the Politburo decided to severely tighten the government's control over the intelligentsia. Henceforth all congresses and All-Russian meetings of any kind were only to be conducted with the permission of the GPU. The GPU was also ordered to examine the reliability of all publications in print (some of which were closed), intensify the filtering of admissions into academic institutions, approve the creation of new artistic unions, and create a special commission for the exile of members of the intelligentsia. The Politburo, the highest Bolshevik organ of power, began to exile dissidents in the summer of 1922. Lenin and the other Bolshevik leaders inspected the lists of exiles.

In 1922 more than 160 outstanding representatives of the motherland's culture, whose presence had prevented the Bolsheviks from forming their own ideological monopoly in society, were exiled. Among them were the philosophers N. Berdiaev, S. Frank, the sociologist P. Sorokin, the historian A. Kizevetter, and the economist B. Brutskus.

The Bolsheviks also struck a mighty blow against the Russian Orthodox Church, which had preserved its own ideological and organizational independence from the regime. The severe hunger of 1921-1922 furnished the occasion. Despite the active assistance of the church to the starving and even Patriarch Tikhon's agreement to sacrifice voluntarily some of the church's unconsecrated objects for these purposes, the Bolshevik leadership decided in March 1922 to confiscate the church's valuables. The process of confiscation basically continued in a peaceful manner. But, taking advantage of the collisions between the faithful and the Red Army at Shuia (where four parishioners were killed and ten wounded), Lenin decided to use the exceptionally favorable and even "single possible moment" (because of the "desperate hunger") to punish the church. ". . . We should now conduct a decisive and merciless battle with the black hundreds of the clergy and oppose it with such force, that it will not forget it for several decades," Lenin emphasized. "The more representatives of the reactionary clergy and bourgeoisie we succeed in shooting on this occasion, the better."

Anticlerical terror began in the country. Approximately 20,000 clerics and believers were arrested, exiled, or shot. Inside the Russian Orthodox Church, with the assistance of the OGPU, a "reform" movement loyal to the Bolsheviks was created, which succeeded in subordinating up to 70% of the parishes to itself. In 1923 a Synod of the Land (*Pomestnyi Sobor*) was set up which approved the socialist revolution and announced that the Patriarch Tikhon, who had been

Library of Congress, Prints & Photographs Div, LC-USZ62-98685

arrested by the Bolsheviks, was an "apostate from the original teachings of Christ and a traitor to the Church." Hoping to save the church from a schism, Tikhon submitted with a penitent letter and the proceedings against him were dropped. The reformers failed to subordinate the Russian Orthodox Church to themselves; their influence fell rapidly, and toward the beginning of the 1930s ceased to exist. Nonetheless the Bolsheviks were able to establish their own control over the church and to guarantee its political loyalty.

The establishment of the Bolsheviks' political monopoly strengthened its position even more in the trade unions. In the spring of 1921 a conflict arose between the Central Committee and some of its members, the leaders of the trade unions (D.B. Riazanov and M.P. Tomsky) who were trying to maintain the trade union's rather significant degree of independence, but the Bolshevik party continued their firm control of the unions directly through communist cells. Nonetheless the transition to NEP somewhat changed the forms and methods of work of the trade unions. They reverted to voluntary, personal membership. The membership fell from seven million in

1921 to 4.5 million in 1922. Later the number of trade unions began to grow rapidly and comprised 9.2 million people in 1926. The scope of the trade unions' functions included the defense of the interests of the workers in the state, cooperative, and private enterprises; participation in the management of the economy (including the discussion of production plans, the promotion of candidates to administrative posts); and taking part in the resolution of workers' disputes up to the level of the organization of strikes. In reality the trade unions did not defend the workers' interests as much as they introduced the "party line" into production.

Voluntary societies, cultural and educational groups, and sport organizations developed extensively during NEP. They included the "Down with Illiteracy" society (ODN), the Society of Friends of the Air Force (ODVF), the Free Society for the Defense of Chemistry (DOBROKhIM), the Red Cross and Red Crescent Societies, the Friends of the Children Society (ODD), the Friends of Radio Society (ODR), the Union of the Godless and the Society of Political Convicts and Penal Colonists. More than ten million people were enrolled in these voluntary societies. All of these social organizations and movements were controlled by the Bolsheviks' party and not infrequently by the secret police (OGPU).

During NEP all power within the Bolshevik party, which had a monopoly on the government of the country, became concentrated in the top leadership. Gradually the significance of the party congresses faded. The decisions undertaken by the Central Committee were more important. In 1921 it consisted of twenty-seven persons and nineteen candidates and met in plenary sessions approximately once every two months. But the Central Committee's Political Bureau (Politburo) was the original center of power, while the informal groups inside of it, to which the more authoritative leaders belonged, were locked in a continuous struggle for power within the country until victory. At the beginning of the 1920s there was the *troika* or triumvirate, while in the middle of the decade there was the *semerka* or septemvirate headed by Stalin. The preliminary meetings of these groups, as a rule, determined the most important decisions of the Politburo, which were later formulated in the decisions of the Central Committee, party congresses, and in due course were reinforced in the decisions of the soviet organs (if they did not relate to internal party matters). The same system operated at other levels—in the republics, provinces, and districts.

During the civil war years the party operated as a militarized war organization. The attempts to democratize the party undertaken in 1921-1924 were inconsistent and blocked by the resolution of the Tenth Party Congress (1921) to prohibit factional activities. Stalin's designation as general secretary of the Central Committee accelerated the centralization process. The structure of the party committees on the various levels became uniform. Secretaries designated by and subject to the leadership and free of control from below were put in charge. A unique "hierarchy" of secretaries under Stalin was created as the strong organizational framework of the party and society. In 1921-1924 even the young communist organization (*Komsomol*) fell under the party's control more and more and gradually lost its organizational autonomy.

The authoritarian political regime of the 1920s characterized by the hierarchical principles of organization and the inertia common to its type was only effective when the authority of the higher level institutions was absolute over the lower ranking ones on the periphery who unconditionally carried out the clear directives of the center. Meanwhile, during the 1930s the national economy fundamentally remained market oriented, with its instability, while the social structure retained its diversity. The impulses from the irregular crises in the functioning of the economic mechanism in the economic chain—the state sector—the state—the party, and also the presence in the party of the representatives of various social groups caused disagreements on the strategic and tactical questions of policy to appear within the party leadership during NEP. The disagreements found expression in the formation of alignments and currents within the party; the struggle between them was capable of paralyzing the authoritarian regime.

In this way a contradiction between the imperatives of political authoritarianism and a pluralistic economy emerged. The contradiction was reduced by the presence at the top of the party-state pyramid of a charismatic leader—Lenin, to whom the most ambitious Bolshevik leaders (Zino-viev, Stalin, Trotsky) deferred. Lenin compensated for the absence of a democratic mechanism for decision-making and considering the rights of the minority. Relying on his own indisputable authority, Lenin either obtained agreements between the warring sides, integrating the different points of view, or won victories over the opposition and thereby led a sufficiently consistent political course.

During Lenin's illness in 1922 and 1923, the situation changed when Stalin and his allies began to decide matters in the top leadership. A paradox took shape: an authoritarian regime without an authoritarian leader, a party monopolistically governing a socially and economically diverse society.

Library of Congress, Prints & Photographs Div, LC-USZ62-98685

Lenin and Stalin at Lenin's summer home in Gorky

Events could have developed in one of two ways. Either the annulment of the Tenth Party Congress's decision to forbid factions, the transition to the social democratic model (allowing the coexistence of different officially recognized policies and platforms) and a pluralistic social order, or the succession of a new leader. But, considering Bolshevism's formation during the struggle with the Russian version of social democracy—the Mensheviks—the conversion of its leaders to social democracy was improbable. The political ambitions of the Bolshevik leaders prevented them from advancing a new leader.

Under the conditions which were taking shape ("without Lenin"), the real authority in the party and state could only belong to the faction which was able to control the party apparatus. As a result, one or the other faction had to gain possession of the party apparatus in order to confirm its own position. On the other hand, with the complex connections between the administration of the party, state, and economy, the struggle between the pretenders for the leadership inevitably took the form of a rivalry between the competing social and economic programs promoted when NEP was malfunctioning. The personal animosity among some of the members of the Bolshevik governing elite (mostly between Trotsky and Stalin) influenced the course of the internal party struggle. All this brought extreme bitterness to the internal party discussions.

The struggle between the leaders for political power during NEP assumed the form of a fight between various currents within the party: the rightists, leftists and centrists. In the socioeconomic area the "leftists" (led by Trotsky) wanted to strengthen the leadership exercised by the state sector in economic planning, develop industry faster, and tax the prosperous layers of the village more heavily. The "rightists" (led by Bukharin), on the contrary, wanted to reduce the scope of economic planning, slow the rate of industrialization, and tax the upper layer of the village less heavily. The "centrists" (Stalin) fluctuated between the "left" and "right" poles, depending on the political situation in the country.

The struggle between the factions within the Bolshevik leadership came out into the open in 1923. Two basic factions became apparent. Trotsky, a member of the Politburo, chairman of the Revolutionary Military Council (RVS), people's commissar for military and naval affairs, headed one; the triumvirate of Stalin, Zinoviev and Kamenev headed the other.

Many representatives of the party's "Old Guard" supported the first faction, who disliked the growth of the bureaucracy, the strength of the party apparatus (the hierarchy of secretaries) and the errors in economic policy. (As a result of the rising price of manufactured goods in 1923 the first crisis of NEP broke out, the "sales crisis" or "scissors crisis.") At the beginning of October 1923 Trotsky wrote a letter to the Central Committee critical of the regime established in the party. The appeal to the Central Committee of forty-six leading party figures (including V.A. Antonov-Ovseenko, A.G. Beloborodov, A.S. Bubnov, N. Osinsky, E.A. Preobrazhensky, G.L. Piatakov, T.V. Sapronov, L.P. Serebriakov, and I.N. Smirnov), which followed shortly afterwards, was the first manifesto of the group which

Zinoviev dubbed the "Trotskyite opposition" in his presentation.

The triumvirate mostly relied on the faithful cadres of the central and provincial party apparatus. To isolate Trotsky and his followers in August 1924 Stalin was able to enlarge and organize his own faction in the Politburo as a "septemvirate" (Bukharin, Zinoviev, Kamenev, Rykov, Stalin, Tomsky, Kuibyshev). Propaganda was disseminated that effectively labeled "Trotskyism" as a petit-bourgeois tendency within the party (the authors themselves did not believe this). The main factor in Stalin's victory was his stable majority in the party apparatus and the passivity of a number of Bolsheviks. As a result the opposition suffered defeat at the October 1923 plenum of the Central Committee, and later, in 1924 at the Twelfth Conference and Thirteenth Congress of the party.

But the oligarchic form did not guarantee the possession of the highest power in the party against additional schisms in the Bolshevik Olympus. For economic and political difficulties did not fail to arise for the regime on a regular basis in 1924 and 1925 (the failure of the harvest, the consumer goods shortage, the exhaustion of the resources to restore industry, stagnation in agriculture, attempts to organize the peasants politically, and the uprising in Georgia). These events forced the leadership of the party and state to undertake new economic and political maneuvers to keep power in their hands. The policy worked out at the end of 1924 and beginning of 1925 was directed to the liberalization of the regime and presumed the revival of the soviets, the democratization of the work of the organs of power, and a struggle against administrative arbitrariness. The restrictions on the growth of peasant farms were removed, repressive measures against private trade were abolished, and craftsmen and artisans received tax exemptions. Private capital began to be attracted and saving was encouraged on the peasant farms.

The policy ardently followed by the "rightists" (Bukharin, Rykov, Kalinin), was supported by Stalin, who moved from the neutral center to the right wing in 1925.

Two members of the septemvirate opposed the present course—Zinoviev and Kamenev, whom Lenin's widow Krupskaia and Sokolnikov supported. They feared Stalin's strength. They also rejected Stalin's concept of "the construction of socialism in one country." In the spring of 1925 this "quadrumvirate" sent the Politburo a series of pronouncements protesting the theoretical innovations of Stalin, Bukharin, and the right wing who had seized the party's leadership. The activities of the quadrumvirate began with the formation in 1925 of the "new opposition." They broke up the "Stalinist septemvirate" and destroyed the distribution of power at the top. But the septemvirate's disciplinary measures against factionalism, which had silenced Zinoviev and Kamenev from time to time, permitted Stalin to make preparations and openly act to eliminate the obvious "dissidents," clearing the path to authoritarian power in the party. Trotsky and his supporters occupied a wait-and-see, passive position in the discussions of 1925.

The climax of the discussions, which opened between the Stalinist "majority" of the Central Committee and the Zinoviev "new" opposition at the end of 1925 and beginning of 1926 occurred at the Fourteenth Party Congress in December 1925.[14] The congress revealed a new kind of general secretary, who stood above the right and left, acting as the supreme arbitrator, the protector of the "maxims" of Lenin.

By the middle of the 1920s Stalin had finally put together his own way of fighting his opponents, which could be seen in the loyal party functionaries' support for the leader in their behind-the-scenes activities, the schism within the opposition forces, the cutting off of "dissidents" from the majority and the extensive utilization of the propaganda apparatus and the secret police (OGPU). The discourse began to lose the character of discussions of various alternative policies within the party. At the Fourteenth Party Congress, commenting on Sokolnikov's speech, Stalin first distinguished between the "general"—"our"—position and the opposition's position, which was "not ours." This stereotype was actively used in the struggle with the opposition. At the same time after 1925 the vociferous praise of Stalin's address became an obligatory ritual of the party congresses.[15]

In 1926 serious movements in the alignment of forces "at the top" forced the opposition to put aside their internal disagreements and act as a unified bloc. In May and June 1927 the "Statement of the Eighty-Three" appeared, which collected the signatures of 1,500 representatives of Lenin's "Old Guard." The signers of the declaration included Trotsky's followers from the opposition of 1923 and 1924 and Zinoviev and Kamenev's supporters from the opposition of 1925 and 1926. Both had the same goal—the desire to change the regime inside the party.

Since the party and state apparatus prevented the opposition from creating a legal faction, it had to use the methods of illegal operation familiar in prerevolutionary times: the creation of a coordinated center, its own channels for the distribution of information, the publication of its declaration, platform, and leaflets, sending its own representatives to local areas and the organization of conspiratorial meetings.

The opposition's need to use illegal methods and directly provoke the secret police provided the occasion for Stalin to toughen the punitive measures against the "unified" opposition. Their attempt to march in the 1927 November Jubilee demonstration under their own banner led to Trotsky and Zinoviev's expulsion from the party by the special decree of the Central Committee and Central Control Commission of the party on November 14, 1927. At the same time Kamenev, Smilga, Evdokimov, Rakovsky, Muralov, and a number of other leading Bolsheviks were expelled from the Central Committee and Central Control Commission.

In this way, the number of potential "heirs of Lenin" grew smaller after every round of internal party discussions. To keep his own legitimacy in the eyes of the hierarchy of party secretaries and the rank and file members, the leading faction did everything to discredit its opponents and represent its own program as the solely legitimate, orthodox one "faithful to Leninism." Maintaining himself on the party's Olympus, Stalin had less and less need to agree with the other leaders.

During the 1920s a one-party political system took shape in the USSR. Although it functioned as a mild regime (in comparison to the preceding and succeeding periods), the number of people who perished in the camps during the suppression of anti-Bolshevik activities during NEP comprised, according to some estimates, almost a million people. Besides, there was no political guarantee that under changed conditions the Bolshevik government would not again turn into labor's "harsh" regime.

Culture

The census of 1920 revealed fifty-four million illiterates in the country. The task of liquidating illiteracy was critical. In 1923 the All-Russian voluntary society "Down with Illiteracy!" was established with M.I. Kalinin as its head. It supported thousands of local circles or schools for liquidating illiteracy (*likbezy*), which enrolled almost 1.4 million adults in 1925. Along with the elimination of illiteracy the government decided to engage in propaganda to indoctrinate the masses in communist ideology. Central Political Education (*Glavpolitprosvet*) undertook the task. The network of workers clubs, village libraries and reading rooms (*izba-chitalnia*) and urban libraries was enlarged. A special series of popular brochures were published on antireligious and revolutionary themes, setting out the official point of view. After 1924 propaganda "on Leninism's foundations" was widely circulated.

The critical lack of financial resources in the early 1920s forced the government to reduce the budget allocated to schools and to introduce funding through local budgets. In 1921 and 1922 unpaid days and weeks of work (*subbotniki*) to assist the schools were introduced, voluntary contributions from the resources of the population. Tuition payments were also introduced as a temporary measure in 1921. The educational institutions of the mid-1920s were part of the following system: the four-year primary, the seven-year urban school, the young peasant's school (ShKM), and the factory-plant apprentice school (FZU) based on the primary school, the secondary schools (grades five through nine) with vocational classes in the eighth and ninth grades in a number of schools.

The factory-plant apprentice schools for preparing workers' cadres took on a massive character between 1921 and 1925. The children of the workers comprised no less than 75% of the student body. The cadres of the lower and middle technical and administrative personnel (craftsmen, team leaders, mechanics) were trained in the technical schools and also in the special trade schools and short-term courses.

The government introduced a class policy in higher education, creating favorable conditions for workers and peasants to enter institutions of higher education and artificially restricting the admission of the children of the intelligentsia and Nepmen. In the 1920s a special form of higher education for the workers arose—the workers' faculties (*rabfaki*), which gave rise to the first generation of Soviet intelligentsia politically and ideologically loyal to the regime. Measures were undertaken to fundamentally change the curriculum in the institutes of higher education (*vyzy*) and universities and remove disloyal professors and instructors. This caused strikes and protests among the students and teachers. At the beginning of the 1920s historical materialism, the history of the proletarian revolution, the history of the Soviet state and law and the economic policy of the dictatorship of the proletariat were introduced as compulsory subjects. According to the Central Committee decree on instruction, known party figures were sent to Moscow University: A.V. Lunacharsky, I.I. Skvortsov-Stepanov and others. In 1921 the Institute of Red Professors (IKP) was set up in Moscow to prepare Marxist cadres to serve as college instructors.

Literature, art, and architecture mirrored the inconsistencies in economics and politics and the complexity of the social processes. The protest of a large part of the intelligentsia against the October Revolution and the exile of many cultural figures did stop the development of art, which had been stimulated at the beginning of the century. Numerous groups and unions belonging to different trends were created.

One of the influential groups, the Serapion Brothers*(1921) included mostly prose writers (K. Fedin, Vs. Ivanov, M. Zoshchenko, and V. Kaverin). Their investigation combined the literary forms and plots which most effectively expressed the content of the postrevolutionary times. Experiments in language and style were connected with them. The literary group "Pass" (*Pereval*), 1923, included such writers as M. Prishvin, V. Kataev, Art. Vesely, and A. Malyshkin. The group's theoretician was A. Voronsky. The members of the group preserved the continuity and tradition of Russian and world literature against rationalism and constructivism.

At the beginning of the 1920s a group of writers (S. Obradovich, V. Kazin, N. Poletaev, and F. Gladkov) separated themselves from the Proletkult and created the union *Kuznitsa* ("Smithy"). In 1923 the Moscow Association of Proletarian Writers and in 1924 the Russian Association of Proletarian Writers (RAPP) rose and became the largest union of the 1920s, pretending to have a monopoly on literature. The activity of RAPP had a openly class, proletarian character. The campaign against the nonproletarian writers (the *Poputchiki*) was conducted on the pages of its journal. M. Gorky, V. Maiakovsky, S. Esenin, A. Tolstoy, and L. Leonov belonged to it.

The representatives of the "Literary Center of Constructivists" (A. Selvinsky, V. Inber, and N. Aduev) called themselves the spokesmen for the "humanism of our transitional era," the preachers of "Soviet westernization" and were oriented toward the Americanization of technocracy. The group "The Left Front of the Arts" (LEF), 1922, included V. Maiakovsky, N. Aseev, S. Kirsanov, who constructed their own esthetics with regard for their theories of the proletkultists and futurists, as well as a concept of "fact in literature" which denied artistic falsehood, psychologism. Some of the prominent writers and poets did not belong to any groups or unions.

At the beginning of the 1920s poetry led in literature; because of the paper shortage, oral poetry became widespread (at literary evenings, concerts, and disputations). Between 1921 and 1923 new stories and novels appeared by the major masters of the prerevolutionary realistic prose: V. Korolenko's *The History of My Contemporary* (1921), A. Tolstoy's *Walking in Torture* (1921), V. Veresaev's *At Dead End*, and S. Sergeeva-Tsensky's *Transfiguration* (1923). The compositions of the symbolists and formalists (A. Bely, E. Zamiatin, and A. Remizov) were widely distributed. Many writers did not seek as much the hero of the times and the ways and means to creatively seize the essence of the times: B. Pilniak's *The Naked Year* (1920), E. Erenburg's *Julio Jurenito* (1921), and F. Gladkov's *The Fiery Horse* (1923). In these works the narration is distinguished by its interruptions and fragmentation as the various pictures pass by rapidly and clearly.

In 1922 and 1923 a revolution occurred in the sense of greater concretization and individualism, opening up some of the aspects of existence. Intimate detective and adventure books began to appear. Social prose also appeared, concentrating on the moral and ethical conflicts inherent in NEP: A. Tarasov-Rodionov, Yu. Lebedinsky, and Vs. Ivanov.

In the mid-1920s the novel again became the leading form of literature. Between 1924 and 1926 a whole series of novels appeared: A.M. Gorky's *The Artamov Business*, A. Serafimovich's *The Iron Flood*, Dm. Furmanov's *Chapaev*, L. Leonov's *The Badgers*, K. Fedin's *The Rebellion*, A. Fadeev's *Chaos*, M. Bulgakov's *White Guard*, F. Gladkov's *Cement*, and others. Works of classical decadence (A. Bely's *Moscow under Assault*) continued to be published.

Works appeared describing the current degeneration of the intelligentsia and youth under the influence of NEP: S. Semenov's *Natalia Tarpova*, Yu. Lebedinsky's *The Birth of a Hero*, and N. Bogdanov's *First a Lass*. Finally, satirical novels with adventurous and socially utopian themes are widely disseminated during the first half of the 1920s: V. Kaaev's *Erendorf Island*, A. Tolstoy's *Nevzerov's Adventure or Ibikus*, A. Platonov's *The City of Cities*, and M. Zoshchenko's stories.

During the second half of the 1920s literature lost its originality, was full of clichés and stereotyped patterns, the range of which was limited. The Resolution of the Central Committee of the Russian Communist Party (The Bolsheviks) "On the Party's Policy in the Area of Artistic Literature" (1925) helped to ideologize literature and art and secure the dictates of the party over artistic creation. Despite its formal condemnation of the activities of RAPP, it contained a call for free competition between groups and trends, while simultaneously setting the task of struggling against the displays of bourgeois ideology in literature, to guarantee the creation of works intended for the mass of readers.

The development of art was also characterized by the struggle between a multiplicity of groups and trends. The Association of Artists of the Revolution (AKhR, 1922) had as its purpose the development of *Peredvizhnik*** traditions in the spirit of "documentary art" and "heroic realism" and had great success with the mass of spectators. The members of the AKhR created many beautiful pictures (the works of I. Brodsky, S. Maliutin, H. Kasatkin, V. Meshkov, and K. Iuon). The AKhR, like RAPP, claimed a monopoly in art and toward the end of the 1920s thanks to the support of the authorities was almost able to completely guide artistic life. The "Society of Easel Artists" (OST), created by the graduating students of the

VKhUTEMAS (art studios), strove to understand the present aesthetically and create pictures which responded to the times not only through their own content but also through their graphic presentation (the works of A. Deinika, D. Shterenberg, and A. Labas).

Professional culture, faithfulness to tradition and at the same time bold inquisitiveness characterized the works of P. Kuznetsov, V. Favorsky, K. Petrov-Vodkin, M. Sarian, E. Bebutov, A. Ostroumova-Lebedeva, V. Mukhina, and A. Shchusaev. In 1927 the "Society of Muscovite Artists" (R. Falk, I. Mashkov, A. Lenulov, and I. Grabar) arose. P. Filonov, whose circle became a complete school in the 1920s, occupied an independent place in the Russian avant-garde.

The founder of the Supremacists, K. Malevich, worked profitably. In 1924 he became director of the State Institute for Artistic Culture (GINKhUK) in Leningrad. The Institute for Artistic Culture (INKhUK) in Moscow was significantly influenced by the ideas of V. Kandinsky. These two unions brought together completely plastic forms, responding to the elevated spiritual idea in an effort to comprehend the laws and logic of artistic practice.

In architecture an intensive search for new styles and innovative forms was conducted. In the first half of the 1920s projects for different types of buildings (residences, labor palaces, workers' clubs, and communal houses) and new architectural forms were worked out. Architectural constructivism, based on the so-called industrial art, developed widely. In 1925 the constructivists joined together in the "Society of Contemporary Architects" (OSA). One other influential trend—the rationalists—gave a special meaning to the search for expressive architectural forms. In 1923 the Association of New Architects (ASNOVA), which was led by their theoretician N. Ladvosky and the famous architect K. Melnikov, was formed.

The placement of monuments created for propaganda purposes was still going on in the early 1920s. A general plan for the reconstruction of Moscow was worked out under the guidance of A.V. Shchusev and I.V. Zholtovsky and for Leningrad under I.A. Fomin.

On the stages of many famous theaters (MKhAT, the Little Theater) along with the classics of the 1920s were the songs of the new playwrights with their revolutionary themes. The work of a whole galaxy of producers (K.S. Stanislavsky, V.I. Nemirovich-Danchenko, V.E. Meierkhold, E.B. Vakhtangov, and A. Ya. Tairov) had enormous significance in the development of the theater during these years. The actors of the old prerevolutionary generation (M.N. Ermolov, A.I. Iuzhin, I.M. Moskvin, V.I. Kachalov, and O.L. Knipper-Chekov) continued to appear with great success. At the same time young talented actors (N.P. Khmelev, A.K. Tarasov, N.P. Batalov, M.M. Ianshin, K.N. Elanskaia, B.N. Livanov, B.V. Shchukin, E.N. Gogolova, and S.M. Mikhoels) gave interesting performances. Many new theaters, theatrical studios, and itinerant theaters were started. The first children's theater in the world appeared.

Very favorable circumstances for the development of modernist trends took shape in the 1920s. But how tragic was the fate of the artists who were oriented toward the values of traditional Russian culture. The outstanding painter V.M. Vasnetsov died in poverty. The great Russian poet S.A. Esenin died in unexplained circumstances. The most talented playwright and writer M.A. Bulgakov was exposed to a subtle defamation of character.

The Contradictions of the NEP Social Model

While the reconstruction period was closing, NEP was malfunctioning more and more. The inconsistencies inherent in the NEP model were becoming immanently sharper.

In the economy the full capacity of the machines capable of producing and the physical wear-and-tear and obsolescence of the basic capital equipment required significant investment to renew the stock of machinery and develop new branches of industry. The capital intensive branches of heavy industry were emphasized, with their long-term turnover of capital: for them to pay for themselves one would have to wait three to five years, the equivalent of paying the working masses "in advance" for a similar period. Major capital expenditures were required. But the Bolsheviks' harsh position on questions relating to the repayment of prerevolutionary debts and the payment of damages to foreign property owners for the nationalization of their property prevented the influx of foreign capital.

The investment of internal capital accumulated by private capitalists was blocked by legislation. Industrial growth required an improvement in the peasant farm's ability to market its produce (to feed the growing urban population, to guarantee raw materials for industry, and to force the export of grain in order to import machinery later). But the development of large-scale commercial farms in the village was inhibited in every way possible.

In the social and political sphere the conflict between a multitude of public interests and Bolshevik authoritarianism became stronger: the village economy was reviving and the private sector was trying to secure political guarantees for its economic interests; all were persistently seeking political channels of expression (during the second half of the 1920s the demands for a "peasants' union" and the bribery of the authorities became more commonplace), which in a one-party system intensified the factional struggle within the Bolshevik party. At the same time the party lost its historic leader (Lenin)—the original guarantor of its integrity.

The antagonism between the economic and political systems was growing. The more dynamic the trend toward a free enterprise-market economy, the faster it produced its own "political grave-digger." In the city the machinists who were unsympathetic to the "Nepmen" filled the ranks of the party, which had a monopoly on political power. In the village, the Bolsheviks' introduction of the "class line" caused the "victims" of the market—the broken peasants (the poor)—to become the most important source for filling the ranks of the party and state apparatus. On account of this one can imagine the "love" of the majority of the party and state functionaries for NEP.

Notes

[1] France against Russia, Austria, and Prussia at the end of the eighteenth and beginning of the nineteenth centuries; France, Austria, and Prussia against Russia in 1812; and Germany against France and Russia at the end of the nineteenth and beginning of the twentieth centuries.

[2] Quoted from *Voprosy istorii* [*Problems of History*], 1991, N 1, p.138. On Lansing's analysis also see above pp. 138,144 as well as the materials in the collection of research articles edited by Viacheslav V. Chubarov, *Rossiia, SSSR i mezhdunarodnye konflikty pervoi poloviny XX veka* [*Russia, the USSR and International Conflicts in the First Half of the XX Century*], Moscow, 1989, especially V.A. Zolotarev, A.E. Titkov, and A.A. Udunian's introduction and V.V. Chubarov's essay international relations in the Far East in the 1920s and 1930s.

[3] See above Chubarov, p. 11.

[4] Up to now it has not been determined whether the letter was a forgery or authentic.

[5] *The History of the Soviet Economy* in seven volumes. vol. 2, Moscow, 1976, p.10. During the period Russia also lost 10,887,000 people. See Yu. A. Poliakov, *Sovetskoe gosudarstvo posle kontsy grazhdanskoi voiny: zemlia i naselenie* [*The Soviet State after the End of the Civil War: Territory and Population*], Moscow, 1986, pp.97-98.

[6] At that time Lenin highly praised a chapter on non-economic coercion from N.I. Bukharin's book *The Economy during the Transition Period*. Among others it included the following statement: "proletariat constraint in all its forms beginning from execution and up to labor conscription is . . . a method of creating a communist mankind out of capitalist epoch people." from Lenin collection, XL, p.424.

[7] V.I. Lenin, *Poln. sobr. soch.*, vol.45, pp. 260-261.

[8] V.I. Lenin, *Poln. sobr. soch.*, vol.45, pp. 263, 119.

[9] L. Martov "Dialectika diktatury" in *Sotsialisticheskii Vestnik* ["The Dialectics of the Dictatorship" in *Socialist Messenger*], 1922, No. 3, pp.3-4.

[10] V.I. Lenin, *Poln. sobr. soch.*, vol.45, pp.379-381, 385-388.

[11] V.I. Lenin, *Poln. sobr. soch.*,vol.45, pp. 379-381, 347-348, 385-386.

[12] At the end of 1923 and the beginning of 1924 membership in the consumers' cooperatives became voluntary (the other cooperatives did not have compulsory membership during the Civil War).

[13] In 1924 and 1925 the revenues obtained from all types of taxes represented from 35% to 52% of the gross income of the private sector.

[14] At this congress the name of the Russian Communist Party (the

Bolsheviks) was changed to the All-Union Communist Party (the Bolsheviks).

[15] The tradition of publicly praising the party leader continued on the whole to the last, XXVIII Congress of the Communist Party of the Soviet Union.

Editor/Translator's Notes:

*The Serapion Brothers were a group of Fellow-Travelers', a term coined by Trotsky to refer to those who sympathized with or did not oppose the goals of the regime. Their name comes from a character in E.T.A. Hoffman's Tales.

** The Peredvizhniks were members of a later nineteenth century school of painters whose works were characterized by their realism.

CHAPTER 4

THE CONSTRUCTION OF SOCIALISM BY COERCION

The World and the USSR in the 1930s

The 1920s was a time of temporary prosperity for the "great retreat" from statism. "War communism," which had been based on the extraordinary centralization of economic life, was dismantled. The New Economic Policy (NEP) was developed, which permitted the reconstruction of the country and the feeding of the population for the first time in many years. After the end of the First World War the West also abolished state intervention in the economy, which businessmen had considered a temporary measure required by the war. The specific conditions for reconstruction were taking shape: passing over onto peacetime tracks the economies of the European countries became geared to the production of light industrial goods, foodstuffs, and later heavy industrial goods earmarked for the civilian sector. At the same time the American loans and reparations from defeated Germany secured the financial resources to reconstruct European industry. The unsaturated market and "easy" money accelerated the volume of economic activity. In 1929 the volume of industrial production of the capitalist world exceeded the prewar level by nearly 1.5 times. Qualitative movements also occurred. Alu-

THE CONSTRUCTION OF SOCIALISM   145

minum and Ford's assembly line technology were widespread. The mass of consumers became familiar with automobiles, rayon, and passenger aviation. Cinematography and the leisure industry, on the whole, experienced extraordinary development.

The prosperity based on the weakly regulated market system of prewar times was temporary. The reconstruction of Europe was completed; the market was saturated; and the flaws in the world market system caused the depression of 1929-1933, the deepest economic crisis in the entire history of capitalism. The volume of industrial production in the capitalist countries fell on the average by 38% while agricultural production fell a third and world trade by two thirds.

The narrowness of the world market and aggressive competition strengthened individual market segments for the leading capitalist countries: international trade and currency blocs were created on the basis of the great powers' colonial spheres of influence. The result was the breakup of the united world market into segments. An agreement for mutually preferential customs for members of the British Commonwealth of Nations was signed at Ottawa in 1932. Other colonial countries followed Great Britain in the formation of exclusive trade zones: France formed a zone for the French franc, Holland a zone for the Dutch guilder, and so forth. World trade was broken up into isolated groups and ensnared in a complex system of trade and monetary organizations. Paralysis of the world financial market completed the picture of the unprecedented destruction of the system of international economic ties.

Social cataclysms shook the western world. By 1932 the number of unemployed exceeded 27 million. Every third worker (16.9 million in all in 1933) was unemployed in the United States. Tens of millions of people in the highly developed countries of the world were facing the threat of hunger. In Germany real wages fell more than 50%, comprising about half of the minimum for survival. Mass strikes in which more than 10 million people participated shook the great powers. The appeal of communist ideas grew. Even in the "nonrevolutionary" United States mass demonstrations of unemployed workers were conducted under the leadership of the Communist Party, and two hunger marches on Washington were organized.

Strengthening the state's intervention in the economy and social life was the most direct way out of the great crisis for the leading powers. The painfulness of a great power's transition to a regulated market economy depended on whether or not it had its own segment of the world market. Thanks to their possession of a developed colonial periphery, Great Britain and to a lesser degree France could implement the structural reform of their economies more smoothly and with a moderate political regime: pumping resources from the dependent countries to the imperial centers did not allow things to reach the boiling point in the "social cauldron." But the crisis was rather more acute in the United States and Germany. The United States, which did not officially possess colonies, effected the transition to a regulated market economy while preserving political freedom because of its strong democratic tradition and an economic safety margin (the financial resources accumulated during the First World War and the 1920s permitted it to conduct a sufficiently flexible social policy during crisis conditions). Moreover the United States was gradually expelling Great Britain from the countries of Latin America, the majority of which were being transformed into economic dependencies of the United States.

In the United States President Franklin D. Roosevelt, who came into office in 1933, proclaimed the new liberal policy of the "New Deal." It, in particular, included 1) the tightening of Federal control over the financial system: the temporary closing of the banks (only "healthy banks" were allowed to be reopened), the expansion of the functions of the Federal Reserve System (a Federal organ created in 1913 to control banking operations) to curb excessive speculation, the abolition of the gold standard, and the devaluation of the dollar. 2) Mandatory self-regulation of industry: trade associations received authority to formulate industry-wide "codes of honest competition," and the President received the authority from Congress to approve them, giving them the force of law. The codes fixed the volume of production, the conditions of labor, and the minimum price level. 3) The regulation of agriculture to increase farmers' income, raising prices through material incentives to reduce the area under cultivation and the herds of cattle. 4) A strong social policy: the organization of public works projects for the unemployed, the extension of the right to organize unions and engage in collective bargaining to the workers, and the setting of the maximum length of the work week and minimum wages. In 1935, for the first time in the United States, a law on social security was passed which introduced a system of old age pensions and unemployment benefits. The New Deal was implemented to preserve and develop political democracy.

Of the world powers Germany was in the most difficult position. A deep socioeconomic and intellectual crisis; the need for structural reform of the economy without colonial reserves; the gulf between her economic potential and her foreign spheres of influence; and, in the final analysis, her "historic" youth, the instability of her democracy, and her bruised national pride—all this pushed Germany to a harsh political regime and to the total mobilization of her reserves to militarize the country and to fight for a redivision of the world.

To some degree all of these factors were also characteristic of Japan, whose need to broaden her sphere of influence was dictated, in particular, by the low technological level of her industry which was unable to maintain competition with the western powers and by the nationalistic and expansionist spirit of the samurai mentality, which was strengthened by the successful wars at the end of the nineteenth century. As soon as "totalitarian" Germany and "authoritarian" Japan were able to win their own spheres of influence, they followed the path of their democratic rivals: Japan formed the commercial zone of the yen, Germany formed a kind of commercial and currency bloc of its own in Southeast Europe. The acquired spheres of influence to a large extent accelerated the stabilization of the regimes in Germany and Japan.

In Germany after the coming to power of the National Socialist German Workers Party (Nazis) in 1933 the processes of stabilization unfolded in the form of a totalitarian regime. Soon after that the remaining parties were prohibited (or "self liquidated"), the press was controlled, and the Reichstag became a ceremonial institution. NSDAP membership spiraled: from 850,000 in January 1933 to 2,450,000 by May 1933 and 6 million in spring 1945. The party headed by Adolf Hitler not only relied on a powerful and widespread terrorist apparatus and the total manipulation of the people but also on numerous mass organizations: 1) the subdivisions of the Nazi party created between 1921 and 1923 were the Storm troopers or SA, the SS units, the Hitler Youth, the Drivers' Corps, the students' union and women's organization; 2) the so-called adjunct groups such as the charitable organization "People's Prosperity," the Doctors' Union, and the Teachers' Union; 3) groups under Nazi supervision: the Unions of Jurists, the Struggle for German Culture, and the original Nazis base in industrial enterprises, the organization of factory and plant cells between 1931 and 1935. After 1933 the number of Nazi controlled organizations grew considerably. The traditional trade unions were dissolved, while all of the German workers were forcibly united into the German Labor Front which also included entrepreneurs. Hitler's plan for the substitution of the "unity of the entire people" for the class struggle was realized. As a result each German found himself involved in an organization reflecting his profession, age, and sex.

State intervention in the economy grew sharply. To coordinate the economy at the macro level the General Council of the German Economy was created. The law on the manditory monopolization of small businesses was adopted. All businesses with less than 100,000 marks of capital were liquidated and the formation of new businesses with less than 500,000 marks of capital was forbidden. The law on the preparation for the integration of the German economy led to fundamental changes in the management of the economy. All of the employers' unions came under the control of the Ministry of Economics headed by the "the fuhrer of the German economy." Even though the post was soon liquidated, the principle of having a boss (fuhrer) for the economy was not forgotten. The Chamber for the Reich Economy was established which included six Reich economic spheres: industry, banking, trade, energy, insurance, and the professions. In addition there were eighteen economic territorial chambers and numerous groups and subgroups. Bosses were placed at the head of each of the units of the vast administrative system—large monopolists with unlimited power to force the production of weapons, assign orders, distribute raw materials, and determine prices.

The fuhrer principle was fully implemented even at the enterprise level. The owner became the fuhrer who was able alone to establish wages, production norms, working hours, fines, and punishments. Everyone who disagreed with the fuhrer's orders in Germany was sent to concentration camps.[1]

The leaders of the Comintern at the end of the 1920s and the beginning of the 1930s saw a clear analogy between the crisis which was developing and the revolutionary situation which had occurred in Europe at the end of the First World War. Without seeing the uniqueness of the situation during the world war and the changes with followed (partially under the influence of the October Russian Revolution)[2] they saw a second wave of proletarian revolution approaching Europe. They thought the reformists, the social democrats who were "clouding the revolutionary consciousness of the proletariat," were the "main enemy." They resembled Lenin who announced an irreconcilable struggle against the "social chauvinists" and "centrists" of Karl Kautsky's type, who was especially dangerous in Lenin's opinion because he had "concealed" his "treason" against the proletariat by his revolutionary language. And so nurtured by these analogies, the Comintern, whose strategy after Bukharin's removal from leadership in 1929 was completely determined by Stalin, embarked on an aggressive struggle with the social democrats, including its left wing.

The potential for mass mobilization of the system and the unrestrained militarization of the country (military spending comprised 58% of the budget before the Second World War) enabled German heavy industry to surpass its pre-Depression level by 150% by 1939 and quickly eliminated unemployment. All of this, in combination with inner stability and foreign policy successes, created massive support for the fascist regime. Obviously the most characteristic features of totalitarian regimes were not only the state's firm control over all spheres of human activity, but also the massive support "from below" which was obtained by ideological manipulation and massive terror, enabling these regimes in a short time to quickly resolve national problems. They shaped the society and the type of person "under them," and they had a definite "nationalist" tint. But the fascists regimes established in a number of European countries on the periphery (Italy, Spain, and Portugal) lacked the intensity of Hitler's

Germany and the even greater intensity of Stalin's Soviet Union.

The Comintern's "liquidation war" with its potential allies in fact was only paving the fascists' road to power. But the Comintern's leaders only realized this fact at the end of 1934. In 1935 the Comintern's Seventh Congress took the course of establishing broad-based popular fronts for the purpose of blocking the fascists and preventing a new world war. But it was already too late. By then the regimes of Germany and Japan, who wanted to redivide the world, were firmly established on the world stage while the conflicts between the USSR and leading western powers all the more caused the planet to resemble a powder keg to which a Bickford fuse was attached.

The first area of international tension appeared in the Far East. 1929 witnessed a conflict on the Chinese Eastern Railway jointly administered by China and the USSR. Chinese militarists supported by White émigrés from Russia tried to seize the railway and intruded into Soviet territory, but they were defeated by the Special Far Eastern Army commanded by V.K. Blucher. In September 1931 Japan moved its troops into the northeastern provinces of China (Manchuria) bordering the USSR. In the summer of 1938 part of the Japanese army crossed the Soviet border in the region of Lake Khasan but was thrown out of Soviet territory after fierce battles. In May 1939 Japan's attack on the Mongolian People's Republic, a Soviet ally, took place on the Khalkhin-Gol River. In August 1939 the aggressors were routed by the troops of the USSR and Mongolia commanded by G.K. Zhukov.

After the victories of Nazism in Germany another hotbed of tension appeared and began to grow in Europe. In 1933 Germany and Japan left the League of Nations to facilitate their preparations for war. In March 1935, having violated the military articles of the Versailles Treaty, the government of Germany introduced universal military conscription. In October 1935, the troops of fascist Italy invaded Ethiopia. In March 1936, in violation of the Treaty of Versailles and the Locarno Pact of 1925, the German army burst into the demilitarized Rhineland and proceeded to the French border. General Francisco Franco's coup against the government of the Spanish Republic began in July 1936. The civil war in Spain heralded the global battle with fascism. The protocol on cooperation between Germany and Italy (the Berlin-Rome Axis) was signed in Berlin in October 1936. In November Germany and Japan signed the Anticomintern Pact. Italy joined it in 1937. And so the military alliance known as the Rome-Berlin-Tokyo "triangle" was created.

In the tense political atmosphere of the 30s the foreign policy of the USSR passed through three definite stages: before the coming to power of the Nazis in Germany in 1933 the USSR's foreign policy displayed a predominantly "pro-German" orientation. From 1933 to 1939 a "prodemocratic" line predominated with its orientation toward an alliance with England and France and attempts to guarantee collective security. From 1939 to 1941 a "pro-German" line was followed again.

In December 1933, the Central Committee of the All-Union Communist Party (the Bolsheviks) decided to work for collective security by concluding a pact on mutual assistance for a large circle of European states. In September 1935, the USSR entered the League of Nations. But because of international opposition and Germany's efforts to amend the conditions of the Versailles treaty, attempts to create a system of European security did not succeed. After German universal military service was introduced in March 1935, the prospect for a Franco-Soviet rapprochement became stronger since they were Germany's natural, continental, geopolitical competitors. In May 1935, a treaty on mutual assistance between France and USSR was signed. Both parties agreed to render immediate assistance and support to each other in case of attack. In September a similar treaty was signed between the USSR and Czechoslovakia. In October 1939, the USSR began to give considerable assistance to the Spanish republicans.

But the British and French leaders (primarily the British) generally conducted a policy of "appeasement" toward Hitler. Having meekly accepted the tearing up of the Treaty of Versailles by Germany, they tried to direct Hitler's aggression toward the east. In March 1938, the fascists occupied Austria (the so-called Austrian anschluss, "union"). The USSR suggested an immediate international conference to undertake measures against this aggression. But the suggestion was not supported by the European democracies.

During the same year Hitler's supporters announced their territorial ambitions in Czechoslovakia. The USSR offered Czechoslovakia military support. On the other hand, in September 1938, British Prime Minister Neville Chamberlain, French Premier Eduard Deladier, and the head of the Italian regime Benito Mussolini visited Hitler in Munich. It was then that Czechoslovakia's fate was decided: it was ordered to transfer the Sudetanland, which was inhabited by Germans, to Germany. The "Munich deal" was supplemented by an Anglo-German declaration which was essentially a nonaggression pact between the two countries. In December Hitler and the French government signed a similar declaration. On March 13, 1939, the Germans occupied the whole of Czechoslovakia. On March 21 they demanded that Poland return the city of Danzig (Gdansk) to Germany. The next day German troops entered the Lithuanian province of Klaipeda. At the end of that month the Spanish Republic fell. Several days later Mussolini's army captured Albania.

The processes taking place in the world at the end of the 1920s and early 1930s directly influenced the internal development of the USSR.[3] The technical and economic backwardness of the Soviet state, the absence of external sources of capital, the fragmentation of the world market, which complicated the utilization of the advantages of the international division of labor, and the growing threat of a new world war forced the Soviet leaders to mobilize the nation's internal resources to accelerate the creation of heavy industry and a developed military-industrial complex (VPK) which in turn increased the brutality of the political regime in the country.

Alternative Ways of Developing Society in the Late 1920s and Early 1930s

Originally the leaders of the party and state implemented an industrialization strategy based on NEP. The need for the accelerated but balanced development of the national economy was the basic premise of the first Five Year Plan for economic development, which was unanimously adopted at the Fifteenth Party Congress in December 1927: the optimum balance between supply and demand,

THE CONSTRUCTION OF SOCIALISM   **153**

the planned development of heavy and light industry, consideration of both the industrial and agrarian sectors.⁴ But, political and economic circumstances immediately destroyed these idealistic plans.

The economic situation in the country deteriorated in the second half of 1927. From this aggravation and the disruption of diplomatic relations with Great Britain, there was talk of war in the air. The Russian population which remembered the bitter experience of privation during the war years rushed to stockpile necessities. The half-forgotten lines appeared again in the shops. As a result the supply of consumer goods was depleted which was earmarked for shipment to the village during the autumn grain purchase campaign to give the farmers an incentive for surrendering their crops. Due to unfavorable weather, winter crops failed in the Ukraine, the Northern Caucasus, and the Crimea. The January 1928 purchase of grain was 128 million puds [a pud equals 16.38 kilograms] less than in January 1927. This endangered the planned grain supply for the towns, the army, and for export.

In this situation the country's leadership took extraordinary measures in early 1928: farmers who refused to sell their grain "surplus" at the low state price were accused of profiteering under Article 107 of the Criminal Code of the Russian Soviet Federated Socialist Republic. The "surplus" was confiscated by the state. In addition 25% of the confiscated "surplus" was distributed among the poorest farmers at a low state price or as a long term credit. Naturally, this incited poor farmers to search for such surpluses in the households of their more prosperous neighbors. These extraordinary measures were accompanied by the closing of country markets and the prohibition of grain trade while special groups watched the roads to prevent the transport of grain; peasant homes were raided in search of grain surpluses.

The grain deficit was eliminated but at a costly price. These administrative measures encouraged the peasants to reduce the area under cultivation on the most productive peasant farms: why sow such a great deal if the entire "surplus" will be confiscated? Likewise massive herds of cattle were slaughtered for the same reason. By cutting their own production the more prosperous peasants were trying to avoid the taxes which were becoming unbearable.

The market reacted to the deteriorating situation in the agrarian sector by increasing the gap between the state purchase price and market price of grain. From March 1928 to March 1929 the price differential for rye increased by 300% in the central industrial area and in the Ukraine. The spiraling price of grain on the market made the cultivation of industrial crops (*tekhnicheskie kultury*) unprofitable, causing a reduction in light industrial production and increasing the hunger for consumer goods which further limited the growth of agrarian production.

At the end of 1928 the rationing of bread and other foodstuffs was introduced. The export of grain fell year after year. In 1926-27 the export of grain reached the record level for the NEP years of more than two million tons (compared to 9.5 million tons in 1913), but it fell to 416.7 thousand tons in 1927-28. In 1929 the Communist Party Central Committee conceded the "almost total collapse of grain export." The decreased level of grain exports lead to an equally severe reduction in machinery imports, which endangered the country's industrialization plans. A modest rise in the purchase price of grain, which occurred in 1928, did not compensate for its production expenses and did not improve the situation.

Stalin once more introduced extraordinary measures in the village in the spring of 1929. The repeated seizure of marketable surplus grain by administrative measures undermined the market stimuli for labor in the village. This was the background of the last major intraparty battle of the 1920s, the struggle with "right-wing deviation." Nikolai Bukharin and Joseph Stalin were the major opponents in the struggle.

The first open disagreements between them became apparent after the April 1928 Plenum of the Communist Party Central Committee and the Central Control Commission to evaluate the causes behind the state's difficulty in purchasing grain. Stalin described the roots of the crisis: the inadequate rate of industrial development had given rise to a consumer goods shortage while the small peasant farms by their very nature were incapable of providing for the needs of the expanding industry. Stalin pointed out the class aspect: the wealthy farmers (kulaks) were exploiters who were sabotaging the state's efforts to procure grain. Bukharin's presentation called attention to the subjective factors behind the crisis: a reserve fund of manufactured goods had not yet been created while the growth of incomes in the village had not yet been balanced by taxes, which was aggravating the consumer goods shortage and reducing the production of agricultural products; the correlation of purchase prices for consumer goods and grain was disadvantageous for the latter. Stalin emphasized the need to accelerate the village's production of agricultural products. Bukharin proposed the normalization of the market as the first task. He thought of collectivization as a secondary task. In addition Bukharin strongly objected to the proposals of M.D. Kondratiev and other economists of the "populist type" to reduce the pace of industrialization significantly, raise the price of grain, and encourage large farms. Bukharin called these suggestions a "frankly kulak program."[5]

By fall 1928 the difference in approaches to economic problems had become even more explicit. Bukharin tried to justify the "American version" of an economy in which the growth of the industrial and agricultural sectors was sufficiently rapid and balanced to create healthy market connections between the town and village without extraordinary measures. He envisioned the development of large collective farms in grain producing areas, and the industrialization of the agrarian enterprise through the creation of small businesses to process crops in the village. But according to Bukharin individual farms would continue to be the basis of agriculture for a long time.[6]

Stalin's model was a variant of the uneven development model (the "Russian variant" in Bukharin's opinion) based on the maximum concentration of resources in heavy industry at the expense of straining the country's economy and pumping resources from the "secondary branches" (agriculture, light industry). After the modernization of heavy industry, the plan envisioned the technological restructuring of the temporarily neglected agriculture and light industry. The first plan stipulated the collective farm (*kolkhoz*) as the form of production to link the town and village. Stalin was sure that there was only an illusory hope of eliminating the consumer goods shortage or industrializing under the conditions of a market equilibrium: "Industrial restructuring involves transferring resources from consumer goods production into the production of the means of production.... It suggests financing the construction of new plants and the growth of a number of towns and new consumers while the new plants will only be able to produce a large quantity of consumer goods after three or four years."[7]

An open fight between the two concepts took place in early 1929. Stalin's control over the party apparatus and the OGPU (secret police) as well as the simplicity, intelligibility, and the "communist attractiveness" (because of its resemblance to the socialist ideal) of his course for the party, workers, and poor peasantry dissatisfied with NEP and its hardships decided the outcome of the discussion. The Joint Plenum of the Communist Party Central Committee and the Central Control Commission and the Sixteenth Party Conference denounced Bukharin's "right wing deviation" in April 1929.

How long would the Bukharin model, which presupposed the harmonious development of the industrial and agrarian sectors, have lasted under these conditions? One must admit that one of the most important elements of the American model was absent, one which permitted the USA at a parallel stage of industrialization in the second half of the nineteenth century to manage without a significant transference of resources from the agrarian economy into industry: the massive influx of foreign capital. In 1843 the US foreign debt was 150 million, in 1899 3.3 billion dollars. In 1896 the major percentage of stock in five out of the nine major US railroads belonged to foreigners. The flow of capital outside of the US did not exceed the influx of capital until the First World War.[8]

The impressive industrial leap in prerevolutionary Russia at the end of the nineteenth and beginning of the twentieth centuries was also to a great extent based on foreign sources of finance. Foreign capital accounted for 35.5% in 1893, 39% in 1900, and 35.2% of all capital investment in securities. In 1913 there were more than 7.5 billion rubles of foreign investment to almost fourteen billion rubles of native investment in securities. There were more than 7.5 billion rubles worth of foreign investments.[9] The defense problem was never as serious in the United States as in Russia and the ideological factor was entirely absent in the United States. In Russia

THE CONSTRUCTION OF SOCIALISM 157

anticapitalism and collectivism had blocked the development of the private-sector trades and small industry in the town in favor of the large farm in the village and the pouring of capital into industry,

Bukharin thought the major error had been the establishment of an unfavorable alignment of purchase prices for grain. But the possibilities for maneuver in that area were limited. In the mid-twenties the alignment was favorable for grain, which caused the production of industrial crops to fall, sharpening the consumer goods shortage. If grain had received priority again at the end of the twenties, the production of industrial crops would have fallen, causing the curtailment of light industry and chaos in the market. It was impossible to implement a substantial price rise for both grain and raw materials without raising the price of industrial goods to compensate the workers for the growing cost of food which would require a new rise in agricultural prices.

The large-scale production farm could function successfully even when purchase prices fell slightly. Bukharin called for an "offensive" against the kulaks (prosperous farmers), but the state did not have the credits or machines to provide an incentive for the peasantry to enter large-scale production collective farms voluntarily. The small poor and middle-level farms could survive on their own only by paying attention to the market situation: the transition from commodity production was less suitable to the cultivation of more profitable crops.

The severe shortage of capital and the decision to create a system of industrial self-sufficiency or autarky (the strategy of building socialism in one country adopted in 1925) made it impossible to balance the development of heavy and light industry and to end the consumer goods shortage by relying on the market to link industry and the individual peasant farms. So it was not by chance that at the November 1929 Plenum of the Party Central Committee Bukharin, Rykov, and Tomsky announced the end of the disagreements. Indeed, it was Bukharin who in February 1930 worked out the theory of collectivization: first socialization of the means of production and then new machinery, and not the other way around, as they had planned before 1929. Bukharin thought that he had made Lenin's concept of inverted (backwards) development more explicit. In October 1917 the Bolsheviks, relying on the minimum material preconditions for socialism, first took power and then began to build an appropriate material basis under it. In 1929 and 1930 they introduced a new production system in the village and then began to build the technical base under it.[10]

The defeat of Bukharin's group, which was caused not only by Stalin's political will and by his skillful intrigues but also for some objective reasons, marked the removal of the last obstacles to the implementation of a strategy of forced industrialization and the formation of a totalitarian regime.

The Anatomy of Stalinist Modernization

Any type of transition to an industrial economy is painful because it is customarily accompanied by the growth of capital (the part of the budget which is earmarked for the expansion of production and reserves), ranging from 5-10% to 20-30% of national income.[11] But in Russia the suffering had complications. First, unlike other countries who settled the problem of capital either with the acquisition of colonies or with the massive infusion of foreign capital—and often both—the USSR had neither colonies nor substantial foreign capital. Nevertheless during the first five year period the percentage of capital accumulated to finance industrialization, which represented about ten percent of the national income in the middle of the 1920s, grew to approximately 29% in 1930, in 1931 to 40%, and in 1932 to 44%. It ranged from 25 to 30% in the later 1930s.[12]

Second, the Soviet model of industrialization did not emphasize the gradual substitution of more and more complicated industry and the gradual integration into the world capitalist economy; it required the immediate development of the most progressive and capital-intensive industries of the age: electrical engineering, metallurgy, chemistry, and machine building.

Under pressure from Stalin, directions were given to industrialize as fast as possible. The State Planning Commission offered the Council of People's Commissars two versions of the first Five Year Plan in early 1929. The "optimal" targets exceeded the "starting"

THE CONSTRUCTION OF SOCIALISM

Joseph Stalin
Library of Congress, Prints & Photographs Div, LC-USZ62-95746

plans by around 20%. In April 1929 the Sixteenth Party Conference approved and in May 1929 the Fifth Congress of Soviets of the USSR adopted the optimal version of the plan for 1928/29-1932/33.

The massive scale of the tasks and the extremely limited material and financial means forced the counting of every copek [100 copeks = one ruble] and each machine. As a result central planning was sharply intensified during the first five year plan. Production plans, resources, and the methods of compensating labor were severely regulated. There was one purpose—to concentrate maximum effort and funding on heavy industry. Out of the 1500 new construction ventures of the Five Year Plan a group of fifty to sixty projects was singled out and guaranteed everything necessary. Their total cost comprised almost half of industrial investments. Fourteen of the favored construction projects received the highest priority. G.K. Ordzhonikidze, the head of the Supreme Economic Council of the USSR (*Vesenkha*) and People's Commissar of Heavy Industry after 1932 paid personal attention to every one of them.

The successful beginning of the Five Year Plans created "dizziness from success" within the ranks of the highest party leadership. Beginning in November 1929 and continuing into the middle of 1932 the plan's goals in industry were raised regularly. It resulted in the inability of transport to cope with the increased volume of work. There were not enough building materials. Construction times were delayed. The rapid growth of the urban population required more and more provisions. The growing importation of machinery demanded higher exports of food and raw materials to pay for them.

But the second half of 1920s witnessed stagnation in agricultural production. The annual growth of the urban population was 4.8% in 1927, 5% in 1928, and 5.2% in 1929, but the corresponding figures for agricultural production were; 2.5%, 2.5%, 2.4%; for the gross grain harvest: 5.9%, 1.2%, and 2.5%; and for centralized grain procurement: 5.2%, 2.0% and 4.9%.[13]

Although market relations in the village were being curtailed more and more, administrative measures so far had been used only for the acquisition of foodstuffs and not for their production, which explains the fall of the gross grain harvest in 1929 and the considerable growth of the procurement of grain by the central authorities. Under these conditions, at the end of 1929 and the beginning of 1930, the course for complete collectivization was adopted,[14] which was accomplished by extraordinary measures, namely: the expansion of the plenary authority of the OGPU (the secret police) which had the authority for extralegal scrutiny of the affairs under it and the mission to evict the kulaks. The choice of this course was determined by the complex interaction of ideological and economic factors.

The party and state documents of the time pointed out that the goal of collectivization was to realize "socialist reforms in the village." But this does not explain the barbaric methods and extremely short time allotted for collectivization. Its forms, methods, and terms are better explained by the second goal of collectivization, about which less was said: to finance industrialization and the uninterrupted supply of the rapidly growing cities at any cost. This required the preservation of low grain prices and a sharp rise in the delivery of supplies to the cities and for export.

As a result massive extra-economic pressure was brought to bear on the village, and the development of the collective farms was carried out by force under threat of denunciation as an enemy of the Soviet power or the war on the kulaks (*raskulachivaniia* or "dekulakization"). The percentage of people deprived of their electoral rights in the village reached 4.1% in 1929 (in 1925—0.74%).[15] This resulted in the fall of agrarian production and an especially massive slaughter of cattle. The total number of horses and large horned cattle in 1929 fell to 9.2 million head,[16] because the peasants

THE CONSTRUCTION OF SOCIALISM   **161**

did not want to surrender them to the state.

The peasants began to openly oppose the authorities. Between January and the middle of March 1930, more than two thousand anticollective farm uprisings occurred, for the suppression of which the army and OGPU were used. To break down the peasantry's resistance and to strengthen the collective farms created after the beginning of 1930—through confiscation of the kulak property—a massive campaign against the kulaks was begun on Stalin's instructions. Anticlerical terror grew stronger at the same time as churches and monasteries were closed. By the end of 1930 up to 80% of all village churches were closed.[17] In 1930 and 1931, according to the documentary evidence, 382,000 peasant families (4.8 persons per family) were dispossessed and settled in remote regions, but in January 1950 the number of expelled peasants was set at nearly 3.5 million. Some scholars calculate the total number of dispossessed families was approximately one million, of which no fewer than half were expelled to remote regions.[18] D.A. Volkogonov thinks that under the "dekulakization" 8.5 to nine million men, women, old people, and children perished.[19] Some of these died en route and some in their new place of residence where there were no constructed shelters nor medicines nor warm clothing (it was seized during the "dekulakization").

To stop the catastrophic decline in agricultural production the process of "socialization" was enforced. It was easier to place tens of thousands of collective farms under administrative control than millions of peasant farms. But the rapid creation of the majority of collective farms without trained managers, material incentives, machinery, suitable investment, and supplies only increased the economic dislocation, as the cattle case shows. In all, from 1928 to 1933/34 the total number of cattle fell from sixty to thirty-three million head,[20] which exceeded the losses during the civil war. The peasantry was deprived of any material incentive for productive labor by irresponsible managers and ruthless extortion of resources; in the chaos, even some of the seed was taken by the state. And the passive resistance (absenteeism, careless labor) of the collective farm peasants, who did not want to work for nothing, grew.

Stalin demanded the fulfillment of the grain requisition plan at any price. Two goals were pursued simultaneously—to force the collective farmers to work and, then, to surrender the grain. In a number of regions the barns were completely empty: the seed and the reserves stored as insurance against a crop failure were taken. As a result a terrible tragedy unfolded in the winter of 1932/1933—famine, which encompassed the North Caucasus, the Volga River area, the Ukraine, and Kazakhstan; the casualties, according to the most conservative estimate, were more than three million (in some estimates as high as five or eight million).[21] In any event the reality of famine was denied in official propaganda. Serious measures to overcome it were not adopted. And the export of grain abroad continued.

The barbaric "total collectivization" and repression against the urban population permitted the creation of a huge, far-flung system of compulsory (really slave) labor, which was an important element of the Stalinist economy. The resolution of July 30, 1930, of the kulak dispossession commission, which was headed by A.A. Andreev, the deputy chairman of the USSR Council of People's Commissars, is an example: "Discussed: The question on additional demands for special migrants and their assignment. Resolved: . . . to require the Supreme Economic Council in three days to give the OGPU their final demands for special migrants. . . . In conformity with these demands to authorize the OGPU to conduct the necessary reassignment according to region and expel the kulaks."[22] The White Sea-Baltic canal was built by 100,000 prisoners; prison labor also constructed the Moscow-Volga canal; the overwhelming mass of prisoners labored practically without pay in the mining and metallurgical industry and in timber-cutting. In 1930 the Labor Camp Administration was created by the OGPU, which in 1931 became a central administrative board (the GULAG or State Labor Camp Administration). The mid-year number of prisoners in the camps of the NKVD (the People's Commissariat for Internal Affairs, which succeeded OGPU as the secret police) rose from 190,000 in 1930 to 510,000 in 1934. According to the current data, on March 1,1940, the GULAG included fifty-three labor camps, 425 corrective labor colonies, and fifty juvenile colonies in which there were 1,668,200 prisoners. By the beginning of the war the number of prisoners was

2,300,000. In addition the expelled kulaks and members of their families were among the special migrants. In January 1932, 1.4 million were counted: a small part of them were occupied in agrarian work, but most worked in the timber-cutting, mining, and metallurgy industries. According to the official, understated figures, between 1930 and 1953 the courts and administrative bodies sentenced 3,778,234 people for counterrevolutionary offenses and crimes against the state, 786,098 of whom were shot.[23]

As a result of complete collectivization an entire system was created to transfer financial, material, and labor resources from agriculture into industry. The basic features of the system were 1) mandatory agricultural deliveries to the state, 2) the purchase of agricultural produce at nominal prices, 3) numerous taxes, 4) provision of the necessities for the Gulag, 5) organized recruitment of workers in the village for industrial enterprises, 6) the peasants lost their passports in 1932, tying them to the land, and 7) the direct interference of the party and state apparatus (district committees, commissioners, political departments of the state farms—sovkhozs—and Machine Tractor Stations) in the production process.

What were the results of complete collectivization? Its effect on agricultural development was catastrophic. In 1929-1932 livestock were reduced by 20 million (by one third), horses by 11 million (one third), hogs by half, sheep and goats by 40%. But Stalin's strategy of rapid modernization, during which all branches of the national economy and all spheres of social life were subordinated to the requirements for the growth of industry, did not require the general growth of agriculture as a whole. Agricultural improvements were introduced only if they could reduce the number of farmers in proportion to the need for industrial workers, to keep food production at the same level by using fewer workers without long periods of hunger, and to provide industry with raw materials for which substitutes were not available.[24]

Collectivization solved these problems. In the mid-thirties the situation in the agrarian sector became relatively stable. Rationing was canceled in 1935. During the 1930s 15-20 million people were released from agrarian work, which increased the working class from 9 to 24 million. The country became self-sufficient in cotton. Although the volume of agrarian production did not grow and the per capita production fell significantly, the production of labor rose somewhat because of severe coercion on the job, cooperation, and later the delivery of machinery to the village. On the eve of collectivization the country's population of 150-155 million annually produced 72-73 million tons of grain, more than 5 million tons of meat, and more than 30 million tons of milk; at the end of the 30s and the beginning of the 40s a population that had risen to 170-200 million only produced 75-80 million tons of grain, 4.5 million tons of meat, and 30 million tons of milk. At the end of the NEP period this amount was produced by 50-55 million private farmers while the output of the prewar years of the 1930s was produced by 30-35 million collective farmers, a third fewer peasants.[25]

A Comparison of Gross Industrial Output of Some Products in the USSR and Capitalist Countries (%)[26]

	USSR/USA 1928:1940	USSR/Britain 1928:1940	USSR/France 1928:1940	USSR/Germany 1928:1940
Electricity	4 : 26	31 : 121	34 : 235	29 : 32
Basic fuel	7 : 27	23 : 105	89 : 437	35 : 133
Iron	9 : 35	49 : 179	33 : 405	24 : 95
Steel	8 : 29	49 : 139	45 : 415	29 : 108
Cement	6 : 25	42 : 77	44 : 127	32 : 75
Cotton	30 : 37	... : 134	... : 187	... : ...

*1937 data

Securing the conditions for the realization of the sudden jump in industrial output was the main result of collectivization, although at considerable cost. Between 1928 and 1941 around 9000 major industrial enterprises were built! The growth rate in heavy industry during the first five-year plans (1928-1940) was two to three times greater than during the thirteen years of Russia's development before the First World War (1900-1913). Even considering that according to recent estimates the average rate of industrial growth

THE CONSTRUCTION OF SOCIALISM

during the 1930s was not 17% (the official figure), but 10.9%, it exceeded the highest rate of growth, which was obtained by Russia during the second half of the 1890s (9.2%). In terms of gross industrial output the USSR at the end of the 1930s occupied second place in the world after the USA while in 1913 she occupied fifth place. The lag behind the developed capitalist countries in per capita industrial output was reduced as well: while the per capita output was 5 to 10 times higher in the capitalist countries in the 1920s, it was only 1.5 to 4 times higher in the 1930s.

As a result, according to a number of parameters the technological backwardness of Soviet industry was overcome. In the 1930s the USSR became one of three or four countries capable of producing any type of industrial product.

The Great Patriotic War was a cruel exam for Soviet economy, an exam which was passed. During the First World War one third to one half of the troops of the central powers fought against Russia and were unable to obtain decisive victory; during the Second World War two thirds to three fourths of the troops of fascist Germany and her satellites fought against Russia and were defeated.[27] The powerful economic potential created in the 1930s was the foundation of the military victory.

But the leap in the development of heavy industry was achieved at the price of rampant inflation (the index of retail prices rose more than 600% between 1928 and 1941), a decline in the standard of living, the underdevelopment of the light and food industries, the stagnation of the rural economy, and the decline of productivity. The growth in the numbers of workers surpassed the growth of industrial production. There was almost no real growth, while the productivity of labor in industry declined between 1928 and 1941. The fall of stock reserves and the growth of the material facilities for production were greater (in terms of the rate of growth and the character of the structural changes) than in the developed capitalist countries during the analogous period at the end of the nineteenth and beginning of the twentieth centuries. The average annual rate of growth of national income between 1928 and 1941 was only one percent according to some estimates.[28]

The use of coercion to industrialize caused the expansion of administrative methods of economic management and bureaucratization. With growth of the scale of the super centralization, the Supreme Economic Council, which united all branches of industry, stopped carrying out its own functions. Around the end of 1931 and beginning of 1932 (when the Supreme Economic Council was reorganized into three ministries called People's Commissariats, *narkomats*) the unrestrained expansion of management began. As new branches of industry appeared and the volume of production grew, more and more new ministries were created from the existing narkomats. Around the end of the 1930s 21 industrial ministries were functioning. Industry became divided into branches functioning as super monopolies. Direct planning was greatly strengthened. During the first five year plan assignments planned in detail were worked out for 50 branches of heavy industry, during the second, for around 120. After 1930 state plans were formulated for the sowing of crops, after 1932 plans were made for the work of the MTS tractors, and after 1935 there were also state plans for cattle breeding and so forth. As a result the number of administrators and managers within the administrative apparatus grew between 1926 and 1937 from 311,000 to 1,353,000, that is by 3.2 times, while the growth in the same period in the countryside was 5.8 times.[29]

In this way the entire administrative-command system of management was formed to strictly and harshly control all sectors of the economy. This was an extraordinary system, which was both a response to and the cause of an emergency situation. The administrative-command system, by practically eliminating private property, formed the foundation of the USSR's political system which was more severe inside the country than the fascist regime in Germany.

The Formation of the Totalitarian Regime in the USSR

The ultimate ideological goal of building socialism in a hostile environment inevitably required the concentration of power in the hands of one "architect and chief construction engineer." Neither the national traditions of strong personal power, nor the political

THE CONSTRUCTION OF SOCIALISM

party which essentially followed the leadership principle, nor the relativist ethics of the Bolsheviks (everything that serves the building of communism is morally sound), nor the most centralized economic structure in the world could in any way limit the concentration of power in the hands of the party leader. In practice the boundaries only depended on his personal qualities, his ambition, and the balance of forces in the party elite, which depended on the leader's political acumen, or more exactly, his ability to manage the apparatus. At the same time Stalin's ambition for supreme power was capriciously interwoven with some of the objective factors influencing the course of development chosen for the country in the 1930s.

The "socialist offensive" which was implemented by force was accompanied by the intensive shuffling of cadres and the fall of Bukharin's supporters and other people unsuitable to Stalin. In 1929 a purge of the party and state apparatus unfolded; 138,000 people who had served the party were removed from their jobs, amounting to a purge of 11% of the party and state apparatus.[30] The percentage of people deprived of political rights in the towns between 1925 and 1929 increased from five to 8.5 percent. As earlier observed, the authority of the OGPU was expanded. Since the mass collectivization had provoked peasant uprisings, Russian émigrés tried to send their own representatives to the USSR and unify the uprisings. In response the OGPU kidnapped the leader of the Russian military union, General A.P. Kutepov and conducted the mass arrest of former officers of the tsarist army who had served (generally honorably) in the Red Army. The political proceedings were falsified; the most important Russian economists and agronomists A.V. Chaianov and N.D. Kondratiev, in particular, were arrested in the so-called Trudovik peasant party affair and the outstanding representatives of the scientific and technological intelligentsia and state apparatus of the Engineering Center (or Industry Party) were victimized. In March 1931 there was an announcement about the uncovering of yet another organization of sabateurs (wreckers), the Bureau of the Central Committee of the Russian Social Democrat Workers Party of Mensheviks.[31] These and other measures not only strengthened Stalin's personal power but provided political support for his social and economic strategy.

The use of coercion to achieve economic growth during a se-

Politburo TsK VKP(B)
Elected at 18th Congress VKP(B)

(Row 1) V.M. Molotov, J.V. Stalin, L.M. Kaganovich
(Row 2) K.E. Voroshilov, A.A. Andreev, M.I. Kalinin, A.A. Zhdanov
(Row 3) A.I. Mikoyan, N.S. Khrushchev, L.P. Beria, N.M. Shvernik

THE CONSTRUCTION OF SOCIALISM   **169**

vere shortage of capital restricted the possibilities for materially stimulating labor and created a gap between economic and social development characterized by a declining standard of living, which could not help but cause the growth of psychological pressure in society.

The acceleration of industrialization and the complete collectivization of agriculture intensified the migratory processes (the movement from the countryside to the town, from the farm to industry, e.g.) and severely disrupted the way of life, changing the values of the great mass of people ("the great turning point," *velikii perelom*). To "condense" the surplus social and psychological energy of the people, to direct it toward the resolution of the key problems of development, and to compensate for the weakness of the material stimulus required strong political and ideological pressure.

The acceleration of industrialization with insufficient funds for material stimulation during the second half of the 1920s, led to attempts to raise productivity and rationalize production at the expense of the workers. The renewal of collective contracts, wage-scale reform, the review of production norms, and the introduction of a passport system in the winter of 1927/28 increased leveling (*uravnilovka*) of labor costs and caused real wages to fall.

The party and state leadership managed to direct the growing discontent of workers against the "technical specialists." The "bourgeois specialists" (*spetsy*) were assigned the role of "wreckers" and perhaps assumed the main guilt for the economic difficulties. The proclamation of the policy of comprehensive acceleration of "social reform" at the end of 1929 was another type of appeal to the class consciousness of the working class. The grandiose nature of the plans exercised a strong stimulating influence on the workers, attracting them to the idea of building a socialist commonwealth and giving them an additional stimulus to develop industry.[32] And so the "two-faced Janus" of the 1930s was born: enthusiasm for work and the struggle against the "wreckers," the "enemies of the people."

The organizers of the campaign against the specialists exploited the antibourgeois attitude prevailing in the worker's movement in the early stages of industrialization which had become particularly strong during the class struggle of the early twentieth century. The thrust of the "socialist offensive" was directed at the "new workers"—representing village youth with little political experience. If arrivals from peasant families accounted for 45% of the working class in 1926-1929, in the following years the peasantry was the absolutely dominant source for filling the ranks of the proletariat.[33]

The emphasis was not on the "depravity" of the peasant roots, but on the rootlessness of the migrants. The "young workers" who had been uprooted from the system of social connections in the village found themselves in a "large and alien world" and were not yet integrated into urban society. They were suitable subjects for political and ideological manipulation. The slogan of "acceleration" promised to the "new workers" (potential migrants from the village) the rapid elimination of unemployment which had been growing in the 1920s which had a great propaganda effect.

In fact the lack of stability and the relative youth of the existing relationships and institutions was one of the reasons for the comparatively rapid introduction of the collective farm system. Collectivization was the fourth agrarian reform in seventy years, including the 1861 reform (the emancipation of the serfs), and the third after the Stolypin reform (the breakup of the commune) and the agrarian revolution of 1917-18 in the twentieth century.[34] The peasants were deprived of any prospects during the NEP years: after reaching a certain profit level, the farm fell under heavy taxation and administrative pressure. The "kulak" was ridiculed in print and deprived of his voice in the soviets, and later in cooperatives and agrarian social societies (*obshchiny*), while his children were denied admission to college (the *vyz* or *vysshee uchebnoe zavedenie*, "higher education institution"). As a result the rate of failure of peasant farms was twice the prerevolutionary index.[35]

By dividing their farms (with all the negative consequences of lost production) the peasants tried to escape kulak status because the latter meant strangulation by taxes and social repression. The peasants were promised that collectivization would give the poor peasants a chance to raise their standard of living and social status. But massive violence against the village finally played the decisive role while the antagonism between the poor and prosperous peasantry was rather skillfully manipulated.

THE CONSTRUCTION OF SOCIALISM   **171**

Who supplied the basic support in society for Stalin's "revolution from above" and to a significant degree for the Stalinist regime? 1) The part of the "old working class" which was full of anti-bourgeois attitudes; 2) the peasants who were no longer part of the peasantry: torn from their past, deprived of the present, existing in a area "outside of a culture";[36] 3) the village poor (in 1927 28.3% of Russian farms did not have horses, 31.6% did not have tools for plowing and 18.2% did not have cows).[37] The regime also managed to rely upon the passivity of a considerable number of middle-income farmers.

Besides the "spores" the Stalin revolution needed a "creator." Only the bureaucratic apparatus, which had already begun to grow during the NEP years, was able to carry out the function of total administrative control of society because of its position in the system of socialized production. On October 1, 1922, there were 1,320,000 Soviet officials, in 1927 3,722,000 (compared to 2,388,000 workers in large-scale industry in 1926-27).[38]

But the customary administrative apparatus was not suited to "revolutionary" activity; they had inherited all of the vices of the traditional Russian bureaucracy, such as sluggishness and corruption. At the end of the 20s and during the 30s the center of gravity shifted to the extraordinary party organizations (the political departments of the Machine Tractor Stations, the collective farms, and transport) and the punitive organs of the NKVD-OGPU.

The Communist party played the major role in political mobilization. The consolidation of the administrative-command system, which was built on the hierarchical principle, led to the final confirmation of the Communist Party as the leader's organization. The transformation of the party, deprived of any independent political role, into the mere instrument of its own leader did not develop automatically. In spite of Stalin's all-embracing power, the curtailment of intraparty democracy, and hyperindustrialism Stalin still encountered opposition within the ranks of the party even after the rout of the "right deviation" which included the top party officials, the "uppers" (*verkhi*). There was the case of the so-called "right-left bloc": V.V. Lominadze, the first secretary of the Caucasus regional party, and S.N. Syrtsov, a candidate member of the Politburo and the Russian republic's sovnarkom chairman (premier), criticized the Stalinist leadership in 1930. There was also the opposition group headed by the secretary of the Moscow Krasnopresnensk regional party committee, M.N. Riutin, who worked out a detailed anti-Stalinist document—the so-called "Riutin platform," as well as the groups headed by D.P. Smirnov, V.M. Tolmachev, and N.B. Eismont.

Although the OGPU ruthlessly suppressed any type of opposition, opposition to Stalin was rife in the party. Despite the loud glorification of Stalin at the Seventeenth Party Congress, in which his former opponents were required to participate, there were about 170 (by some estimates 270) votes against Stalin in the secret elections to the Central Committee. In all 1225 delegates at the congress were able to vote. The leader of the Leningrad party organization, S.M. Kirov, an advocate of a somewhat more moderate policy, was advanced as a more popular figure in the party. A number of Bolsheviks wanted to elect him as general secretary instead of Stalin, but he refused. (Later, of the 1961 delegates at the Congress, 1108 were purged and of the 139 persons elected to the Central Committee, 98—70%—were removed.) On December 1, 1934, Kirov was assassinated under very strange circumstances. This assassination, which in all probability was initiated or directly organized by Stalin, was the beginning of the mass repression that touched every layer of the population, but the burden fell upon the party and state elite, "the Old Guard."

Extremely simple and summary rules for the conduct of terror cases were adopted, and they tried to apply them to every major political offense. The accused were not allowed to participate or appeal and action was taken within ten days. Mass meetings and demonstrations of workers were held demanding harsh summary justice against the accused. In January 1935 the first political trial was held against the former leaders of the "new" opposition: G.V. Zinoviev, L.B. Kamenev, and G.E. Evdokimov. A secret letter from the Central Committee was circulated around all of the party organizations demanding the mobilization of all forces to uproot the "counterrevolutionary nest" of enemies of the people. Mass arrests and exiles were conducted. On March 8, 1935, a law was promulgated on the punishment of the members of the families of traitors of the country, which essentially introduced a system of hostage-taking (*zalozhnichestvo*). In April 1935 the Central Executive Committee, which carried out the functions of a head of state, issued a decree to make children twelve and over accountable. The purge of the party actually continued up to 1936. In August 1936 new "open" judicial proceedings—the show trials—were conducted against the leaders of the opposition, the so-called "Trotsky-Zinovievite terrorist center," in which the accused received death sentences. A new, even broader wave of repression was connected with the new head of the NKVD, N.I. Yezhov, who had replaced H. Yagoda. In January 1937 the so-called "parallel center"—Iu. L. Piatakov, K.V. Radek, G.Ia. Sokolnikov, L.P. Serebriankov, N.I. Muralov and others—were tried and proceedings were conducted against Bukharin, N.M. Krestinsky, A.M. Rykov (Lenin's successor as USSR sovnarkom chairman), Kh. G. Rakovsky, Yagoda, and others (the so-called "anti-Soviet right wing monarchist bloc"). The majority of the accused were given death sentences. Similar proceedings and cases of mass summary justice occurred all over the country. By torture and moral pressure the majority who were sincere communists, or at least supporters of the soviet power, were demoralized by the very fact of their arrest. They not only admitted their guilt which was actively used in propaganda but also confessed the names of their "associates" which widened the scope of the repression even more. The major weapon was the NKVD apparatus. Although the waves of repression touched it too (20,000 people were victims of the repression), the membership of the NKVD, including internal troops, rose from 271,000 to 366,000 between 1937 and 1939.[39]

The repression even extended outside of the boundaries of the USSR. The leadership of the Comintern and of many foreign communist parties was destroyed by Stalin. Even Soviet intelligence lost almost all of its members. An agent of the NKVD murdered L.D. Trotsky in Mexico in 1940. The total number of victims of the repression is unknown. According to scholarly estimates there were five million arrests alone between 1937 and 1939, during the peak of the repression, of whom 800,000 to 900,000 were shot.[40]

As R. Medvedev wrote, Stalin surpassed all of the records of political terror known to history. The victims of the inquisition numbered 360,000 during the entire time of its existence while during the century of the persecution of the Huguenots only 200,000 were eliminated and the oprichnina terror of Ivan the Terrible (Ivan Grozny) claimed the lives of several tens of thousands in all.[41]

The great terror of 1937-1939 and the purge of the party between 1933 and 1936 had the following goals: 1) The elimination of all opposition and, more than that, of every possibility of its appearance; 2) the liquidation of the "Old Guard of the Party," who had used their own traditions and knowledge of Bolshevik history to oppose Stalin; 3) the suppression of localism and the annihilation of the functionaries corrupted by often uncontrolled authority; 4) the removal of social tension by the punishment of the "pointsmen" (*strelochniki*) who were falsely, but sometimes truthfully, blamed for the mistakes and negative aspects of social life.[42] The number of party members grew significantly in comparison to the 1920s, despite the fluctuations caused by the purges. In 1926 there were 1,086,000 members, in 1930—about 2 million, in 1941—more than 3,876,800 members.[43]

At the end of the 1920s the party regime became extremely harsh while the last survivors of internal party democracy and openness were being liquidated. And so the stenographic accounts of the Plenums of the Party Central Committee and the working plans of the Politburo and Orgburo ceased to be sent to the local organizations in 1928; and the publication of the informational journal *The Proceedings (Izvestia) of the Central Committee* was terminated in 1929. Party congresses, conferences, and plenums of the Central Committee were held less often: the Twelfth Congress in 1923, the Thirteenth in 1924, the Fourteenth in 1925, the Fifteenth in 1927, the Sixteenth in 1930, the Seventeenth in 1934, and the Eighteenth in 1939. At the Seventeenth Congress of the Central Control Commission—Workers' Control Commission—which had plenary authority to control the organs of the party and state at all levels, was reorganized into the Party Control Commission under the Central Committee of the Communist Party and the Soviet Control Commission under the Council of People's Commissars, that is, into organs which were subordinate to and could not control the Central Committee and Sovnarkom, which guaranteed the control of the

THE CONSTRUCTION OF SOCIALISM   **175**

"center" over the "periphery." The practice developed of selecting party committee members from lists of approved candidates.

The now monolithic party strove to subordinate the entire society to its total control. Between 1930 and 1932 party committees, shop cells, and party groups organized in teams were created in all industrial enterprises where more than five hundred communists worked. Party cells were created on collective and state farms and in Machine Tractor Stations (in the summer of 1930 there were 30,000 party cells in the village; in October 1933 there were 80,000). The Komsomol ("Young Communist League") whose membership grew from three to more than five million between 1935 and 1938 alone, operated under the strict control of the party.

The trade unions were the other "transmission belt," in addition to the Komsomol, from the party to the masses which helped to mobilize the masses to carry out the tasks of coerced technological modernization. Their membership grew more than 200%: on April 1, 1930, there were around 12 million members, in 1940 nearly 27 million members. The structure of the trade unions became more fractured: in January 1931 45 unions were created instead of 22; there were 154 trade unions in 1934, 182 on January 1, 1941. In 1937 the regional, city, provincial, area, and republican intertrade union bodies—trade union councils—were liquidated. The absence of horizontal connections and the extreme fractionalization of the structure made it easier for the party to control the workers.

In a situation where the real political power was concentrated in the committees and extraordinary and punitive organs of the Communist Party, the soviets carried out secondary functions relating to cultural organizations and the economy. The population's participation in the electoral process finally became a mere test of political loyalty.

During the reelection of the soviets the average percentage of voters in the country was 50.7% in 1927, 63.2% in 1929, 72% in 1931 and 85% in 1934; in the elections to the Supreme Soviet of the USSR on December 12, 1937, 96.9% of the electorate participated while 99.21% participated in the elections to the local soviets in 1939. In a situation where the official authority—soviets—had practically no power and democracy was wiped out in the true organs of power (the party committees and especially, the NKVD—the People's Commissariat for Internal Affairs, which had assumed the functions of the old OGPU) the new Constitution of the USSR adopted on December 5, 1936, which was relatively democratic in context, was a declaration which did not reflect the real situation in society.

The harsh political regime of the 1930s, with its periodic mass repressions and the purges of cadres, was genetically connected to the chosen model of industrialization and the administrative-command system: the center exercised continuous control over production operations as well as social functions.[44] The system was only effective with the prompt and steady fulfillment of the planning directives and the commands of the center. Moreover, the excessive concentration of resources in some sectors implied the excessive squeezing of other sectors, which gradually created the danger of a social protest by the "stepsons" (*pasynki*) of economic growth, on the robbery of whom the entire development strategy was based. In order to root out the discontent, a widespread system of informers was created for punitive purposes. To a significant degree the scale of the repression was also connected to the despotic, vengeful, cruel, and suspicious character of the "communist dictator" J.V. Stalin, who had grabbed absolute power.

However, the practical impossibility of controlling everything and everyone from the center somewhat tempered the repression and administrative control; besides, given the dubious economic efficiency of the system there was a potential threat to the political stability of the regime. During the 1930s mighty waves of administrative coercion and massive repression occurred, alternating campaigns against leveling with material stimulation to neutralize the destructive influence of Stalin's sudden changes on economic development, without touching the foundations of administrative and political control or the essence of the terrorist regime.

1929-1930: The spread of administrative control, with the sharp increase of planned tasks in industry, the escalation of violence in the village, the distribution of goods and services for the purpose of leveling (*uravnilovka*), and the party purge of 1929-30.

1931 to mid-1932: the "rebound" of the profit-and-loss business methods (*khozraschet*)—the struggle against leveling, the absence of personal responsibility for production in conformity with Comrade Stalin's "six conditions," the movement of the self-supporting brigades,[45] and the development of collective farm trade.

Mid-1932 to 1933: The intensification of administrative control: the adoption of the draconian "Law on the Five Ears of Wheat," [46] famine, the creation of extraordinary party organs in villages: the political departments of state farms and MTS, the establishment of tight control over the payroll fund in 1932, the introduction of the passport system, and the party purge of 1933-34.

1934-36: The struggle between "profit-and-loss business methods" and the growing inclination toward coercion. The acceptance of realistic directives in the preparation of the Second Five Year Plan at the Seventeenth Party Congress (1934); the stabilization of the situation in villages; the liquidation of village political departments; the cancellation of rationing; the Stakhanovite movement, which was based on piece work; the new, relatively democratic constitution of 1936, and the simultaneous growth of repression after S.M. Kirov's assassination on December 1, 1934.

End of 1936 to 40: The "Great Terror"—the party purge of 1937-38, the new repressive laws in industry,[47] the struggle with "the squandering of collective farm lands,"[48] and the introduction of state procurement (*zagotovka*) by per-hector allotment in the village.

1941: The "rebound of profit-and-loss business methods," interrupted by the Great Patriotic War. The decision of the Eighteenth Party Conference (February 1941) to increase material incentives in industry.[49]

How did the party and state leadership during the course of the 1930s succeed in maintaining the high spirits and enthusiasm for work of a significant part of the Soviet people, keeping them in a state of preparedness resembling mobilization? Total ideological manipulation is thought to have been the key factor which gave the people the feeling, or more precisely the illusion, of being masters of their own country. The illusion was enhanced by revolutionary traditions and Russian patriotism and reinforced by massive repression; it aroused the population to make material sacrifices to create a strong industrial power and an "enlightened" socialist future. Fear for their own lives, families, or careers served not only as a powerful stimulus for labor—compensating for the insufficient monetary incentive—but it also made people (voluntarily or involuntarily) unreceptive to any information which undermined the basis of the official ideology.

The industrial achievements of the USSR and some improvement in the material well-being of the people in the second half of the 1930s helped considerably. The standard of living had fallen catastrophically at the end of the 1920s and beginning of the 1930s. Millions of peasants died of starvation, in the towns real wages were sharply reduced, and rationing was introduced. But unemployment was eliminated at the beginning of the 1930s. Rationing was abolished in 1935, the supply of consumer goods significantly improved, and the per capita consumption of necessities by the collective farmers (*kolkhozniks*) increased more than 200% after 1933. In 1931 and especially in 1932-33 large rural areas were struck by famine. Hundreds of thousands of peasant families suffered a life of humiliation in labor camps or special labor settlements. The situation in the cities was better but even there great growth of population created serious supply difficulties. Agrarian technology was introduced on a large scale in the village. Toward the conclusion of the Second Five Year Plan the USSR occupied first place in the world in the number of students and in the pace and scope (not always the highest quality) of agronomists' training.[50] Absolute indices of economic growth were not as important to the population as the relationship to the preceding period (1929-1933) to support the growing awareness that "life is changing for the better." The evidence of this social-psychological phenomenon was expressed by the German writer L. Feichtwanger who visited Moscow in January 1937: "For many years Soviet people have suffered privations.... Now ... they see that, as promised, they have a lot of things which they could hardly dream of two years before...."[51] The most important fact was that millions of ordinary people now had access to a higher education and had become accustomed to social and political work; they had improved their own social status. They became qualified workers, technicians and engineers, farm mechanics, officers, and servants of the party-

THE CONSTRUCTION OF SOCIALISM   **179**

state apparatus which was growing and renewing during the course of the purges and repression. For many the party-state apparatus was their authority.

Certainly the attitude of the victims of the oppression and of those who possessed a clearly defined political outlook and had knowledge of the flaws of the Stalinist regime was different. But even a significant number of these, under the influence of Bolshevik ideology with its faith in the historical correctness of constructing socialism and the infallibility of the party, the genuine achievements of the USSR, and the psychology of the "fortress under siege" shared many of the typical illusions. Some, even though they turned up in the camps, believed in Stalin as much as before and constructed various explanations for themselves for the causes of the terror and other negative phenomena.

Propaganda was specially emphasized. Relying on its monopoly over the means of mass communication and actively taking advantage of the real or imaginary successes of the country, the Stalinist regime put out a broad spectrum of appealing slogans and replaced one propaganda campaign with another. They played on the best and the worst of human nature. There were appeals to the traditions of revolutionary struggle, to class consciousness, to the feeling of proletariat internationalism (the campaign of solidarity with Republican Spain, for example). There was extensive reliance on patriotic feelings and an appeal to the traditional: a list of historical questions to accompany literature and the movies; the broad development of historical education. Heroism, the cult of the working man: there was widespread propaganda on the achievements of the Stakhanov, Chkalov, and Papanin teams. Then there were the frenetic searches for "the enemies of the people," the periodic waves of protest against the specialists, the *spetseedstvo* (setting the people against the intelligentsia), the postwar antisemitism, and the cultivation of the psychology of the "fortress under siege." Later, reliance on the traditional xenophobia of the Russian masses which was reinforced by foreign intervention between 1918 and 1922, the Second World War, and the cold war; this attitude became the cornerstone of the mentality of the Soviet man. All of this rested on the goal-oriented indoctrination of the people,[52] which was conducted on a grandiose scale after the *Short Course on the History of the All-Union Communist Party [The Bolsheviks]*, the original catechism of Stalinism, was published in 1938.

In life these orientations of human and inhumane factors coexisted, strengthening one another, forming a contradictory but single whole. To keep the flame of an almost religious faith in the "approaching communist future" which helped the common person to carry the burdens of daily life and stimulated enthusiasm among the masses for the work, new, even more perverted explanations, which were always concrete and easy for simple people to understand, were found for the causes of industrial accidents, the shortages of consumer goods, and the interruption of food supplies. At first the "kulaks" or "bourgeois specialists" were blamed; then the representatives of the exploiter class who had wormed their way into the party and state organs and even into plants or collective farms; later it was Trotskyites "recruited by foreign intelligence agencies."

By punishing the "captains," the government satisfied the feeling for social justice which was being wounded by the unequal realities; Soviet society in the 1930s was not egalitarian, having significant differences in levels of incomes, in the ways of life of the peasants, workers, a significant part of the intelligentsia, and the nomenklatura.[53] Around the better educated members of society who were suitable for work and capable of independent decision-making an atmosphere of social distrust was created (the terms "rotten intelligentsia" and "bureaucrat" were used and repression was a constant threat). This nipped any opposition and separatism in the bud and minimized corruption and the shadow economy.

At first glance Stalin's idea of aggravating the class struggle on the way to socialism seemed absurd but it was undertaken to resolve the doubts in the minds of the masses about the causes of the low standard of living, the increasing intensity of labor, and the spread of repression. The difficulties grew over time so that the "wreckers" and the "enemies of the people" expanded their sabotage, thereby sharpening the class struggle and moving the population closer to socialism. At the same time those who tried to find another explanation were thrown into the GULAG for reeducation.

In the short-term, the idea of a rapid but rocky road to a bright future without any problems could have been a greater mobilizing force than Bukharin's concept of a gradual "growing" into socialism and the presence in it of nonantagonistic contradictions about which Lenin wrote. If, in the long-term, the complexity, injustice, and misfortunes were perceived to be an integral part of socialism, who then would want to sacrifice himself for it? It is a different matter if one's life should be sacrificed for the happy future of one's own children, the Motherland, or humankind: The great Soviet poet Vladimir Mayakovsky wrote: "Let the socialism built in these struggles be our common memorial." Thus, socialism (and later communism) joins sacrificial Marxism, Christian expiation, and Orthodox "purification through sufferings" as an other-worldly-ideal, perhaps, but not an achievable socioeconomic program.

"The worship of suffering and the inclination toward it could appear only in Russia," writes Valentin Rasputin, a great contemporary writer. In front of us the phenomenon of distorted illusory consciousness, a kind of massive "anti-religious religion," which as well as any religion reconciled a person with the imperfection of the present-day world for the sake of an ideal future, doomed heretics to slaughter, emotionally tied the mere mortal to the teacher of the faith, the leader, the bearer of paradise, the secular incarnation of the Absolute.

In Russia the church has always held a subordinate position to the monarchist state (caesaropapism).[54] But with the rapid destruction of the traditional social and economic structures in pre-and-post revolutionary times, the various social cataclysms (three wars, three revolutions, and collectivization in the first third of the century), and the systematic antireligious campaign of the Bolsheviks the legitimacy of traditional religion in the eyes of a significant part of the population was severely compromised . Nevertheless, the need for faith remained, and for the time being it was filled with faith in the communist party and its ideals. This new semireligion formed the foundation for the attitude of *joie de vivre* on the part of a significant part of the Soviet people.[55]

Culture in the 1930s

The demands of socialist modernization and the "education of the new person" required the rapid education and acculturation of the broad masses. In 1926, 43% of the people between the ages of nine and forty-nine and a majority of the older people were illiterate. After 1930, the task of "providing universal compulsory primary education and the liquidation of illiteracy" was identified and four years of compulsory primary education was introduced and in workers' centers seven years was required. (As a point of comparison, compulsory primary education in the German-speaking parts of Austria-Hungary was introduced in the eighteenth century, in Sweden in 1842, in Switzerland in 1848, in France in 1882, and in England 1891).[56] By 1939 the percent of literate people above nine-years-old reached 81.2% (the level of Belgium and France in 1900), which was a great achievement in one decade. Industrialization and the need to create a nonbourgeois intelligentsia required the rapid development of intermediate, special, and higher education. In 1940, around 4600 higher education institutes and technical schools were operating in the country. The Soviet Union was first in the world in the number of students.

Significant successes were attained in the natural sciences and technology. In the USSR at the end of 1932 more than 1150 scientific institutes were operational, while in 1941 there were 1821 (including branches). Founded in particular were such major scientific centers as the All-Union Academy of Agronomic Science *(Vsesoiuznaia akademiia selskokhoziaistvennykh nauk—VASKhNIL)*, composed of twelve institutes (the president was Vavilov); the Lebvedev Physics Institute; and institutes of organic chemistry, physics, and geophysics.

S.V. Lebedev's development of an original method for deriving synthetic rubber from ethyl alcohol around 1928 was a major achievement. New branches of industry were created around this discovery. Significant discoveries were made in nuclear physics: D.V. Skobeltsyn developed a method for detecting cosmic rays, D.D. Ivanenko proposed the theory that an atom's nucleus was composed of protons and neutrons, A.F. Joffe invented a multiplastic insulator, and N.N. Semenov successfully worked on the theoretical problems

THE CONSTRUCTION OF SOCIALISM

of chain reactions. The studies of K.E. Tsiolkovsky ("The Cosmic Rocket," 1927; "The Cosmic Rocket Train," 1929; and "The Jet Plane," 1930) won the USSR over to giving priority to the conquest of the cosmos. In 1930 the first jet engine in the world, which operated on petroleum and compressed air, was constructed by F.A. Tsander; P.K. Oshchepkov constructed radar equipment before Great Britain and the United States developed that technology. The noted Russian psychologist I.P. Pavlov continued his studies until his death in 1936. And the selectionist I.V. Muchyrin had great successes.

But the oppressive atmosphere of the totalitarian state threatened the development of science. Many outstanding scientists were repressed, including N.I. Vavilov, S.P. Korolev (the future father of Soviet space science), P.I. Oshepkov, the physicist L.D. Londau, the aviators A.N. Tupolev, V.M. Petliakov, and V.M. Miasishchev. Some branches of science, such as sociology, were destroyed while the development of rocket technology, radar, and other important, progressive developments in science and technology were interrupted. The goal of the party and state leadership to create a new socialist culture, to promote conformity, and to mobilize the masses to modernize by coercion required that a parallel effort go into the manipulation of perception—the ideological factor. After the decision of the Central Committee of the Communist Party in 1931 in the journal *Under the Banner of Marxism* (*Pod znamenem marksizma*) and Stalin's letter "On the Work of the Communist Academy," social studies was finally placed in the service of ideology and lost its scholarly function.

The appeal to the revolutionary, and later to the national traditions, became the most important direction of indoctrination. In the 1930s—guided by Stalin's specific requirements—historiography took a radical course: history education was introduced in the intermediate and high school to "shape" historical perceptions; and history students, in general, learned to suppressed or outright falsify "unsuitable facts." To substantiate the official slogan "Stalin is the Lenin of Today," Stalin's role in the history of Bolshevism was greatly exaggerated, confirming the concept of "two party leaders." At the same time the names of the famous Bolsheviks who had been repressed by Stalin disappeared from the textbooks and essays. Of the twenty-one members of the Bolshevik Central Committee in 1917 eleven had been proclaimed "enemies of the people," seven had been killed or died before the end of the 1920s, and only three were "unblemished in the 1930s: Stalin, Lenin and Kalinin.⁵⁷ The actual information on Trotsky, Bukharin, Zinoviev, Kamenev, and many others was not accessible to the Soviet public until more than a half century had passed. The "class struggle" in relationship to scholarship reached the absurd. Entire schools of thought were crushed in philosophy and history. The scholars subjected to repression included the historians N.M. Lukin, H.H. Vanag, V.G. Druzhinin, S.A. Piontlovsky, and S.F. Platonov; the philosophers Ya.E. Sten, N.A. Kareev, and I.L. Luppo, as well as many other representatives of the historical, philosophical, and economic disciplines.

An even more tragic situation took shape in the area of literature and art. In April 1932 the Central Committee of the Communist Party accepted a decree "On the Reform of Literary Organizations." Instead of the numerous literary groups a single, rigid Union of Soviet Writers led from above was created (the First All-Union Congress of Soviet Writers occurred in 1934). The ruling party attempted to drive all of the multifaceted literary forms into the Procrustean bed of "socialist realism." These famous writers and poets were suppressed: O. Mandelshtam, S. Tretiakov, I. Babel, B. Yasensky, N. Zabolotsky, O. Bergolts, and N. Kliuev. But during these years significant work was produced both within the confines of the prevailing school ("socialist realism") and outside of it. Many compositions of the second type became known to the people much later: Mikhail Sholokov's *The Silent Don* and the first part of *Virgin Soil Upturned,* M.A. Bulgakov's *The Master and Margarita*, the verses and poems of A.A. Akhmatova, P. Vasiliev, N. Kliuev, O.E. Mandelshtam, and M.I. Tsvetaeva, and the novels and tales of A.M. Gorky, A.N. Tolstoy, N.A. Ostrovsky, A. Fadeev, I. Ilf, and E. Petrov.

Soviet cinematography developed and became established over the years. The outstanding productions of Soviet film included "The Battleship Potemkin," S. Eizenshtein's "Aleksandr Nevsky," A. Dovzhenko's "The Land," H. Ekk's "A Start in Life," "The Happy Children," G. Aleksandrov's "Circus," V. Petrov's "Peter the Great," S. and G. Vasiliev's "Chapaev," E. Dzigan's "Those of Us from

Kronstadt," and the trilogy on the Maxim (a machinegun) ("The Youth of Maxim," "The Return of the Maxim," and "The Vyborg Side") of G. Kozintsev and L. Trauberg. Stalin, being a great fan of movies, personally controlled this sector and saw practically every new film. During the period of mass repression from the 1930s to the beginning of the 1950s the victims of his policy, even by rough estimates, numbered more than one hundred cinematographers and outstanding figures of the theater: V. Meierkhold, L. Kurbas, and N. Sats. The editors of the majority of central and regional newspapers and a thousand other cultural figures died. But cultural life did not entirely die even after being thinned out and deformed.

The following were active in painting and sculpture during these years: A. Deineka, M. Nesterov, P. Korin, M. Grekov, P. Konchalovsky, Yu. Pimenov, V. Andreev, V. Mukhin, and I. Shadr; in music V. Asafiev, R. Glier, Yu. Shaporin, and D. Shostakovich.

Summary

By the end of the 1930s an integral social system—*state socialism*—had taken shape in the USSR. Theoretically state socialism seems the only type of socialism possible. It was socialism because the socialization of production and the abolition of private property occurred. It was state socialism because the socialization was unreal, an illusion: the functions related to the disposition of property and political power were denied the majority of society and exercised by Stalin personally and the party and state apparatus. The "construction of socialism" was the major historic task accomplished (but at the price of an enormous number of victims) and socialism in Russia itself was implemented by coercion to complete the transition from an agrarian to an industrial society. The system may be defined as a "leftist totalitarian regime" in the terminology of several scholars.

How well does this society fit the model of socialism worked out by Marx and Engels and developed by Lenin? Does it represent a perversion of the socialist ideal or is it the logical result of its practical realization? One may consider the Soviet society of the

1930s to be the legitimate realization of the ideas of Marx and Lenin on nonmarket socialism which was to be attained through the revolution and dictatorship of the proletariat. The abolition of production for the market and market ties under socialism, proposed by the "classicists," and the denial of parliamentary democracy and the rule of law—an essential feature for Lenin—could not be realized without depriving all of the members of society of their economic and political rights and creating a totalitarian regime. Nevertheless, some of its features and the scale of the repression were conditioned by the results of the intraparty struggle, which was completed by Stalin's victory, and they bore the stamp of his personality.

Characterizing the social system of the USSR in the 1930s as "materialized ideology" is simplistic. In the broad historical context the creation of "state socialism" in the USSR coincided with the painful and critical stage of global structural reform which was being experienced by the world—the transition to a regulated market economy. The Soviet system represented one of the last, extreme variants of social development, the *ultraleft model,* in contrast to the *ultraright* or fascist model, and in opposition to the new liberalism of Western Europe and North America. The specific conditions which prevailed in the country and in the world in the 1920s and 1930s which made the rapid technological modernization of the economy necessary and therefore caused the expansion of the state's role as the leading agent of development, were not the only factors affecting Russia's choice of a development model. The revolutionary tradition (especially war communism) and the Russian traditions of many centuries connected with the hypertrophic role of the state, the conscious "antiliberalism" of the masses, and the popularity of collectivization were all factors contributing to the new model which essentially reproduced the features of the "autocratic-state-serfdom" period of Russian feudalism: despotic power relying on the bureaucracy and determining the role of the state in social relations ("the enserfment of the estates"), and the complete dominance of Marxist ideology which was actually being transformed into a substitute for religion .

THE CONSTRUCTION OF SOCIALISM

Notes

[1] *Istoriia fashizma v Zapadnoi Evrope* [*The History of Fascism in Europe*], Moscow, 1978, pp. 220-230.

[2] The share of national income allocated for social needs, grew in Western Europe from 2.6% in 1900 to 11.3% in 1938. Unemployment insurance was introduced in all of the major parliamentary countries. Social security was introduced in twenty-five countries, health insurance in twenty countries.

[3] In particular, foreign sources guaranteed during the pre world war one period no less than fifty percent of the requirements of industry in terms of equipment, but internal sources in the 1920s and 1930s (during the first five year plan) financed almost 75-80%.

[4] Fifteenth Congress of All Union Communist Party (b), stenographic account, vol.2, Moscow, 1962 pp.1441-1454.

[5] N.I. Bukharin. *Uroki khelbozagotovok, shakhtinskogo dela i zadachi partii* [*The Lessons of Grain Storage, of the Shakhtinsk Deal and the Tasks of the Party*]. Leningrad,1928, pp. 37-38.

[6] Bukharin N.I. *Zametki ekonomista. N.I. Bukharin, Izbr. proisvedeniia* [*Economist's Notes in N.I. Bukharin, Collected Works*], Moscow, 1988, pp. 391-418.

[7] J.V. Stalin. *Sochineniia* [*Works*], vol. 2, p. 267.

[8] See G. Andreev, *Eksport amerikanskogo kapitala. Iz istorii eksporta kapitala SShA kak orudiia ekonomicheskoi i politicheskoi ekspansii* [*American Capital Export. From the History of American Capital Export as a Means of Economic and Political Expansion.*] Moscow, 1957, pp.55-57.

[9] Counted according to V.I. Bovikin, *Rossiia nakanune velikikh sverzhenii* [*Russia on the Eve of the Great Achievement.*] Moscow, 1988, pp. 66-67.

[10] N.I. Bukharin, *Velikaia rekonstruktsiia. [Great Reconstruction]* Pravda, Feb. 2, 1930.

[11] L.A. Gordon and A.V. Klopov. *Chto eto bylo?* [*What Was It?*], Moscow 1989, p. 53.

[12] See Gordon and Klopov, p.53.

[13] Yu. A. Moshkov, *Zernovaia problema v gody sploshnoi kollektivizatsii seliskogo khoziaistva* [*The Grain Problem in the Years of the Complete Collectivization of Agriculture in the USSR (1929-1932)*], Moscow, 1966, p.34.

[14] On the course of collectivization see *Dokumenty svidetelstvuiut [The Documents Testify]*, Moscow,1989.

[15] A.K. Sokolov, *Sovety: ot vlasti illiuzii k illiuzii vlasti: Formirovanie administrativno-komandnoi sistemy, 20-30-e gg. [The Soviets: From the Power of Illusion to the Illusion of Power: The Formation of the Administrative-Command System]*, Moscow, 1992, p. 175-176.

[16] *Istoriia SSSR s drevneishikh vremen do nashikh dnei [The History of the USSR from Ancient Times to Our Days]*, vol. 8, Moscow, 1967, p. 543.

[17] R. Medvedev, *O Staline i stalinisme [On Stalin and Stalinism]*, Moscow, 1990, p. 201.

[18] R. Medvedev, *O Staline*, p. 205.

[19] D. Volkogonov, D. *Triumf i tragediia. Politicheskii portret J.V. Stalina., [Triumph and Tragedy. A Political Portrait of J.V. Stalin.* Book I, Part 2*]* Moscow, 1989, p. 19.

[20] Gordon and Klopov, p. 74.

[21] Dokumenty svidetelstvuiut, pp. 40-45; V.P. Danilov, Diskussiia v zapadnoi presse o golode 1932-1933 gg. "demograficheskoi katastrofe" 30-40-kh godov v SSSR ["Discussion in the West on Famine of 1932-1933 and the `Demographic Catastrophe' of the 1930s and 1940s in the USSR"], *Voprosy istorii [Problems of History]*, 1988, No. 3. Zh. B. Abilkhozhin, M.K. Kozibaev and M.B. Tatimov, Kazakhstanskaia tragediia ["Kazakhstan Tragedy"], *Voprosii istorii*, 1989, No. 7 and I.E. Zelenin, O nekotorykh "belykh piatnakh" zavershaiushego etapa sploshnoi kollektivizatsii ["On certain 'white spots' of the final stage of all-around collectivization"], *Istoriia SSSR [USSR History]*, 1989, No. 2; R. Conquest, Zhatva skorbi ["Harvest of Grief"] *Voprosii istorii*, 1990, Nos. 1, 4.

[22] *Pravda,* August 25,1989.

[23] Nekrasov V.F. Desiat "zheleznykh" narkomov ["Ten Iron Commissars"]. *Komsomolskaya Pravda,* September 29,1989; "Arkhipelag GULAG: glazami pisatelia i statistika. Interviu s V. Zemskovym" ["GULAG Archipelago": A Writer and Statistician's View. Interview with V. Zemskov] in *Argumenty i fakty [Arguments and Facts]*, 1989, No. 45; Dolumenty svidetel'stvuiut [The Documents Testify], p. 49; N.K. Dugin, GULAG, otkryvaia arkhivy ["The GULAG: Opening the Archives."] In *Boevoi post [The Military Post],* December 27,1989; O. Khlevniuk, Prinuditelnyi trud v ekonomike SSSR, 1929-1941 gody ["Compulsory Labor in the Economy of the USSR, 1929-1941] in *Svobodnaia misl [Free Thought]*, 1992, No. 13; V Komitete gosudarstvennoi bezopasnosti SSSR ["Inside the USSR Committee on State Security" (KGB)], *Pravda,*

Feb.14,1990.

[24] See Gordon and Klopov, p. 78.

[25] See Gordon and Klopov, p. 80.

[26] See Gordon and Klopov, p. 64.

[27] See Gordon and Klopov, p.64; A.I. Denikin, *Ocherki russkoi muty* ["Essays on the Russian Troubles"], *Voprosii istorii,* 1990, No. 3, p. 137.

[28] See G.I. Khanin. *Dinamika ekonomicheskogo razvitiia SSSR [Dynamics of the Economic Development of the USSR.],* Novosibirsk, 1991, p. 146-152, 174-178.

[29] V.B. Zhiromsky, *Kadry reshaiut vse! Administrativno-upravlencheskii apparat v 20-30-e gg. po dannym obshchikh i spetsperepisei [Formirovanie administrativno-komandnoi sistemy [Cadres Decide All! The Administrative-Managerial Apparatus in the 1920s and 1930s on the Evidence of the General and Special Censuses (The Formation of the Administrative-Command System)],* p. 211.

[30] See Sokolov, p. 179.

[31] See *Nashe Otechestvo: Opyt polikticheskoi istorii [Our Motherland: The Experience of Political History],* Part II, Moscow, 1991, pp. 291-295.

[32] G.A. Bordiugov and V.A. Kozlov, *Istoriia i koniuktura [History and Circumstances.]* Moscow 1992, pp.73-74.

[33] See O. Latzis, *Perelom: Uroki gorkie, neobkhodimye [The Turning point: Bitter but Necessary Lessons.]* Moscow, 1988 p. 88.

[34] *Neuslyshannye golosa. Dokumenty Smolenskogo arkhiva. [Unheard Voices. Documents of Smolensk Archive.]* Book 1,1929. *Kulaks and Party Officials.* Ann Arbor,1987 p.20. Traveling around regions of total collectivization at the peak of the *velikii perelom* ["turning point], E.A. Preobrazhensky, one of former leaders of left opposition, had a conversation in a dining room in the marketplace with two middle class peasants: "I asked the first one: " How are things with the collective farm in your village, has it already been formed?" "Not yet, but people have already started talking about it." I asked again in an indifferent tone: "Do you believe anything good will come out of it?" "I don't think so. But the authorities want it. And you can't go against the authority. . . ." So I asked the second one and he remarked: "If a tree is planted anew three times in a different way its roots will be damaged, so what's the use? After the revolution the land was redivided. Later in 1918 the land was divided anew. Still later the land was divided into individual farms. Now they want to change that into collective farms. If you ask me all-around collectivization is better. Let's see what will happen. One can't start dividing

the land again." *Pravda*, 1930. In those answers one can see the natural common sense of a Russian peasant who is sure that "nothing will come out" of the next venture of the bureaucrats but is tired of the endless "restructuring" in the village; and there is the traditional fatalism: "one can't go against the authorities", "let it happen."

[35] N.D. Kondratiev, *K voprosu o differentiatsii derevni. Puti sel'skogo khoziaistva [Concerning the Problem of Differentiation in the Village. Agricultural Methods.]* 1927, No. 5, p. 136.

[36] I.M. Kliamkin. Eshche raz ob istokakh stalinizma. ["Again on the lessons of Stalinism".] *Politichiskoe obrazovanie [Political Education].* 1989, No. 9, p. 44.

[37] *Istoriia sovetksogo krestianstva [History of the Soviet Peasantry.]* Moscow, 1986. vol. I, p. 330.

[38] See XII RCP(b) Congress. Stenographic account. Moscow 1923 p. 207; XV VCP(b) Congress. Vol.1 pp. 68, 442-443.

[39] V. Zhiromskaia, p. 213.

[40] D. Volkogonov, pp. 19-20.

[41] R. Medvedev, p. 404.

[42] R. Medvedev, *O Stalina i stalinizme [On Stalin and Stalinism],* Moscow, 1990, pp. 252-64.

[43] *Istoriia SSSR s drevneishikh vremen [The History of the USSR since Ancient Times],* Vol. 8, Moscow, 1967, pp. 192, 394.

[44] The administrative command system was sufficiently effective in resolving those tasks which were then assigned to it: It was quite possible to control the construction and work of comparatively few key objects from the center or to introduce there the achievements of world science and technology. See: G.H. Popov, S tochki zreniia ekonomista ["From an Economist's Point of View."] in the book *Uroki gor'kie, no neobkhodimye [Bitter but Necessary Lessons],* p. 78.

[45] O.V. Khlevnjuk, *Uradniki pervoi piatiletki [First Five Year Plan Shockworkers.]* Moscow, 1989, pp. 49-58.

[46] The law of August 7,1932 on the defense of socialist property, which was written by Stalin, introduced "execution with property confiscation as a measure of jurdicial repression for misappropriation or theft of collective farm or cooperative property. In case of extenuating circumstances the sentence could be changed to ten years imprisonment with property confiscation." Amnesty was not permitted in such a case. 54,645 people were sentenced according with the law in the next five months." *Dokumenty svidetelstvuiut. [The Documents Testify],* p. 41.

[47] The resolution of the USSR Soviet of People's Commissars, Com-

munist Party Central Committee and Trade Union Council of December 28,1938 introduced harsher measures concerning responsibility for violating labor discipline: if a person was twenty minutes late for work, he was dismissed. The decree of June 26, 1940 established an eight hour working day, seven day working week; workers were prohibited to resign. Resignation was punished with two to four months imprisonment, absenteeism without a good excuse brought up to six months of corrective labor at the place of work (25% of wages were confiscated). The decree of July 10, 1940 regarded the production of substandard, incomplete or non-standard merchandise as sabotage with all ensuing consequences. See: V.A. Kozlov, O.V. Khlevniuk, *Nachinaetsia s cheloveka [It Begins with a Person],* Moscow, 1988, p. 183; *Istoricheskii opyt i perestroika [The Historical Experience and Perestroika],* p.120; O.V. Khlevniuk, *26 Iiunia 1940 goda; illiuzii i realnosti administrirovaniia* ["June 26,1940: The Illusions and Reality of Administrative Coercion"] in *Kommunist [Communist],* 1988, No. 9.

[48] The decision of May 1939 of the plenum of the Central Committee of the Communist Party ordered the withdrawl of land from the peasants' private plots in excess of the norms fixed by the Statute on the Agrarian Artel, which had consisted of 1/4 to 1/2 hector, in some regions up to one hector, of land adjacent to the farm houses. At the same time a minimum number of work days, ranging from sixty to a hundred per year depending on the region, were made obligatory for each collective farm. Violators were considered to have left the collective and forfeited their rights as a kolkhoznik. See *Istoricheskii opyt i perestroika [The Historical Experience and Perestroika],* p. 118. On measures for preserving the common lands of the kolkhoz from squandering see the decree of May 27, 1939 in *KPSS v rezoliutsiiakh i resheniiakh c"ezdov, konferentsii i plenumov. Ts.K., [The CPSU in the Resolutions and Decisions of its Congresses. Conferences and Plenums. CC.]* Part III, 1930-1954, Moscow, 1954, pp. 396-402.

[49] See *Istoricheskii opyt i perestroika [The Historical Experience and Perestroika],* pp.124-126, and *O zadachakh partiinykh oreganizatsii i oblasti promyshlennosti i transporta [Rezoliutsiia po dokladu tov. Malenkova, priniataia konferentsiei edinoglasno 18 Fevralia]* in *KPSS v rezoliutiakh...* Part II, p. 432. ["On the Tasks of the Party Organizations in Industry and Transport [the Unanimously Adopted Resolution on Comrade Malenkov's Report, Conference of February 18]" in *The CPSU in Resolutions.*]

[50] *Istoriia sotsialisticheskoi ekonomiki v SSSR [The History of the*

Socialist Economy in the USSR], vol.3, p.85; Gordon and Klopov, p.87-88.

⁵¹ L. Feikhtvanger (Feichtwanger). *Otchet o poezdke moikh druzei [An Account of the Visit for My Friends]*, Moscow 1937.

⁵² Indoctrination is the inculcation into the consciousness of a definite doctrine (theory), in the present case, "Stalinism," a specific variant of the Marxist ideology.

⁵³ The so-called decile coefficient is normally used to characterize income differentiation. This is the ratio of the salary level above which the top ten percent of the highest paid workers are found to the salary level below which the lowest paid ten percent of the workers are found. In 1989 the ratio in the USSR was 3.5:1, in Stalin's time it was 8:1.

⁵⁴ N.A. Berdiaev, *Istoki i smysl russkogo kommunisma* [Sources and Essence of Russian Communism], Moscow 1990, p.110.

⁵⁵ There is evidence of this attitude. The French writer A. Zhid, who visited the USSR in 1936, observed a great deal of "negative factors" (poverty which sometimes came close to destitution, the suppression of any difference in opinions and the total power of the secret police); nevertheless he stated: "But the fact is that the Russian people seem to be happy . . . in no other country do the people met in the streets (especially the young people), factory workers enjoying their leisure in the parks, look so radiant and smiling. How can one link this visible expression with the horrible life of the overwhelming majority of people? . . . One can see a lot of hungry people who smile and look glad, their happiness . . . rests on "trust, ignorance and hope." *Dva vzgliada iz-za rubezha [Two Points of View from Abroad],* Moscow, 1990, p. 136.

⁵⁶ L.E. Kermont. *Istoriia kul tury stran Evropy i Azii [The History of the Culture of the Countries of Europe and Asia],* Moscow, 1987, pp. 120-121.

CHAPTER 5

THE SOVIET UNION IN THE SECOND WORLD WAR (1939-1945)

The Sources of the World Conflict

The Second World War had its own special causes and features which distinguished it from the First World War. Nevertheless, in terms of their remote causes and the definite continuity of the geopolitical paradigm (right up to the rough similarity of the leading participants in the opposing blocs[1] and the late alignment of the United States with the anti-German coalition), both world wars may be considered as waves of global crisis in the system of international relations at the end of the nineteenth and the first-half of the twentieth centuries.

The roots of this crisis go back to the last-third of the nineteenth century when the principal geopolitical changes which changed the balance of power in the world arena began. The most important factor was the rise in the center of Europe in 1871 of a powerful German Empire and its later turbulent economic and military growth which forced repartitioning of the foreign political and colonial spheres of influence to adjust to the existing world order and to Prussian militarism. The annexation of the French province of Alsace-Lorraine in the course of the formation of the German

Empire, just as much as the existence of a strong and aggressive neighbor, made France the "natural" enemy of Germany. The threat of German hegemony united France and Russia.

The growing opposition between Russia and Austria-Hungary, both allies of Germany, in the Balkans complicated the situation. The fragility of the "rag-tag" Austro-Hungarian Empire, the shift of Russian foreign policy from the Far to the Near East and to Europe (after the Russo-Japanese War), and also the intensity of the complicated Balkan problems inevitably caused the clash of the great powers on the Balkan peninsula.

The chief cause of the growing instability of the system of international relations at the beginning of the twentieth century was the relative weakness of its basic guarantor—the British Empire. Despite its vast possessions (nearly thirty-two million square kilometers and 434 million people) and its financial and military strength, this nineteenth-century superpower lost more and more in economic competition with the United States and Germany. In terms of industrial development, she had been driven back to third place in the world by the beginning of the new century. The commercial and political expansion of Germany, the construction of her fleet of unprecedented speed, and the rearmament of the army threatened the existence of the British Empire. The disturbance in the international balance of power forced Britain to abandon her traditional policy of "splendid isolation" as the world arbiter and conclude an alliance with France and Russia. But the division of Europe into two hostile blocs did not prevent the descent to a global armed conflict.

Mankind did not understand how to regulate and neutralize the "opposite sides" of progress: growing internationalism, technical achievements, and the gradual involvement of the broad masses in public policy gave the conflict a world scope. W. Churchill wrote: "The unification of the world into large states and empires and the awakening of the people's collective consciousness permitted the planning and realization of bloodshed on such a scale and with such a persistence that had been unthinkable earlier." And so the achievements of civilization were permitted for a long time "to convert the energy of entire peoples to destruction."

The results of the First World War, which were embodied in

the Versailles-Washington system of international relations (1919-1922), did not permit the restoration of a stable balance of power in the international community nor did the victory of the Bolsheviks in Russia. As a result, the relative integration of the world achieved toward the beginning of the century was lost. The world was broken into the socialist (Soviet Russia, the USSR) and capitalist parts, and the latter was broken into the triumphant, victorious powers and the humiliated, fenced in, defeated countries. The two largest powers and the most rapidly recovering economies—the USSR and Germany—were treated as if they were international "pariahs," outside the system of civilized states. Their rejection of the common human values of "bourgeois democracy," the Versailles-Washington system, and their aspirations for a utopia (in Germany's case a nationalist one) brought together these two totalitarian regimes. They were "genetically" related by the fact that the global crisis in the system of international relations was an important prerequisite for the victory of the Bolshevik and fascist regimes and, for the most part, a condition for their existence.

The difference between them was that the immediate operations of the First World War facilitated the Bolshevik victory, while its results and the growth of the Communists' influence consolidated fascism. German National Socialism in contrast to Bolshevism, in fact, did not pretend to fundamentally reconstruct the social and economic basis of society and was to a much greater degree oriented to the "outside." The formation of a totalitarian regime in Germany only took three years in comparison with two decades in the Soviet Union. Rapidly resolving its own internal political problems, the fascists placed their hopes on foreign political expansion. Hitler openly proclaimed war as the means of implementing their ideological doctrine of "Aryan" racial superiority over other peoples and of resolving their political and economic problems. In 1933 Germany withdrew from the League of Nations, and in 1935, disregarding her obligations under the Versailles Treaty, she reintroduced universal military conscription and took back the Saarland through a plebiscite. In 1936, in violation of the Versailles Treaty and the Locarno Pact, German troops entered the demilitarized Rhineland. In 1938, the *Anschluss* (union) with Austria was proclaimed. Fascist

Italy in 1935-36 occupied Ethiopia, and in 1936-39 carried out a massive military intervention along with Germany in the civil war in Spain[2] where the leftist democratic community of the world and the USSR were the first to oppose them.

Conditions were deteriorating in Asia also. In 1931-32 Japan annexed Manchuria and, in 1937, began a massive war against China, occupying Peking (Beijing), Shanghai, and other important centers of the country. Nearly seventy regional wars and local armed conflicts occurred during the "interwar" period.

The weakness of the powers who were interested in keeping the Versailles-Washington system contributed to the growth of international tension. The traditional Franco-Russian alliance, which had contained Germany, was destroyed after 1917 while isolationism prevailed in the United States. As a result, the Versailles system relied on Britain and France alone. The efforts of these countries to preserve the status quo in Europe were paralyzed by the their disagreements and the ruling elite's unwillingness to take decisive action to deter any aggressors or "violators" of the treaties. The last attempt was undertaken in 1923 when, in response to Germany's nonpayment of reparations, French and Belgian troops occupied the Ruhr. The desire to use Germany against the Bolshevik threat was also a factor. This is why they adopted the "appeasement" policy which actually stimulated Hitler's growing appetite. Its climax was the Munich agreement (September 1938) which authorized the transfer to Germany of the Sudetanland, the most important industrial and military region of Czechoslovakia, leaving the country practically defenseless.

Munich was the most important strategic miscalculation of western diplomacy which opened the road for the military expansion of fascism and brought the beginning of the "big" war closer. In March 1939, German troops occupied the Czech lands of Bohemia and Moravia (a puppet state was created in Slovakia), and the Lithuanian port of Klaipeda (Memel) was taken later. On March 21, Germany issued a demand for Poland to transfer Gdansk (Danzig) to it. In April, Italy occupied Albania. In Spain, the civil war ended with the victory of Franco's fascist regime. The German army rapidly grew in numbers and strength. The weapons seized in Czecho-

Adolf Hitler and Benito Mussolini, Venice, June 1934

slovakia enabled Hitler to arm up to forty of his own divisions, while the factories of "Shkoda" produced as many weapons as all of Great Britain. The balance of power in Europe had been decisively changed.

In response, Great Britain and France had to push their own weapons programs, conclude mutual assistance treaties, and guarantee some of the European countries against possible aggression. The smell of war was in the air. But a significant part of the ruling elite of Great Britain and France still expected a conflict between Germany and the Soviet Union, even after the occupation of Czechoslovakia.

Meanwhile, Germany was not ready for a major war with the USSR, and Hitler chose the western option. On March 8, 1939, the strategy for the further expansion of fascist Germany was set out in a secret conference with the Fuhrer. It presumed that after the occupation of Czechoslovakia, Poland would be seized before autumn; France's turn would come in 1940 and 1941 and then Britain's. The "unification" of Europe and the establishment of fascist hegemony on the American continent was proclaimed as the final goal. In April, Hitler approved the plan to attack Poland.

The governments of Britain and France bore most of the responsibility for the nearsighted policy of appeasement. But they were not the only ones. The general failure to accurately evaluate the fascist threat, fear of communist expansion, and, finally, the well-known "national egoism" of the leading European peoples were also contributing factors. The first public opinion survey conducted in October 1939 showed that 57% of those questioned approved of the Munich agreements while only 37% were against them. The American magazine *Time* announced Hitler as "man of the year" on January 2, 1939; before this only Franklin Roosevelt and Mahatma Gandhi had received a similar honor.

Dramatic changes also occurred in the USSR's foreign policy. Although they were slow to recognize the danger of fascism, in the mid-1930s the Soviet leaders tried to establish relations with the western democracies and create a system of collective security in Europe. As we observed earlier, the USSR entered the League of Nations in 1934 and concluded treaties on mutual assistance with France and Czechoslovakia in 1935. But the military convention with France remained unsigned. The League of Nations had proven ineffective in the peace struggle, and the USSR found itself in political isolation after the Munich agreement. The military assistance offered by the USSR to Czechoslovakia was refused. Moreover, the USSR found itself facing the threat of a war with Japan. In the summer of 1938 Japanese troops penetrated the Soviet Far East in the region of Lake Khasan, while in May 1939 they invaded Mongolian territory. The Bolshevik leadership began to vacillate.

After sharply criticizing Britain's and France's policy at the Eighteenth Party Congress on March 10, 1939, Stalin unexpectedly announced that these powers—and not fascist Germany—were actually the chief warmongers. On April 17, 1939, the Soviet government proposed to Britain and France a Tripartite Pact of mutual assistance in case of aggression. Their motive was to exploit the "insight" into the fascist threat which was beginning to surface in western public opinion and simultaneously to pressure Germany into improving its relations with the USSR which had become strained after 1933. At the same time Hitler, trying to prevent the formation of a western bloc that included Russia, proposed the conclusion of a "Four Party Pact" between Britain, France, Germany, and Italy.

The USSR's negotiations with Britain and France were on the skids. The western governments were not interested in achieving a genuine agreement with the Soviet Union as much as exerting pressure on Hitler and calming public opinion. Thus, in the great diplomatic game beginning in Europe, each of the three sides was trying to outplay the other and paralyze the others.

The USSR was largely interested in obtaining some kind of agreement guaranteeing its own security. On May 3, 1939, the People's Commissar for Foreign Affairs, M.M. Litvinov—a proponent of an alliance with the western democracies and a Jew—was replaced by V.M. Molotov. This was undoubtedly a symptom of the change in tone of the USSR's foreign policy. On May 30, the German leadership indicated its readiness to improve relations with the USSR. On May 23, Hitler finally confirmed the plan for a armed conflict with France and Britain on the western front and, therefore, his interest in a temporary alliance with the USSR. In contrast to the leaders of Britain and France, he was prepared to make real concessions. At the end of July, Stalin decided to begin negotiations and improve political relations with Germany. But he did not yet refuse contacts with the western democracies. Intelligence reports on the deployment of German troops against Poland, which was supposed to be completed between August 15 and 20, stimulated Soviet diplomacy all the more.

Upon the USSR's initiative of August 12, 1939, in Moscow negotiations began with the military missions of Great Britain and France. The western representatives' unwillingness to assume definite obligations was immediately apparent, as the extreme "modesty" of the British position later revealed. While the USSR was prepared to place 136 divisions against the aggressor, Great Britain was only ready to deploy six. Since Poland refused to allow Soviet troops to pass through its territory, joint military operations against Germany were extremely difficult. This finally confirmed Stalin's opinion of his democratic partners' lack of seriousness. Hitler not only expressed his clear readiness to conclude a treaty with the USSR, but the success of his earlier policy recommended itself. In Stalin's eyes, the decisiveness and strength of the Fuhrer, which presented such a clear contrast with the western powers' weak policy of appeasement, was an important argument for an alliance with Germany. Thanks to the efforts of Soviet intelligence, Stalin already knew in March 1939 about fascist Germany's plans for the attack on

Poland and the war with Britain and France. The agreement with Hitler therefore permitted him to delay the USSR's entrance into the war. It not only made it possible to preserve the inviolability of the Soviet borders, which would also have occurred in the event of successful negotiations with Britain and France, but also to significantly expand them. The latter was important to Stalin not only because of the strength of his imperial ambitions—his goal of regaining the territory earlier belonging to the Russian Empire—but also for ideological reasons. Stalin understood that the failure of the revolutionary movement in the West, a strategic goal of the Communists, probably had prevented the expansion of socialism from within the European countries and would require the military and political might of the USSR instead. As a result, a treaty with Germany promised a double advantage which transcended the ideological disadvantages and the risk inherent in an agreement with the fascist aggressor.

Convinced of the failure of negotiations with Britain and France (on August 14 even the head of the British mission, Admiral R.A. Drax, expressed this opinion), Moscow accepted the persistent proposals of the Germans to negotiate a Soviet-German agreement. On the night of August 20, a trade and credit agreement was signed in Berlin. On August 21, the head of the Soviet delegation, K.E. Voroshilov, broke off negotiations with the French and British military missions for an indefinite period. On the same day an agreement was made for the German foreign minister, J. von Ribbentrop, to come to Moscow to sign a nonaggression pact.

On August 23, 1939, after three hours of negotiations in Moscow, the "Ribbentrop-Molotov Pact" was signed. To the nonaggression treaty was attached a secret additional protocol which provided for the "delineation of spheres of mutual interest in Eastern Europe." To the USSR's sphere of influence belonged Finland, Estonia, Latvia, Eastern Poland, and Bessarabia [now Moldova].[3]

These documents fundamentally changed Soviet foreign policy and the situation in Europe as a whole. From here on the Stalinist regime was transformed into an ally of Germany for the purpose of dividing Europe. The last obstacle to the attack on Poland and, through it, to the beginning of the Second World War was removed.

The appraisal of the pact of August 23, 1939, and of the Soviet

Union's rapprochement with fascist Germany is the subject of sharp disagreement. The arguments of the supporters of the pact are based largely on the danger of the rise of a single anti-Soviet front, joining the fascists and democratic powers, or on the threats of war in the West against Germany and the East against Japan. The supporters of the pact also cite the delay of the Soviet Union's entry into the war and the expansion of the Soviet Union's boundaries on the eve of the fascist aggression, achieved by the agreement with Germany.

But in reality, with the exception of the slight possibility of the creation of a single anti-Soviet front, which had not even been achieved in 1917-1920, the remaining arguments are far-fetched. It turns out that Germany could not have begun a war against the USSR in 1939 in any event because it did not have any common boundaries on which it could deploy troops and launch an offensive. More than this, it was totally unprepared for a great war.[4] The USSR was therefore actually protected from a war on two fronts. The rout of the Japanese troops at Khalkin Gol, which Stalin knew about on the eve of the signing of the pact, also forced the eastern neighbor of the USSR to be more cautious. The advantage "in time and space" was weakened even more by fascist Germany's ability to use the twenty-two months from the beginning of the Second World War to the beginning of the Great Patriotic War much more effectively than the leadership of the USSR, whose attention was not focused on the systematic improvement of defensive capabilities but on the realization of foreign political expansion and the difficult and bloody war with Finland. With individual exceptions, the new territories which entered the USSR could not be secured militarily, and almost all of them were lost during the first days of the war.

The possibilities for continuing the negotiations with Britain and France were not yet exhausted. On August 21 the French representative General J. Doumenc received full authority to sign a military convention with Russia. By not signing the pact with fascist Germany, the USSR not only could have preserved its own prestige in the world but also could have safeguarded itself from an outside attack, which occurred in spite of the pact and the general rapprochement with Germany. Besides this, Hitler's hands would have been tied in Europe. Of course, this would not have had immediate concrete advantages for the USSR. The "Munich attitude" was too strong among the leadership of Britain and France. Finally, the Stalinist regime had just completed the annihilation of the flower of the army command staff and was trying with all its strength to delay the war, if only for a short time, so that it could expand the sphere of its own dominance and choose a path which was to its benefit, ostensibly a rapprochement with fascist Germany. The consequences did not follow immediately.

The Beginning of the Second World War

On September 1, 1939, Hitler attacked Poland. The Second World War had begun. The Polish troops prepared themselves faster for war with the USSR than with Germany. On the Soviet borders thirty units were deployed, while there were only twenty-two units on the border with Germany. The tank columns of Hitler's army and the aviation units, which were concentrated in the direction of the main attack, ground up the poorly organized defense and successfully overwhelmed the Polish army's heroic but poorly coordinated operations. On September 17, when there was no doubt about the outcome of the battle in Poland, the Red Army occupied the western Ukraine and Belorussia, incorporating them into the Soviet state.

On September 3, France and Britain declared war on Germany. Despite the overwhelming superiority of their forces on the western front (ninety French divisions against only twenty poorly equipped German divisions, almost without any tanks and artillery), France and Britain conducted themselves with extreme passivity and gave practically no assistance to Poland. The last seats of Polish resistance were suppressed by the beginning of October.

The "phony war" continued on the western front. France and Britain clearly demonstrated their unwillingness to fight. The number of automobile accident casualties exceeded the French army's war casualties. On what did the western powers hope? Mostly on the strength of the French defensive "Maginot" line and the supremacy of the British and French fleet at sea. All this, it seemed, promised success in a difficult war with Germany through an economic blockade. In addition, after the seizure of Poland and the withdrawal of Hitler's troops to the boundaries of the USSR, some western leaders cherished the hope of a Soviet-German confrontation. Some circles in France, General Charles de Gaulle remembered, "sooner saw Stalin than Hitler as the enemy."

But Hitler himself believed that he could attack Russia only when he had "freed himself" in the West. He was able to utilize effectively the time given to him for preparing an offensive on the western front and to increase the army. Its numbers were increased by more than a half million men, while the number of tank units doubled. At the same time Hitler did not have overwhelming superiority in forces and hoped, therefore, for a surprise attack, using the tactics tried in Poland: the concentration of the major tank and air forces in the direction of the main attack, the rapid breakthrough of the defense, and the deep penetration and envelopment of the enemy's forces [deep strategic penetration]. This calculation proved justified. On April 9, the German army occupied Denmark almost without a shot and began the invasion of Norway. They were quickly able to suppress the resistance of the Norwegian army and the expeditionary forces sent by Britain and France. The strategic platform, guaranteeing control over all of northern Europe and the important sea communications had been seized.

On May 10, German troops attacked the Netherlands and Belgium. When the French and British armies moved to assist Belgium, the German tank corps struck further to the south—through the Ardennes forest, which was considered impenetrable for major tank units, on the flank of the "Maginot" line. Having broken through the defense, the Germans proceeded to LeMans and surrounded the main forces of the allied armies in Flanders. Thanks to Hitler's decision to save his tanks for the decisive thrust, 330,000 British and French troops facing the sea were able to be evacuated from Dunkirk to England; the outcome of the war with France was obvious.

France still had significant military force, but the morale of the society and especially of the country's leadership had been crushed and defeatist attitudes had sapped their strength. On June 14, the Germans entered Paris which had been declared an open city by the government. On June 16, the new premier, Marshal Petain, asked

Hitler for an armistice. It was signed on June 22, 1940, in the woods of Compiegne, in the same railway car where the armistice ending the First World War had been concluded in 1918.

The sole country in Europe that continued the courageous, but apparently completely hopeless, struggle with fascist Germany was Great Britain. Although she did not dispose of any significant land forces and was not ready for a defense of the islands, the government of Winston Churchill, which had come to power on May 10, 1940, categorically denied the possibility of any peace agreement with Germany and energetically worked for the mobilization of all of the country's resources for the enemy's defeat. Despite massive bombing and the severe losses of the fleet from German submarines, the morale of the British was not destroyed. Fascist Germany did not succeed in conquering the British superiority in the air and on the sea, which made it almost impossible to mount an invasion of the British isles.

On July 31, 1940, Hitler announced that the overriding goal from now on was a war with Russia, the outcome of which also would decide Britain's fate. On December 18, 1940, the plan of attack on the USSR ("Barbarossa") was approved. The transfer of troops to the East began in deep secrecy.

What was the Soviet Union's policy after the beginning of the Second World War?

In 1939-1940 Stalin was mostly concerned about the USSR's annexation of the territory in eastern Europe "assigned" to him by the secret agreements with fascist Germany and a further rapprochement with Hitler for the purpose of carrying out expansion and delaying the onset of the war with Germany as long as possible. Efforts were simultaneously made to enhance the military and economic potential of the USSR.

On September 28, a treaty was signed with Germany "On Friendship and Borders" to which three secret protocols were attached. In these documents both sides were obligated to conduct a joint struggle against "Polish agitation" and to carve out their own spheres of influence. Relying on this agreement, Stalin demanded the Baltic States conclude "mutual assistance" treaties and permit the establishment of his military bases on their territories. In September and October 1939 Estonia, Latvia, and Lithuania had to agree to this. On June 14-16, 1940, after fascist Germany's defeat of France, Stalin sent an ultimatum to the Baltic states informing them of the introduction onto their territories of contingents of Soviet troops "to guarantee their security" and on the formation of new governments who were ready to "honorably" carry out the treaties concluded with the USSR. Several days later "people's governments" were created in Estonia, Latvia, and Lithuania which established Soviet authority in the Baltic states with the help of local Communists. At the end of June 1940, Stalin acquired Bessarabia, which Rumania had occupied in 1918.

Stalin had a somewhat more difficult time with Finland. The Finns would not agree and would not sign a mutual assistance treaty, nor would they alter their borders. Stalin, in particular, wanted to move the border away from Leningrad which was only thirty kilometers from the border with Finland and to acquire a base on the Hango peninsula and on the Finnish part of the Rybach peninsula in exchange for territory in Soviet Karelia. On November 30, 1939, using the pretext of a border incident, the USSR began military operations against Finland. In advance he had prepared a "People's Government" for Finland which would transform the country into another "Soviet Socialist Republic" within the USSR. At the head of this "government" was the Communist O.V. Kuusinen. But Stalin could not achieve a rapid victory over the four million Finns. Despite consistent superiority of force, especially tanks and planes, the Red Army was unable to defeat the stubborn Finns for a long time. Only in February 1940, at the price of huge sacrifices, was the Army able to break through the Mannerheim defensive line. On March 12, a peace treaty was signed under which the USSR received the territories it wanted.

On the whole the results of the war were not very comforting for the Soviet Union. Only the conclusion of peace saved it from an armed confrontation with Britain and France, who were ready to send their own troops to help the Finns. The Red Army lost 127,000 men killed and 270,000 wounded or frostbitten, while the Finnish army lost 48,000 dead and 43,000 wounded or frost-bitten. The "Winter War" revealed the poor combat readiness of the Red Army which caused its international prestige to fall sharply. In the spring of 1940, Hitler explained to his generals that the failure of the Soviet troops was the result of internal repression and that it was important not to give Stalin time to correct the deficiencies in the Red Army. As a result the timetable for fascist Germany's attack on the Soviet Union, originally planned for the spring of 1942, was moved up by a year.

For Stalin, the relative weakness of the Red Army in the Finnish War was a powerful incentive for avoiding a Soviet-German confrontation and for a even greater rapprochement with Hitler's regime. In 1940 and the first half of 1941, economic ties with Germany were rapidly growing. Having undermined the trade blockade, the USSR made huge deliveries of oil, cotton, grain, nonferrous metals, and other strategic materials urgently needed by the German economy. After a long interval in the 1930s, Soviet-German cooperation in military affairs was resumed. The Soviet leadership gave the fascists a naval base on the coast of Murmansk, but after the seizure of Norway Hitler withdrew from it. In the official communiqués of Stalin and Molotov, fascist Germany was portrayed as a peacemaker, while Britain and France were chastised as warmongers who supported the continuation of the conflict. Upon the occasion of France's defeat Molotov "warmly congratulated" the Hitler regime on behalf of the Soviet government.

The tone of the Soviet press and all of the ideological propaganda inside the country was changed accordingly. All antifascist subjects and statements were removed from the repertoires of theaters and radio stations while Soviet-German friendship and cooperation became the propaganda line. Moreover, Stalin turned over to Hitler 800 German and Austrian antifascists who were found on the territory of the USSR. Public opinion inside the country was disoriented. Abroad, Communists and others who were sympathetic to the USSR were shocked. It is not surprising that right up to the defeat of France the western powers had planned to send an expeditionary corps to help Finland and to bombard the Soviet oil fields in the Caucasus.

At the same time efforts were made in the USSR to expand the military-industrial complex as much as possible. From 1939 to June

1941, the share of military spending in the Soviet budget increased from 26% to 43%. The output of military production at the time was more than twice the general rate of industrial growth. In the eastern part of the country defense plants were constructed at a rapid rate, doubling the number of enterprises. By the summer of 1941, they comprised almost a fifth of all military plants. The production of new types of military machinery became routine, some forms of which (the T-34 tanks, the BM-13 rocket mortars, and the IL-2 attack planes) exceeded all similar weapons produced abroad. The Red Army went from a mixed, territorial organizational system, which was introduced in the mid-1920s out of economic necessity, to a regular system. On September 1, 1939, a law was adopted on universal military service. The size of the armed forces from August 1939 to June 1941 increased from two million to 5.4 million people.

But for the most part the physical and moral terror established in the country during the 1930s reduced the major efforts that had been undertaken to expand the military-industrial complex. This caused the USSR to delay the transformation of the economy to military production and the reorganization of the army; moreover, the work itself was accompanied by major errors and miscalculations. The production of new types of weapons lagged. Many designers and engineers had been arrested; some later worked in a special designers' bureau, created from prisoners (the "*sharashki*").* Whole branches of the defense industry were in a fever from this repression. As a result, in 1939-1941, the USSR produced more airplanes than Germany, but the overwhelming majority of them, in contrast to the German machines, were outdated designs. The tanks are a prime example of this armament chaos: because of the Stalin's arbitrary decisions before the Great Patriotic War, the seventy-six millimeter and forty-five millimeter guns were removed (the output of which later had to be urgently resumed). Because of the personal opposition of the Deputy People's Commissar for Defense, G.I. Kulik, and other Stalin loyalists, who had living memories of the civil war, the development of mortars and submachine guns was delayed. People's Defense Commissar K.E. Voroshilov called the replacement of horses in the army by motor vehicles a "bad theory."

A terrible blow fell on the army. Stalin's repression resulted in the liquidation of most of the army high command, almost all of whom were skilled generals and military theoreticians. Of eighty-five senior officers—the members of the War Council at the People's Commissariat of Defense—seventy-six were purged. The purge also involved a significant number of the middle- and junior-level officers. 43,000 officers were purged in 1937 and 1938 alone. One should also remember that the purges of the officers began in the mid-1920s and that by the mid-1930s forty-seven thousand officers had been dismissed, many of whom were executed or sent to the camps. The repression continued between 1939 and 1941 and even during the Great Patriotic War, although on a smaller scale. As a result, in 1941 the number of commanders (66,900) for the land forces was insufficient while the deficit in the composition of flight technicians in the air corps reached 32.3%. The quality of the military personnel sharply deteriorated. Only 7.1% of the commanders had a higher education in military science. At the beginning of the Great Fatherland War 75% of the commanders had been in their offices less than a year.

On the eve of the war the army was practically without leadership. The losses in the high command from the Stalinist purges greatly exceeded the later losses in the war with Germany. As a result the level of the Soviet military readiness fell sharply. Surely it had been one of the best in the world up to the mid-1930s. The Soviet theory of "deep operations" presupposed the carrying out of an assault on the entire depth of the enemy army's formation with the utilization of large tanks massed in mechanized units with the support of planes and landing parties. Hans Guderian, who created a similar system of offensive operations for Germany (the "lightning war" or *Blitzkrieg* later used successfully in western Europe and in the USSR in 1941), borrowed many of the ideas of Soviet military theorists. Indeed, the Red Army was the pioneer in the creation of large mechanized units at the brigade and corps levels. But during the second half of the 1930s the development of the military art was not only stopped but was set back. The mechanized corps were disbanded and only re-created on the eve of the war. The reorganization of the army after the Soviet-Finnish War, which included the replacement of the People's Commissar for Defense by S.K. Timoshenko, the reform of the troop training system, and other measures could not change the situation, not only because of the shortages of the period but also because of the continuing anxiety and fear connected with the ceaseless search for the "people's enemies" which encouraged unscrupulous behavior and blind submission to authority.

This was especially apparent concerning the question of when fascist Germany might attack the Soviet Union. In November 1940, Soviet intelligence agents, despite the preceding purges that had touched the majority of the foreign residents, began to report concrete information on the attack being prepared by Germany against the USSR. There were dozens of such reports composed from very different military and diplomatic sources. Moreover, even Churchill and the German ambassador to Russia, F. Schulenburg, who was an opponent of the war, warned Stalin about the preparations for the invasion of Russia. But Stalin considered all of the arguments of the intelligence agents, diplomats, and foreign leaders to be disinformation. Of Richard Zorg, the brilliant intelligence agent stationed in Japan, Stalin remarked: "We have only found one 'solicitor' [pimp], who in Japan has provided himself with prostitutes and brothels and has been pleased to inform us that the date of the German attack is July 22. How can we believe him?" A communiqué of *TASS* was published on June 14, 1941, in which statements about a German attack on the USSR in the foreign, and especially the British, press were "exposed." Attempts to elevate the combat readiness of the border troops in June 1941 were frustrated by Stalin's orders not to allow any activities which could be construed as preparations by the USSR for a war with Germany. In his panic Stalin feared provoking the conflict. "To prevent provocations" flights of Soviet aircraft within ten kilometers of the border zone were forbidden up to ten days before the beginning of the war.

What caused Stalin's blindness and cost the Soviet people so dearly? There were several closely interwoven factors which reinforced one another. Knowing the Red Army's lack of readiness compared to Germany's military machine, Stalin feared the war and wanted to delay it in every possible way. He presumed that Hitler would not risk repeating Germany's sad WWI experience of a struggle on two fronts and would not attack the USSR while Britain remained unconquered. The numerous warnings of an imminent attack by Hitler seemed the result of an extensive campaign of disinformation planned by the British leadership, which was known to be anti-Soviet, whose purpose was to "cause trouble" between the USSR and Germany. These assumptions time and again confirmed in Stalin his own farsightedness and infallibility, and all the rest were unable or unwilling to dispute this position.

The sources of the tragic miscalculations of the Soviet leadership between 1939 and 1941 were rooted in the country's totalitarian system. Being totally centralized, the system did not permit any kind of democratic mechanism for decision-making, for considering alternative proposals (if the charismatic leader did not want to), or for "correcting" the dictator. The system did not permit the effective management of the country's accumulated military and economic potential and became the cause of new tragic errors, even in wartime.

The Peak of Fascist Aggression: The Beginning of the Great Patriotic War

At dawn on June 22, 1941, Germany attacked the Soviet Union in violation of the nonaggression treaty. The Great Patriotic War had begun. It was the most important component of the Second World War because, to a great extent, Hitler's attack on the USSR changed the course of the war. From the very beginning the war was distinguished from the conflict in the West by its vigor, its bloodshed, the extreme tension of the struggle, and the unprecedented atrocities of the fascists upon prisoners of war and the civilian population. Emphasizing that the campaign in the East would be "something greater than a mere armed struggle," Hitler demanded a war of "annihilation." The Nazis planned to destroy the "Russian people as a nationality," to subvert their "biological strength" and destroy their culture. They envisioned the deportation of tens of millions of people and every kind of genocidal attack on reproduction, on "inoculations and other health improvement measures," and on education "of the non-German population."

In accordance with the plan, "Barbarossa" prescribed a short campaign of approximately ten weeks to annihilate the main forces of the Red Army "by means of the deep and rapid advance of tank columns." The blow would be dealt in three directions: against Leningrad, Moscow and Kiev. "The final purpose of the operation," the fascist orders noted, "was the creation of a curtain barrier against Asiatic Russia along the common Volga to the Archangel line." Hitler allotted the overwhelming part of his land forces for the attack on the USSR. Together with his allies (Finland, Rumania, Hungary and Italy) the invasion army numbered 5.5 million men, 3,800 tanks and 4,600 planes. They were opposed by 3.3 million Soviet troops supported by 10,400 tanks and 8,600 aircraft. But the vast majority of this equipment was obsolete, and personnel training left much to be desired. The suddenness of the attack gave an enormous advantage to the fascists as did their combat experience in contemporary warfare and the high offensive spirit of the soldiers intoxicated by their victories in Europe. On the first day of the war they destroyed 1200 Russian planes, mostly on air bases.

During the first hours of the war the Germans without difficulty suppressed the disorganized opposition of the Soviet forces on the border and drove a deep wedge into Soviet territory. In two days the German tanks had forced their way 230 kilometers inside the border. Hundreds of thousands of Russian servicemen were killed or wounded. In the Belostok-Minsk region alone thirty-eight Soviet divisions were routed and 288,000 prisoners were taken. Minsk fell on June 28. By the middle of June the Germans held almost all of the Baltic states, Belorussia, and the Right-Bank Ukraine. To the German leadership it seemed that the war was going well. The border district troops were defeated and the permanent losses comprised more than 700,000 men.

Soviet society experienced a severe shock. According to Marshal G.K. Zhukov's memoirs, which were first published without censorship in 1992, at dawn on June 22 Stalin could not believe that the invasion of German troops was not a provocation but the beginning of war. "Hitler absolutely knows nothing about this," he said. After the official declaration of war by Germany he dispatched a directive to the troops, emphasizing that they were not to violate the German border! The dictator fell into a severe depression and even announced his renunciation of the leadership of the country. The administration of the troops of the border regions was disorganized. The commanders and the Red Army were completely unprepared for such a turn of events. Brought up on the official slogan that there would not be a war with Germany in the near future and that when it did begin military operations would be conducted on the enemy's territory "with little bloodshed," they were often unable to understand what was occurring and easily could have given in to panic. This situation happened in the fall when twenty German submachine gunners took nearly four hundred Red Army servicemen as prisoners.

At the same time, from the very beginning of the war against Russia the German generals perceived that the enemy troops would defend themselves with greater tenacity than in the West. Cases of self-sacrifice were not rare: aerial breakthroughs, for example, where pilots steered their damaged planes into enemy troops and blew themselves up along with the enemy tanks or soldiers. Heroic resistance was directed against the Germans at Brest where a small, completely surrounded garrison fought on for a month, at Diepa, Peremysl, and the Lutsk-Brody-Rovno where the first tank counterattack was organized. Gradually the leadership of the country got the situation under control. On June 22 mobilization was announced, on the 23rd the Headquarters (*Stavka*) of the High (later Supreme) Command was created, on the 30th the State Committee on Defense was established. Stalin headed both of these organs. The reform of the administration was begun with regard to the troops, war industry, and the evacuation of enterprises and the population from occupied territories.

The losses of German soldiers grew as a result. Toward the middle of July German loses comprised nearly 100,000 men—much less than the Soviet losses, but greater than the Wehrmacht's losses in France (50,000), Poland (16,000), and other European countries. The losses in tanks in Russia reached 50%. The Chief of the General Staff of the German Army, F. Halder, observed in his diary on July 20, 1941, that "the loss of spirit in our leading echelons is well known," caused by the fierce fighting and the great exhaustion of the troops. The two month battle at Smolensk, the defense of Kiev

(70 days), Odessa (73 days) and finally, the counteroffensive of the Red Army at Elna in the beginning of September, during which eight German divisions were routed, broke the momentum of the German offensive and put the rapid completion of the war in Russia in doubt.

Nevertheless the enemy was still strong. Having regrouped his forces, on September 30 he began a general offensive against Moscow. The Germans obtained major success at Viazma, where more than 660,000 men were surrounded on three Soviet fronts. In October Orel, Kaluga, Kalinin, Volokolamsk, and Mozhaisk were seized. German newspapers printed maps of the Moscow region, where the forward movement of the Wehrmacht was shown approaching the capital of Russia. But despite the significant superiority in personnel and planes (1.5-to-1) and in tanks (2-to-1), the fascists were unable to overcome the heroic resistance of the mixed group successfully assembled by the command of the Red Army. Moreover, the war acquired the character of the people's, the Motherland's war. In the summer and autumn of 1941 nearly 10 million peacetime citizens, mostly women, participated in the construction of border defenses and about 2 million people entered the people's militia. Each step forward for the Germans was made all the more difficult.

Only in the middle of November, after new reserves had been brought up, could the Wehrmacht renew the offensive. The enemy came as close as twenty-five to thirty kilometers of Moscow. Stalin, who was already prepared for the worst, anxiously asked Zhukov: "Do you believe that we can hold Moscow? . . . Speak honestly. . . ."

"We will unconditionally hold Moscow," Zhukov answered and it came true. The defenders of the capital and its last southern outpost—Tula—were able to stop the enemy and bleed him white. The offensive spirit of the German units waned. They were unprepared for the frosts, and the forces of resistance were growing daily.

Despite the loss of vast territories on which 40% of the population of the USSR lived and on which 60% of the steel and 70% of the coal was produced before the war, and despite a 50% decline in industrial production, the output of tanks during the second half of 1941 grew 2.8 times, of airplanes—1.6 times, of arms—nearly three times. This helped to partially compensate for the colossal losses of weapons in the preceding period. It was no less important to replenish the unprecedented human losses. At the end of the year they comprised, according to the most conservative estimate, 3.1 million, but according to some data, more than five million people (90% of the size of the prewar army). In any event, according to the German documents, Soviet prisoners of war alone amounted to 3.9 million people of whom only 1.1 million were alive by the beginning of 1942. Mobilization, a voluntary militia, and the intelligence agent Zorg's report that Japan would not join the attack on the USSR in the near future permitted the reinforcement of the troops. As a result Moscow at the decisive moment succeeded in bringing in fresh Siberian divisions.

Library of Congress, Prints & Photographs Div, War Information Collection, LC-USZ62-94366

General Georgy K. Zhukov

Although it would seem that the Red Army did not have the preponderance of forces needed to mount an offensive, on Zhukov's initiative a counteroffensive was prepared near Moscow. The right time was chosen. The offensive which began on December 5 and 6 drove the enemy back 100 to 300 kilometers. Attacks were launched at Tikhvin and Rostov-on-Don while an expeditionary force was landed on the Kerchensk peninsula. As a result of the battle for Moscow thirty-eight enemy divisions were routed and their losses reached half a million people. Soviet losses were even greater—514,000 people.

The problems which had arisen during the counteroffensive were far from being resolved. Stalin wanted to destroy the enemy's main force which, of course, was a fantastic idea. The Soviet troops could not break the blockade of Leningrad which began in the fall of 1941. Leningrad remained under siege for 900 days at a cost of

800,000 residents who died of deprivation or hunger. During the battle for Moscow, Leningrad not only drew away major German and Finnish forces but, despite the evacuation of a significant part of the population (1.7 million between June 1941 and March 1943) and enterprises, the city continued to produce weapons, especially cannons and mortars which were sent by plane to Moscow.

All the same the victory at Moscow had enormous significance. As a result of it the immediate threat to the capital was eliminated and the German army lost the first major battle since the beginning of the Second World War. The plans for "lightning war" were broken and it was clear that German intelligence and the General Staff had miscalculated the USSR's military potential. They assumed that Stalin would be able to bring in only fifty-nine additional divisions, but actually 324 divisions were sent to the front during that summer! It is not surprising that Hitler dismissed more than thirty of his own generals. At the same time the successful counteroffensive of the Soviet Army raised the spirit of the army and the people, breathing new life into them. The international position of the USSR was remarkably strengthened too. During the battle of Moscow the anti-Hitler coalition was formed.

On June 22, 1941, Prime Minister Churchill and, on June 24, President Roosevelt announced their support of the Soviet Union. On July 12, a Soviet-British agreement on combined operations against fascist Germany was accepted, and on August 24, the USSR joined the Atlantic Charter (originally signed by Roosevelt and Churchill) in which the goals of the anti-Hitler coalition were set out. At the Moscow Conference of September 29 to October 1 tripartite decisions were reached on the supply of weapons to the USSR and of strategic raw materials to Britain and the United States. On November 7, Roosevelt expanded the operation of the Lend Lease Act for the Soviet Union. Although during the war years the supplies under lend lease only comprised 4% of the USSR's war production, in a number of instances they had great significance. In particular the supplies of Studebaker and Willys Jeeps helped to motorize the Red Army. Nonetheless before December 1941 the allies had serious fears for the fate of the USSR. "President Roosevelt was considered a very bold man when he announced in September

1941 that Moscow would not be taken," Churchill remembered.

The counteroffensive of the Soviet troops at Moscow and the entry of the United States into the war (on December 7 the Japanese attacked Pearl Harbor, on December 11 the United States declared war on Germany and Italy) seriously changed the situation. On January 1, 1942, in Washington the representatives of twenty-six states signed the United Nations Declaration which completed the basic formation of the anti-Hitler coalition.

But besides the USSR only Great Britain was conducting a real struggle with the fascists—in North Africa and on the Atlantic Ocean and Mediterranean Sea. The war with Japan in the Pacific began extremely unsuccessfully for the United States. At Pearl Harbor the Japanese destroyed or damaged eight American battleships and, having won superiority on the sea by this means, seized the overwhelming part of Southeast Asia and even threatened Australia in the spring of 1942.

Considering the difficult position of the USSR, the allies decided to open a second front in Europe in 1942. But, in fact, a second front in Europe was not opened in 1942 for a number of reasons: because of the risk of landing in France, possibly, because of political considerations (as early as October 1942 Churchill had anxiously written about the threat of Russia in postwar Europe), and because the America army was unprepared. The soldier, in the opinion of Dwight Eisenhower, still "did not understand the basic causes of the war," or "why a conflict between two European countries had any relationship to America." Instead the Americans landed in North Africa. It goes without saying that this was not an exchange of equal value. In addition, as became apparent later, operations in Africa complicated the offensive through LaManch even in 1943. The problem of a second front became at this time one of the most critical problems in the relations of the USSR with the United States and Great Britain.

Meanwhile on the eastern front the German troops were preparing themselves for *revanche*. Not being in a condition to go on the attack on every front, they concentrated the main blow in Southern Russia: in the direction of Stalingrad (now Volgograd) and the northern Caucasus. Hitler tried not only to destroy the entire southern flank of the Soviet forces and seize the wealthy oil and grain production regions but also to acquire an entrance to the Near East. The miscalculations of the military and political leadership of the USSR facilitated the realization of these plans. Reevaluating his own forces, Stalin insisted on lauching an offensive instead of being limited to a strategic defense of the entire front from Leningrad to the Crimea. And Headquarters and the General Staff calculated that the main blow would be directed by the Germans against Moscow.

In fact, all of the "forestalling" offensive operations which were undertaken in April and May 1942 failed and led to a new military disaster. Especially tough defeats were suffered by the part of the Red Army in the Crimea which led to the fall of Sevastopol on July 4. It had conducted a heroic defense for 250 days, attracting large enemy forces to itself. Kharkov was also defeated, where the Soviet forces lost 230,000 men. The route to the east was opened and the German troops began to move forward rapidly. The loss of the Crimea and the defeats at Barvenky, Voronezh, and in the Donets Basin were "difficult for the morale of the people and troops," Zhukov remembered. In units of the Red Army "attitudes of panic and violations of military discipline occurred." After the second half of July all the world with its heart in its mouth followed the progress of the Germans toward Stalingrad. In the south they came to the main ridge of the Caucasus and planted their flag on Elbrus. On July 28, the remarkable Order No. 227, "No Retreat," was published which provided for the creation of penal companies and battalions (actually of condemned men) and also of defensive detachments in the rear of the units who had to shoot those who were retreating. One of Hitler's commentators observed that to retreat to the Soviets is too far and there is nowhere to go behind the Volga.

What was the cause of the severe defeats of the Red Army between the spring and autumn of 1942 which again brought the USSR to the brink of destruction?

Besides the strategic errors and the deficit in manpower and weapons, the Stalinist regime, economically and especially politically and psychologically, could not adapt itself to the new type of warfare. Although the reform which was planned began during the first days of the Great Patriotic War, in 1942 Stalin himself and the old military cadres who had survived and had been promoted during the period of the great terror were tied to the customary stereotypes and continued to rely on the command system and repression. In July 1941, Stalin blamed the defeat of the army on a number of commanders and shot the commander of the Western Front D. G. Pavlov, A.D. Loktionov, who commanded the Baltic military district, and P.V. Rychagov, the administrative head of the Air Force and chief of the Supreme War Council (*VVS—voenno vozduchnye sily*), along with other generals. In August, on the orders of Headquarters those who were imprisoned were declared traitors, and the families of deserters or imprisoned commanders were subject to arrest (the families of the soldiers were deprived of state support and assistance). In September those taken as hostages were considered "accomplices" of the Hitlerites. In October and November 1941, with the Germans approaching Moscow, "scorched earth" tactics were used for the first time. By order of Headquarters it was decreed that "all population points in the rear of the German forces at a distance of forty to sixty kilometers in depth from the front line and twenty to thirty kilometers to the right and left of the road should be destroyed and burned to the ground." At the same time, relying on the experience of the civil war, in July 1941 Stalin introduced commissars or political instructors into the army. Undoubtedly these harsh measures to some degree accelerated the restoration of discipline and the introduction of order into the army. At the same time these "prewar" methods stifled initiative, kept tactics at a primitive level, and gave rise to new problems. The night of July 22, 1941, is characteristic: many commanders, who were in a state of panic and feared every kind of accusation, waited to the last minute for orders from above and did not prepare their units for war even though they could hear the noise of motor vehicles and the clamor of the goose step on the other side of the border. Stalin's panic and his preference for the old revolutionary scheme ("Lenin's experience at Brest"), perhaps, is rather clearly shown in his attempt to conclude peace with Germany. Influenced by the severe defeats of the Red Army, he directed Beria to establish a connection with Berlin and proposed "to cede to Hitler's Germany the Ukraine, Belorussia, the Baltic States, and the Karelian isthmus, Bessarabia and Bukovina upon the termination of hostilities." But Hitler had no need of peace.

The defeats in 1942 accelerated the renewal of the leading cadres who determined the psychological reconstruction of the regime. Stalin's gradual abandonment of faith in his own infallibility in military strategy (of which he, in fact, had a poor understanding) and the abolition of the institution of war commissars in October 1942 are examples of this.

Industry, which was placed on a war footing at this time, very rapidly increased the output of weapons. As a result, by the middle of November 1942 the advance of the German units was successfully stopped.

The Turning Point in the War

For the first time since the beginning of the war the Soviet leadership succeeded in obtaining the general superiority of forces over the German forces: 6.6 million men against 6.2 million; 78,000 guns against 52,000; 7,300 tanks against 5,000; and 4,500 planes against 3,500. Since Hitler was still trying to seize Stalingrad and the Caucasus without regard for the shortage of forces and against the advice of his own generals, the Soviet command had favorable opportunities to deal the counterblow. Under Zhukov (deputy of the Supreme High Command) and A.M. Vasilevsky (Head of the General Staff) an operation was planned to surround the enemy's forces at Stalingrad. Thanks to careful planning and tight security, which was unprecedented before that time, the preparations were successfully kept secret from the Germans.

The offensive began on November 19, 1942. Because of powerful attacks on the German flanks by the Soviet forces, 330,000 fascists were successfully surrounded. The Germans' attempt to break out was frustrated, and by February 1943 the surrounded army group headed by Field Marshal von Paulus was routed. 91,000 soldiers were taken prisoner. The total losses to the German forces during this huge battle were 1.5 million. Perhaps as much equipment was lost as during the entire preceding struggle on the Soviet-German front. Four days of mourning were declared in Germany.

Some historians believe that Stalingrad was the greatest defeat ever suffered by the German army. As far as the Second World War was concerned, Stalingrad was undoubtedly the turning point.[5] To farsighted politicians it was already becoming clear that Germany was doomed to defeat. Similar views grew stronger in the countries of the fascist bloc. The international reputation of the Red Army flew to new heights.

Having seized the strategic initiative, the Soviet forces launched a general offensive. They liberated the northern Caucasus, broke through the siege of Leningrad, and routed the German army groups in the central sector of the front. The Wehrmacht could only answer with one, although a rather considerable, counterattack at Kharkov.

Nevertheless the forces of fascist Germany were still not destroyed. Introducing total mobilization (all males from sixteen to sixty-five and women from seventeen to forty-five), Hitler was able to replenish to some extent the huge losses in manpower and to sharply increase the output of military equipment (70% per year), including new models. In the summer of 1943, taking advantage of the absence of a second front in Europe, Hitler was able to concentrate large forces in the region of Orl and Belgorod—in the Kursk Bulge. Up to fifty divisions and more than two-thirds of the tanks and planes found at the Soviet-German front were tied down there. With the blows concentrated on the Kursk Bulge he hoped to surround and annihilate the Soviet forces which were dispersed along the Bulge and open up the road to Moscow. This was a desperate attempt to change the course of the war in one battle (there was no greater force).

The ever-increasing skill of the Soviet commanders was displayed in their anticipation of Hitler's plans and in having arranged for a preponderance of force. Headquarters decided to deliberately defend the Kursk Bulge in order to bleed the enemy white, in the first instance his tank forces, and then to proceed to the counteroffensive. On the whole this plan succeeded.

Beginning on July 5, and for approximately a week, Russian forces defended the Bulge and stopped the enemy. But during the battle the Germans, with an unprecedented concentration of forces in separate sectors, were able to drive a wedge in the Soviet defenses of ten to thirty-five kilometers. The culmination of this gigantic struggle was the largest tank battle in world history near the village of Prokhorovka on July 12, in which 1200 tanks from both sides dueled. From this time on the Soviet forces were on the offensive. As a result of the fierce battle on the Kursk Bulge the Wehrmacht lost half a million men, 1600 tanks, and 3700 planes. Germany was unable to make up these losses: here, as at Moscow and Stalingrad, the flower of the German forces perished. The Kursk victory marked the final passage of the strategic initiative into the hands of the Soviet forces.

The German command tried to secure the Dnieper. But by October 1943 Soviet forces were able to take the river by force and on November 6 they entered Kiev, timing the liberation of this ancient town, on Stalin's instructions, to coincide with the anniversary of the October Revolution. Continuing the offensive, the Soviet forces liberated the central Ukraine and besieged the Germans in the Crimea. At the same time the liberation of Belorussia was begun. Between November 1942 and the end of 1943 about half of the territory of the USSR seized by the Germans had been liberated. The enemy had been driven back about 600 to 1200 kilometers to the west. Two hundred eighteen divisions had been destroyed.

The partisans, whose numbers reached 250,000, inflicted a great loss on the Germans, but the fascists conducted a ruthless struggle against them. In the course of punitive operations, in which not only part of the SS, but also the Wehrmacht participated, whole villages were liquidated including children and the elderly. And there was no "amateur performance" from the fascists who were intoxicated by blood. The soldiers followed Keitel's order: "the troops must employ all sorts of measures without limit, even directing them against women and children." But despite the massive terror the fascists were unable to finish off the partisan movement. Moreover, the mass desertion which occurred at the beginning of the war in the Baltic area and the Ukraine, which was in part a quiet protest against the Stalinist regime, was redressed by the intensity of the partisans' struggle against the German occupiers, brought on by the cruelty of the occupation. In 1943 alone the number of diversions by the partisans increased by approximately 500%. The "rail war" unleashed by the partisans during the battle of Kursk seriously complicated the transport of the German troops.

The turning point in the war was secured by the unprecedented heroism of the workers of the Soviet rear, and also to some degree by the advantages of the extremely centralized system for managing the economy. As a result of the system, during the first six months of the war 1,500 industrial enterprises were evacuated to the East in record time. The Kramatorsk factory was able to begin production a mere twelve days after its arrival at the new location. Sometimes machines were put in a field, connected to electricity, and the factory walls would rise around them. At the end of 1942 the economy of the country was placed on a war footing and the output of machinery grew at an extremely rapid pace. At this time the production of machine-producing factories in Western Siberia in comparison to 1940 grew 7.9 times, in the Urals by 4.5 times, and in Uzbekistan by 5.1 times. Having on the whole less industrial potential than Germany and the European countries working with her, the USSR produced more armaments and machinery during the war years.

Moreover women comprised more than half of the workers in the economy. Beside them on the collective farms and in the factories were hundreds of thousands of adolescent workers. Often boxes had to be placed under their feet so they could reach the machines. From hunger and chronic exhaustion people would faint, but they did not abandon any work. Russian patriotism, belief in the justice of their cause and, for some, faith in Stalin helped the people to hold on, without being broken by this harsh tension.

The critical conditions of the war evoked changes in the social and political policies of the Stalinist regime and in the consciousness of society. The classic totalitarian paradigm of the INFALLIBLE LEADER—HARSH ADMINISTRATORS—OBEDIENT MASSES changed in all respects. Stalin became more flexible and attentive to the voices of subordinates (mostly military men). Extensive replacements were made in military and administrative cadres. Among the promoted were talented people, capable of making and effectively implementing decisions on their own. Among such commanders were Zhukov, Vasilevsky, and K.K. Rokossovsky (who had been released from internment). Among the civilians were N. Voznesensky, A.A.

Kuznetsov, A.N. Kosygin, and others. The initiative of the masses was also emancipated, but within definite limits. The critical conditions and the upswing in patriotism made it possible for many of them to make personal choices and experience a certain degree of self-realization. The military disasters of 1941 and 1942 forced people to reevaluate some of their values and to critically examine the leadership and the system which existed before the war. Of course, these changes in the consciousness of the masses did not become revolutionary and were far from universal. Nonetheless their influence was felt not only during the years of war, but after.

Even the official ideology experienced some corrections. The creation of the anti-Hitler coalition dampened the "anti-imperialist propaganda." Gradually within society certain traditional Russian and even imperialist values began to return, which, obviously, Stalin considered more useful under those conditions than the usual party clichés. In his radio statement on July 3, 1941, the dictator turned to the people with an entirely "non-ideological" appeal—"brothers and sisters." The officer class was also restored (the generalitet before the war), the shoulder straps, guards, and nonrevolutionary orders: of Suvovov, Kutuzov, and even Aleksandr Nevsky (ignoring the fact that the latter was considered a saint before the revolution.) The rehabilitation of the Orthodox Church began slowly but surely. In September 1943 and in April 1945 Stalin personally met with the church hierarchy. Thanks to the changed relationship with the authorities, a number of registered parishes of the Russian Orthodox Church grew by 500%, reaching 14,500 between 1941 and 1951.

However, the Stalinist regime preserved the features of the system which it had formed. The political terror was continued. Moreover, on Stalin's order, acts of repression were conducted against entire nationalities. In 1941 more than a million Germans from the Volga region were deported, in 1943 more than 93,000 Kalmyks and 68,000 Karachaevtsy. In 1944 around half a million Chechentsy and Ingush, 37,000 Balkartsy, 183,000 Crimean Tatars, 12,000 Bulgars, and 91,000 Turks, Kurds, and Khemshils were resettled. The deportation was accompanied by frequent shootings of peaceful people, with the insults of the NKVD soldiers over them. It is difficult to calculate the major sacrifices endured by the deported peoples during resettlement, in new, barren places such as Siberia, Kazakhstan, and Central Asia.

According to the evidence at hand, the number of prisoners (excluding convict settlers) reached 2.4 million in 1941. Despite the continuous "renewal of quotas," in 1945 their number exceeded 1.7 million. The total number of people serving a sentence in prisons, camps, and in exile comprised, according to some estimates, 5 to 7 million people which was comparable to the numbers in the regular army serving on the Soviet-German front. It is not surprising that V. Schellenburg planned to land expeditionary forces close to the major Stalinist camps and, after liberating the prisoners, to deprive Stalin of laborers and influence the country through propaganda. The protest against the regime would encourage the Russians and representatives of other nationalities to cooperate with the Germans and to enter Russia as liberation armies. The total number of collaborators with the Germans reached a million people according to estimates. The problem of the relationship between idealistic and "sordid" motives among them awaits its own researchers.

At the end of 1943 the Soviet military art attained a higher quality, which in the person of its own best representatives was second to none and probably exceeded the German skill. Stalin became somewhat better at understanding strategy. But the results of the military campaign of 1943 could have been rather more impressive and the losses of the Soviet troops less, but for the haste of the Supreme High Command and its passion for a frontal assault—for "pushing out" the Germans, instead of deep envelopment and the encirclement of the enemy. It is significant that in 1945, when fascist Germany was beginning to experience her death-throes, the entire American command avoided frontal attacks, considering them a "difficult and costly affair."

In the autumn of 1942 the British began the struggle against the German and Italian forces in North Africa. On October 23 the battle of El Alamein began which completed the rout of the enemy whose losses in dead and wounded reached 55,000 men. On November 8, the landing of American and British forces began in Morocco and Algeria. But, despite their superiority in manpower and equipment, the allies were only able to rout the enemy's Afrika Corps in May, taking 240,000 prisoners. In July and August 1943, the Anglo-American forces landed in Sicily, and in September in the Apennines. In July 1943, the government of Mussolini was overthrown, and in October Italy declared war on Germany (and was occupied by the Germans). The war in Southern Italy proceeded slowly; by winter the allies had entirely passed over to the defense. From the fall of 1942 in the Pacific Ocean the Americans had begun to go on the offensive against Japan and won a number of great naval battles.

Undoubtedly, the operations of the allies in Africa and the landing in Italy made a contribution to the completion of the war against fascism. Everyone understood that the fate of the war would be decided on the eastern front, and the North African and Italian theaters of military operations bore a distinctly secondary character. While only seventeen Italian and German divisions fought in Africa in 1942-43, on the eastern front 260 fascist divisions were fighting. More-

Library of Congress, Prints & Photographs Div, War Information Collection, LC-USZ62-104520

**Joseph Stalin, Franklin Roosevelt, and Winston Churchill
Teheran Conference, 1943**

over, from September 1942 to October 1943, Hitler (ignoring the operations of the allies) transferred forty-nine divisions from the west to the Soviet-German front! This process continued later. It is not surprising that in the first conference of the "Big Three," (Stalin, Roosevelt, and Churchill) in Teheran at the end of November and the beginning of December 1943 the problem of opening up a second front in Europe was decisive. As a result of the discussion the decision to land in France was made (Churchill insisted on the Balkans, wanting to cut the USSR out of Europe). It was planned for May 1944. At the Teheran Conference the fate of postwar Germany was also discussed. The allies insisted on her division. Stalin did not consent. The question of Poland's future boundaries was decided also.

The Victory over Fascism

On the eastern front, 1944 proceeded under the control of the overwhelming superiority of the Soviet Armed Forces and the realization of the largest strategic offensive operations on the entire length of the front. 6.3 million men, 5,300 tanks, and 10,200 planes participated. In January Soviet troops finally broke the siege of Leningrad and, having destroyed the German army group "North," drove its remnants into the Baltic states. An attack on the Ukraine was launched almost simultaneously. In the spring the Right-Bank Ukraine, Crimea, and Moldavia were liberated. Army group "South" was destroyed.

Under these favorable conditions, on June 6, 1944, the Anglo-American troops under the command of D. Eisenhower began the largest expeditionary operation in history through LeMans. Using their superiority of forces, they landed in France without much difficulty. At the same time the Soviet troops mounted a new strong attack. On June 10 it began in Karelia, on June 23 in Belorussia, and on July 13 in Western Ukraine. As a result of these operations the army group "center" was routed, and Belorussia, Western Ukraine, and the overwhelming part of the Baltic states were liberated. In the fall of 1944, the Soviet forces were waging war on the territory of Poland, Rumania, Czechoslovakia, and Norway. Rumania and Finland left the war and later declared war on Germany. As a result of the uprising of November 9, Bulgaria also freed herself from her profascist government and declared war on Germany.

The liberation campaign of the Soviet army in Eastern Europe, which kept expanding until the end of 1944, was gradually being transformed into a struggle for spheres of influence and could not help but aggravate the disagreements between the USSR, the United States, and Great Britain. According to the testimony of one of the Yugoslav Communist leaders, Milovan Djilas, Stalin candidly declared in one of his conversations with him that "everyone imposes his own social system wherever his army is able to advance." Roosevelt on the whole understood the aspirations of the Soviet leadership to form friendly governments in the countries that were neighbors of the USSR. At the same time Churchill was extremely upset by this. But in the autumn, he was able to conclude with Stalin a gentleman's agreement on the demarcation of spheres of influence in southeastern Europe (the so-called "percentage agreement"), which for the time being reduced the disagreements among the allies. In February 1945 at the conference at Yalta the big three generally agreed on the future of Europe.

Meanwhile the Anglo-American troops, having with great difficulty repelled the German's counteroffensive in the Ardennes at the end of 1944 and the beginning of 1945, went on the attack. In March they forced their way across the Rhine; in April they surrounded and then captured a large German unit in the Ruhr. Almost without encountering opposition, they began to advance to the East. These successes were conditioned by the fact that the main forces of fascist Germany were still concentrated on the eastern front. In January 1945, the Soviet troops began an offensive. Breaking the enemy's defense in February, they liberated Poland and Budapest and reached the Oder River, just sixty kilometers from Berlin. Berlin was surrounded on April 24; the fight for the streets had begun. Hitler ended his life by suicide on April 30, having named Admiral Doenitz as his successor. The latter's attempts to conclude a separate peace with the United States and Great Britain were unsuccessful. On May 7 at Reims the preliminary protocols of the capitulation were signed and on May 8 in Berlin, under the chairmanship of Marshal Zhukov, the document on the unconditional surrender of fascist Germany was signed. Meanwhile, having taken Berlin and seized 480,000 prisoners, the Soviet forces proceeded to the assistance of Prague, which had risen in revolt. Its liberation on May 9, 1945, was the real Victory Day for the peoples of the USSR.

The problems of the postwar organization of the world were discussed in detail at the Potsdam Conference in July and August 1945. Its decisions determined the fate of Europe for almost four and a half decades, laying the foundation for the geopolitical division of the continent and the entire world into the two blocs which were later formed under the leadership of the superpowers that had arisen during the war—the United States and the USSR. During this period the disagreements between the allies which had existed from the beginning became sharper, beginning the gradual disintegration of the anti-Hitler coalition. Ideological antagonisms did not cause this as much as the liquidation of the main factor which had caused the formation of the anti-Hitler bloc, namely the struggle for hegemony in Europe. The coming into office of President Harry Truman, who replaced Roosevelt after the latter's death in April, played a definite role. Besides this, the inertia of allied relations and the interest of the United States in the armed forces of the USSR for the struggle with Japan did not permit an open confrontation yet. The American War Secretary, G. Stimson, wrote to his own president that upon landing in Japan the American troops could expect a tougher battle than in Germany, and the expected losses could reach a million men. At the same time General D. MacArthur believed that the American forces should not land on the Japanese islands until the Russian army had begun to operate in Manchuria.

The Defeat of Japan

Fulfilling the obligations of an ally, the USSR in April 1945 denounced the neutrality treaty with Japan and on August 8 declared war on her. The next day Soviet troops under the command of Vasilevsky (1.8 million men, 5,000 tanks and 5,200 planes) began a swift offensive against the Kvantun army (800,000 men, 1,200 tanks, and 1,900 planes). Utilizing an overwhelming superiority in troops, weapons, and tanks, our forces in only three weeks completely defeated the Japanese, taking 600,000 prisoners and liberating China, North Korea, South Sakhalin, and the Kurile Islands.

On August 6 and 8 the Americans subjected Hiroshima and Nagasaki to atomic bombardment. The total number of casualties up to now has not been established. According to some estimates, it totaled 300,000 people. The use of atomic weapons against the Japanese cities was caused not only by military, but also by political considerations and most of all the urge to demonstrate (and to test in real conditions) the trump card to put pressure on the USSR. On September 2 in Tokyo Bay on board the American battleship "Missouri" the document on the unconditional surrender of Japan was signed. The Second World War, the bloodiest in the history of mankind, which had carried off more than fifty million people, ended six years and a day after its beginning.

For the peoples of the USSR the war cost at the very least twenty-seven million lives, of which civilians comprised the overwhelming part. The USSR lost approximately 30% of its national wealth. 1710 cities, more than 70,000 villages and 32,000 industrial enterprises were destroyed. On the whole the country was deprived of approximately half of its urban residences and nearly 30% of the homes of rural dwellers. 6,000 hospitals, 82,000 schools, and 43,000 libraries were annihilated. The production of grain was reduced to half, of meat to 45% in 1945.

This heavy price was the payment not only for the defeat of the best military machine in the world and for the fascist genocide, but also for the "expenses" of the totalitarian regime, which had not been able at the beginning of the war to effectively manage its own military potential and which right up to the final victorious days subordinated the people's losses to the attainment of its own purposes.

At the same time, all of the possibilities of the totalitarian regime were able to be realized in the war. Overcoming the original shock, the Stalinist regime was able to "build itself up" and utilize the supercentralized administration, the vast natural and human resources, the absence of personal freedom, the patriotism of the people, and finally the charisma of the leader to definitely direct all of the country's forces, to mobilize it for the struggle. The victory in the war was exploited for the "transference" of a similar system to other, contiguous countries.

Notes

[1] Of the major powers only Japan and Italy changed blocs (Italy from the pro-German to the anti-German in the First World War, Japan from the anti-German to the pro-German in the Second World War). Besides this one must consider that Japan was acting no so much as a participant in the blocs, but as a state following its own specific interests, which were outside of the basic conflict, which was going on in Europe. Italy was a member of the Triple Alliance up to the beginning of the First World War.

[2] Besides weapons and equipment Italy and Germany sent assistance to Franco's partisans in the form of 250,000 of their own soldiers and officers (while the republics of the USSR sent around 3000 "volunteers.")

[3] The fact of the existence of secret Soviet-German protocols was denied on the Soviet side up to the end of the 1980s. In later years the Gorbachev regime keep the existence of the original protocols from the society, claiming that they had not been preserved in the archives.

[4] Even the war with small (in comparison to the USSR) Poland required the concentration of the principal armed forces of Germany against it, while the losses suffered, costing up to 15-20% of the tank units, made a long period of reconstruction necessary. The German generals therefore opposed Hitler's efforts to begin the attack on the West in the fall of 1939. It began, as is well-known, only after eight months of "phony war" which Hitler used to elevate the combat readiness of the army and strengthen the economic potential for war.

[5] President Franklin Roosevelt recognized this immediately. In a congratulatory message sent to Stalingrad in the name of the American people, he expressed his admiration for the defenders of the city and observed that their victory "had stopped the tide of invasion and was the turning point of the war of the United nations against the forces of aggression."

Editor/translator's Note:

*The *sharashki* were workers in a shady enterprise or "mickey mouse office," the *sharahskina kontora*. See Stephen Marder, *A Supplementary Russian-English Dictionary*, 1992, 505.

CHAPTER 6

THE CLIMAX OF TOTALITARIANISM: THE USSR (1945-53)

From the Anti-Hitler Coalition to the Cold War

The Second World War fundamentally changed the situation in the world and the very climate of international relations. The victory over fascism joined the nations and dampened ideological disagreements. Relations between the allied powers seemed to have the character of a partnership, even a friendship. Between 1945 and 1948, as a result of the large-scale demobilization, the size of the armed forces in the United States was reduced from 12 to 1.6 million people, in the USSR from 11.4 to 2.9 million people. American military spending fell from 81.6 to 13.1 billion dollars; the share of military spending in the Soviet budget fell from 43% to 17.9%. The creation of the United Nations in San Francisco in April-June 1945 and the Nuremberg proceedings in 1945-46, which punished the German war criminals and demonstrated the relative unity of the victorious powers, instilled hope. The USSR's major contribution to the victory in Europe caused a wave of sympathy in the West, superseding dekulakization and the "great terror." The attitude toward the communist parties in the West softened, thanks to their selfless struggle with the fascists and the dissolution in 1943 of the Comintern. They were not seen as subversive organizations of the

Kremlin, and their membership grew 2.9 times between 1939 and 1946. In 1945-1947 Communists were in the government of thirteen "bourgeois" states in Europe, Asia, Latin America. In such states as Italy and France they were close to coming to power.

For the Soviet Union the war was the first opportunity to discover the West. Having been abroad for the first (and probably the last) time, millions of Soviet people (in the regular army—seven million in Europe, 1.5 million in the East and another 5.5 million repatriates) could see and compare the achievements of western civilization for themselves. The extensive cooperation with the "imperialist countries" in the struggle with a common enemy and the weakening of ideological manipulation during the war years weakened the old stereotypes and generated interest and sympathy for the West.

These changes at first suggested some hope of finally overcoming the schism in the world, creating a new harmonious system of international relations which would integrate the USSR and capitalist powers. But the hopes and changes in the consciousness of the masses did not form the future shape of the world; it was shaped by the interests of the leading powers instead.

The war radically changed the balance of power in the world. Thanks to its overwhelming economic strength (more than half of the world's industrial production, gold, and monetary reserves), to the creation of a first-class army, and an extensive military presence in the world (which seemed temporary then), the United States became the undisputed leader and chief architect of the postwar system of international relations. Germany and Japan disappeared from the ranks of the leading states for a long time, and the European states were weakened significantly by the war and later by the gradual breakup of the colonial empires. Burma, India, Indonesia, Lebanon, Syria, Ceylon (now Sri Lanka), and other countries had received independence by the early fifties.

The USSR's military and political influence also grew. It not only emerged from its international isolation but also became recognized as a great power, playing one of the key roles in international affairs. The number of countries with which the Soviet Union had diplomatic relations doubled in comparison to the prewar period from 26 to 52. Together with the United States, Great Britain,

France, and China, it became one of the five permanent members of the United Nations Security Council. In the general context of postwar territorial changes, the great powers recognized the right of the USSR to part of East Prussia, Southern Sakhalin, the Kurile Islands, and the need for a military presence in China. Even more important was the recognition of Soviet interests in Eastern Europe which was confirmed at the Yalta and Potsdam conferences. The powerful Soviet military, political, and economic influence took shape when the Red Army liberated those regions (and also North China and Korea) from fascism and Japanese militarism. So by the end of the Second World War one could see the outline of the two new "super-powers" and their potential blocs.

With the disappearance of the deadly threat of fascism, which had rallied the world's nations, the inherent inconsistencies within the anti-Hitler coalition and the geopolitical interests of the participating states led to the breakup of the coalition and a new split into two hostile blocs. Since the principal changes in the balance of power after the war were incomplete and had not assumed their final shape, the great powers tried to tilt the unstable balance to their advantage.

Although the inertia of allied relations kept them together until 1947, as early as the spring of 1945 the lack of unanimity between the USSR and the other participants in the anti-Hitler coalition was clearly visible in their struggle for geopolitical supremacy and, most of all, in the division of Europe. The disagreements became so severe that the possibility of a military conflict emerged. Prime Minister Winston Churchill ordered Field Marshal Bernard Montgomery, the commander of British troops in Germany, to collect German weapons to arm the German prisoners in case the Russians continued their march further to the West. As early as the autumn of 1945 the strategic military and intelligence agencies of the United States were beginning to work out plans for a future war after changing their estimate of the USSR's military potential. The Joint Committee on War Planning on December 14, 1945, (N 432/D) suggested a plan for bombing the basic industrial centers of the USSR. 196 nuclear bombs were to be dropped on twenty Soviet cities. The plans were continually updated and acquired a massive character.

The American and British leadership justified these steps on the grounds that (1) the USSR had ignored some of the Yalta and Potsdam decisions, such as the obligation to organize free elections in Poland and other East European countries, and (2) the strong Red Army which stood in the center of Europe, ready to attack the allies and quickly reach the English Channel and Pyrenees, posed a threat. Speaking on March 5, 1946, at Fulton, Missouri, in the presence of President Harry S. Truman, Churchill for the first time openly blamed the USSR for having fenced in Eastern Europe with an iron curtain and called for organized pressure against the Soviet Union to obtain foreign policy concessions and domestic changes. It was essentially a call for an open and tough confrontation with the Soviet Union. A year later Truman officially announced the obligations of the United States to Europe which were directed toward the universal "containment" of Soviet expansionism.

We have no documents confirming the USSR's readiness to attack its allies in Europe at the end of the war or soon after it. Probably such documents do not exist at all. But there is V.M. Molotov's sincere belief that Stalin knowingly refused to carry out certain obligations of the USSR as an ally, merely orienting itself to the balance of forces, and that the foreign minister's main task was the extension "of the boundaries of our Motherland." In Molotov's opinion, the "tough" Churchill and not the "soft" Roosevelt accurately evaluated the foreign policy strategy of the USSR.[1]

Still Stalin's main goal was not territorial claims. Despite the "boldness" of his demands (the USSR claimed Iranian Azerbaijan, part of Turkish Armenia, control over the Black Sea straits, and even Libya!), the goal was to sound out the firmness of the West's position. In Europe, Soviet attention was concentrated on the construction of its own socialist bloc which was considered the main achievement after the October Revolution in Russia. The growing confrontation with the West, in many respects, grew out of and at the same time accelerated this process.

Taking advantage of the mistakes of Western foreign policy during the war, such as its slowness in understanding Stalin's real intentions and its insufficiently firm position, the Soviet Union was taking positive steps to confirm its influence in Eastern Europe. The Soviet leadership and the military administration in those countries

THE CLIMAX OF TOTALITARIANISM   235

supported procommunist forces, including the physical (often perfidious) destruction of the opposition leaders as, for example, in Poland. The Eastern European countries were already dependent on the USSR before 1945. Under its growing control they coordinated their foreign and their domestic policy to restore the economy. Stalin did not always use coercion to introduce the Soviet system. In Yugoslavia, for example, the new power base formed during the struggle against the German occupation and the Communists were essentially the only national organizations capable of forming a new type of state. A similar situation existed in Albania and, partially, in Bulgaria. In 1945-1947, as a rule, not purely Communist but coalition governments existed in Eastern Europe. The open introduction of Communist power and the formation of the Soviet bloc paralleled the growing confrontation with the West.

1947 was the turning point. In that year the USSR refused the Marshal Plan for itself and for Eastern Europe, although it (and most Eastern European states, with the exception of Yugoslavia) had been inclined to accept before 1947. In the fall of 1947 the Information Bureau of Communist and Workers' Parties (Cominform) was set up as a sort of successor to the Comintern, which Stalin had decided in the summer of 1946 not to restore because of the danger of Western sanctions. Also in 1947, on Moscow's orders, Communist governments were established in Eastern Europe (in Czechoslovakia—in 1948). These steps, as well as the break with Yugoslavia (whose leader Joseph Broz Tito wanted comparative independence), the division of Germany, and the formation of the Council of Economic Assistance (Comecon) in 1949 were the landmarks in the development of the Soviet bloc. And, of course, the Western, pro-American bloc was formed at the same time.

At the end of the 1940s and the beginning of the 1950s major political trials occurred in these Eastern European countries, during which prominent politicians were accused of state treason and sentenced to death. Among the Communist leaders whose reliability was doubted by the Soviet leadership were Wladyslaw Gomulka (Poland), Laslo Raik, Janush Kadar (Hungary), Traicho Kostov (Bulgaria), Jan Klementis, Rudolph Slansky (Czechoslovakia) and Anna Pauker (Rumania). These purges were directed at the removal of the slightest deviation among the leaders of the Communist party and state. The people who came to power unconditionally supported the political line of the Soviet Union. In addition, the acts of repression and the public trials were a weapon of influence over the masses to instill fear and to suppress freedom. The imposition of Communism cost Eastern Europe dearly. According to recent evidence, in Eastern Germany more than 122,000 persons were repressed between 1945 and 1950, in Poland around 300,000 between 1944 and 1948, and in Czechoslovakia around 150,000 between 1948 and 1954. In the Polish People's Republic in 1953 the apparatus of political repression grew in comparison to prewar Poland by 1000%, reaching 325,000. There was one informant for every 250 people in Poland while in the German Democratic Republic one for every eighty people.[2]

The military-political alliance of the states of central and southeastern Europe, headed by the Soviet Union, opposed the alliance of the countries of Western Europe and North America headed by the United States. On April 4, 1949, the latter alliance was legally formed by the signing of the agreement on the creation of the North Atlantic Treaty Organization (NATO). The treaty participants did not conceal their orientation against the Soviet Union and the countries of the Soviet bloc. Thus, the military organization of the North Atlantic Treaty came into existence and American troops in Europe became a reality for an indefinite time. Dozens of military bases were erected along the borders of the Soviet Union. Essentially, the steps taken in these years which were supposed to integrate the western zones of Germany into the European state system gave the green light to the rearmament of Germany.

The growing international confrontation and, to some extent, the economic difficulties caused by the sudden reduction in military spending and the conversion of production to peacetime accelerated the movement to the right in the domestic policies of the great powers. In May 1947 Communists were removed from the French and Italian governments. But the domestic policy of the United States became especially firm. On March 22, 1947, Truman signed an order for the examination of the loyalty of government workers. Lists of "subversive organizations" were made; for membership in these organizations people were fired and subjected to social ostracism. The House of Representatives' Committee for the Investigation of Anti-American Activity started pursuing Communists and others who simply had leftist views. On June 23, 1947, the Congress approved the Taft-Hartly Act that seriously restricted strikes and trade union activities. The judicial pursuit of the leadership of the American Communist Party began in 1948. The strength of the anti-Communist war hysteria and espionage rapidly changed people's attitudes. The number of survey respondents who believed that a new war was inevitable rose from 3% in 1946 to 32% in 1948.

The Korean War (which cost America 54,000 lives) escalated the United States' struggle against the Soviet Bloc. In 1950, Senator McCarthy started his active search for "Red" (Communist), "pink," and other disloyal officials in government circles, in trade unions, and in the intellectual community. The survey of a reporter from a local newspaper in Madison, Wisconsin, shows how much stress the Americans were under. During the course of the questioning, all but one of the 112 respondents were afraid to sign some selected paragraphs from the Bill of Rights because they considered them Communist propaganda.[3] Although the scale and severity of the repression was much smaller (140 American Communist party leaders were arrested and 400 foreign Communists were expelled between 1948 and 1954), the "witch hunt" in the United States and Eastern bloc countries had several common aims connected with the reorientation of social consciousness and preparations for armed conflict.

International relations involved more than propaganda campaigns and acute polemics in the United Nations. The Berlin crisis broke out in 1948 and continued for about a year. It brought the opposing states close to a military conflict. In 1946-1949 there was a civil war in Greece in which Great Britain, Yugoslavia, and Bulgaria actively interfered. Germany became the victim of confrontation when it was broken into two states in 1949: the Federal Republic of Germany and the German Democratic Republic. The attempts of the victorious powers to work out some common principles in relation to Germany finally failed in 1951-1952.

The Soviet Union, which created a bloc of European states under its aegis, was guided by its security interests and by the creation of firm guarantees in the event of an armed conflict with any of the great powers. But Stalin's imperial expansionist plans were of primary importance. He proceeded from the firm conviction that there would be armed conflict with the United States.

By the end of the forties the attention of the Soviet government was slowly turning to the East. The completion of the basic division of Europe and the final confirmation of Soviet hegemony over the countries of central and southeastern Europe facilitated this; so did the formation of the Communist regimes in North Korea and especially in China where the Chinese People's Republic was proclaimed on October 1, 1949, after a long civil war.

These conditions opened up the possibility for the Soviet bloc and China to change the balance of world power to their own advantage. At the end of the forties world socialism embraced more than a third of the planet's population and 26% of its land area. Relying on the strength of this alliance and the support of the international Communist movement, the leaders of the bloc believed that they had been given an opportunity to consider the question of liquidating the opposing military and political camp headed by the United States through military means.

Stalin remarked during a reception for the Soviet delegation in Yugoslavia in April 1945 that after its inevitable defeat, Germany would recover quickly in twelve to fifteen years. He categorically stated: "The war will soon be over, we will have recovered in fifteen to twenty years, and then again!" One of the witnesses of the scene, the Yugoslav Communist leader Milovan Djilas, said: "There was something horrible in his words: the cruel war was still going on. On the other hand one could not but be impressed with his confidence in choosing the direction to go, his realization of the inevitable future that was in store for the world where he lived and the movement that he headed."[4]

So Stalin was sure that military conflict was unavoidable and necessary and was consciously preparing for it. Five years after the end of the world war the dictator's decision to cut short the time before the expected beginning of the new war became clear. He liked accelerating events and it is probable that the condition of his health, his analysis of the combat readiness of both sides, and the feeling of superiority so important for victory pushed him to the final decision. He realized that the people and society had not had time to become "soft" and relax after the Great Patriotic War; it was a significant advantage for the USSR that he did not want to lose.

1949 is known for the serious steps taken by the United States to prepare for a possible military conflict. In that year the United States adopted the "Dropshot" plan outlining massive nuclear attacks against the Soviet Union in 1957 and its subsequent occupation by the combined armed forces of the Allies. The "Dropshot" plan was based on the assumption that the United States would retain a nuclear monopoly for a relatively long period of time. But contrary to the prognosis, the monopoly was already lost by 1949.

The end of the nuclear monopoly of the United States changed the entire geopolitical situation and the balance of power between the great powers. After talks with Mao Tse-tung in February 1950, Stalin agreed to North Korea's attempt to "reunify" the country by military means. Under the flag of the United Nations, troops from the United States and fifteen other countries became involved in the armed conflict in which Chinese troops and Soviet airmen and advisers also participated on the side of North Korea. During the battles the scales tilted both ways. When there was a threat that the American forces, which had been driven back toward Pusan, would be thrown into the sea, Stalin sent a secret message to Mao Tse-tung: "America's defeat is unacceptable." Having strained international tension to the limit, Stalin decided it was impossible to use the full strength of the USSR and China in an armed conflict in Korea. He thought of it as sort of a proving ground for the combined operations of Chinese soldiers and Soviet military hardware.

Stalin believed that the time for a direct conflict between the Soviet Union and United States had not yet arrived. He hoped for a success in the development and stockpiling of nuclear weapons and for the rapid development of jet aviation and missiles which would more effectively resolve the problem of the delivery of nuclear weapons. The huge expenditure of manpower and diplomatic maneuvering occupied an important place in the strategic plans of the Soviet and Chinese leaderships.

Stalin's statements at the end of 1952 that a war between the capitalist countries because of the "irreconcilable contradictions of imperialism" was more probable than an armed conflict between the Soviet and American blocks perplexed world public opinion and diplomacy. These statements were a kind of "smoke screen" to cover the USSR's military preparations and calm public opinion in Western Europe and the United States. Moreover, in his December 24, 1952, interview with the *New York Times* Stalin expressed his readiness for cooperation and diplomatic actions by the United States and Soviet Union, among other things, to end the Korean War.

All of the attention of world opinion and NATO military planning was focused on armed conflict in Europe. Here serious conflicts had occurred and here everyone expected the main strike, including the possibility of powerful tank and aviation attacks in the center of Europe. There had never been a single conflict on the immediate Soviet-American border in the region of the Bering Strait and Alaska.

But the armed forces of the Soviet Union were not only increased in Europe. Since the early fifties military bases and air fields quickly rose on Chukotka, Kamchatka, and on the coast of the Arctic ocean, that is, comparatively close to Alaska. Stalin exercised personal control over the construction of new military machines capable of operating in the tundra and forest-tundra.

In spring 1952, to the surprise of the air force high command, Stalin decided on the formation of a hundred new divisions of jet bombers. The high command thought that sixty were enough in case of war. More than 10,000 bombers above the production plan had to be built in the shortest possible time. Life was assuming a wartime rhythm once more. This affected other branches of military production. Active preparation for the coming war began not only in Europe but close to the American border. A war in Alaska posed for America the direct threat of air strikes and an invasion of land forces. Mankind was on the brink of the Third World War with all of its monstrous consequences.

As early as the 1930s Stalin had extricated himself from having to inform anybody of his plans or having to explain his decisions and actions. He made all the key decisions unilaterally. They were never set down on paper in any complete form, and the motives for them were never clearly known. All of Stalin's long-term military intentions were kept secret even from the high command. There was much conjecture about Stalin's intentions during the last years of his life. One thing is certain. He did not merely react to the events which were unfolding in the world, but he acted with firm conviction and a general plan. A new world war was part of the design, to all outward appearances.

The Reconstruction of the Economy of the USSR and the Choice of an Economic Development Model

The USSR paid a high price for the victory over fascism. The storms of war raged over the main regions of the most developed part of the Soviet Union for several years. The majority of the industrial centers of the European part of the country were attacked. The flames of war also engulfed the major grain-producing areas—Ukraine, Northern Caucasus, and a significant part of the Volga region. So much was destroyed that reconstruction could last many years, even decades.

About 32,000 industrial enterprises lay in ruins. On the eve of the war they provided the country with 70% of its steel production, 60% of its coal. 65,000 kilometers of railways were out of order. About half of the urban residences and 30% of the rural dwellings were destroyed. In 1945 the production of grain was half, of meat 45%, of the prewar figures. But by far heavier was the loss of people's lives. Practically every Soviet family lost somebody in the war.

The postwar devastation and the hardships of rebuilding the economy were aggravated by the severe drought of 1946. From starvation (which was not officially recognized) and illness around a million people died.[5] But the export of grain was not stopped. The consequences of this included the further deterioration of the peasant's farms. The conditions of life in the village became even more difficult, but the collective farmer was unable to leave the collective farm legally without the special permission of the authorities. The consequences of the drought of 1946 were aggravated by the government's policy in the village which basically considered the farm as a source for the accumulation of savings for the reconstruction of the towns and industry. The poverty-stricken peasants were ignored. The country needed changes: renovation of the system, more freedom for people, and favorable social conditions for freer life, creative work, and increased well-being.

Unlike the countries of the West, who received nearly 13 billion dollars from the Marshal Plan, the USSR relied on its own resources to restore its economy. German reparations played an important role, financing about half of the new industrial equipment (worth 4.3 billion dollars) and accelerating scientific and technological progress in several branches.[6] But the majority of this equipment was obsolete, and the considerable assistance rendered by the USSR to the socialist countries sharply reduced the balance between the import and export of resources.

Only the efforts of millions of people could restore the devastated towns and factories and rebuild the infrastructure. The labor of the Soviet people was sincere and honest; they managed to live with the difficulties which characterized their existence.

Thanks to the people's unselfish labor and the general concentration of resources in the restoration of heavy industry, the volume of industrial output reached the prewar level in 1948. (By comparison, Great Britain reached this level in 1947; in France 1948, in West Germany 1950).

The harvests of 1947 and 1948 somewhat improved the supply of food for the population of the country. At the end of 1947 the card system for rationing food and consumer goods was canceled and a monetary reform was implemented which reduced the amount of money in circulation. Although it was a hardship for the population, it promoted the stabilization of the country's financial situation. Consumer goods prices fell by 80% between 1947 and 1950. Later on this process took on a life of its own and was remembered by the people as "Stalin's policy of constant retail price reductions."

During the transition from war to peace the problem concerning the path of the country's future economic development, of its structure and administrative system, was resolved. The matter not only concerned the conversion from wartime to peacetime production, but also the expediency of preserving the economic model which had already taken shape. That model was formed during the extraordinary conditions that had prevailed at the end of the 1920s and in the 1930s. The coercive aspects of the existing economic model were displayed during the war years, especially the very high mobilization potential, the ability within a short time to organize the mass production of high-quality weapons and to secure the resources needed by the army and the VPK (the military-industrial complex, *voennyi promyshlennyi kompleks*), at the expense of the remaining sectors of the economy. But the war with all its force underscored the weakness of the Soviet economy: the high relative weight of manual labor and the low productivity and quality of nonmilitary production. What was bearable in wartime required resolution in peacetime.

So the question was whether the state should return to the prewar economic model with its hypertrophic military sectors, the unrestricted planning in detail of the activities of every enterprise, the complete absence of any of the elements of market exchange, and strict control over the work of management.

After the war, some of the party economists and managers wanted to reorganize the managerial system, to soften the features that restrained the initiative and independence of the enterprise, and in particular to reduce the degree of hypercentralization which was suppressing the initiative and autonomy of individual enterprises. Some suggested that some elements of market relations and a private sector in the area of service and small-scale production could be officially sanctioned. Ordinary citizens sent similar proposals to the central organs. The President of the Council of Ministers of the RSFSR, M.I. Rodionov, and a number of other party and soviet leaders, including those at the regional level, came out in favor of softening the harshness of the administration.

One may look for an explanation of these ideas in the conditions which took shape during the war. With the conversion of the work of the basic branches of industry to secure the requirements of the front, the output of peacetime production fell sharply. Local authorities began to be predominantly occupied with protecting the lives of the people, with supplying consumer goods and services, organizing small-scale production, drawing handicraft workers and artisans into the production of consumer goods. A cottage industry developed as a result, bringing private trade to life not only in the production of foodstuffs but also in the production of consumer goods.

The war taught many managers at all levels to exercise a definite amount of independence and initiative. After the war local authorities attempted to develop consumer goods production not only in small workshops but in big enterprises directly controlled by central ministries. In 1948, the Russian Federation Council of Ministers together with the Leningrad region authorities organized a fair in the city in which enterprises from Russia, Ukraine, Belorussia, Kazakhstan, and other republics sold materials surplus to them. The fair opened up the possibility of establishing independent economic ties between the industrial enterprises, excluding the center, and partially expanding the sphere of activity of market relations.

Such ideas influenced the USSR's State Planning Commission which was headed by N.A. Voznesensky. There were indications in the plan drawn up for the period between 1945 and 1950 which opened up the prospect of developing the basic branches of the economy without undue restraint, reserving some independence for individual enterprises and the industrial sectors. But the hopes for managerial reform were unrealized.

At the end of the forties the former policy of accelerating industrial development by strengthening the administrative-command method of management was resumed.

To understand the choice one should realize the dual task of the USSR economy. From the very beginning it was oriented to function under wartime conditions. All the plants built before the war had simultaneous civilian and military profiles. Therefore, the selection of an economic model rested on one key question: whether the economy was going to be a peacetime one or remain a two-faced Janus as before—a peacetime economy in words and a wartime one in fact.

All the attempts at changes went against the logic of the cold war that had developed in the world and stumbled on the imperial ambitions of Stalin. As a result the Soviet economy returned to the prewar model.

Despite the partial conversion of the war industry, the military-industrial complex experienced further development. Huge resources were concentrated on the completion of the atomic project supervised by the all-powerful L.P. Beria. Thanks to the efforts of Soviet scientists and the secret service which was able to steal important atomic secrets from the Americans, the A-bomb was created in the USSR in an incredibly short time in 1949. And in 1953 the Soviet Union became the first country in the world to create a thermonuclear bomb. The thirty-two year old academician A.D. Sakharov was one of its fathers.

The realization of the nuclear project demanded new production sites and industries, even some general economic restructuring. Uranium mines were needed and plants to manufacture enriched uranium began to operate in the Urals. The machine tool industry, which was responsible for the rapid realization of the nuclear project, was practically built anew. Great strides were made in electrification which insured the priority supply of power to the factories involved in the nuclear project and in military programs.[7]

Immediately after the war technical rearmament took place in the army which was saturated with the newest type of aircraft, small arms, artillery, and tanks. The creation of jet aviation and missiles for all of the branches of the armed services required great efforts. Tactical and then strategic and antiaircraft defense missiles were developed in a short time.

Under the most difficult postwar conditions, the expansion of the military production, to which the rest of industry was subordinated, created an imbalance in the development of the economy. Military production, which sharply limited the prospects for raising the people's standard of living, was a heavy burden for the country's economy. But Stalin thought it was necessary to accelerate the pace of industrial and military development. In 1949, the head of Gosplan, Voznesensky, was blamed for the low expectations of the plan for the reconstruction and development of the economy between 1945 and 1950. Voznesensky was tried and executed. And in the same year, on Stalin's order but without evaluating the real prospects for the country's development, new targets were determined for the basic branches of industry. These arbitrary decisions exerted extreme pressure on the economy and slowed its rate of growth which depressed the people's standard of living once again.

By means of political and administrative pressure and the ideological stimulation of labor, 6,200 industrial enterprises were restored or built between 1946 and 1950 (by comparison 9,000 enterprises were put into operation between 1928 and 1941), but the price was the unconcealed robbery of light industry and agriculture. According to official data, industrial output in 1950 exceeded the prewar level by 73%. The output of heavy industry increased by 200%, while light and food industry increased only by 23%. But agriculture did not even reach its prewar level; according to the Five Year Plan it should have increased by 27%. Antiquated methods and an unwillingness to embark on any kind of reform which would have weakened the government's harsh control were especially painful for the peasants. In general the government relied on noneconomic coercion. Each peasant had to perform a definite amount of work on the collective farm. For failure to fulfill his quota, the collective farmer could be deprived of his freedom or his personal plot of land around the house (*pridebnyi uchastok*) which, as a rule, was his primary source of sustenance. The government decrees of 1946 set up strict dimensions for plots around the peasant's house which had been enlarged somewhat during the war years because of the opening up of empty lands.

The "violations of the statute on the agrarian artel" was announced for the purpose of reallocating resources away from agriculture and tightening the control over collective farmers by reducing the dimensions of the private plots of the rural residents. A policy of transforming the collective farms (formally agrarian cooperatives) into state enterprises was adopted.

The situation in agriculture significantly complicated the supply of provisions for the population and of raw materials for light industry. Even though the food ration was especially severe for the people, the government of the Soviet Union exported grain and other agrarian products, especially to the countries of central and southeastern Europe, who had begun "to build socialism."

The meager resources allotted in the budget did not permit the implementation of extensive social development projects. The stan-

THE CLIMAX OF TOTALITARIANISM 247

Soviet collective farming, ca. 1955

dard of living in the towns in 1928, which was close to the 1913 level, was only reached again in 1954. Nonetheless, compulsory primary education was restored and steps were taken to introduce compulsory but incomplete secondary education. By comparison, in the leading Western European countries, the transition was made at the end of the nineteenth and beginning of the twentieth centuries. The number of educational institutions was considerably increased, and measures were taken to strengthen and expand the network of preschool institutions. The system of rest homes, sanitariums, and health resorts was reestablished and expanded. But housing construction developed very slowly in spite of the housing crisis.

The previous management model was implemented with even greater severity than it had been during the years of the prewar five year plans. Consistent with Stalin's plan, a society characterized by the elimination of market relations and the complete subordination of the individual to the political and administrative authorities was finally achieved.

Grandiose projects for building huge electric power stations on the Volga and Dnieper were proposed in the early fifties, as well as canals in the Kara-Kum desert and between the Volga and the Don rivers. These projects diverted vast resources, drained the government's already meager treasury, and introduced new tension into society by reducing the standard of living and ruining agriculture. Russian peasants did their best to leave the village by getting jobs in the towns at new building sites.

Looking for a way out of the crisis, the Soviet leadership tried again to broaden the use of forced labor. The amount of work carried out in the GULAG, the system of labor camps where the imprisoned worked, grew by several times after the war. They built, but did not finish, the Baikal-Amur Railway from Lake Baikal to the shores of the Pacific Ocean and the Northern Railway along the coast of the Arctic ocean from Salekhard to Norilsk. Nuclear industry units, metallurgical enterprises, and electric power stations were built. According to the only available documents, the number of people imprisoned in the camps and colonies of the GULAG between 1945 and 1953 grew from 1.5 to 2.5 million, and this does not include convicts in prisons and so forth. According to some estimates, as a result of the postwar wave of repression, the total number of prisoners and convicts reached 5.5 to 6.5 million people.[8]

The system of political repression and the expansion of criminal punishments were used to suppress the regime's opponents and to utilize a cheap labor force in industry, especially in the uninhabited regions. In the long run, such labor was not economical and the system of concentration camps did not justify itself as a reserve labor force, but the system was an important lever for the political regime.

The Time of Unrealized Hopes

The Soviet people, who had suffered the privations of the prewar years and the unprecedented burdens of the war years, hoped that the victory they had attained through so much work and sacrifice would fundamentally change the life of the people for the better. The world changed in front of the eyes of the Soviet people and they were full of hope that these changes would affect their lives too. Their aspirations were not limited to the improvement of their material welfare, which was undoubtedly their main priority; they believed the need for political and ideological restrictions would end, too. Rumors circulated among the people about the future breakup of the collective farms. The intelligentsia hoped for the weakening of ideological control over society and increased prospects for creative endeavors.

As the leader of the Soviet state, Joseph Stalin, appealed to the citizens of his country, to his "brothers and sisters" as he called them, for help and support in the difficult moment of the catastrophic defeats of 1941. The people answered the appeal and after the victory had the right to expect a corresponding response from "brother Stalin."

Not only ordinary workers but a layer of political and industrial managers placed their hopes on the relaxation of the extreme measures that existed in industry and agriculture during the prewar and war years. Everybody expected a decline in the physical, ideological, and political tension. During the (closed) discussion of the projects for a new Constitution for the USSR and the Communist Party Program, many progressive proposals were made by the workers in the nomenkaltura: the decentralization of management, the liquidation of the wartime courts and tribunals, the expansion of internal party democracy, and the preparation of rules for the rotation of cadres.[9] But Stalin did not choose to make concessions. New acts of repression were his answer to the people's hopes and aspirations for democracy and freedom.

With the return to peacetime labor the authorities tightened their control over all areas of intellectual life. Between 1946 and 1948, Communist Party regulations were adopted which imposed strict ideological control over the creative intelligentsia, especially in literature, drama, theater, and music. "Discussions," which resembled a pogrom, began in 1947 in philosophy, biology, linguistics, and political economy. The campaigns that followed one another were directed against the influence of Western ideology, against any sign of originality, independent thought, or creativity. Such outstanding figures as the writer M. Zoschenko, poetess A. Akhmatova, the composers D. Shostakovich, Yu. Shaporin, S. Prokofiev, the producer S.

Eizenstein, and others were persecuted. Some of them were expelled from their professional associations, and their activity was severely restricted or stopped altogether. Some scholars and even whole branches of science suffered. Essentially, genetics was ruined while such sciences as cybernetics and psychology were considered "bourgeois."

The loud ideological campaigns were accompanied by the actions of the security organs whose activities remained secret and were not publicized. Mass arrests gripped the country.

Between 1945 and 1948 a broad wave of repression was conducted against those people who had been in fascist prisons during the war. (Of the 5.7 million Soviet prisoners of war, 3.3 million or 57.8% perished.) Hundreds of thousands of people who were liberated from camps by the Red Army and those who were liberated earlier and managed to participate in battle were sent to prison or exile again. It was done to terrify those who might prefer imprisonment to death in the next armed conflict. Besides, Stalin believed that the prisoners' return to their families and work collectives would cause undesirable attitudes. The stories about the circumstances of their being taken prisoners would restore the tragic events of the beginning of the war to the people's memory and would cause them to discuss the causes and authors of the catastrophe of 1941 and 1942. Stalin preferred to make a large number of those unfortunate people who suffered the horror of the Hitler camps suffer years of slave labor and torture again, deprived of their freedom and separated for many years from their families and friends. Other prisoners of war were accused or suspected of collaboration with the German authorities in the prisoner of war camps. Among those were many people who did some work for the service of their own comrades in the camp. And, finally, everyone who joined the army units who fought the Soviet Army on the side of Germany were court-martialed.

Harsh punishments were given to civilians who collaborated with the German occupation authorities in one way or another. These punishments were not only inflicted on those whose guilt was proven but on those who were only suspected of collaboration. The number of people convicted from this population group was large. Some of

THE CLIMAX OF TOTALITARIANISM   251

them were sent into exile without any trial or investigation, merely on an order from the security organs.

On February 21, 1948, the government decided that everyone who had served time in prison after the "great terror" of the thirties should be sentenced again or sent into perpetual exile. Even the victims' children who had come of age by that time were included. The prisons were full again; multiple columns of prisoners were taken to the North, to Siberia, and to the Kolima peninsula.

To some extent the acts of repression, which assumed a special scope after 1948, were generated by the growing dissatisfaction of the population between 1946 and 1947. After the victory the people saw that everything remained as it was and there was almost no improvement in life. The revocation of the ration cards, the monetary reform, and the reduction of the size of the private plots caused the situation to deteriorate again. Many did not want to put up with it. The security organs discovered those who had sharply criticized the highest leaders and at times expressed doubt about the legitimacy of the Soviet government's policy. According to a well-known Russian writer Varlam Shalamov, who suffered though the horrors of the GULAG, "those who remembered the wrong things from modern history were imprisoned." But few were critical of Stalin or of socialism. In 1946-1948, underground youth groups appeared in some places. In the secret meetings, these young idealists, who had grown up during the war and were less burdened by stereotypes, were trying to discuss the basis for the construction of a just socialist society and condemned Stalin's policy. Such groups existed in Moscow, Voronezh, Sverdlovsk [Ekaterinburg] and Leningrad [St Petersburg]. Their participants were sentenced to long years of imprisonment in the GULAG.

The early postwar years witnessed a cruel repression of nationalistic underground groups in the country's western regions, especially in the Ukraine and the Baltic region. The nationalist movement was so strong that it took the form of armed resistance, and for a long time it was difficult to cope with since it relied on the support of part of the local population. The members of the underground movement used bloody reprisals to subjugate all of the local population, sparing neither children nor the elderly. Every form of collaboration with the Soviet power, every refusal to participate in armed conflicts against Soviet power and the Soviet Army was punished with bloody revenge. The security forces of the Soviet Union just as mercilessly punished not only the armed insurgents but also those who had given any support to them.

The movement was generally suppressed by the 1950s. Its participants, members of armed groups, and the part of the population accused of supporting the armed underground were either subjected to imprisonment in the GULAG or sent into exile in the northern regions or to Siberia. By this time, the review of the cases of former prisoners of war and those people who were condemned again after the conclusion of their punishment on the basis of the verdicts of the 1930s was completed.

But even then peace did not come to the Soviet land. The campaign against the "cosmopolitans," against "those who admire everything foreign," began in 1948. In January 1949, a large group of theatrical critics were accused in print of antipatriotism, of trying to denigrate the success of the Soviet people, to slander it. The campaign against antipatriotism and cosmopolitanism rapidly embraced all spheres of social life. It was soon clear that the term "cosmopolitanism" only concealed the true intention of the campaign. The term "cosmopolitans without a family" referred to the Jewish population of the country. The campaign was intended to "brainwash" the population, to prepare it ideologically for more severe measures than discussions in print or at meetings. Open discrimination and the restriction of the rights of persons of Jewish nationality, the humiliation and abuse of the "cosmopolitans without kith or kin" in print, were accompanied by increased measures of repression.

In January 1948, state security agents in Minsk murdered the outstanding actor S. Mikhoels who was the Chairman of the Jewish Antifascist Committee. The committee was set up during the war years to mobilize the Jewish population of the country in the struggle against the enemy. Prominent scientists, writers, actors, political figures, engineers, and physicians were among the committee members. The authorities highly appreciated their work. The committee was in touch with progressive circles in other countries, especially in the United States.

At the beginning of 1949, all the committee members were arrested, including Deputy Foreign Minister S.A. Lozovsky, academician L.S. Stern, the writers and poets P. Markish, L. Kvitko, D. Bergelson, D. Hofstein, S.Z. Galkin, and S.D. Persov. The number of arrests grew. Investigators of the Ministry of State Security (MGB, later the KGB) were continually looking for prominent Jews who could be represented as important figures of "the anti-Soviet underground." The state security organs were gathering evidence on "the nationalist activity" of V.M. Molotov (his wife, P. Zhemchuzhina, a Jew by nationality, was arrested and sentenced), L.M. Kaganovich, and the author I. Erenburg.

Antisemitism became an open state policy. The victory in the war contributed to the growth of the Soviet people's patriotism, and their pride in their own power. Stalin skillfully played on those feelings, turning them into a tool for the further ideological indoctrination of the population.

A large group of generals were arrested in the second half of the forties. Their number included the closest colleagues of Marshal G.K. Zhukov. Zhukov himself was dismissed from the post of Deputy Defense Minister and sent to command the military district at Odessa. Air Marshal Novikov, Minister Shakhurin, and a number of the leaders of the aviation industry were imprisoned.

The acts of repression also touched some of the party functionaries. Stalin was afraid of their aspirations for independence and for greater autonomy from the central authorities. Attempting to nip their aspirations in the bud, Stalin chose the Leningrad organization of Communists for an example. It had always aroused Stalin's annoyance with its search for independence, its sense of its own self-importance, and the high qualifications of its managerial cadres and party functionaries. Early in 1948 almost all of the Leningrad party officials were arrested on the accusation of trying to establish a separate Russian Communist Party in opposition to the All-Union Communist Party and to transfer the capital of the Russian Federation to Leningrad. Some time later the same thing happened to the Russian Federation Council of Ministers chairman, M. Rodionov, Politburo member and USSR Gosplan head Voznesensky, and All-Union Communist Party Central Committee secretary A. Kuznetsov. All of them were convicted and executed in 1950.

This was not the first cadre shake-up undertaken by Stalin after the war. In 1946, he sent G. Malenkov, who was a prominent figure among the Soviet leadership, into exile in Central Asia. Malenkov had been responsible for all personnel questions. After him A. Kuznetsov (up to that time first secretary of the Leningrad regional party committee) and N. Patolichev (first secretary of the Cheliabinsk regional party committee) handled personnel problems. At the same time the leaders of the central committees of Belorussia, P. Ponomarenko, and Ukraine, N. Khrushchev, were dismissed from their posts. Gusarov, who had worked before this as secretary of the Perm regional party committee, and L. Kaganovich, the former Deputy Chairman of the USSR Council of Ministers and Politburo member, were designated as their respective replacements.

Some time later G. Malenkov was pardoned and returned to his former job. Kaganovich was returned to Moscow and N. Khrushchev was given his post again. A high position in Moscow was designated for P. Ponomarenko.

Such shake-ups and acts of repression were one of the ways of maintaining Stalin's power, fighting different trends of thought, and avoiding the possibility of opposition to the regime. All party and state functionaries from the lowest to the highest had to live in constant fear and anxiety.

The facts show that steps were being taken to prepare a new great terror. Many of the measures implemented by Stalin were similar to his conduct in the mid-thirties. The head of state security was changed; the former Minister of State Security, Abakumov, was arrested. The new head (S. Ignatiev) came from the party apparatus and had not been connected earlier with the security organs. In 1936 Ezhov, a secretary of the Central Committee, replaced Yagoda, who was arrested. A purge of the personnel in the security organs began. Many of them were arrested.

As in the thirties, an "enemy" was found. This time it was the Jewish population of the country. Stalin gave instructions to the security organs to consider every Jew a potential American spy and enemy of Soviet power. In party circles it was explained in this way: before the Second World War, Germany was the most probable Soviet opponent and every German was considered a potential spy. In the future war the chief enemy of the Soviet Union could only be the United States of America. And if one considered the significant role of the Jews in the political and financial life of that country, then each Soviet Jew could be considered a potential spy for the United States. And so, during the preparations for the purge, on the one hand, the Jews were seen as a group as enemies of the Soviet people, while on the other hand, the United States was designated as the future opponent.

The campaign expanded, the courts abandoned leniency, and extra-legal acts of repression ranging from execution to exile touched many thousands of people. In the summer of 1952 the War College of the Supreme Court of the USSR considered the cases of fifteen members of the Jewish antifascist committee. One of the accused died during the trial; all but one of the others were given death sentences which were carried out on August 12, 1952.

Stalin succeeded anew in exercising firm control over the entire society. He exterminated the attitudes and ideas that he thought opposed or were dangerous to his dictatorship. This was facilitated by Stalin's clever use of the stereotypes of the "besieged fortress," the constant search for "the enemies of the people," and some improvement in the people's standard of living at the end of the 40s and beginning of the 50s. The organs of state security were still the most important instrument of Stalin's authority and policy. They always had been under Stalin's personal control, but at the end of 40s and the beginning of the 50s his guidance became more direct.

In the summer of 1951, Stalin appointed a new state security minister, S. Ignatiev, a little known party functionary. With his help Stalin carried out a purge of the security organs in which the leadership of the Ministry of State Security (MGB) was completely renewed. Hundreds of personnel of the central apparatus, who had worked earlier alongside the former Minister of State Security, Beria, were dismissed, arrested, and convicted. Almost all of his protégés were removed from the central apparatus of state security.

The Ministry of State Security had a complex branch structure with many departments managing various types of operations, beginning with foreign intelligence and ending with surveillance over the country's citizens. As in the 30s Stalin practically took over the central part of the secret police—the Division for the Investigation of Especially Important Cases. It was there that the documents were made, documents "of special importance," which laid the foundation for the major state cases. Stalin developed the whole plot. He determined the characters, prepared the list of questions for the arrested, and indicated what answers and evidence they had to give. He gave personal orders to use torture to get the evidence he wanted from prisoners. The intelligence apparatus used all means to obtain the "necessary" evidence. The investigation protocols were written later, and the falsified documents were sent to the highest state officials and party functionaries as important evidence of the existence of a plot or proof of intelligence activity. Self-incrimination, a confession obtained by torture, was the basis of these documents in the overwhelming majority of cases.

The secret police—the Ministry of State Security—was controlled directly by Stalin and was the real source of his power. That is to say that through the MGB Stalin exercised his leadership of the country. In the bosom of this institution Stalin's plans were concretely formulated and formally documented.

The second weapon of Stalin's essentially autocratic power was the Communist party. It remained divided into two unequal parts. The first part included millions of party members who were united in primary organizations fully removed from the actual resolution of state and party matters, but who were actively involved in propaganda and the implementation of decisions. The other part was a narrow hierarchy of secretaries with a powerful, well organized, and experienced apparatus that had in its hands authority over the country and the fate of every individual; but this authority could only be realized through Stalin's power. The Central Committee and Politburo formally existed as the highest collegial organs of the party in which the most important problems of internal and foreign policy had to be discussed.

No congresses had been convened for 13.5 years, from March 1939 to October 1952. Central Committee plenums had not been held for 5.5 years, from February 1947 to October 1952. Even the Politburo (10 members and 4 candidate members) was almost never convened with its full membership. Stalin always determined who was to be invited to a meeting. All authority in the party was concentrated in structures created by Stalin which were not subject to control by the leading elected bodies of the party. Stalin used the party organs extensively to control the activity of any state official or party functionary.

To control the party apparatus, a special department of the secret police (MGB) existed in the Central Committee of the party, directly subordinate to Stalin. There was a special prison and procurator's office (the Party Control Commission) for party functionaries. The commission chairman, M. Shkiriatov, conducted the investigation, handled interrogations, and signed arrest and imprisonment orders without the knowledge of the civilian organs of justice.

The party and the organs of the Soviet state were for Stalin only a cover which formed the decor of the political arena. They were set up to symbolize the existence of "socialist" democracy, respect for the people's will, and the party's leading role. Actually there was only the guiding will of Stalin which was exercised either through the soviets or through the party, but the organs of repression (the MGB) remained Stalin's chief instrument for governing the state.

As a result, step by step Stalin was preparing a new round of "shake-ups" in the top echelon of power. At the end of the 40s he began preparations for the dismissals of Molotov, Mikoyan, Kaganovich, and Voroshilov. They were not always invited to the sessions of the Politburo, important meetings which were conducted by Stalin. The state security organs collected materials to accuse them of being spies and enemies of the people. Stalin's attitude toward Beria changed radically in summer of 1951. He was removed from participation in the affairs of the state security organs. His protégés were arrested one after another in 1952. Soon after the so called "Mingrel case" was staged through which many people close to Beria (he was a Mingrel by nationality) were accused of espionage and anti-Soviet activity. Stalin personally conducted the investigation and trial of the case. Beria's activity in the organs of state security between 1938 and 1941 was investigated in deep secrecy.

The Twenty-Ninth Party Congress took place in October 1952;

the personnel changes implemented by it showed Stalin's desire to free himself from most of the old members of the Politburo. The party's newly established top organ, the Presidium, had twice as many members as the Politburo. But not all of the old Politburo members became part of the expanded Presidium. Besides that, a Bureau of the Presidium was created which excluded Molotov, Mikoyan, and Voroshilov. In fact during the last months of his life, Stalin functioned almost entirely within a tight circle consisting of Malenkov, Khrushchev, and Beria.

Members of the group vied for Stalin's favor; thus he could play one of his aids against the other, making it impossible for them to plot against him. The desire to please Stalin caused intense competition within Stalin's inner circle.

All ideological propaganda was directed to the general reinforcement of Stalin's personality cult. The propaganda penetrated the activity of all organizations—party and state alike, science and education, literature, and art.

The end of the 40s and the beginning of the 50s were marked by the development of an imperialist ideology and a more open display of state antisemitism. The idea of Russian statehood was becoming more important in official propaganda in the social sciences and in education. During and immediately after the war many old civil and military titles (officer, general, minister, etc.) abolished by the Revolution were restored. There were great changes in the Army. It received a new name. Instead of the Workers and Peasants Red Army it was called the Soviet Army. The "gold shoulder straps" which were despised during the Revolution were restored as insignia for generals, officers, and sergeants. After the war the People's Commissariats (cabinet departments) became known as Ministries and a number of old cities renamed during the five year plans reverted to their old names (Ordzhonikidze to Vladikavkaz, Voroshilovsk to Ussuriisk). The same thing happened to a number of main thoroughfares in Russia's big cities.

On the eve of the Twenty-Ninth Party Congress, Stalin organized a new provocation known as the Doctors' Plot that was to become the signal for the beginning of a broad wave of repression.

In September 1952 the arrest of the top administrators and physicians of the Kremlin hospital as well as family physicians of the Politburo members began. A large group of prominent specialists were arrested, including Professor V. Vinogradov who treated Stalin. The doctors were accused of involvement in a plot to murder the leaders of the state and party by means of obviously incorrect treatments. Trying at any cost to conclude the investigation quickly and obtain confessions from the arrested physicians, among whom the elderly predominated, on Stalin's orders they were subjected to torture; even before the investigation was concluded, an announcement was made in the press on January 13, 1953, of the exposure of a "group of doctors-terrorists" whose spying and terrorist activities had already been proven. It was supposed that the trial of the physicians would be public. It should have taken place in March. All the accused were to be sentenced to death. The execution was to take place publicly on one of Moscow's squares. Although the arrested included not only Jews, but also Russians and Ukrainians, the affair immediately assumed an antisemitic character; the more so because the published news directly reported that the arrested physicians conducted their terrorist and espionage activity on orders from foreign intelligence services and under the guidance of Jewish nationalist organizations found in the United States.

All over the country meetings were organized at which the participants demanded the death penalty for the "physician-assassins" and called for the strengthening of "Bolshevik vigilance." The physicians affair was to have served as the signal for the beginning of a mass terror which would touch all layers of society.

After the public trial of the physicians a significant part of the Jewish part of the big industrial centers of the European part of the country were to be deported to the uninhabited regions of Central Asia and Siberia. Special camps and closed zones were prepared for the deportees. The organs of repression were preparing for massive repression. In December 1952 a plenum of the Central Committee specifically addressed the question of the work of the Ministry of State Security which was mobilizing its personnel to conduct the major operations. The flywheel of repression was taking up speed.

In organizing the great terror, Stalin had in mind not only the terrorizing of the people and the suppression of even potential opposition but also the psychological preparation for a new war. The creation of the image of the enemy who would be the opponent in a future war became the dominant theme in the mass media and state propaganda. And there was no secret about who the enemy would be. The leading themes in a number of art forms were anti-American. The major state officials who controlled the activity of the cultural institutions, who held the instruments of mass communication in their hands, gave direct orders to create literary and musical compositions on anti-American themes. As the poet Konstantin Simonov testified, he received his commission directly from Stalin. Theaters, movies, concerts, plays, and poetry were full of anti-American subjects. In the consciousness of the masses the image of the America as an enemy of the Soviet people was beginning to form.

The climax of the anti-American campaign was to be the case against the official Varfolomeev and some personnel of the American embassy in Moscow who were accused of organizing an attempt on Stalin's life and the lives of other members of the Politburo. The American ambassador, George Kennan, who was at the time outside of the USSR, was declared "persona non grata" and the American embassy in Moscow was without an experienced leader.

The growing anti-American sentiments, the massive acts of repression among the people, and the confrontation between the Soviet Union and the United States helped to keep society in a state of tension, ready for mobilization.

But Stalin's sudden death changed the whole situation. The political leaders who came to power had their own ideas about the Soviet Union's domestic and foreign policy, and the country entered a new period in its development.

Notes

[1] See *140 besed c Molotovym* ["A Hundred Conversations with Molotov"]. *Iz dnevnik F. Chueva [From F. Chuev's Diary]*. Moscow, 1991.

[2] Voprosy istorii [Problems of History]. 1993, No. 2, p. 187.

[3] N.V. Sibachev, E.F. Iazkov. *Noveishaia istoriia SShA [The Newest History of the United States]*. Moscow, 1980, p. 197.

[4] M. Djilas, *Litso totalitarizma [The Personality of totalitarianism]*. Moscow, 1992, p. 85.

[5] *Otechestvennaia istoriia [History of the Fatherland]*, 1993., No. 1, p. 43.

[6] G.I. Khanin, *Dinamika ekonomicheskogo razvitiia SSSR [The Dynamics of the Economic Development of the USSR]*, Novosibirsk, 1991, pp. 186, 187, 264 and 265.

[7] In 1946-1950 electrical stations with a total capacity of 8.4 million kilowatts were restored and built which equaled the country's total electrification capacity in 1937. See *Istoriia SSSR s drevneishikh vremen do nashikh dnei [The History of the USSR from Ancient Times to Our Day]*, vol. XI, Moscow, 1980, p. 136.

[8] See V.N. Zemskov, op. cit., pp. 152,153; D. Volkogonov, op. cit., Book II, part 2, Moscow, 1981, p. 70.

[9] See *Nashe otechestvo. Opyt politicheskoi istorii [Our Fatherland. An Essay of Political History]*. Part 2, Moscow, 1991, pp. 431,432.

CHAPTER 7

THE USSR DURING THE THAW

The Collective Leadership and the Rise of Khrushchev (1953-58)

The Death of Stalin and the Beria Plot

Stalin died on March 5, 1953. The absence of a reliable, legitimate mechanism for the transfer of power caused a crisis of power and a long struggle for its possession. During Stalin's administration the party, which *officially* determined the development of society, was shoved aside by the executive, predominantly repressive, state organs and the real power was in the hands of Stalin. As a result, the relative strength of the pretenders to power was determined not only by their posts, but by their proximity to the deceased dictator and their personal connections within the elite of the party, state, and armed forces. The fates of two hundred million people were decided behind their backs by a small group of people who ruled the country.[1]

After Stalin's death "collective leadership" officially came to power which included the dictator's inner circle—G.M. Malenkov, V.M. Molotov, L.P. Beria, N.S. Khrushchev, L.M. Kaganovich, A.I. Mikoyan, N.A. Bulganin, and K.E. Voroshilov.[2] But based on the alignment of forces at the time of Stalin's death, the struggle for power would rage around the "younger generation" who had fallen into Stalin's immediate circle in the 1930s. Three key figures were discernible during the struggle: Malenkov, Beria, and Khrushchev. It is significant that, although most of the members of the "collective leadership" supported various changes in state policy, these three were probably the most disposed toward reform. The struggle for power which unfolded between them was a struggle for a particular version of social reform.

Having inherited the traditionally important (after Lenin and Stalin) post of head of government, Malenkov controlled the most important levers of power, along with Beria. After Stalin's death Malenkov actually seemed to be the first person in the party and presided at sessions of the Presidium of the Central Committee (the new name of the Politburo after 1952). But Malenkov and his then weaker competitor Khrushchev and the entire "collective leadership" feared and hated Beria, feeling the insecurity of their own positions in his strength.

The "Beria affair" was the most mysterious of all of the post-Stalin "palace revolutions."[3] His personal position was questionable. The traditional and rather elaborate version is that Beria had prepared a plot to establish a personal dictatorship. According to another version, Beria understood that neither the other leaders nor the army would support him as Stalin's successor and was not striving to establish an openly personal dictatorship immediately. It seems that he had convinced Malenkov and Khrushchev that he would be content with the secondary role of *eminence grise*. From here the outcome of the struggle for power depended on which of the two leaders—Malenkov or Khrushchev—Beria preferred. But he miscalculated. Dragged into a double game, he gave them reason to suspect him of being "unfaithful" and of making his own dictatorial plans, just as he had earlier inspired fear among his own colleagues. This, it is believed, decided Beria's fate. Yet another version exists—that of Beria the reformer, punished by the nomenklatura for his attempt to implement large-scale reforms.

The latter version seems rather less believable. Yet after Stalin's death Beria (in tandem with Malenkov) actually supported some very radical proposals. He knew "the painful part" of the system better than others and information on what the people did not particularly like was collected for him by the organs of state security. But concern for the state and people were not the chief motives of his activity. If one can believe anything, it is Beria's complete amorality. Beria obviously thought that to strengthen his position he had to clean up his bloody image more than the other members of the collective leadership, distancing himself from Stalinism (even more than he had done in recent years by removing himself from the leadership of state security and by not assuming responsibility for the "fresh" acts of repression).

It was mostly Beria and Malenkov who acted against the continuation of the cult of Stalin. As a result the leader's name began to disappear from the pages of newspapers and journals shortly after his death. From the end of May to the end of June he was only mentioned once in the editorials of *Pravda*. The publication of the collected works of Stalin was discontinued. Upon Beria's proposal of May 9, 1953, an unprecedented decision was made by the Presidium of the Central Committee requiring party organizations to refrain from forming columns of demonstrators and designing buildings with portraits of party leaders. Later, at the July (1953) plenum of the Central Committee, Beria was imputed "to have worked against the cult of personality in the first days after comrade Stalin's death" because he "wanted to bury the name of comrade Stalin."

Beria undertook some measures to soften the repressive nature of the system. On his initiative on March 27, 1953, a decree of amnesty was issued under which 1,184,000 people, mostly imprisoned criminals, were freed. The amnesty, which was unforgettable in its scale, significantly destabilized the situation in a number of regions (which Beria may have considered one of his tasks). In April, on Beria's suggestion, the "doctor's affair," in which he had not been involved, came to a close. Simultaneously he undertook a reform of the internal affairs organs. On March 6 he was given instructions for the transfer of the GULAGs to the Ministry of Justice, and the transfer of all of the construction offices under the USSR Ministry of Internal Affairs (MVD) to their corresponding ministries. In June 1953 Beria introduced a proposal to the Presidium of the Central

Committee to limit the rights of the Special Conference at the USSR MVD.

Being first deputy chairman of the Council of Ministers of the USSR, Beria tried to carry out a number of economic reforms. In his statements he called into doubt the effectiveness of collective farm productivity and denounced the establishment of collective farms in the "countries of socialist democracy" (Communist Eastern Europe). This was a feeler for raising a similar question with regard to the USSR. He discontinued the construction of grandiose but uneconomical projects; these included the Central Turkmen Canal, the Volga-Baltic Waterway, the Volga-Ural Canal, and the Chum-Salekhard-Igarka Polar Railway.

Lavrenti Beria

Library of Congress, Prints & Photographs, NYWT&S Collection, LC-USZ62-107297

Realistically evaluating Stalin's nationalities policy and hoping to strengthen his own position among the cadres of the nationalities, Beria proposed reverting to the "Leninist policy of the indigenization" of the party and state apparatus of the republics. The first secretaries of the Central Committees of the Communist Parties of the Ukraine and Belorussia, L.G. Melnikov and N.S. Patolichev, were removed. The Ukrainians A.I. Kirichenko and the Belorussian M.V. Zimianin were appointed to replace them. Similar measures were outlined for the other republics. Beria proposed the establishment of republican orders and other awards bearing the names of the national heroes and cultural figures along with the all-union medals. (All this was declared to be a "perversion of the

Leninist-Stalinist nationalities policy" in July 1953.)

Beria favored the redistribution of the governing power from the party organs to the state. To the Hungarian leader M. Rakozi he directly stated: "Let the Council of Ministers decide all, while the Central Committee is occupied with cadres and propaganda." His foreign policy innovations looked even bolder. He supported the normalization of relations with Yugoslavia and the unification of the German Democratic Republic (East Germany) with the Federal Republic of Germany (West Germany). The apparatus of MVD representatives in the German Democratic Republic was reduced to one seventh of its former level. In addition, attempts were made to establish contacts with supporters of the idea of "democratic socialism" in the west. All this was attributed to Beria, who was accused of contacts with the enemies of the socialist state and even of "spying" for the interests of "world capitalism."

Beria could hardly have been guilty of espionage, but this was the usual political propaganda. And these Stalinist labels catered to the conservatism of the majority of the members of the collective leadership frightened by the decisiveness of Beria the reformer, who was infringing on the pillars of the system. After Beria's arrest Stalin's name appeared again in print, and Beria's guilt was established by the assertion that his propositions would have led to the "degeneration" of the Soviet society, to the creation of a "bourgeois order, which would have satisfied the followers of Eisenhower, Churchill, and Tito." This rich set of accusations was expressed at the July (1953) Plenum of the Central Committee of the CPSU. But Beria's fate was decided earlier.

At some risk to himself Khrushchev was able to unite all of the upper leadership against Beria and attract the army to his side.[4] According to another, less popular, version, Malenkov did this, but in any event without his active participation this agreement could not have been realized. On June 26, 1953, at a session of the Presidium of the Council of Ministers of the USSR, which was transformed in the course of business into a session of the Presidium of the Central Committee, Beria, to his surprise, was accused of a number of crimes and arrested there by Zhukov (the Deputy Defense Minister), K.S. Moskalenko, and a number of other generals and officers. After a trial, which was short for such a matter, Beria was convicted and shot as an "enemy of the Communist Party and Soviet people" in December 1953.

Could an "alternative to Beria" have won? Putting aside the question of whether his policy would have corresponded to the reformers' plans had he come to power, the prospects are remote. The fear of Beria, whose executioner's reputation was not unfounded, united the country's entire leadership against him and deprived him of mass support while his position in the state security organs had been shaken during Stalin's last years. Besides, the people as a whole were not ready for radical social reform. Moreover, the innovations proposed by Beria were identified in the minds of the masses not with him, but with the entire leadership that succeeded Stalin which made it possible for Malenkov and Khrushchev to continue the reforms.

Beria's removal weakened Malenkov's position relative to his political rival—Khrushchev. Malenkov deprived himself not only of a dangerous but also strong ally. The organs of the MVD-MGB (Ministries of Internal Affairs and State Security) were placed under the party's control. As a result Malenkov, as the chairman of the Council of Ministers (in contrast to his predecessors, Lenin and Stalin) was unable to use them to support his authority. At the same time Khrushchev, who had become first secretary of the Central Committee of the CPSU in September 1953, received substantially expanded power. As early as the July plenum, the Central Committee had noticed the need to strengthen the party leadership in all branches and the need to suppress any attempts by its departments and cadres to escape party control.

At the same time Malenkov still possessed significant power and had the advantage of the military's support with which he could have tried to obtain sole power. But Malenkov did not travel along this path. The matter was not only decided by his "failure to possess all of the qualities needed for leadership" but also by the decisive role played by the entire post-Stalin leadership. Any attempts to establish a personal dictatorship would have aroused the decisive opposition of the remaining colleagues who understood that only limited authority which was capable of being controlled could protect each of them from the repression of the stronger and more successful. Therefore, like it or not, the "heirs" had to transform a regime based on personal authority and abandon the leadership model of the past before the parameters of the future power structure were set. The vagueness of their position on this fundamental problem and the relative balance of power inside the new "triumvirate" (Malenkov, Khrushchev, and Bulganin) were expressed in the principle of "collective leadership."

At the first Central Committee Presidium after Stalin's funeral on March 10, 1953, Malenkov declared the need to abolish the "politics of the personality cult." At first the problem of surmounting the cult tradition was centered on the reform of propaganda and the Central Committee preferred to limit reform to that subject. But in July, at a Central Committee plenum, Malenkov took the further step of explaining that "the problem not only concerns propaganda," but the very principles of leadership. "Stalin's cult of personality in the daily practice of leadership assumed the forms and dimensions of an illness, the methods of collegiality in work were thrown away, criticism and self-criticism were absent in our highest leadership echelon," Malenkov stated. "We have no right to conceal from you that such a deformed personality cult . . . in later years began to inflict serious damage on our party and state leadership." In addition, everything in the plenum spoken about, debated, or disputed by the participants was concealed from the people. After Stalin's death society did not expect changes as much as it hoped for continuity of policy. Considering these attitudes, the party leadership had to act in general as "Stalin's successors."

It is difficult to say whether Malenkov would have been a reformer had he governed in a calmer period. But the situation in 1953, despite the external stability, required decisive and immediate action. A source of social unrest was being created by the continually expanding scope of forced labor, which was concentrated in the GULAG and collective farm village. At the beginning of the 1950s, despite some increase in the number of products produced per work day, the exhausting labor of the collective farm on an average day only provided 20.3% of the family's income, while 22.4% of the collective farms in 1950 were paying wages on a per diem basis.

And so the collective farm did not represent the peasants' means of support. Rather, the peasant busied himself in his free time, when he did not have to work on the collective farm, on his own private plot, which provided him both subsistence and income.

After Stalin's death the hope of amnesty and rehabilitation was aroused among the inmates of the GULAGs. These attitudes played the role of detonator in the disorders and uprisings which spread through the camps in 1953 and 1954. The decree on amnesty of March 27, 1953, which gave freedom "to the criminal element," without touching those judged guilty of "counterrevolutionary activity," did not reduce, but only aggravated the problem. To many, especially after the Beria affair, the innocence of a majority of these people was clear. The resolution of the rehabilitation problem promised an enormous political gain by establishing confidence in the new leadership inside the country and also in the eyes of world society. But, to decide on such a step it was necessary to surmount the psychological barrier: to fight the fear of the future and the fear of possible disclosures. Malenkov was the first to cross the line, Khrushchev took the step later, and there was no going back for either of them.

In September the Special Conference with the MVD of the USSR and the other extra-judicial organs ("the "threesome" or *troika* and the "five" or *piaterka*) was discontinued by the Decree of the Presidium of the Supreme Soviet of the USSR. Upon the procurator-general's appeal, the Supreme Court of the USSR received the right to review the decisions of the highest boards of the OGPU, "the three," and the special conferences of the NKVD-MGB-MVD of the USSR. In April 1954 the Supreme Court of the USSR reviewed the "Leningrad affair" and rehabilitated the leaders of the party and administrators who had been found guilty. This was a direct blow to Malenkov who had been a participant in the affair. The rehabilitation of the victims of the political trials of the 1930s and early 1950s began a year later. Between 1954 and the beginning of 1956 the War College of the Supreme Court of the USSR rehabilitated 7679 people, many of whom were dead. Tens of thousands of people had already been released from prison or labor camps before the Twentieth Congress of the CPSU.[5]

The cases of Beria, V.G. Dekanazov, B.Z. Kobulov, and the other leaders of the NKVD-MGB-MVD were reviewed in December 1953. The case of the former minister of State Security of the USSR, V.S. Abakumov, was reviewed in December 1954. According to the court's verdict all were shot. A significant change in cadres in the organs of repression took place. In 1954 the Ministry of State Security was transformed into the Committee of State Security [*Komitet gosudarstvennoi bezopastnosti* or KGB] of the Council of Ministers of the USSR.

The corresponding economic decisions underscored the change in policy. On April 1, 1953, the sharpest postwar reduction in the price of food and other necessities was implemented. At a meeting of the Supreme Soviet of the USSR in August 1953, Premier Malenkov outlined a new economic course, which for the first time in Soviet history gave priority to the development of light industry—the production of the consumer goods needed by the people. The policy of socially reorienting the economy as rapidly as possible embodied consumer goods, housing, and salary raises.

Solving the food problem and extricating agriculture from its lingering crisis was the other main goal of the economic program. The government expected to achieve this by reducing the collective farm tax (it fell by 250% in 1954), writing off the collective farms' arrears, increasing the size of the collective farmers' private plots, raising the purchase price of agricultural commodities, and expanding the opportunities for the development of the collective farmers' market. The government also intended to significantly raise the level of capital investment and the delivery of machinery. The opening up of the virgin and fallow lands in Kazakhstan, Siberia, and the Lower Volga was recognized (through Khrushchev's influence) as an important means of raising the production of grain. As a result the average annual rate of growth of agrarian productivity was 8% for the period between 1954 and 1958 instead of the 1.6% for the period between 1950 and 1953. The incomes of collective farmers between 1953 and 1958 grew by more than three hundred percent!

Aside from the socioeconomic effect, the policy drew a broad political response. Contemporaries remembered the newspaper with Malenkov's report that "we have reached the abyss in the village" and the simple peasant who lived in poverty said "here that man is for us." Even after a quarter century and despite the silence in the official propaganda, the collective farmers still have a high opinion of Malenkov's policies and his efforts to improve the people's lives. Malenkov's position on the village was not only determined by economic and propaganda considerations. The village, essentially, was his sole support, his social base, through the consolidation of which he finally could have been confirmed as leader of the state.

As early as 1953 Malenkov in his "inaugural" address to a meeting of party and managerial workers at the Central Committee was subjecting the apparatus to unusually sharp criticism for its bureaucratism, disregard for the people's needs, moral degradation, and graft.[6]

In the final analysis this miscalculation ended Malenkov's political career. Khrushchev at the time avoided this trap, using the support of the apparatus to consolidate his own position, but years later he also violated the principle of compromise and fell into the same trap as Malenkov.

As is often the case with major political leaders, the authority of Malenkov was greater abroad than at home. His new foreign policy was the principal reason. In an August 1953 address Malenkov introduced the world "détente" (*razriadka*) which later spread around the world. And in March 1954 he made an unprecedented announcement: "The Soviet government stands for the further weakening of international tensions, for a genuine and long peace, and decisively rejects the policies of the Cold War because the policy involves preparing for a new world war, which," Malenkov affirmed, "would, given the methods of modern warfare, mean the ruin of world civilization." This announcement made a significant impression on the apparatus and on a major part of the "Soviet society" who were influenced by the ideological dogma of those who saw the world through the prism of the mortal combat between socialism and capitalism and could not reconcile themselves to the idea of the impossibility of a military victory over the latter.

With his conciliatory attitude Malenkov's unstable position steadily deteriorated. At the January 1955 Plenum of the Central Committee, Khrushchev accused Malenkov of lacking "sufficient zeal and firmness for a Bolshevik leader" and said that he was only pretending to lead the activities of the government and the Presidium of the Central Committee and was trying to achieve "cheap popularity" among the masses. He remembered his close relations with Beria and his participation in the "Leningrad affair." Khrushchev denounced the premier's statement at the August 1953 meeting of the Supreme Soviet of the USSR as a "parliamentary declaration," an opportunist speech. His pronouncements on the changing relationship between the rate of productivity of Group A [heavy industry] and Group B [light industry] and his thesis on the ruin of world civilization in the event of a third world war were declared erroneous.

Malenkov himself recognized his own errors, although he did not give them political significance. He was unable to fight. Tvardovsky remembered him on that day: "The impression was grave, as in half an hour the man faded away, all his importance disappeared, and he was simply a stout man at the rostrum of the presidium, with the index fingers of his outstretched hands pointing at him, stumbling in his speech, repeating himself, 'somber,' bewildered, very nearly lost . . . lost and without hope for his later fate. That he understood."

In February 1955 at the session of the Supreme Soviet of the USSR, Malenkov officially "requested" his removal. The request was, naturally, granted. Nikolai A. Bulganin replaced him as premier. Although Malenkov was appointed Minister of Electric Power Stations and at the same time Deputy Premier, his political career was essentially over.

The tragedy of the reformer Malenkov mostly consisted in his mistakes in the power struggle. His policy was not furnished with the strategic rod (the "key" in Tvardovsky's expression) and the major key was a reliable political base. But many of the ideas which sprang from the statist mind of Malenkov were ten years ahead of their time. For the most part, thanks to his efforts, the economy in the mid-1950s began to turn toward the consumer, farm production grew rapidly, and international relations were normalized.

Khrushchev, partially because of the power struggle, proceeded much further in the liberalization of society and the dethronement of Stalin, but was unable to preserve some of the important initiatives of Malenkov in the social and economic sphere.

The Twentieth Party Congress

On February 25, 1956, at the final proceedings of the Twentieth Congress of the Communist Party of the Soviet Union (CPSU), Nikita Khrushchev, unexpectedly for the vast majority of those present, came to the rostrum with a report "On the Personality Cult and Its Consequences." Reflecting on his own election in 1956, Khrushchev recognized that "these questions had ripened, and it was necessary to raise them. If I had not raised them, others would have raised them. And that would have been the downfall of the leadership, who was not paying sufficient heed to the dictates of the period." Although the session was closed and the delegates had been informed earlier about the secrecy of the proceedings, the secrets which had surrounded the name of Stalin for many years ceased to exist from that moment. First the deviations from the principles of socialist democracy, the gravest violations of legality, the mass repressions, and the greatest errors and vicious methods of the leadership that proved Stalin's guilt were disclosed. The explanation of the causes of these events was mostly given within the confines of the old tradition, writing off the failures to the existence of capitalist encirclement and the difficulties of constructing socialism in one country. Together with this, enormous significance was given to Stalin's personality. Essentially, the origin of the negative phenomena in the practice of constructing socialism was attributed to the influence of Stalin's character flaws. Stalin's activity itself was divided into two periods—the "progressive" (the period of the struggle against the opposition, the time of the industrialization, collectivization, and the Great Patriotic War) and the "negative," when Stalin's character, simply speaking, began to degenerate. Thus the new term "the period of the cult of personality" appeared in history. This period, with its very inexact chronological boundaries, was understood as a "zigzag" or "accident" in the victorious history of the Soviet nation.

The address on the truth about Stalin, delivered from the rostrum of the congress, shocked contemporaries regardless of whether the facts and judgments presented to them were a revelation or a long expected restoration of justice. Ilia Erenburg remembered that "several delegates fainted during Khrushchev's speech during the second session on the 25th, which was closed. . . . I did not cut out: reading the report, I was in shock, you know the rehabilitated did not speak of this even among friends, but the first secretary of the Central Committee was talking about it in the party congress. February 25 was for me, as for all of my compatriots, a great date."[7]

Gradually the content of the documents of the Twentieth Congress on the problem of the cult of personality became the possession, first, of the party and, later, of the general public. It seemed that the people's view of the world and their hearts had been shattered. The universal intellectual confusion stimulated some to develop ideas while others lost their "bearings."[8] During one of the sociological surveys of the 1960s on people's attitude toward the various events in their lives, the following response was characteristic: "I am going to name the worst event. Everything is connected with the criticism of Stalin and the party's work during that period. No other event has been as difficult to bear, not even the failures of the first months of the war with Fascist Germany." Here is other evidence: ". . . A week had already passed before our party organization became familiar with the materials of the Twentieth Congress on the cult of personality and the entire time I was deeply impressed. . . . During the first days it irritated me that we were judging a dead man, and so we wanted during our lifetime Joseph Vissarionovich Stalin to remain in our memories as the just and honorable man that we had portrayed him as for more than three decades. . . . And now that his worst crimes were known, it was difficult, very difficult to hold in our heart this great love, which had been so strongly rooted in the entire organism."

The concentration of attention on Stalin's personality was not accidental. One of the peculiarities of the Russian, and especially the Soviet, political culture was the inclination to personify the bearer of evil ("Who was guilty?"—"the class enemy"—"the people's enemy") and the efforts of the ruling elite to avoid linking socialism to the evil itself; hence, the assertion that the cult of personality did not change the nature of the system. They were also interested in getting themselves off the hook, since the denunciation of the cult had been made by the politicians who had willingly or unwillingly participated in its crimes. The character of the discussion of the cult was set at the Twentieth Congress and in the printing of subsequent materials. The cult of Stalin was the cause of the failure of the first period of the Great Patriotic War, the cult of Stalin was the source of the use of "naked administrative coercion" (*administirovanie*), and the cult of Stalin was the original cause of the stagnation in intellectual life.

There was undoubtedly a rational core to this position. But then something prevented society from consciously accepting it as the undisputed truth. One of the letters in an edition of the journal *Kommunist* expressed the general attitude of the doubters: "They say that the party's policy was correct, but here that Stalin was wrong. Who guided this policy for decades? Stalin. Who formulated the basic political positions? Stalin. How can the one be accepted without the other?" This and similar discussions testified not only to the fact that society was gradually turning away from the mechanical acceptance of orders discharged from above to the actual evaluation of what was going on, but also to the fact that the process of this evaluation from below sometimes went beyond the "personality theme," which had been proposed in the beginning.

The people began to think about how the personality cult and the orgy of tyranny could have been possible. According to the evidence of contemporaries, our society had not known such a mass movement for a long time. Meetings, informal discussions, debates, and discourses took place. I. Erenburg remembered, "Stalin was spoken about everywhere—at the apartment, at work, in the cafeteria and in the metro. Upon meeting, one Muscovite said to another: 'Well, what do you say?' . . . He did not expect the answer: there was no explanation for the past. After supper the head of the family discussed what he had heard at the meeting. The children listened. They had known that Stalin was wise and kind . . . but suddenly they heard that Stalin had murdered his own close friends . . . that he had absolute faith in the word of Hitler, who had approved the nonaggression pact. Son and daughter asked: 'Papa, how could you not know anything.'" The return en masse of the rehabilitated from the camps complicated the situation even more.

The political leadership was unprepared for the scope of events. The Hungarian crisis of 1956 played a negative role in the further unfolding of the criticism of the cult and on the liberalization of society. It caused the Soviet leadership to have misgivings about the possible repetition of a similar occurrence in the USSR itself. At the party meetings which were taking place in the entire country the Communists did not always express support for the introduction of troops into Hungary, and even occasionally connected the events unfolding in Hungary with the need for more radical social reform. An automobile factory designer, Kiselev, remarked at a meeting in January 1957: "If the former leadership of the workers' party in Hungary had made errors, they were only some of our mistakes." The observation was made at a meeting of the active members of the Leningrad party that some of the party workers were in a state of panic in connection with the events in Hungary; rumors were spreading around town that someone was going from house to house compiling lists of communists. The effort to avoid the possibility of spontaneous mass activities led to a whole series of overcautious measures formulated under the slogan of "the struggle against the revisionists."

The Presidium of the Central Committee of the CPSU created a special commission under the leadership of L.I. Brezhnev who prepared the draft of the Central Committee's letter to party organizations "On the strengthening of the work of party organizations by the suppression of the attacks of the anti-Soviet, enemy elements." As examples of the weakening of vigilance were cited the statements of K. Paustovsky in a discussion of V. Dudintsev's novel *Not by Bread Alone*, O. Bergholts for his criticism of the dogmatic pronouncements of the Central Committee of the CPSU in the journals *Star* and *Leningrad*, and K. Simonov for his "revision" of the fundamental principles of the party leadership in literature and art.

On the general tone of the letter one of the Communists said: "The letter was read in such a tone and with such hints—either be silent or we would go our way." Different level party apparatchiks reacted to the letter in their own way. "If the Communist's fear of being accused of not suppressing criticism and of not opposing those who allowed demagogic and anti-Soviet statements was evident in the earlier reports coming to the Central Committee Presidium, the Central Committee's letter left no doubt on that question and armed the party organizations for the struggle with the demogogues, slanderers, and hostile elements." The prosecution of those who had a different points of view than the party began. The Leningrad regional committee of the CPSU, for example, were removed from the party and exiled from Leningrad. Among the exiles many veterans of the party were repressed.

It was decided to discontinue temporarily the reading of Khrushchev's secret speech in order to prevent the intrigues of western propaganda and to carry out preparatory work among the Communist party members, in some of whom "incorrect attitudes" had arisen toward "unhealthy statements." It seemed that the criticism of the cult of personality had caused "exaggerations," leading on the one hand to the appearance of spontaneous meetings and on the other hand to attempts to overthrow the authorities.

The various exaggerations were the product of logic: if the party opposes the idolization of the leader, then why in this day and age are there memorials to living leaders and why are towns, collective farms, and enterprises named after them? A special situation had begun to take shape in society. By toppling Stalin from his pedestal, Khrushchev removed the halo of inviolability from the leader and his general circle; in many respects the system of total fear had been destroyed. The strong faith in the infallibility of the supreme authority had been badly shaken.

The Twentieth Congress was the starting point for the critical and agonizing reexamination of the practice of socialism in the world and the development of the international communist movement. "We had too willingly supposed that the great task of building socialism could be realized without serious errors," said one of the leaders of the Communist Party of the USA, Eugene Dennis. "We refused to believe in any reports in which serious injustices in the socialist countries were spoken about, and read such reports as slander."

The process begun at the Twentieth Congress later led to a schism within the practically monolithic Communist movement, excluding the Yugoslavian Communists and Trotskyites. The groups of parties which were formed included: (1) Those who recognized some of the "errors" of Stalin and were oriented toward the Soviet Communist Party. (2) Those who did not recognize the criticism of Stalin and were oriented toward the Chinese Communist Party. (3) The Eurocommunists who proceeded further than everyone else in their comprehension of Stalinism as a phenomenon and engaged in the most thorough reexamination of the concept of socialism and the means of its attainment. The Twentieth Party Congress marked the beginning of the crisis of the world communist movement from which it was not fated to extricate itself.

The Liberalization of the Political Regime

The overthrow of Stalin, the pillar of the political regime which had existed for so long, inevitably required the correction of the political ties and structures and the destruction of the excesses which were the rather obvious consequences of his administration. The process started soon after the dictator's death. It was decided to decentralize the state's administrative system, limit the power of the bureaucracy, develop the people's activism in strictly controlled forms, and promote their participation in some managerial functions. In January 1957 the previously decorative role of the soviets was enhanced. In the Central Committee's decree "On the Improvement of the Activities of the Soviets of Workers' Deputies and the Strengthening of Their Ties with the Masses" measures were undertaken to broaden the competence and expand the material and financial base of the local soviets to overcome bureaucratization and involve the society in the work of the soviets.

While continuing to run only one candidate for each deputy's seat, the Central Committee decided to discuss the nominees in meetings of workers and collective farmers to limit in a small way the despotism of the party and the state nomenklatura. In March 1957, 60% of 1.5 million deputies of the local soviets were workers and collective farmers compared to 55% in 1955. A similar increase in the number of representatives from these social categories occurred in the elections to the Fifth Supreme Soviet in February 1958—(from 40% in the Fourth Supreme Soviet to 60% in the Fifth Supreme Soviet). The tendency to expand the proportional weight of the workers who were immediately involved in production among the deputies reflected the course adopted by the party leadership under N.S. Khrushchev to expand society's support for the reforms which were being conducted. But the place of the soviets in the political system was nearly unchanged. They continued to be deprived of most of the prerogatives of real power.

Khrushchev tried to arouse social organizations out of their bureaucratic lethargy in order to broaden the base of support among the masses for his reforms, to develop the "socialist" initiative of the masses, and in part to create a kind of counterweight to the apparatus. In 1957, as a result of the reorganization of the All-Union Central Council of Trade Councils (VTsSPS) the trade unions of 47 branches of industry were reorganized into 23. The administrative personnel of the VTsSPS and the central committees of the trade unions were reduced to a third of their former level. The overwhelming majority of the first union organizations were headed by activists instead of workers "freed from work." The rights of trade unions were significantly expanded. The wave of social activity which began with the "thaw" touched young people most of all and revived the activity of the Komsomol. Around 350,000 young people went to cultivate virgin lands out of the one million who applied to local Komsomol groups. Answering the CPSU and Komsomol "call," another 300,000 went to work at the largest building sites all over the country. Khrushchev's policy of expanding international contacts was reflected in the formation of the Committee of Youth Organizations in 1956 and the holding of the World Youth and Students' Festival in Moscow in 1957 which was an unprecedented event for a "closed" society.

A lot of attention was paid to other public organizations working under the guidance of local soviets: there were street and apartment committees, public commissions for cooperation in household management, brigades for assisting the militia, parents' councils in schools and household management, sanitation teams, club councils, guardianship councils at orphanages, and councils of retired workers. These bodies developed elements of communal self-government, but all of them were under party-state control.

Khrushchev somewhat limited officials' privileges and abolished Stalin's system of "packages"—tax exempt monetary sums which were secretly distributed to the top officials of the apparatus, media, and scholarly institutions above their regular salaries. He frequently tried to close down the special distribution center, officially known as the "health food cafeteria," for the top members of the nomenklatura on Granovsky street in Moscow and to restrict rights to personal cars. But most of his innovations failed and set the nomenklatura against him.

After the Twentieth Party Congress, the process of rehabilitating repressed peoples not only assumed a massive and general character, but also worked to restore the rights of entire nationalities who had suffered during the Stalinist period. In February 1957, the national autonomy of the Balkar, Chechen, Ingush, Kalmyk, and Karachaev peoples, which was abolished in the war years, was reestablished. In the RSFSR the Chechen-Ingush Autonomous Republic was restored, the Kalmyk autonomous region was formed which was later (1958) transformed into an autonomous republic while the Kabardine Autonomous Republic became the Kabardine-Balkar Autonomous Republic and the Cherkes (Circassian) autonomous region became the Karbardino-Cherkes autonomous region. But some peoples who suffered during the Stalinist period were not rehabilitated. The rights of the Germans of the Lower Volga, the Crimean Tatars, and the Meskhetine Turks were not restored.

The competence of the union republics was significantly expanded. Approximately 15,000 mostly small enterprises were transferred to their jurisdiction between 1954 and 1956. The percentage of tax revenues allocated to the republics' budgets was increased. A number of union ministries (communications and education, for example) were reorganized into union republic ministries. The number of all-union ministries was reduced from 30 in 1953 to 23 in May 1957 while the number of union republic ministries increased from 21 to 29. In May 1956, the functions relating to the administration of the judicial institutions and organs of justice were placed under the control of the union republics, and the Ministry of Justice of the USSR was disbanded. In 1957-1958 the rights of the union republics over their own legislation and the internal administration of their own territory were expanded.

In that way some liberalization of the totalitarian bureaucratic system was introduced in the middle of the 1950s. But on the whole these measures had a transitory character. The scope and direction of the succeeding steps depended on Khrushchev, on the balance of forces in the leadership, on the public reaction to the measures which had been realized, and on the slogans which were proclaimed.

The Power Struggle

Khrushchev's decisive actions concerning Stalin's exposure and the rapid growth of his personal influence accelerated the formation of an anti-Khrushchev opposition within the leadership which was later called the "antiparty group." In fact they were not against the party; moreover, they cannot be considered fully pro-Stalinist. In addition to the core (Malenkov, Molotov, and Kaganovich) many different people who did not have much sympathy for one another (Pervukhin, Saburov, Shepilov, Voroshilov, and Bulganin) were either members of or inclined to support the group. Their fear of further exposures (which did not affect everyone) was not the only factor joining them; they were also more conservative in their whole attitude and disagreed with Khrushchev on several concrete policy issues. Khrushchev's unequivocal attempts to confirm his position as the sole leader, without a "collective leadership," was the most important factor in bringing the group together. The implementation of his plans would have meant political oblivion for all of Stalin's former associates and also for the people placed by them into responsible posts in the party and state (in that world "whose" person you were was always more important than the "kind" of worker you were).

This was first and foremost a power struggle in which political disagreements were closely interwoven with the goal of self-preservation. The web, which was typical of any political struggle, was of special importance in a totalitarian state. On June 18, 1957, the struggle turned into direct opposition when a majority of the Central Committee's Presidium (the Politburo before 1952 and after 1966) decided to dismiss Khrushchev from the post of First Secretary of the Central Committee of the Communist Party of the Soviet Union. But a considerable part of the renewed apparatus of the party Central Committee, the army commanded by Marshal G.K. Zhukov, and the KGB supported Khrushchev. A Plenum of the Central Committee (June 22-29) was convened with their assistance and the activities of the members of the opposition were determined to be factional and the group was branded as antiparty. Malenkov, Kaganovich, Molotov, and Shepilov were dismissed from the Central committee and its Presidium.[9] Bulganin was severely reprimanded; he was dismissed from the post of chairman of the Council of Ministers (premier) and dropped from the Presidium of the Central Committee when Khrushchev assumed the premiership in 1958.[10] There were new examples of liberalization: for the first time in many decades the Plenum of the Central Committee rather than the narrow circle of Presidium (Politburo) members made the decision, and the opposition members not only retained their personal freedom but their party membership. Malenkov, Kaganovich, and Molotov were expelled from the party only after the Twenty-Second Congress in 1961.

The next act of the political struggle, which was intended to secure the party and state officials from a strong and popular personality in the army and among the people, was the dismissal of G.K. Zhukov from the post of Minister of Defense and his expulsion from the leadership organs of the party. On October 29, 1957, a Plenum of the Central Committee adopted a statement "On the Improvement of the Party's Political Work in the Army and Fleet." G.K.Zhukov—an outstanding general of the Great Patriotic War who made an indispensable contribution to Beria's removal and the liquidation of "antiparty" group—was accused of "breaching Lenin and party leadership principles in the Armed Forces; conducting a policy of diminishing the work of the party organizations, political organs, and Military Soviets; and destroying the leadership and control of the party, its Central Committee, and the government over the Army and Navy."

The Premiership of N.S. Khrushchev (1958-64)

Ironically, Khrushchev's defeat of the conservative opposition and his advancement to the position of exclusive leader (he held Stalin's old offices of First Secretary of the Communist Party's Central Committee and Chairman of the Council of Ministers) had quite contradictory consequences for "the thaw." After defeating the right wing opposition, Khrushchev rapidly turned to the "left." The significant advances "of the great decade" and the boisterous campaigns of those years began at this time. It is possible that the situation would have corrected itself in time and created a counterforce to the First Secretary's personal power, but Khrushchev blocked this path as his move to the left stopped, precluding the possibility of further liberalizing of the regime.

The obvious retreat in 1957 and 1958 from the policy of democratic renewal, which had been conducted under the slogan of de-Stalinization, meant the completion of the first stage of social reform, which could be characterized as the stage of emotional criticism. Over night the problem of moving "from the democratism of the mass meeting" to the long-term practical realization of a reform program became obvious. But on a practical level Krushchev sought other objectives: the concentration of power (in Khrushchev's hands), the curtailment of the democratic process, and attempts at a gigantic leap to communism.

In 1959 the extraordinary Twenty-First Party Congress which was convened to approve the Seven Year Plan for the development of the economy of the USSR decided that socialism in the USSR had attained a complete and final victory. It followed from this that the Soviet Union was entering into the period of the full-scale construction of communism. At the Twenty-Second Party Congress, which took place in October 1961, a new Program for the Communist Party of the Soviet Union was accepted—the program for the construction of communism. The goals, which were presented in the third Program of the party for the creation of the material and technical basis of communism before 1980 seemed unrealistic even at the moment of their adoption. The plan called for (1) the attainment during the course of ten to twenty years of superiority in per capita production over the leading capitalist countries, (2) the elimination of heavy physical labor, and (3) the attainment of material and cultural abundance. Still they were received positively by society on the whole. The target of a high standard of living, of democratization, and the transition from government administration to a self-governing society gave rise to new illusions on the part of broad layers of the population and renewed faith in "the enlightened ideals" proclaimed by the ruling party. The conclusion contained in the congress's materials on the replacement of a state governed by dictatorship of the proletariat with a state governed by all of the people and the policy of broadening the scope of self-management in society marked the end of Stalinist theory and practice and promoted greater initiative and enthusiasm on the part of the masses. Society's enthusiasm was expressed by a renewed vigor of socialist competition (soon cooled by the bureaucracy), and the movement for a communist attitude toward labor. The grandiose nature of the goals was intended not only to renew the moral, political, and ideological values of society, which were somewhat shaken after Stalin's discrediting, but also to use the enthusiasm of the masses as an important stimulus for development. The first manned space flight in 1961 confirmed people's confidence that there was nothing impossible for the Soviet Union.

Economic and Social Development

In the economic sphere it was clearly felt that the government of the country had embarked on a massive, long-term project without having a well-thought out program in mind. A similar situation had been encountered in world and especially Russian history. But in the USSR in the 1950s the situation was more critical because of the negative consequences of Stalin's policy of "annihilating" the independent scientific thought of social science teachers and the general deterioration in the intellectual potential of society which was a consequence of the massive repression against the intelligentsia and the conditions of moral terror. This was also reflected in the composition of the top leadership. Khrushchev, who possessed a sharp mind and practical wisdom, nevertheless, had an incomplete middle school education; he could not even write grammatically; and unlike Stalin he never seriously engaged in self-education.

The conceptual vacuum pushed Khrushchev, especially after the elimination of "collective leadership," toward rash actions that were dictated by momentary interests and an attitude of impatience. All of this encouraged a persistent search for a "panacea," a miracle remedy for solving complex problems. Although all of Soviet history is marked by searches for a "philosophical foundation" (the class theory as the only way of understanding contemporary society; the concept of "the key link in the chain" in specific policy; the method of shock work, *udarnost,* in building socialism), it seems that the search for a panacea was especially prevalent in the fifties. Administrative reform was considered the possibly decisive method of industrial growth; opening up the virgin lands and the "corn campaign" were considered the only way of agricultural development; and the aggregate of social problems could be solved by the forced advance to communism on a wave of popular enthusiasm.

In the 50s it became obvious that the concentration of authority for most of the operating functions of management and petty restrictions on the activity of the individual enterprise only complicated production at the local level. In 1957 a reform of the management of the economy began with the replacement of the branch by the territorial principle. During the course of this movement a People's Economic Council was created in every economic region. Of the 105 councils, seventy were in the RSFSR, eleven in the Ukraine, four in Uzbekistan, nine in Kazakhstan, and one in each of the other republics. One-hundred-forty-one All-union, Union-republic, and autonomous republic ministries were abolished. The adoption of a single economic policy, the preparation of long and short-term plans, and control over the maintenance of deliveries was reserved for the State Planning Commission of the USSR. State committees on airplane equipment, automation, machine-building, and radio-electronics were created within the Council of Ministers of the USSR to provide scientific and technological guidance for those branches.

The reform included all the basic ideas of the previous years: the implementation of decentralized management, the creation of conditions to secure the control of the work of the economic organs from below, the maintenance of the complex development of the economy within the boundaries of the specific territories, and a reduction in the size and cost of the administrative apparatus.

The reorganization of the managerial system gave a significant stimulus to economic development: the removal of bureaucratic barriers and greater administrative efficiency caused the rate of national income to rise from 7% in 1957 to 12.4% in 1958, all of which strengthened specialization and the scope of cooperation within the economic-administrative regions and accelerated the process of the technological reconstruction of production. Significant economies were obtained by reducing the size of the administrative apparatus, but the effect of the reorganization was temporary.

At the very beginning of the creation of the sovnarkhozs, the experts made an interesting observation: during the interval between the abolition of the ministries' authority and the creation of the regional economic councils, when the firms were on their own, they not only maintained their rate of productivity but actually began to function significantly better. The same effect could be observed in the entire economy. This situation continued as long as the new organs were weak and had not yet formed a stable system. Having preserved the substance of the administrative mechanism, the reform replaced the shortcomings of the branch management system with the soon apparent defects of the territorial system: its lack of balance between the sectors of the economy and the parochial tendencies of the sovnarkhoz.

Later many sovnarkhozes were repeatedly expanded and numerous branch committees were set up at the center. The logic of the development of an administrative system combined with the territorial principle of industrial management demanded the further evolution of economic management in the direction of the vertical centralization of the sovnarkhozs. The basic stages included the formation of republican sovnarkhozes (SNKh) in June 1960, the Higher Economic Council in March 1963, and the Economic Council of the USSR in June 1963. The system of state economic planning was consistently becoming more complicated.[11] In the final analysis there was a definite tendency to restore the branch managerial system of economic administration within a territorial framework, while the extension of the process of centralization and the mechanical growth of similar organizational units at the beginning of the 1960s were evidence of the development of a crisis connected with the reforms of 1957. At the same time, the managerial model created by the reform still possessed some organizational potential.

A substantial part of Khrushchev's economic course, especially the extension of the social orientation of the economy, followed Malenkov's policy in many respects. But the accents were shifted in favor of extensive methods in hopes of a rapid return from "shock" measures. In agriculture the shock measures included bringing virgin and fallow lands under cultivation and, in residential construction, the transition to industrial methods and the large-scale construction of the urban "Khrushchevas." The new homes carrying that nickname were intended to last for two decades, but they soon became run-down and could not compare with the "better planned homes." At the end of the 50s and the beginning of the 60s such a residential construction policy (essentially the first planned mass residential construction during the Soviet period) helped ease the housing problem for tens of millions of citizens just as the grain from the virgin lands helped to solve the food problem. Another path would hardly have been able to yield such rapid results in raising the people's living standard in the second half of the 1950s; however, the efforts undertaken in this sphere were not adequate in comparison to the resources of the economy.

In the 1950s the intensive factors in the development of industrial growth attained the highest rate of increase in comparison with the prewar and later periods. This can be explained by the rapid growth in the supply of workers' tools, the increase in the level of qualified blue-collar and white-collar workers, and some improvement in planning and management, in particular, the definite growth of the economic independence of the regions and, to some extent, of the individual firms. In the 1960s the increasing number of workers became more significant than the increase in productivity and the increase in the volume of industrial production.

The development of the Soviet economy in the mid-1950s was characterized by technological progress. This was basically the beginning of the scientific and technological revolution in the USSR. Space exploration, the chemicalization of the economy, the development of electronics, and many other important scientific and technological trends during these years were supported by major government programs. The Twentieth Party Congress paid great attention to technological progress by setting the goal of raising the technological level of production. The State Committee of the Council of Ministers of the USSR on New Technology (*Gostechnika USSR*) was established to supervise the introduction of the new machinery and technology into the economy.

The growth rate of industrial production was high. According to G.I. Khanin's data, which is more accurate than official statistics, the average annual rate of growth of Soviet industry was higher than in the overwhelming majority of capitalist countries (except Japan): in 1951-55—8.7%, in 1956-60—8.3% and in 1961-65—7%.[12] A slight reduction in the rate of growth occurred at the beginning of the 1960s, but numerous factors and the slowing rate of growth caused a turn-around in the late 1960s. The national income growth figures in the 50s also were better than in the previous or following decades. The rate of national income growth began to fall in the first half of the 1960s.

For the first time the country succeeded in securing a massive improvement in the standard of living of the population which was accelerated by the increase in productivity and the reduction in the armed forces and defense spending in the mid-1950s. Between 1956 and 1960 blue-collar and white-collar workers received a seven-hour working day while those underground and in dangerous work received a six-hour working day. The work week was shortened without a reduction in workers' wages. The wages of underpaid blue-collar and white-collar workers were increased in 1957. Social security was significantly improved in 1956. On the whole the real income of blue-collar and white-collar workers grew by 60% between 1950 and 1958, while the real income of collective farmers grew by 92% during the same period.

The situation in agriculture was rather more complicated. After a short period of prosperity in the mid-1950s, when annual growth rate was 8% (1954-1958) and agricultural investments rose by nearly a third in comparison to a fifth at the beginning of the 1950s,[13] the situation in the countryside deteriorated again. The rate of productivity slowed down sharply. A shortage of food products began to be acutely felt in the country. In 1963 the USSR began regularly and on an increasing scale to import grain from abroad. The exodus from the farms to the cities grew stronger.

The reasons for the agricultural crisis which became a constant feature of the Soviet economy from that time on were complicated and numerous. First was the lack of adequate financing for the village. While the country was beginning its giant "leap to communism" and developing large scale social programs (mostly in the cities), agriculture and the branches servicing it became an economic "stepson." 30.7 billion of the 97 billion rubles allocated by the state to agricultural development were used to cultivate virgin lands. After a brief period of growth (between 1956 and 1958 the state received more than half of its grain supplies from the virgin lands), the harvest fell sharply because of soil erosion and other unforeseen negative phenomena, which struck most of the 36 million hectares of virgin and fallow lands under cultivation between 1954 and 1956. The retreat from Malenkov's policy of a cautious, concerned attitude toward the village was replaced by innumerable administrative reorganizations, including Khrushchev's campaigns. The "integration" of the economy, the reform of farm administration, the transformation of 15% of the collective farms into state farms, the reorganization of the state's machine tractor stations through the sale of their machinery to the collective farms, the planting of corn even in regions where it could not ripen, and other shock measures all helped destabilize the entire agrarian economy. But the fundamental causes of the agrarian crisis were found in the demoralization of the collective farm system, which began after Stalinist repression ended. The distribution of passports to the peasants permitted them the freedom of movement to liberate themselves from the Stalinist ties to the land and to move into the city where there was a much higher standard of living and a social and cultural infrastructure. The elimination of the threat of repression for not fulfilling the set number of "working days" in the collective farm undermined an important stimulus for labor on the "socialist farm," since work on their private plot located near their cottage was much more profitable. At the beginning of the 1950s labor on the collective farm only represented 20.3% of the peasant's income, which did not secure for him adequate provisions as much as the right to feed himself through his private plot.[14] Probably this situation and the goal of reaching a fully socialized communist agriculture pushed Khrushchev into liquidating the peasants' private plots, which was not only a major blow to agricultural productivity, but it also pushed millions of peasants into the towns and served as an important stage in the "depopulation of the peasantry of the Soviet village."

Significant developments in the sociodemographic structure of the population occurred. According to the 1959 population census, the number of people stood at 208.8 million—eighteen million more than the population on the eve of the Great Patriotic War (World War II). The proportional weight of the urban population was 48% compared to 33% in 1939. The population of old towns had grown while hundreds of new towns had arisen. Blue-collar and white-collar workers comprised two thirds of the population, while the weight of the peasantry had been reduced to 31.4% of the population. The bias and cohesion of the social structure bore an artificial character which appeared to be a consequence of the social practice of the totalitarian regime. But the dynamics of the social structure also reflected significant positive movements connected with the growth of industry, science, technology, and education. In 1959, 39% of the blue-collar workers and 21% of the collective farmers had a secondary school or higher education, while in 1939 among manual laborers only 4.3% had such an education.

The growth of workers' salaries continued at the beginning of the 1960s. The first pensions for collective farmers were introduced in 1964. The consumption of manufactured goods and foodstuffs was growing. The fund of housing available in the country significantly increased, rising forty percent during the Seven Year Plan.

The Development of Culture

Significant developments occurred in culture. Polytechnical schools expanded. Boarding schools were created in 1956 and priority was given to orphans, children of invalids from the Great Patriotic War and labor, and children from low-income parents and single mothers. In December 1958 a law was adopted under which a universal compulsory eight-year education was introduced instead of the seven-year education. The graduation of specialists from institutions of higher education significantly increased. In 1958/59 Soviet institutions of higher education graduated three times as many engineers during the academic year as the United States.

The number of research facilities reached 3,200 in 1958. A reorganization of the Academy of Sciences took place under which institutions of applied scientific research were removed from its jurisdiction. At the same time institutes and laboratories conducting theoretical research were created, especially in the area of physics and mathematics. In May 1957 the government of the USSR decided to create a major research center in the eastern part of the country—the Siberian division of the USSR Academy of Sciences. The construction of a scientific town in the region of Novosibirsk soon became the largest academic center and there the world's most powerful elementary particles accelerator—synchrophasatron—became operational in 1957.

In 1956 a major international research center—the Unified Nuclear Research Institute—was built in the town of Dubna. The works of Soviet physicists—academicians L.D. Landau, I.E. Tamm, M.A. Leontovich, N.N. Bogolubov, and others—received world wide recognition. Domestic computer production began. The works of academicians L.A. Artsimovich, M.V. Keldish, and M.A. Lavrentiev were of great theoretical and applied importance, finding their application in the area of nuclear synthesis theory, field theory, and in hydrodynamics, aerodynamics, and other areas of science. In July 1956 the country's first jet plane, the TU-104, designed by the team headed by A.N. Tupolev, rose into the air. At the end of the 50s and beginning of the 60s the USSR became the world leader in space exploration: the first multi-stage intercontinental ballistic missile was launched in 1957. The first Soviet Sputnik (satellite) was launched into space orbit on October 4, 1957. On April 12, 1961, the Soviet astronaut Yury Gagarin completed the first manned space flight in history. The systematic exploration of near-Earth space with the help of artificial satellites began.

"New" mass media was developed between the mid-1950s and early 1960s. Radio service covered the whole country. In 1958, 53 television centers were in operation in the country and the number of television sets reached 3 million, while in 1953 there were only 3 television centers and television sets only just exceeded 200,000.

Complicated and contradictory processes were developing in literature and art. On the one hand party decisions rehabilitated scientists, artists, and writers who were repressed in Stalin's time and errors in the evaluation of a number of works of art were corrected. In 1958 the Central Committee of the Communist Party of the Soviet Union adopted a resolution "On Correcting the Mistakes in Evaluating the Operas *The Great Friendship, Bogdan Khmelnitsky,* and *From the Depth of the Heart.*" New artistic unions were established—the USSR Union of Cinematographers, the RSFSR Writers' Union, and the RSFSR Artists' Union—and new magazines began to come out. On the other hand the appearance of a number of critical works of fiction and poetry were branded as slander against socialist reality. Among them were the following anti-Stalinist works: V. Dudintsov's *Not by Bread Alone*, A. Yanshin's *Levers*, D. Granin's *One's Own Opinion*, and S. Kirsanov's *Seven Days of a Week*. The persecution of the Nobel laureate Boris Pasternak, whose novel *Doctor Zhivago* had been published in the West, was real and far-reaching. Some artists whose works Khrushchev did not like were severely criticized. The totalitarian regime continued its control of intellectual life by establishing rigid boundaries between what was and was not permissible.

Foreign Policy

Contradictory tendencies appeared in international relations as well between the mid-1950s and mid-1960s. With the formation of the North Atlantic Treaty Organization (NATO) and the Warsaw Treaty, the split between the social systems became formalized in the form of military and political blocs. The Cold War continued although in a somewhat milder version. The inconsistency of Soviet foreign policy was revealed by contradictory steps. On the one hand steps were taken to relax international tension. At the Geneva meeting of government heads from the USSR, the USA, Great Britain, and France (July 18-23, 1955) the Soviet delegation presented a draft of a general European treaty on collective security in Europe which was rejected by the Western powers who had proposed the resolution of the problem of German reunification as a precondition. In May 1955 the Austrian State Treaty was concluded guaranteeing her development as a sovereign, democratic, and neutral state. The USSR proposed a number of disarmament initiatives. In August 1955 the Supreme Soviet of the USSR resolved to reduce the armed forces by 640,000 men as a unilateral action. The other socialist countries of Europe also proceeded to reduce their armed forces. In May 1955 the USSR withdrew its troops from the territory of the Port Arthur naval base. On May 14, 1956, the Soviet government decided during the course of a year to implement a more significant reduction in the size of its armed forces—another 1,200,000 men above the reduction carried out in 1955. In 1957 in the United Nations the USSR introduced a number of resolutions on banning the testing of nuclear weapons, on accepting the obligation not to use atomic and hydrogen weapons, and on reducing the armed forces of the USSR, the USA, and China to 2.5 million, and then 1.5 million men, and on the removal of military bases from foreign territories. In 1958 the USSR unilaterally stopped nuclear testing expecting the West to follow the example, but in vain! Soviet relations improved with Turkey, Iran, and Japan, with whom the USSR signed a declaration in 1956 ending the state of war and restoring diplomatic relations. The USSR conducted two-party negotiations with Great Britain and France in 1956 and concluded an agreement with the United States concerning cooperation in cultural and economic areas and the exchange of delegations of scholars and cultural figures. Relations with Yugoslavia were normalized. Relations with most socialist countries become stronger. But relations deteriorated with China and Albania who did not accept the Soviet Union's exposure of the Stalin cult.

On the other hand, not all of the Soviet Union's foreign policy steps contributed to the relaxation of tension between the East and the West. Some of those steps were caused by the international situation, others were shaped by the ideological orientation of the Kremlin leadership. The democratic, anti-Stalinist Hungarian revolution in October and November 1956, in which the diplomatic efforts of a number of European countries as well as the USSR failed to achieve a peaceful resolution, had a very negative influence on international relations. The direct use of Soviet troops to resolve a social and political crisis in a sovereign state was an extreme form of intervention in the internal affairs of Hungary which deepened the schism and distrust between the two social camps although the USA, the German Federal Republic, and other European states had not abstained from intervention in other ways. Together with the exposure of Stalinism at the Twentieth Party Congress, the Hungarian events of 1956 diminished the Soviet Union's prestige in international affairs as well as the popularity of communist ideas in the world, undermining the world communist movement.

The official view on the inappropriateness of exporting revolution clashed with practice when the USSR dictated the social structure of the countries of "the people's democracy"—its own allies. The entire world felt Soviet ideological pressure. If the capitalist states first used economic and political measures to secure their influence, the Soviet Union first used ideology. The USSR gave considerable assistance to young nation-states like Egypt, Iraq, Syria, India, and Indonesia, actively helping them to secure their political and economic independence while also strengthening its own geopolitical position. Diplomatic relations were established and cooperation developed with Burma, Cambodia, and Nepal; a trade treaty with Pakistan was concluded. The collapse of the colonial system, a process which the USSR supported, accelerated the change in the alignment of forces in the world.

Soviet-American relations experienced a series of severe crises. In 1960 an American U-2 spy-plane was shot down near the city of Sverdlovsk (now Ekaterinburg). The flights of spy-satellites over Soviet territory began at the beginning of the 1960s. In 1961 the Berlin Wall was erected which was long the symbol of the opposition between the West and East.

The Caribbean (Cuban Missile) Crisis of the fall of 1962 showed how fragile the peace was and how close mankind came to the brink of a nuclear war. In response to the deployment in Europe and Turkey of new American missiles which altered the military and political balance in behalf of the United States, and also in response to the threat to Cuba where the revolution was successful in 1959. Soviet rockets were secretly placed on the island. The United States could not accept that and the world found itself on the brink of a third world war. At the same time the experience of conflict resolution (the USSR removed its missiles from Cuba, the United States removed its missiles from Turkey and promised not to intervene in Cuba) encouraged both sides to avoid dangerous direct confrontations in the future.

On the whole the postwar world achieved a certain degree of stability toward the middle of the 1960s. The opposing systems headed by the Soviet Union and United States emerged from the major conflicts which threatened military confrontation and acquired experience in mutual coexistence under the new conditions caused by the formation of military and political blocs, nuclear weapons, and the appearance of numerous independent states from the ruined colonial system. The disarmament talks did not move the world forward, but they were an important step in limiting the nuclear arms race, which also had ecological significance: On August 5, 1963, the Nuclear Test Ban Treaty, which forbid the testing of nuclear weapons in the atmosphere, outer space and underwater, was signed in Moscow.

Politics and Society in the Early 1960s and Khrushchev's Dismissal

Some elements of the democratization of social life, such as (1) the attempts to resolve the housing problem which was the most serious issue, (2) the rise in the wages and pensions of many categories of workers, (3) the reduction in the length of the work day, and (4) the ambitious targets to raise the standard of living inspired a broad layer of the Soviet people. These processes promoted the growth of activism among the workers and brought to life many initiatives on the part of labor. That form of social activism was

Nikita Khrushchev and Leonid Brezhnev in 1962

welcomed by the authorities on a political level.

But there were other displays of social activity outside the bounds of the system's ideological orientation. In those cases the system reacted with cruelty and ruthlessness in the spirit of the Stalinist repression, regardless of the fact that the social activity emerged from the same working class whose interests the system was supposed to represent and protect. In October 1959, an uprising of 1,500 workers occupied in the construction of the "Kazakhstan Magnitka" was suppressed with the assistance of troops. The workers who had come to the city of Temirtau from the European part of the USSR were dissatisfied with their extremely poor living conditions, which sharply contrasted with the accommodations occupied by the citizens of the countries of Eastern Europe who worked alongside of them. In June 1962 a demonstration of 7000 people, most of whom were workers who were demanding better living conditions, was fired on in Novocherkassk. There is evidence of numerous victims of the armed suppression of workers' uprisings in three cities of the Donbas region (Donetsk, Artemovsk, and Kramatorsk), of the bloody suppression of strikes in Kemerovo and the other cities of the Kuznetsk coal field, and of collisions with the police at an agricultural machinery plant and a textile mill in Ivanovo. The workers' uprisings in June 1962 were directly connected with an increase in the price of meat and butter, which, given the low standard of living and the food problem, touched off a spontaneous rebellion.[15]

During the period which is today conventionally called the "thaw," there were many other disturbances, partially caused by the arbitrariness of the authorities, which were spontaneous uprisings against various developments in central or local government policy. Almost all of the disturbances were severely suppressed and ended with judicial proceedings against their participants, who could scarcely have understood that acting against the authorities' concrete acts of repression was protesting against the very system that had caused them. But the totalitarian bureaucratic machine could by no means change its nature, and having denounced the crimes of the bloody dictator, it continued to employ the same methods at the slightest threat to its existence. The spontaneous attacks on authority by the workers who were officially proclaimed the social base of the "socialist state" actually represented a much greater threat to the totalitarian one-party system than the individual acts of dissident intellectuals. However, both social streams opposing the system, the spontaneous workers' uprisings and the activity of dissident intellectuals, failed to reach the political level and never intersected with one another. But they created an element of instability within the system which along with Khrushchev's organizational experimentation did not suit the bureaucracy.

The processes which were destabilizing the system were also occurring on another level—within the organizational structure of management—the source of which originated in the upper political leadership, with Khrushchev personally. Many reorganizations characterized the period of the late 50s and early 60s. In November 1962, the plenum of the Central Committee of the CPSU agreed to restructure party organizations according to the production principle: independent industrial and agricultural party organizations were created. The frequent changing of the leading cadres took place. This provoked the displeasure of the party and the state apparatus, which desired stability and safety for its position. It is no accident that the first decision of the party leadership after Khrushchev's dismissal in October 1964 from the posts First Secretary of the Central Committee of the CPSU, member of the Presidium of the Central Committee of the CPSU, and Chairman of the Council of Ministers of the USSR was the cancellation of the first article of the Party Statute which restricted the occupancy of the leading offices of the party to two terms.

The "October Coup" of 1964 was the natural result of the activities of N.S. Khrushchev—a reformer who threatened the system which had given birth to him and which right up to the end kept him in a prison of ideological dogmas and myths, only some of which he was able to surmount. The political boldness of this remarkable leader turned into unreasoned, sometimes adventurist actions; his civic courage was combined with a narrow world view and the absence of culture, his innovative decisions often were overturned by campaigns organized by the administration, the arbitrary nature of the bureaucracy, and voluntarism. With all of Khrushchev's angry zeal for anti-Stalinism, he continued to serve faithfully the system formed by the dictator—the party's bureaucratic apparatus. But he failed to suit that bureaucracy as a leader.

Khrushchev's dismissal proceeded under the banner of the struggle against voluntarism and support for consistency in reform. The October Plenum recognized the error of the further concentration in one person of the duties of First Secretary of the Central Committee and Chairman of the Council of Ministers of the USSR. The Plenum underlined the necessity of the collective leadership principle, denounced subjectivism, management by orders and decrees, and rash voluntarist decisions. The nomenklatura did not need the innovations that threatened their well-being and the stability of their position under an energetic, but impulsive, unpredictable leader. The October Plenum rearranged the cadres, which actually meant a change in course. The Plenum chose L.I. Brezhnev as First Secretary of the Central Committee. At the same time the Presidium of the Supreme Soviet appointed A.N. Kosygin Chairman of the Council of Ministers of the USSR.

Notes

[1] For the details about the atmosphere of the first post-Stalin years and historic figures of the period see: Burlatski F.M. "After Stalin," *Novyi Mir [New World]* 1988 N10; Burlatski F.M. *Leaders and Councilors* Moscow 1990; Adzhubei, A. *Those Ten Years,* Moscow 1989; *Light and Shadows of the Great Decade: N.S. Khrushchev and his Time.* Leningrad 1989; Medvedev R.A. *They Surrounded Stalin,* Moscow 1990; Medvedev R.A. *N.S. Khrushchev: Political Biography,* Moscow 1990; *From the Thaw to Stagnation,* Moscow 1990.

[2] On March 6, 1953 at a joint meeting of the Plenum of the Central Committee of the Communist party of the Soviet Union, the Council of Ministers of the USSR, and the Presidium of the Supreme Soviet of the USSR the following members of the Presidium of the Central Committee of the KPSS were confirmed: G.M. Malenkov (from March 15 President of the Council of Ministers—Prime Minister), L.P. Beria (First Deputy Prime Minister and minister of internal affairs and state security), V.M. Molotov (First Deputy Prime Minister and minister of foreign affairs), K.E. Voroshilov (from March 15 President of the Presidium of the Supreme Soviet of the USSR—head of state), N.S. Khrushchev (Secretary of the Central Committee of the Communist Party, from September 1953 First Secretary of the Central Committee), N.A. Bulganin (First Deputy Prime Minister and minister of defense), L.M. Kaganovich (First Deputy Prime Minister), A.I. Mikoyan (minister of trade), M.V. Saburov (chairman of the USSR Gosplan) and M.G. Pervukhin (minister for electrical power stations and the electrical industry).

[3] See *Nashe otechestvo (Opyt politicheskoi istorii) [Our Motherland (The Experience of Political History)],* Moscow, 1991, pp. 440-442.

[4] According to Khrushchev's version, Beria had prepared himself to seize power and set aside the other "heirs." Khrushchev discovered his plot and prepared a preventive strike, discussing Beria's arrest with the other members of the Central Committee Presidium, who supported his initiative. The discussions took place without Beria's knowledge and the arrest was a complete surprise to him. In contrast to Khrushchev, Malenkov gives a different explanation of the "surprise" factor. Beria had actually prepared a coup and was planning to arrest Malenkov and assume the premiership. Beria shared his intention of replacing Malenkov with Khrushchev. But the latter, thinking things over and realizing that he could be next, told everything to Malenkov. Then the two with Marshal

Bulganin's assistance, turned the tables on Beria; in the Presidium of the Council of Ministers Beria was arrested instead of Malenkov. Beria knew about the discussions Khrushchev was having with the members of the Presidium, knew that a plot was being prepared, only thought that it would be to his advantage. As a result Beria conducted himself relatively calmly at the session of the Presidium, right up to the appearance of Marshal G.K. Zhukov, the immediate organizer of the arrest and his own dire enemy. As in all events such as this, there are a number of versions.

[5] For the documents and materials on the course of the rehabilitation see *Reabilitatisiia: Politicheskie protsessi 30-50-kh godov [Rehabilitation: Political Trials from the 30s to the 50s]*, Moscow, 1991.

[6] "The main spirit of his speech," S.M. Burlatsky, who was present, observed, "was the struggle against bureaucratism right up to his complete defeat. And this was the matter, such negative descriptions resounded on his lips as the degeneration of several elements of the state apparatus, the removal of several organs of the state from the party's control, total neglect of the people's needs, and graft and the corruption of the moral character of a Communist. It was necessary to see the faces of the people who were present. Surprise turned to embarrassment, fear to resentment. There was deadly silence after the speech, which the lively, it seemed to be, cheerful voice of Khrushchev interrupted: 'All this is so true in the long run, Georgi Maksimillionovich. But the apparatus—this is our support'. And only then was friendly applause heard, which continued for a long time."

[7] I. Erenburg, Liudi, gody, zhizn' ["The People, the Years, the Life"]in *Ogonok [The Little Light]*, 1987, No. 23, p. 22.

[8] During one of the sociological surveys of the 1960s, the purpose of which was to explain the people's attitude to various events in their own lives, the following answer was characteristic of those received back: "I myself consider it bad. All the events connected with the criticism of Stalin's activity and the work of the party are in this period. No other event in my life has burdened me as much as the failures during the first months of the war with Fascist Germany." Here is other evidence, relating to the first reaction after the discussion of Khrushchev's report: "... A week had passed before our party organization became familiar in detail with the documents of the XX Party Congress on the cult of personality and the entire time was impressed with them. ... In the first days it was irritating that the court had passed judgment over a dead man and so we wanted to continue to remember Stalin as a just and honorable man throughout his life, as he had been represented to us during the course of

more than three decades. . . . But then, when his greatest mistakes were known, it was difficult, very difficult to extinguish in our heart this great love, which had been so firmly planted in our organization."

[9] Plenum TsK KPSS 22-29 iiunia 1957 g. *KPSS v rezoliutsiakh i resheniiakh sezdov, konferentsii i plenumov TsK.* ["The Plenum of the Central Committee of the Communist Party of the Soviet Union of June 22-29, 1957" in *The Communist Party of the Soviet Union in Resolutions and Decisions of the Congresses, Conferences and Central Committee Plenums.*] Moscow, 1960, ch. 4., pp. 271-277.

[10] For the details of the power struggle see R.A. Medvedev, *N.S. Khrushchev*, pp. 117-123.

[11] The State Scientific-Economic Council of the USSR Council of Ministers was set up in February 1959; the functional role of the State Planning Commission of the USSR (Gosplan) was changed in January 1963; the mechanism for territorial planning through the planning commissions of the large economic regions of the USSR was developed after December 1963.

[12] G.I. Khanin. *Dinamika ekonomicheskogo razvitiia SSSR [The Dynamics of the Economic Development of the USSR].* Novosibirsk, 1991, p. 146.

[13] *Istoriia SSSR s drevneishikh vremen do nashikh dnei [The History of the USSR from Earliest Times to the Present]*, vol. XI, Moscow, 1980, p. 498.

[14] *Istoriia SSSR [USSR History]*, XI, 208.

[15] *Stolitsa [The Capital],* 1991, No. 4, pp. 20-21.

CHAPTER 8

THE PATH TO GLOBAL CRISIS: THE USSR UNDER BREZHNEV (1964-82)

New Reform Attempts

The late 1950s and early 1960s marked the end of the period during which the administrative command system created by Stalin attempted to mold the USSR into an industrial society. The alternatives of a scientific-industrial or postindustrial society opened up for the country. But development along either of these paths was impossible under the existing social and economic system, ideological orientation, and political structure. The radical renovation of the entire system was necessary for a new round of social progress.

Of course, the end of the period did not mean the end of the country's economic and cultural development. There was still a reserve of time during which the industrial economy could be successfully developed since the process of industrialization had proceeded unevenly in the various regions of the country and in specific sectors of the economy. Only the major sectors which did not touch all areas of life were fully developed; in other sectors progress was still possible. But the authorities' failure to take the appropriate measures in time, threatened a future of stagnation and crisis. The alarming symptoms of this were already apparent in the first half of the 1960s, when even according to the official statistics the average annual rate of growth of national income slowed from 10.2% in the 1950s to 6.5% while the rate of labor productivity fell from 8% to 6%.[1]

Although the preconditions for change were present, they were not reinforced by the readiness of the society to change. What circumstances complicated radical social reform?

1) The party and state nomenklatura in which all economic and political power was concentrated was not interested in any serious change.
2) The self-regulating market and the diverse forms of self-management within society were annihilated in the 1920s and 1930s and were, therefore, incapable of serving as an alternative to the state monopoly over power and property.
3) The massive repressions which occurred between the 1930s and 1950s, as well as ideological brainwashing, caused millions of Soviet people to form not only a conservative approach to their environment but a fear of taking the political initiative.
4) Years of totalitarianism had molded a generation that had little or no awareness of the democratic traditions of their own country or the world beyond the frontier.
5) Stalin's vulgarization and oversimplification of the concepts of socialism led to a distorted view of its ideals and values. Under the rubric of "collectivism" there remained no place to nurture the rights and interests of the individual; the idea of leveling was transformed into equality in poverty while outrageous privileges and benefits were reserved for the party and state elite. The idea of a messianic route to socialism had to be used to justify the numerous victims and the misery of Stalin's system. All this convinced the majority of the Soviet people that socialism could only be this way and that it was necessary to endure it for the sake of a bright future, if not for oneself, then for one's children and grandchildren.

And so the problem of changing the existing system mainly rested on significant layers of the population who were not ready for change, which explains the failure to complete the process of industrialization and the burden of the Stalinist inheritance. This also explains the contradictory character of the "reforms from above" undertaken in the 60s.

After Khruschev's fall, the new leadership (the CPSU Central Committee First Secretary L.I. Brezhnev, the Council of Ministers Chairman A.N. Kosygin, and USSR Supreme Soviet Presidium Chairman N.V. Podgorny) advocated economic reform. There was the usual attempt to stimulate industrial and agricultural production without changing the basis of the administrative-command system of management or relinquishing noneconomic coercion.

The new economic reform started in May 1965 when measures were undertaken to resolve the social problems of the village by the partial utilization of economic methods of management and the elevation of the purchase price for agricultural produce. But the main emphasis in agricultural policy was placed on expanding the role of the agricultural ministry in planning and managing agricultural production, while capital investment in the agrarian sector increased and the collective farm debts were written off. Nevertheless as a result of the reforms the aggregate rate of profitability on the collective farm was 22% and 34% on the state farm.[2]

With the curtailment of the policy of coercion, peasant productivity diminished and by the 1980s the collective and state farms became unprofitable despite the expenditure of many billions of rubles on capital investment. About 400 billion rubles were invested in agriculture between 1966 and 1980. The backwardness of social conditions in the village caused an outflow of population to the cities. The introduction of stable wages for farmers caused the growth of dependent attitudes and the collapse of the stimuli for labor. As a result within the 25 year period between 1964 and 1988 the amount of arable land under cultivation fell by 22 million hectares. The waste of agricultural produce represented 20% to 40% of the harvest,[3] and the country faced serious interruptions in food supplies.

In September 1965, the party leadership proclaimed an industrial reform which was the most radical of the entire Soviet period. Changes in planning and the intensification of economic incentives for greater industrial productivity were intended. The number of planned targets was cut to the minimum. New indices for securing product quality were introduced while preserving unrealistic targets for gross output. To provide an economic incentive for the producers, part of the proceeds were left to the disposal of the firm; the proceeds were divided into three funds: the financial incentives fund, the social, cultural, and consumer development fund (for the construction of housing, entertainment centers, and vacation guest houses), and the factory's self-financing fund. The practice of correcting planned tasks "from below," by the firms themselves, was introduced. The supervisory levels were not allowed to change plans during their implementation. At the same time the branch principle of industrial management was restored and the rights of ministries were expanded which maintained the vertical line of departmental supervision and inevitably contradicted the intended "autonomy" of the firms.

Even this halfway reform managed to stimulate economic growth. During the eighth Five Year Plan the annual rate of national income rose from 6.5% to 7.7%, and the rate of productivity increased from 6% to 6.8%.[4]

No sooner had the reform started than it was emasculated by the wing of the party and state leadership that feared even a partial transition to a market economy and advocated the preservation of the existing system of economic management without change. The group's prospects were favorable since it was headed by the CPSU General Secretary, Leonid Brezhnev, who had been accumulating power. The victory of his policy of curtailing reform became evident after the defeat of "Prague spring" in 1968, when the attempts to give a "second wind" to socialism in Czechoslovakia by using market mechanisms turned into a massive movement for social reform and frightened both the conservatives of the Czechoslovak Communist party and the Soviet leadership. After the economic reforms in the USSR stalled, economic indicators dropped: the annual rate of national income growth dropped from 7.7% during the eighth Five Year Plan to 3.5% between 1981 and 1985; the productivity growth rate fell from 6.8% to 3% during the same period.[5]

The leadership attributed the situation to purely objective factors: 1) the unfavorable demographic situation and the decline in the percentage of the population capable of work which made it impossible to secure the labor force required to continue the extensive development of the economy; 2) the exhaustion of the traditional raw materials base, mostly fuel and energy, and the rising cost of mining and transporting raw materials; 3) the physical wear-and-tear and the obsolescence of machinery, some of which dated from the 20s and 30s; and 4) the significant rise in military spending. All of these conditions had a negative impact on the USSR's economic development. But the crisis in the "socialist organization of labor" itself was no less an important cause of the deplorable situation. In the early 1980s the Academician T. Zaslavskaya stated that the main reason for economic failures was the inability of the existing system to guarantee the effective use of human resources and the intellectual potential of the individual in society.

While to the leaders of the country the way out of the potential crisis lay in expanding the number of branch ministries and departments (by the early 80s there were more than 100 union and 800 republican ministries, for the maintenance of which nearly 40 billion rubles were set aside)[6] and in the concession of newer rights to them, it was obvious to many people that without changing the economic system to include economic incentives for labor, it was impossible to avoid an economic crisis. The material incentives introduced by the economic reform of 1965, considered sufficient by the leadership, were actually unable to stimulate labor because the incentives comprised only 3% of their wages.

The existing system also did not provide an incentive for scientific and technological progress without which it was impossible to pass from an industrial to a scientific-industrial society. Despite the loud pronouncements on the "merger of scientific and technological progress with the advantages of socialism" toward the end of the 1970s, when the advanced western states were beginning the road to a post-industrial society, in the USSR only 10% to 15% percent of the industrial workers were employed in the most primitive forms of scientific-industrial economy.[7] At the same time 40% of the industrial workers, 55% to 60% of the construction workers, and up to 75% of the farmers in the USSR were employed as manual laborers.[8] By 1985, when 1.5 million mainframe and seventeen million personal computers were in operation in the USA, no more than several tens of thousands of mainframes and personal computers were in operation in the USSR and most of these were out of date.[9*]

As a result, by the middle of the 1980s, as in the 1920s, the USSR faced the danger that a new gap with the western countries would develop in stages. It could not be avoided if the existing system were preserved.

Authority and Society from the Mid-Sixties to the Early Eighties

After the leader of the party and the state changed in October 1964, a new generation (in comparison to Stalin's circle) came to power whose average age was between fifty-five and fifty-seven years. Leonid Brezhnev became the new party leader. In the opinion of the participants in the events of those years, Aleksei N. Kosygin, who was appointed head of the government, was a genuine alternative. This fact largely explains the strain in their relations. One of Brezhnev's closest associates, N.V. Podgorny (the former First Secretary of the Central Committee of the Ukrainian Communist Party), was elected Chairman of the Presidium of the Supreme Soviet of the USSR to replace Anastas Mikoyan. At first the central committee secretaries M.A. Suslov, A.N. Shelepin, Yu.V. Andropov, and N.G. Ignatov had the greatest authority in the new leadership, but as Brezhnev's power gradually became stronger, personnel transfers took place. The new leader's relatives, old colleagues, or people who expressed their unlimited support for him occupied more and more positions in the power structure. According to A.N. Shelepin's testimony, whole new ministries were set up to provide jobs for Brezhnev's relatives. By the end of the 70s and the beginning of the 80s only two of the people who had brought Brezhnev to power in 1964 remained in the leadership, Yury Andropov (the KGB chairman) and Marshal Dmitry Ustinov (the Defense Minister).

During the first months after Brezhnev's accession to power under the slogan of "the struggle against Khrushchev's subjectivism and voluntarism," the fight against the principal directions of his policy began. In the economy, the former system of centralized management not only returned but even expanded. The number of personnel in the managerial apparatus grew by 3 million between 1976 and 1983 alone, reaching 18 million people.[10] By this time there was one administrator for every 6 or 7 people in the country, for the maintenance of which tens of billions of rubles were needed annually. The curtailment of economical methods of management and the expansion of the state apparatus strengthened the role of the Communist Party in the state organs.

The party's control over all aspects of social life became stronger during these years. At the Twenty-Third Party Congress (1966) all of the innovations in party life accepted under Khrushchev, including the rotation of the party nomenklatura, were canceled. The right to control the administrative activity not only over production (which the party had earlier) but over scientific research, educational, cultural, and public health institutions was strengthened in the Party Statute at the Twenty-Fourth Party Congress in 1971. The party's control over the activities of the apparatus of state organs, ministries, and departments was also strengthened. The Constitution of 1977, for the first time in the country's history, assigned the guiding role in society to the Communist Party of the Soviet Union which was defined as a "nucleus of the political system."

To a greater degree than Khrushchev, Brezhnev used purely administrative methods in his work: like his predecessors he relied on the Secretariat of the Central Committee for preliminary discussions of questions prepared in advance, which effectively predetermined the decisions. The most important decisions for the country were made by a narrow circle of people, as in Stalin's time. Under the slogan of the "struggle for party unity," any point of view which did not coincide with the "general line" was suppressed and criticism and self-reliance were curtailed. Under Brezhnev dissenting speeches of members of the Politburo and secretaries of the Central Committee at plenums and party congresses were secretly forbidden. The practice of requiring the Secretariat's permission for the travel of the members of the elected party organs around the country was introduced and the text of official addresses had to be agreed upon before a party leader spoke in public. The regulations reached the peak of absurdity when, on Brezhnev's personal request, Podgorny had to stand and applaud during his speeches in large auditoriums to set an example for the audience. Later during the presentations of the work-of-the-party and Komsomol congresses, the groups of people assigned to provide "sound effects" in the hall were seated in various parts of the Kremlin Palace of Congresses.

The campaign to glorify Brezhnev began in the late 60s and grew stronger with the passing years. A special decision was made that Brezhnev would appear on television at a ratio of three times to one over the other members of the leadership. In 1973, a resolution on "elevating the authority" of the leader was passed. After that Brezhnev was granted the rank of an Army general; soon after, he became a Marshal of the USSR. He was decorated several times with the stars of a Hero of the Soviet Union and Hero of Socialist Labor, with the Order of Victory, two Orders of the October Revolution, two international Lenin Prizes, and numerous foreign awards.

Brezhnev's policy on "the stability of cadres," which received official confirmation in the decisions of the party congresses, meant not only a "reserved place" for the workers of the nomenklatura but also the preservation of the status quo. This approach provided all ranks of party leaders with freedom from punishment, encouraged the spread of corruption, promoted the abuse of their position of service, and created an even greater rift between word and deed.

Brezhnev became the most consistent spokesman for the interests of the party and state nomenklatura, so his rule turned into a "golden age" for them.

For an ideological foundation to curb the democratic impulses of "the great decade" (1953-1964), Brezhnev's circle first campaigned against Khrushchev's subjectivism and voluntarism, and later against the concept of "developed socialism." The assertion that the USSR had entered into this phase of development was first heard in 1967. The concept was based on the idea of the complete, although relative, uniformity of the Soviet society; the absence of any real internal contradictions, and, therefore, the presumption of its development without conflict. This in turn led to the formation of a complacent and self-soothing perception of the state of affairs on the part of the leadership of the CPSU. The concept of developed socialism rested upon the premise that an industrial society had been created in the USSR, which was the result of the construction of developed socialism. One of its main characteristics was " the further progress of socialism on its own base" (i.e., on the foundation of an industrial society).

About half a year after Khrushchev's dismissal, the period of Stalin's secret "rehabilitation" began. Not only his name but his very image began to appear (even becoming central) in fiction, films, memoirs, and periodicals. On the eve of the Twenty-First CPSU Congress such outstanding scientists and public figures as P. Kapitsa, I. Tamm, M. Leontovich, V. Kataev, K. Paustovsky, K. Chukovsky, O. Efremov, I. Smoktunovsky, G. Tovstonogov, and M. Romm wrote a letter to Brezhnev expressing their concern about the intended "partial or indirect rehabilitation of Stalin."[11] The address of the first secretary of the Moscow committee of the CPSU, N. Egorychev, answered the letter, stating: "Lately it has became a fashion . . . to look for some elements of the so called "Stalinism' in the country's political life and to use the latter as a bugbear to frighten the public, especially the intelligentsia. We tell such people: 'It won't do, gentlemen!'"[12]

The conservative ideological goals and the rather radical economic reform of 1965 were, it would seem, incompatible. Naturally such a situation could not last long. The end of the 1960s saw the curtailment of economic reform and the final appearance of a definitely conservative course. This occurred at a time when realistically the authorities should have been guided very little by ideological considerations and mostly by common sense, since the scientific and technological gap between the Soviet Union and the West was becoming more significant by degrees.

And so, after Khrushchev's dismissal, a sort of rebound to Stalinism and the Stalinist model of development occurred, but without a charismatic leader equal to Stalin and without the massive repression. The authorities did not seem to notice the changes that were taking place in the society. And those were quite considerable. In the 60s and 70s the demographic situation in the country seriously changed. As a result of "the second echo of war" the country's birth rate fell by 25%, while the mortality rate increased by 15%.

Population growth only occurred in Middle Asia and the Caucasus.

The completion of industrialization intensified the processes of urbanization. Within 25 years (1960-1985) more than 35 million rural residents moved to the city. The number of cities with a population over 3.5 million rose from 3 to 23. Seventy percent of the urban population was employed in industry, construction, and transport.

The educational level of the population grew significantly. In the 1960s and 1970s the transition to a comprehensive, full secondary education was completed. As a result, more than 64% of the population had a secondary or higher education by the end of the 1970s (compared to 17% in 1959).[13] At the same time the average level of culture still left much to be desired.

In comparison to the semihunger of the 1930s and 1940s, the standard of living of the population had improved significantly: workers' wages were constantly growing; a comprehensive pension system was functioning; separate apartments became the predominant type of urban housing; television sets, refrigerators, and radios came into everyday life; nutrition improved. The intensification of production, however, did not play a significant role in this; instead the wealth came from the export of large quantities of oil and gas to the West. During the 1970s and the first half of the 1980s, the country received 450 billion United States dollars from the export of energy reserves. But the money was spent mostly on food and the necessities of daily life. The half-way policy of improvements in the material position of the population proceeded from the limited nature of the changes in the entire social system. In the absence of a market mechanism, the steady growth of the production of food and other necessities was impossible. In the making of political decisions connected with the structure of production and the distribution of national income, the political system should have defended the interests of the workers; however, trade unions and youth organizations did not participate. The traditional structures of power continued to give priority to defense and the development of heavy industry. It was becoming obvious that without genuine democratic management of the economy, change for the better was impossible. In the absence of such changes, consumption only represented about

35-38% of the USSR's national income according to some figures (70-75% according to official statistics), compared to 65-82% in the developed countries of the West. Even in those countries of the socialist camp, where at least the elements of the market and democratic traditions were functioning, the standard of living was higher than in the USSR.

Social processes connected with the transition to postindustrial labor were occurring. In the 1970s the working class became the largest group. By the end of the 1970s workers represented as much as 65% of the population. The next group included white-collar workers and the intelligentsia (20-30%). The educational level of the workers and the inclusion of a significant part of the engineering and technological intelligentsia in industrial work continued to progress. A social and cultural environment, which created the preconditions for a postindustrial society, began to take shape; but these social and cultural changes were, on their own, insufficient to effect a transition to postindustrialism. These processes, which were not reinforced by full-scale economic and political reforms directed toward changing the entire system of socioeconomic and political relations, only led to individual breakthroughs and could not ensure the USSR's genuine transition to the postindustrial stage of development.

A deep moral crisis was one of the restraining factors. The preservation of a pseudodemocratic system under the slogans of democracy and humanity and the gap between the declarations and slogans of the official propaganda, on the one hand, and real life, on the other, not only hampered the formation of a morality suitable to the new conditions but also destroyed the norms of social conduct which were then in existence.

The contradiction between the existing political system and the new necessities and requirements of the country's population, whose intellectual and cultural attitudes were rapidly maturing, was the main conflict between the authorities and society during these years. The leaders were unable to perceive these new objective requirements and to accomplish these qualitatively new conditions of life. But if in former years the punitive machine of the OGPU-NKVD-MGB (successive names for the secret police) had protected the regime from opposition activities, under these new conditions there was much less fear of punitive organs, although the repression, which had lost its massive character and bloodiest forms, was still present.

With the curtailment of the processes of de-Stalinization and the spread of moral decay in society, the seeds of opposition against the system sprouted. They were most visible in the intelligentsia. The writers Yu. Daniel and A. Siniavsky were arrested in 1965 and sentenced in 1966. The poet Yu. Galanskov and journalist A. Ginsburg were arrested in 1967. The authorities' first measures against dissidents utilizing the potential of "specialized psychiatric clinics" were taken in 1968. In August 1968 K. Babitsky, L. Bogoraz, V. Delone, V. Dremliuga, and V. Fainberg were arrested as organizers of a demonstration in Red Square protesting the introduction of Soviet troops into Czechoslovakia. In 1969 the poet I. Gabai and demoted general P. Grigorenko were arrested. The first Soviet Open Public Association—the initiative group for the protection of human rights in the USSR (N. Gorbanevskaya, S. Kovalev, L. Plushch, P. Yakir, and others)—was set up in May 1969. Academician Andrei Dmitrievitch Sakharov had begun his campaign for the protection of human rights in 1965. In 1974 A.I. Solzhenitsin was deported to the West. In 1976 a group promoting the implementation of the Helsinki Accords in the USSR was established in Moscow under Yu. Orlov and he was arrested with the other Soviet leaders of the group in 1977. Almost all of the leaders and active participants in the human rights movement in the USSR were arrested or exiled by the end of 1979 and early 1980, including A.D. Sakharov who was exiled to the city of Gorky, now known by its former name of Nizhni Novgorod. It was the end of open associations in the country.

Nationalist movements and organizations also operated in the USSR: the Ukrainian national movement, the Lithuanian national-democratic movement, the Estonian national-democratic movement, the Armenian national movement, the Georgian national movement, the Crimean-Tatar movement for their return to the Crimea, the Meskh movement to return to the motherland, the Jewish movement for emigration to Israel, and the Soviet Germans' movement for emigration to the German Federal Republic. All of them taken together represented the dissident movement.

The meetings and demonstrations of thousands of people in favor of the nationalist opposition took place in Erevan (1965), Andizhan and Bekabad (1966), Frunze (1967), Chimkent (1967), Nalchik (1967), Tbilisi (1968,1978), Grozny (1973), Vilnus (1977), Tallinn (1980), Mtskheta (1981), Ordzhonikidze (1981), and other places. The resistance to the totalitarian regime and re-Stalinization of society was quite strong. According to the KGB data in 1968-1972 3,096 organized groups of "nationalist, revisionist, and other anti-Soviet deviations" were uncovered and, for participation in which, "precautionary measures" were taken against 13,602. The data refutes the view of those who saw in the dissident movement no more than "a few CIA paid operatives." The movement's geographic spread was rather wide. According to the same KGB documents, the above mentioned groups were found in the cities of Moscow, Sverdlovsk [Ekaterinburg], Tula, Vladimir, Omsk, Kazan, and Tiumen and in the Ukraine, Latvia, Lithuania, Estonia, Belorussia, Moldavia, Kazakhstan, and other places.

In 1975 the second in command at the antisubmarine ship *"Storozhevoi"* [Patrol], third captain V.M. Sablin, arrested the ship's commander, took his place at the bridge and led the ship into neutral waters where he addressed a revolutionary appeal to the country's leaders. He did not oppose Soviet power or the "Communist point of view"; he warned of the pernicious nature of the policy being conducted in the country. The appeal ran: "Citizens, the Motherland is in danger! Embezzlement and demagogy, deceit and window-dressing are undermining it. . . . Return to Lenin's principles, to democracy and social justice. . . . Respect a person's honor, life and dignity. . . ." In his farewell letter to his wife, the political officer wrote: "The iron state and party machinery is really made of steel, any open blow to the front will turn into empty sounds. . . ." The fighter planes stopped the "Storozhevoi." Sablin was courtmartialed and shot.

The authorities' responded to all of these actions by perfecting the apparatus of repression. With the accession to the leadership of the KGB of the party secretary Yury V. Andropov, the struggle against dissidents began to be conducted on a "scientific" basis. At his suggestion the Fifth Department of the KGB was set up to work against dissidents. Its employees were placed in all or almost all youth, religious, national, social, and political institutions, organizations, and movements. They conducted secret and open investigations of human rights activists and their potential associates and monitored their telephone conversations. The scale of punishments changed, too: in most cases dissidents were tried not for their political activities but for criminal offenses. Many of them were sentenced to forced "treatment" in specialized psychiatric institutions found on the payroll of the Ministry of Internal Security (MVD). In 1972, on Andropov's initiative and with the consent of the Politburo of the Central Committee of the CPSU, the Supreme Soviet of the USSR issued a decree authorizing the security organs "in necessary instances" to give dissidents an official warning in the name of the proper authorities demanding the cessation of the "politically harmful activities" being conducted by them. If the person warned in this way later committed a "political offense," the official record of the previous warning was included with his criminal record and, as a rule, the punishment was more severe.

Censorship was tightened again during Brezhnev's period of power. Many interesting books, articles, and films did not see the light of day between the middle of the 1960s and the early 1980s because of their ideological character. On the other hand, B. Okudzhava, V. Vysotsky, A. Galich, and Yu. Kim were recognized in those years. Theater and movie productions by T. Abuladze, A. German, Yu. Liubimov, G. Volchek, A. Tarkovsky, A. Efros, and M.Zacharov opened new horizons in theater and movies. V. Voinovich, V. Aksionov, B. Nekrasov, V. Dudintsev, A. Rybakov, and others wrote books which broke out of the mold of "socialist realism." The art works of A. Shilov, I. Glazunov, and others created a lot of interest and for a time caused spirited discussion among the intelligentsia.

In those years economists who saw success in the development of the economy through its transition to a market system suffered persecution. In various years the authorities also obstructed the historians of the "revisionist school"—P. Volobuev, K. Tarnovsky, M. Gefter, and others who had their own view of the historical development of Russia and the world in the twentieth century.

Representatives of the creative intelligentsia found themselves in a more severe bind than during Khrushchev's time. The rehabilitation of the victims of Stalin's repressions was practically stopped.

All of these measures were based on the program of the official ideologists to intensify the struggle between the two systems during peaceful coexistence which was nothing more than a variation on Stalin's thesis on the intensification of the class struggle along the road to socialism.

And so the development of the totalitarian system between the mid-1960s and early 1980s deepened the gulf between the authorities and society. All of the attempts at moderate political reform undertaken by Khrushchev were interrupted for a long time by Brezhnev and his circle. The symptoms of stagnation in the economy were accompanied by a tendency toward stagnation in political life, in culture, and in the social development of the USSR.

The USSR and the World in the Brezhnev Era

The new Soviet leadership's shifts in internal policy could not help but influence the direction of its foreign policy. Despite the stabilization of relations between the East and the West by 1964, Brezhnev's heritage in international relations was nothing to envy: the unity of the socialist camp was broken by the "schismatic activities" of the Chinese leadership; relations with the West became complicated because of an open American involvement in Vietnam; the USSR's role and influence in the third world countries did not bring the expected results and did not justify the huge expenditure. Therefore, the three tasks of Soviet foreign policy during the entire period of Brezhnev's rule remained: 1) stopping the disintegration of the world socialist system, 2) normalizing relations with the West, and 3) supporting "friendly regimes" and movements in the third world countries.

The greater emphasis on ideology was the major characteristic of the USSR's foreign policy during these years. Khrushchev's successors strayed from his idea of "peaceful coexistence" and competition between countries with different social systems. The idea itself was not rejected under Brezhnev, but it was given a somewhat different interpretation. The foreign policy was based on the ideology of confrontation, which implied that peaceful coexistence between the socialist camp and capitalist states could not endure because of the very nature of capitalism. In addition, in their attempts to justify their departure from the former interpretation of the concept of peaceful coexistence, the party ideologists announced that it was nothing more than a new form of class struggle between labor and capital, and the idea of the continual intensification of the ideological struggle between the two systems was introduced.

These theoretical positions were invoked to explain not only the strengthening of the regime's support for radical movements in the countries of the West and Third World but also the severity of the policy of persecuting dissidents inside the USSR and in socialist countries. The ideological basis of Soviet foreign policy strengthened the paternal relationship between the USSR and other countries and complicated its relations with the West, which was interested in the economy rather than ideology. All this only complicated the international position of the USSR.

Brezhnev's administration continued to derive its foreign policy from the thesis on the radical change in the balance of forces in the international area connected with the weakening of the global position of the United States and her allies. This, in turn, was explained by the two systems' achievements of strategic military parity (consequently, depriving any country of the possibility of victory in a nuclear war), and by the growth of the revolutionary struggle in the developing countries. The Soviet leadership considered the partnership of the western countries with the USSR in détente as a sign of their weakness, a necessary measure.

Actually the West agreed to détente for other reasons. By the early 1970s the nuclear arms race had led to the oversaturation of their arsenals, rendering the conduct of nuclear war impossible. The attitude of the public of the western countries toward their governments' policies had changed. The policy of "the containment of communism" (for example in Vietnam) had resulted in huge spending and human casualties, a decline in the international prestige of the United States, and, as a result, to a change in the social and political climate in the countries of the West. The sensible policy of the Soviet government toward the war in Vietnam and the Middle East crisis of 1967 also played a role in the achievement of détente.

Acknowledging international détente, the USA and its strategic allies proceeded from the idea that the totalitarian and authoritative regimes of Eastern Europe probably could preserve their strength during a serious military confrontation. Thus the dismantling of the totalitarian power structures in the USSR and the other countries of the socialist camp was considered one of the possible results of détente.

In this way, by the end of the 1960s and beginning of the 1970s, after a whole decade of crises, the gradual normalization of the relations between the East and West began.

In 1969 the Warsaw Treaty states proposed the convening of the Conference on Security and Cooperation in Europe (SBSE). On August 12, 1970, the Soviet-West German treaty was signed which confirmed the final postwar frontiers in Europe and gave up the use of force. A similar treaty between West Germany and Poland was signed in December 1970, and in December 1973, between West Germany and Czechoslovakia. West and East Germany recognized each other in December 1972.

September 1971 witnessed the signing of the agreement between the United States, the USSR, Great Britain, and France on West Berlin which was also based on the idea of the peaceful, diplomatic settling of the problems of the status of the city.

The first visit to Moscow of an American president in the history of Soviet-American relations took place in May 1972 with the arrival of Richard Nixon. The Treaty on Limiting Antiballistic Missile Defense Systems, the Temporary Agreement on Limiting Strategic Missiles (SALT-1) and "The Basic Principles of Soviet-American Relations" were all signed. Those documents together with the Agreement on the Prevention of a Nuclear War (signed in 1973 during Brezhnev's visit to the United States) meant a turn from confrontation to détente in the relations between the two leading world powers.

In May 1975, the Convention Banning the Production and Stockpiling of Bacteriological and Toxic Weapons and On Their

Elimination was implemented. In 1976, a Soviet-American treaty limiting underground nuclear tests for peaceful purposes was signed. A whole series of documents were signed on the development of cooperation between the USSR and United States in other areas. In summer 1975, the joint space flight of the spaceships "Apollo" and "Soiuz" took place. The exchange of commodities between the United States and Soviet Union grew by 800% between 1971 and 1976. The fact that forty of the one hundred treaties and agreements concluded since 1933, when diplomatic relations between the USSR and the United States were first established, were signed between 1972 and 1975 shows the intensification and success of the negotiation process during the period.[14]

The climax of the détente policy was the signing of The Final Act of the Conference on European Security and Cooperation in Helsinki on August 1, 1975. The core of the document was the Declaration of Principles for Mutual Relations between the Member-States, that recognized their sovereign equality, the absence of force or threats of force, the inviolability of postwar borders, the territorial integrity of member states, the peaceful resolution of conflicts, noninterference in internal affairs, and respect for human rights.

Yet the détente did not last long. The main reasons for its failure were not only the diametrically opposite understandings of its motives and prospects, but the resulting attempts to use détente to change the balance of power in the world in one's favor. In 1976, the Soviet Union began to deploy medium range nuclear missiles on the territory of Czechoslovakia and the German Democratic Republic. This created an additional threat to the Western European states and changed the strategic balance of power between the East and West in favor of the USSR. Confrontation between the United States and Soviet Union also arose in regional conflicts (Angola, Mozambique, Ethiopia, and Nicaragua). The final collapse of détente occurred in December 1975 after the introduction of Soviet troops into Afghanistan. "Brotherly assistance" to the Afghan people cost the Soviet Union dozens of billions of rubles and brought death to 15,000 Soviets and over one million Afghans.

The steps taken by Brezhnev's leadership considerably undermined the USSR's authority and for a long time postponed its admittance into the world community as a full and equal member. The new round of the arms race placed the economies of the USSR and other socialist states into a very critical situation that facilitated the growing global structural crisis in those states.

Simultaneously the policy of détente gave birth to and strengthened many antitotalitarian processes in East-European states. The attempts of the Czechoslovak leaders to make their society more democratic in 1968 with the help of economic and political pluralism, the evolution of their ruling party, and genuine popular self-government ended with the introduction of Warsaw Treaty troops and the termination of the "Prague spring" by force. But under détente the Soviet government did not dare to use armed intervention to interfere in their allies' affairs. However, other measures were developed to preserve Soviet influence over them and maintain the status quo in Eastern Europe. A whole series of interstate treaties and agreements, setting up almost thirty interstate offices, provided for the close economic and military integration of the Comecon and Warsaw Pact states. That considerably limited the states' sovereignty and increased the role and importance of the USSR in the "socialist camp." In the West these measures were called "the Brezhnev doctrine."

Yet despite the operation of the doctrine, the situation was slowly moving out of Moscow's complete control. The mass actions of Polish workers in 1970 resulted in the formation of the Solidarity independent trade union. It was the first organized mass social and political force in the "socialist camp" that did not arise as a result of reform "from above" but from a mass movement "from below" and became a genuine alternative power. Despite the introduction of martial law in December 1981 (at the climactic moment of the antigovernment activities), its strength led in the final analysis to the fall of the Communist regime and its leader, Lec Walesa, became the first democratically elected Polish president in the postwar period.

China, Albania, Romania, Yugoslavia, and the Korean People's Democratic Republic finally drifted away from the USSR in those years. Their complicated relations with the USSR were conditioned by their significantly independent internal and foreign policies.

Thus, the foreign policy of the Soviet leadership in 1965-1985 traveled a complicated road from harsh confrontation with the West (during the second half of the 1960s) to the relaxation of international tension (during the détente of the 1970s), which was followed by a new period of confrontation in the late 1970s and early 1980s that took mankind to the brink of nuclear war. The mutual distrust between the East and West and the continuation of the arms race was not the only cause of this; the extremely ideological nature of Brezhnev's foreign policy was also responsible. All of these reasons caused the failure of the USSR and other socialist states to enter the world community, which had seemed possible in the mid-1970s. This failure postponed the prospect of a transition to a postindustrial society for many years. As in domestic policy, the totalitarian regime whose time had passed long ago was the main obstacle.

Notes

[1] G. Khanin, Ekonomicheskii rost: alternativnaia otsenka ["Economic Growth: Altnernative Estimates"], *Kommunist,* 1988, No. 17, p. 85.

[2] M.S. Gorbachev, *Ob agrarnoi politike KPSS v sovremenniykh usloviakh* [*On the CPSU Agrarian Policy under Contemporary Conditions*]. Moscow, 1989, p. 14.

[3] Gorbachev, p.5.

[4] Khanin, *Ekonomicheskii rost,* p.85.

[5] Ibid.

[6] *XIX Vsesoiuznaia konferentsiia KPSS* [*XIX All-Union CPSU Conference*], Vol. I, pp.46-48.

[7] See Narodnoe khoziaistvo SSSR za 70 let. *Iuibileinyi stat. ezhegodnik* [The USSR National Economy for 70 Years. *Anniversary Statistical Almanac*], Moscow, 1987, p. 89.

[8] See above pp. 109, 126.

[9] See *SSSR i zarubezhnye strany, 1987 [The USSR and Foreign Countries, 1987],* Moscow, 1988, p. 110.

[10] *Novyi Mir [New World],* 1988, No. 5, p. 187.

[11] See *Ogonek [The Small Light],* 1988, No. 25, p. 30.

[12] See XXIII sezd KPSS. Sten. otchet. [The XXIII Congress of the

CPSU. Stenographic Report], Moscow, 1966, vol. I, p. 126.

[13] See *Chislennost' i sostav naseleniia SSSR: Po itogam Vsesoiuznoi perepisi naseleniia* [*The Number and Composition of the Population of the USSR: According to the Figures of the All-Union Population Census of 1979*], Moscow, 1984, p. 23.

[14] *Istoriia diplomatii* [The History of Diplomacy], vol. V, book 2, Moscow, 1979, pp. 218-219.

***Editor/Translator Note:** In Russian the computer is usually called an EVM or *elektronnaia vychislitelnaia machina*]

CHAPTER 9

"PERESTROIKA" THE NEW RUSSIA (1985-1994)

The Pre-History of Perestroika

By the end of the 1970s part of the Soviet leadership and millions of rank and file citizens had already recognized that without radical changes the existing system was doomed.

The limited, conservative economic reform of 1979, designed to strengthen the role of centralized planning and management, did not prevent the stagnation of production and the further widening of the scientific and technological gap with the West. In 1981, the total production in some sectors was lower than 1980.[1] Indeed, there was no growth of labor productivity. During an inspection in 1979 and 1980 of the technology of almost 20,000 types of machines and tools produced by native mechanical engineering, one out of three had to be removed from production or fundamentally modernized.[2] False claims reached unbelievable levels. In Uzbekistan a "record" of some kind was obtained: false reports on the sale of cotton reached 600,000 tons, which cost the state hundreds of extra rubles annually.[3]

External factors also exercised a harmful influence on the economy. The accelerated arms race and the ruinous and unpopular Afghan war strained the economy; up to 45% of the industrial budget was spent on the military-industrial complex, and not only did war expenditures account for 3 to 4 billion rubles[4] annually but approximately 15,000 Soviet and 1.5 million Afghan solders were killed. The West refused to cooperate with the USSR in technical and technological fields and the sharp decline of world oil prices in the early 80s stopped the influx of petrodollars. In the 70s, 180 billion petrodollars in American currency were used to import food and consumer goods instead of for industrial development.[5] The combination of all of these influences resulted in an extremely difficult situation for the Soviet economy.

In the early 80s a social crisis similar to the one between 1966 and 1970 became apparent. The national income declined to 46.3% of the previous figure, in real per capita income to 35.7%, in retail turnover to 38.4%, and in the provision of services to 35.7%.[6] Every year the gap between the effectiveness of Soviet medical and educational equipment and the world standard became more evident.

While the hardships associated with the economic decline were shared by the "lower" part of the social pyramid, the party and state "managers" had their own strictly guarded system of benefits and privileges. Corruption and embezzlement were increasing, all of which led to growing social apathy and declining morals. In the early 70s academician A.D. Sakharov wrote: "Our society is infested with apathy, hypocrisy, petty egoism, open cruelty. Most representatives of its upper layer—the party and state managers, the highest circles of prosperous intellectuals—firmly hold on to their secret and open privileges. They are deeply indifferent to human rights' violations, the interests of progress, the problems of security and the world future."[7]

By the late 70s and early 80s stagnation was quite evident in all spheres of social life. The figures of L.I. Brezhnev, the country's leader who was physically frail and decorated with all kinds of awards, and his "immortal" Politburo personified the decay of the existing political regime. Even part of the ruling elite admitted that the oppressive social atmosphere in the country had reached its limit. According to N. Ryzhkov the morals of society "could be compared to the verses of the old folk song "Today Is the Last Day I Play. . . ."[8]

After Brezhnev's death in 1982 the country's new leader Yu.V.

Andropov made the first attempts to get out of the quicksand. He introduced measures to establish elementary order and to get rid of corruption. But his actions were intended to preserve the system. As A.N. Yakovlev said, Andropov stood only for "cleaning off the dirt when the level exceeded the limits of sanitation."[9] At that time a group of comparatively young leaders (M.S. Gorbachev, E.K. Ligachev, N.I. Ryzhkov) began to gain power. Those who struggled for power were prepared to continue the renovation of the system. Although the dissident movement was defeated, people treated Andropov's activities with sympathy and hope. His modest theoretical innovations paved the way for social thought. Masses of people gained hope of coming changes for the better. Probably the main result of Andropov's fifteen month rule was a kind of moral stimulus. The influence of that reforming impulse was felt even after Andropov's death in February 1984.

After Andropov's death the balance of power in the Politburo, on which much but not all of the country's political life depended, was against his closest associates. The majority of the elderly Politburo members decided Andropov's "saving" mission was fulfilled. They were afraid further reform would threaten their personal power.

Seventy-two year old K.U. Chernenko became General Secretary of the CPSU Central Committee and later Chairman of the USSR Supreme Soviet Presidium. Many people who knew him considered his election a mistake[10] or an accident, at least an absurdity.[11] But from the point of view of the leaders of the CPSU who were striving for the "quiet" life and for strengthening their positions, or from the scholar's point of view it was neither a mistake nor an absurdity. A. Toynbee once came to the conclusion that "a symptom of collapse and the reason for a schism within society is the degeneracy of the minority who used to be able to manage things because of their creative potential, but who now retain power only because of the use of rough force."[12] The election of elderly, mortally ill Chernenko as the leader of the party and the state, instead of the young dynamic Gorbachev who Andropov intended to be his successor, served as "a glaring signal of total system failure, its lack of vitality."[13] The absence of change contributed to the "ripening" of public opinion as people began to clearly understand the need for changes. The prospects of the reformers coming to power increased with the progress of Chernenko's illness. Gorbachev became the second person in the party and, therefore, in the state—not only formally but in fact. According to Ryzhkov's frank confession, a group of reformers had already been formed, and to start reforms "just had to wait . . . for him [Chernenko] to die." [14] At the time of Andropov's death there had been a strong consensus that M.S. Gorbachev was the only worthy successor to the dying leader. It was also understood that "the country wouldn't stand another Chernenko, a person of his views, his intellectual and political weakness."[15]

K.U. Chernenko died on March 10, 1984. A day later a plenum of the Central Committee of the CPSU elected M.S. Gorbachev the party's General Secretary. At that time nobody could imagine that he would be the gravedigger of the system that brought him to power. He did not suspect it either.

The Search for Ways to Perfect Socialism

The April 1985 plenum of the Central Committee of the CPSU proclaimed the acceleration of the country's social and economic development as the strategic goal of the Soviet leadership and of all Soviet society. The main engine of the acceleration was to be scientific and technological progress, the technical renovation of machine-building, and the activation of the "human factor": better labor discipline and more initiative on the part of all working people. The Communist reformers hoped to overcome such dangerous tendencies as the corruption and irresponsibility of the nomenklatura, as well as the lack of authority of party and state leaders. The absence of the term "perestroika" in the political vocabulary of 1985 is interesting. Later Gorbachev admitted that at first he had only foreseen the perfection of a stagnant society and the correction of "certain defects" in socialism.[16]

The renovations mostly touched economics, where the symptoms of the coming crisis were most acute. Certain measures were undertaken to put the economy in order, to strengthen labor discipline and improve technology, to increase personal responsibility, and to extensively change senior and mid-level managers. People greatly supported measures that could not help but improve the situation. In 1985-1986, the growth of labor productivity in industry and construction was 1.3 and in agriculture 3 times greater than the annual figures from the eleventh five year plan. Investment in social programs also increased significantly.[17] But the first results caused the leaders to become euphoric and strengthened their faith in the power of decrees and correct orders. The "new edition" of the Communist party program adopted by its Twenty-Seventh Congress, which asserted the new policy of "perfecting" socialism after the failure to build Communism by 1980, contained new and quite challenging tasks, including the provision of an apartment or house for each family by the year 2000. No serious preliminary calculations had been made nor substance given to such a task. In May 1985 a large-scale antialcoholism campaign began which was supposed to overcome the centuries-old traditions through administrative measures of prohibition. A secret article in a party-state directive regulating the annual decrease in the amount of alcohol production brought the figure to the lowest level in years, depriving the economy of 70 billion rubles after only the first 4 years of the campaign. Moonshining increased considerably and a sugar shortage developed.

In general the country's economy continued using the old working scheme—extensive use of coercion and orders, political campaigns, rush work, plan corrections, and the opening up of additional resources. The administrative-command system of management and the huge bureaucracy (more than eighteen million people with a total annual salary of 40 billion rubles) choked the political innovations, rendering them ineffective. In 1987, the country's leadership started speaking conservatively of putting the brakes on reform. The January (1987) plenum of the CPSU Central Committee proposed the new goal of democratizing social life instead of economic acceleration. The replacement of the nomenklatura continued. But there was still no understanding of the contradiction between the large-scale goals and the perceived stability of the economy and political life because of the general failure to understand the influence of the global crisis on social and political structures.

Mass media played an important role in society's intellectual emancipation by openly reconsidering its past and present life. Thanks to the policy of "glasnost" the mass media became one of the most influential instruments of change, expressing ideas and attitudes that heretofore had no place in political structures monopolized by one party. The Chernobyl nuclear catastrophe in April 1986 forced people to think anew about the status quo.

Slowly the painful realization grew that the economic model had to be changed instead of perfecting the old system. Production and, therefore, administrative and political changes were needed.

In June 1987 the plenum of the CPSU Central Committee approved the first reforms under perestroika, proclaiming the transition from administrative to economic management. But the reform mechanism was not consistent with its goal. In fact the mechanism did not allow different forms of property, did not affect the basis of the existing administrative-command system in the economy or the ministries, and did not affect the people's attitude toward labor. In addition, the half-way reforms contributed to the growing economic distress. They were destroying the old economic system without building a new one. But that only became clear much later. Thanks to Gorbachev's position the party retained its role as the "initiator" and "moving force" of reform.

In 1988 the Twenty-Ninth All-Union Conference of the CPSU put forward the question of deep political reform for the first time during the Soviet era. The roots of the "braking mechanism" which slowed down the innovations were being concealed by the country's political system. Even the preparation for the conference was unusual: the election of the deputies was relatively democratic (some were otherwise) because the party supported the reform policy. The people's faith was strengthened by the idea that the party could guide innovations. Almost all of the important reformers, the so-called "perestroika superintendents," were CPSU members then and some of those who were not, such as Sobchak and Stankevich, joined it. The CPSU's radical political course was explainable. On the one hand the country's leaders needed to find new ways of "innovation" as the old ones turned out to be ineffective. On the other hand, under the influence of democratic processes, new economic and political alternatives appeared and their "authors"—the new political forces—

threatened to explode the CPSU's political monopoly.

The conference decided to merge "socialist values," including the "historically formed" one-party system, with some of the elements of liberalism: a state based on law ("socialist" legal norms), a Soviet parliamentary system, and even a division of powers. The CPSU was to become the fourth and the main power. But the party leaders overestimated their flexibility and adaptation skills and the unnatural merger did not help the CPSU. However the merger excited the masses of people who did not know much about liberal values. It contributed to the formation of new political structures, such as reformed soviets. And Gorbachev wanted to use them as a new "motivator" for perestroika, as the party's effective assistant.

Perestroika in Crisis

The halfway, inconsistent reforms aggravated the social and economic situation in the country. In 1989 it became clear that the USSR was entering an economic crisis: faster growth of per capita incomes, the consequences of the antialcohol campaign, food and consumer goods shortages. The CPSU lost the initiative because the democratization of the party lagged behind that of society, and its authority declined because of its timidity and indecisiveness. The initiative passed to the soviets renewed during the quasidemocratic election of 1989 and 1990 and to the newly emerging political parties and movements. The deputies who were elected included such reform-minded democrats as A.D. Sakharov, G.H. Popov, B.N. Eltsin, Yu. N. Afanasiev, and others who advocated radical social reform in addition to the usual nomenklatura officials.

In May 1988 the Democratic Union, whose initial membership was around 2,000 and whose leader was V. Novodvorskaya, proclaimed itself the first opposition party to the CPSU. In April 1988 the first independent organizations—Popular Fronts—appeared. By the middle of 1989 the Estonian Popular Front had 60,000 members, the Latvian Popular Front had 115,000, and the Lithuanian Sajudis had 180,000 members. Later similar organizations materialized in all of the union republics and autonomous subdivisions.

1989 was the year when many new parties came into being in the USSR. Most of the social forces that are active now emerged in 1989 or early 1990.

The newly formed parties revealed all the leading political ideas. Demsoiuz (the Democratic Union) represented the ultraliberals who stood for the radical and uncompromising change of social models. The Russian Christian Democratic Movement, the Christian Democratic Union of Russia, the Christian-Democratic Party of Russia and other groups belonged to this political wing. The first representatives of liberal ideas were the Democratic Party of the Soviet Union, later known as the Conservative Party, which was created in August 1989, the Democratic Party, the Liberal Democratic Party, and three constitutional-democratic parties. The largest and the most genuinely liberal party—the Democratic Party of Russia—was formed in May 1990 and led by N. Travkin. Its original membership ranged between 25,000 and 30,000 members. The Republican Party of the Russian Federation appeared in November 1990. It had 30,000 members; its co-chairmen were V. Lysenko, S. Sulakhshin, and V. Shostakovsky. Many of these parties, public organizations, and liberal movements were united in the massive social and political organization known as Democratic Russia created in October 1990 on the basis of the electoral movement that emerged during the spring 1989 election of USSR People's Deputies.

Social democracy was represented by two major organizations—the Social Democratic Association and the Social Democratic Party of Russia. Anarchists organized the Anarcho-Syndicalist Confederation and the Anarcho-Communist Revolutionary Union.

In the fall of 1990, radical right-wing political parties, such as the Russian National Democratic Party, began to form. The monarchists formed a separate party of state traditionalists who later joined with other right-wing groups.

Political pluralism even touched the Communist Party of the Soviet Union, where five different points of view emerged, but on the whole the party still favored its own General Secretary.

With all of the diverse organizations which were springing up, the "Communists" and "democrats" were the movements and parties at the center of the political struggle. The latter promoted decisive reforms: the privatization of state property, the creation of a full parliamentary system, and security for political rights.[18] Gorbachev and the "Communists" worked for the "renewal of socialism" and called for the preferential development and reform of socialist property, collective forms of social relations, and self-management. The truth about the mechanisms of socialist reform was spoken of in a very general way.

Mikhail Gorbachev

With the appearance of political opponents, Gorbachev's "revolution from above" had to deepen the reforms. But the reformers did not receive extensive support for their own projects from the upper and middle ranking nomenklatura. In contrast to China, in the USSR the party apparatus was unable to work out a well-thought-out concept of reform. Responding to demands for the elaboration of a whole program of changes, Gorbachev announced that "in these demands there is the echo of the past, an echo of a long period of dependence" and that it was absolutely enough "to determine what matters: socialism, the interests of the people, democracy, glasnost, and the party as the generator of ideas and the organizing force."[19] This was evidence of the exhaustion of the celebrated potential of the Communist reformers in the USSR. But while the army, KGB, MVD, and basic means of mass information remained under the control of the party and state nomenklatura, it used these entities to keep power in its own hands. With the weakening of the Communist Party's position and the appearance of an opposition, the problem of authority became especially serious.

In Ryzhkov's opinion, Gorbachev "felt, as things went to pieces, that he had lost his perspective and therefore his strength and authority in the country," but the President of the Supreme Soviet of the USSR (Gorbachev occupied this post after October 1988), where the constitutional authority was concentrated, was unable to resolve the problems of state administration; in reality he was a speaker in a parliament.[20]

To compensate for the failure of the government's authority the post of President was introduced at the Third Congress of People's Deputies in March 1990. Gorbachev was the first and, as it turned out, the last President of the USSR. He did not understand that the essentially mechanical introduction of the presidential post, while preserving the system of soviets—thereby joining constitutional and executive functions—did not lead to a division of power but to a conflict between authorities. But this conflict only became apparent after the demise of the Communist Party of the Soviet Union. Nevertheless, the introduction of the post of President and Gorbachev's activities in this post did not prevent the further deterioration of the situation.

The beginning of the disillusionment of the masses with Gorbachev and his policy was connected with the gap between the high-sounding statements, the leader's promises, and the absence of positive changes in the actual lives of the people. Moreover, in December 1989, the absolute value of the volume of industrial production began to fall, continued to fall throughout 1990, and fell more rapidly in 1991. The union budget deficit reached 92 billion rubles in 1989 (almost 10% of the gross national product).[21] According to some indices, such as the extraction of oil and coal and the smelting of metal, by the end of 1990 the country had the same productivity as in the early 1980s. A fourth of the enterprises were unable to fulfill their contractual obligations.[22] The production and consumption of foodstuffs fell. Consumer goods disappeared from stores, standing in line (queuing) grew. But the major factor was the decline in Gorbachev's moral authority. All this, together with the fear of repression by the authorities, led to the appearance of a strike movement in the country. In March 1991, there were strikes at 542 enterprises. Direct and indirect losses for that month from miner's strikes alone exceeded 4 billion rubles.[23] Then the union republics, who were trying to find an independent path out of the deepening crisis, began the "sovereignty parade." Ignoring some of the decrees of the center, proclaiming the priority of republican laws over union ones, the republics not only tried to solve their own problems, but also to exert pressure on the center. The paralysis of authority in the country grew.

An important cause of the radicalization of the masses and the fall of the Communist Party was the rupture of the information blockade, which brought numerous facts to light on the crimes of Stalin and, later, of the CPSU leadership as a whole. Then, for the first time, the timid, often disguised, criticism of Lenin began. These conditions created a base among the masses for the formation of a single opposition, joining everybody who wanted to genuinely reform society. Such an opposition, which received the "democratic" designation, in reality could more accurately be called anticommunist. The "democrats" from the intelligentsia and some of the more adaptable and progressive representatives of the nomenklatura, who had proposed the radical reformation of society and had been expelled from the party apparatus, headed it. One of the prominent former CPSU leaders, Boris Eltsin—a former candidate member of the Politburo of the Central Committee of the CPSU, secretary of the Central Committee, and first secretary of the Moscow City Party—became its leader. In the fall of 1987, as a result of a conflict with the majority of the Politburo, he had been removed from his posts but he attained growing popularity with the people. In March 1989 he was chosen a people's deputy of the USSR.

Despite the efforts of the central authorities and the leadership of the CPSU, Eltsin, reacting against the inconsistent course of the country's leadership and favoring radical reform and the abolition of the nomenklatura's privileges, was elected Chairman of the Supreme Soviet of Russia in May 1990. One of the first steps of the new leadership of the largest republic of the union was the acceptance on June 12, 1990, of the Declaration on Sovereignty, proclaiming the priority of the republican over the union constitution.

Significant changes occurred in the consciousness of the masses. The absence of positive results from the activities of the leadership of the CPSU and the destruction of information barriers led to the rapid growth of skepticism about the possibility of "improving" and "completing the development" of socialism, as well as the feasibility of further movement within the boundaries of the socialist choice.

The erosion of the former ideological and moral values, in which generations of Soviet people had been raised, was tantamount to a spiritual drama. From 1990 on, sociologists found evidence, on the one hand, of the growing popularity in society of new ideas and spiritual values, identified in former years as "bourgeois," and, on the other hand, of the growth of pessimism, political apathy, and a lack of confidence in tomorrow. The truth is that for many this pessimism was connected with the deterioration of their economic situation.

Marking time in these conditions, Gorbachev, who was bound to the "socialist choice" and its lack of confidence in "democracy," experienced sharp criticism from both the right and left flanks. The "democrats" judged him for indecisiveness and inconsistency, while conservative circles indicted him for "betraying the cause of socialism" and "bourgeois degeneration." While 52% of the participants in a sociological survey supported Gorbachev's activity in December 1989, only 21% supported him in October 1990.[24] At the Fourth Congress of People's Deputies of the USSR (December 1990) Ryzhkov declared that perestroika in the form in which it was conceived in 1985 had suffered defeat.

The struggle between the two fundamental political lines appeared with new strength in the summer and autumn of 1990. The "democrats" demanded rapid transition to a market economy and the state's divestiture of its ownership of the means of production. During preparations for the Twenty-Eighth Congress of the CPSU the conservative wing of the party advanced its own program, "The Platform of the Working People in the CPSU," whose economic sections were oriented toward reform and the defense of socialist property.

The Centrists, including Gorbachev, submitted their own project entitled "Toward a Humane, Democratic Socialism," which formed the basis of discussion at the CPSU congress. The discussion resulted in the acceptance of the document which declared that the single "alternative to the administrative-command system, which had outlived itself, was a market economy."[25] This thesis was very important as a platform statement since, with definite reservations, Gorbachev took the position of the democratic forces on this fundamental question. This, it seemed, made their cooperative activity possible, despite the conservative attitude of the congress's majority.

Under these new conditions the democratic opposition changed tactics. Instead of the former scheme in which the apparatus conducts a reform and the opposition "presses" against it, the idea of a left-center coalition was advanced. As it had done earlier, the apparatus would continue to occupy the key positions while the representatives of the opposition would participate in the power structures. The coalition's program had to be worked out jointly. Even Gorbachev and Eltsin approved such a compromise. At their meeting on July 31, 1990, an agreement was reached on working out an alternative to the government's economic program. A commission was created for this under the leadership of academician S. Shatalin and the Deputy Chairman of the Council of Ministers of the RSFSR, G. Yavlinsky. The commission (mainly Yavlinsky) prepared the project, estimating that the USSR's transition to a market economy would take 500 days. The project created a genuine economic basis for a union of the republics. But under conservative pressure and the lack of confidence in "democracy" syndrome (the CPSU thought that the "democratic" alternative itself was mostly a power struggle between specific individuals) Gorbachev withdrew his support of the program. An emasculated, still-born "compromise" program was adopted. The coalition that had been formed with the "democrats" was dissolved. Under these conditions Gorbachev became all the more inclined to an alliance with the conservatives. An index of the strength of their position was the retirement of Foreign Minister Eduard A. Shevardnadze as a protest against the impending dictatorship (December 1990) and the bloody events at Vilnius (January 1991) caused by an attempt to militarily crush the independence movement, which had intensified its attacks on reforms in Russia. In December 1990, the President of the Council of Ministers of the USSR, Ryzhkov, was replaced with V.S. Pavlov. At the same time a reorganization of the government was implemented.

But the need to quickly sign a new union treaty between the republics and the mass demonstrations of workers organized by the Democratic Russia movement forced Gorbachev to veer toward the left again. Gorbachev had already affirmed the impossibility of using strong methods against those republics that had declared sovereignty. On April 23, on the initiative of the President of the USSR, a meeting was held with the leaders of the RSFSR, Ukraine, Belorussia, Uzbekistan, Kazakhstan, Azerbaijan, Kirghizia, Tadzhikistan, and Turkmenistan. The meeting, which took place at Novo-Ogarevo, near Moscow, seemed to mark the beginning of the process of stabilization of conditions in the country. The combined search for a political compromise for the preparation and acceptance of a new union treaty had begun.

It was all the more obvious that deep reforms were impossible without the assistance of the West. The question of the degree to which the world community was interested in the changes taking place in the USSR and how prepared they were to assist became increasingly important. A group of Soviet economists headed by Iavlinsky and his colleagues from Harvard University worked out a program for the USSR's transition to a market system by 1997. The draft proposed by the scholars included an enumeration of the areas requiring foreign assistance. But because of Gorbachev's lack of desire for radical market reforms, Iavlinsky's "Harvard Plan" did not form the basis for the assessment of the prospects for the development of "East-West" relations at the London meeting of the seven major industrial countries with the Soviet president in July 1991.

Internal opposition to the course of radical reform continued. It took new turns during the preelection campaign for the President of the RSFSR (May-June 1991). Essentially, the platforms of the candidates (V. Bakatin, B. Eltsin, V. Zhirinovsky, A. Makashov, N. Ruzhkov, and O. Tuleev) presented various proposals for the realization of economic and political reforms. Around 57% of the participants voted for Eltsin and the radical reform platform. For the conservatives who were concentrated in the ruling structures of the state, the CPSU, and the RSFSR Communist Party created in 1990, this was a danger signal. At the plenum of the Central Committee of the CPSU on April 24, 1991, the question of lack of confidence in Gorbachev and the need to introduce a state of emergency in the country was publicly circulated for the first time.[26] Gorbachev announced his resignation from the post of General Secretary of the Central Committee of the CPSU, but after a hastily summoned meeting of the Politburo he rescinded his own declaration. On June 17, immediately after Eltsin's victory in the presidential elections in Russia at a meeting of the Supreme Soviet of the USSR, Prime Minister Pavlov, referring to the deterioration of the situation in society, demanded the government be given full emergency power, but this decision was not made because of Gorbachev's intervention. At the plenum of the Central Committee of the CPSU in July 1991, the question of Gorbachev's resignation from the post of party leader was proposed. On the eve of the plenum, 32 of the 72 secretaries of the regional committees of the Communist Party of the RSFSR announced the need to "summon Gorbachev to account."[27] It was becoming obvious that the political struggle over the content, pace, and methods of social reform was entering the decisive phase.

Glasnost and the "Revolution of Minds"

If "perestroika" began in economics when the goal of "accelerating social and economic development" was proposed, its leitmotiv in intellectual and political life was "glasnost'" (openness).

Glasnost was understood in the Russian language as "publicity" (*izvestnost*), "public opinion" (*obshchestvennost*), "publication" (*oglashenie*) and "publicity" (*oglaska*).[28] The party used the term before perestroika to refer to one of the principles of "socialist competition" which required the results of the competition to be made available to all of the participants. The term "glasnost" was first used in reference to new policy directions in Gorbachev's speeches at the Twenty-Seventh Congress of the CPSU (February 1986) when it was proclaimed that "without glasnost there is none and cannot be any democracy."[29] The term, like the policy of developing glasnost, appeared because the serious opposition of some of the members of the old nomenklatura had forced the reformers to rely more actively on public opinion. Therefore the major content of the concept, in Gorbachev's opinion, signified nothing more than the renewal of Communist ideology. The movement originally paraded under the slogans: "More democracy, more socialism!," "The Return to Leninism," and so forth. From the very beginning glasnost was clearly limited by boundaries. Gorbachev frequently affirmed in the name of the party leadership: "We stand for the broad development of glasnost, but in the interests of society, socialism, and the people."[30] The "chief ideologue" of the party, Ligachev, saw the attempts to reevaluate Soviet history on the pages of print, as a "campaign of slander"[31] and proposed "placing our history in the service of the Soviet society, its interests." The leader of the Russian Communists, I.K. Polozkov, proclaimed the need for the CPSU's monopoly over glasnost.[32] He explained that "it is difficult to live and work with a man with split consciousness."[33] The leaders of the ruling party who feared such a "split personality" were uneasy because "attempts to attack the CPSU could be undertaken as a form of glasnost."[34] But it was impossible to stop the emancipation of consciousness that had begun.

The policy of glasnost acquired a special dimension after the January (1987) plenum of the Central Committee of the CPSU. At the end of 1986 and the beginning of 1987 literary pieces began to be published in the country which had not been allowed in print during the re-Stalinization of the Brezhnev period—A. Rybakov's *Children of the Arbat,* B. Dudintsev's *White Dresses,* D. Granin's *The Die-Hard,* Yu. Trifonov's *The Disappearance,* V. Grossman's *Life and Fate,* and A. Pristavkin's *The Precious Cloud Slept.* The works of native men-of-letters which had been banned for a long time were published—E. Zamiatin's *We,* B. Pilniak's *The Tale of the Unredeemed Moon,* A. Platnov's *Chevengur, The Foundation Pit,* and *The Juvenile's Sea,* B. Pasternak's *Doctor Zhivago,* M. Voloshin's verses, M. Gumelev's poetry, the work of V. Khodasevich, N. Shmelev, and V. Nabokov who was unknown to the broad mass of Soviet readership, the memoirs of N. B. Verberov, N. Mandelshtam, A. Tsevaeva, L. Razgon, A. Larina (Bukharina), E. Drabkina, and A. Zhigulin. The works of Russian philosophers—N. Berdiaev, V. Soloviev, P. Sorokin, V. Rozanov, V. Lossky, and A. Losev—were made available again to the native reader. After this the works of the èmigrè "Third Wave"—N. Brodsky, A. Galich, V. Nekrasov, A. Aksenov, and V. Voinovich were published. One of the brightest events was the publication of A. Solzhenitsyn's *Gulag Archipelago.*

The policy of glasnost touched other spheres of cultural life besides literature—cinematography, the fine arts, music, and theater. In all of the artists' unions the abolition of the earlier "recommended" by the departments of the party's leadership occurred. The years of perestroika were marked by the appearance of the antitotalitarian films—"Repentance," "Tomorrow There Would Be War!" "The Cold Year of Fifty-Three," "The Solovetsky Regime," "Balthazzar's Banquet," "The Servant," and "One Cannot Live So." The plays of M. Shatrov, "The Peace of Brest," "Farther . . . Farther . . . Farther!" were performed in the country's leading theaters. The return of cultural figures to prerevolutionary events and the fates of historical figures, including the tragic murders of the Tsar's family, were discussed. Television began to transmit live more often. New popular programs appeared on television and, thanks to their openness and their controversial nature, won great affection from viewers ("Opinion," "Before and After Midnight," "the Fifth Wheel," and so forth). The live broadcast of sessions of the Twenty-Ninth Party Conference of the CPSU and the Congress of Peoples Deputies of the USSR, which caught the attention of a huge number of people, were unique phenomena.

The best literary compositions and scientific studies of western authors which uncovered the nature and sources of the totalitarian regime were published—G. Orwell's *1984*, R. Conquest's *The Great Terror*, K. Popper's *The Open Society and its Enemies*, A. Rabinowitch's *The Bolsheviks Come to Power*, R. Tucker's *Stalin: The Path to Power*, S. Cohen's *Bukharin*, and Zh. Zhelev's *Fascism*.

Within the party leadership there was no single opinion on the purposes, tasks, and "extent" of glasnost. The conservative wing, represented by Ligachev, was inclined toward suppression of the criticism of totalitarianism. The Centrists, including Gorbachev, supported glasnost, but "within the limits of the socialist choice." Much for the real development of glasnost was accomplished by A.N. Yakovlev who was considered its "father" and most consistent supporter among the CPSU leadership. From 1987, he headed the Commission of the Politburo on the Rehabilitation of the Victims of Political Repression, and in 1989, he headed the Commission of the First Congress of People's Deputies of the USSR on the Political and Legal Evaluation of the Soviet-German Nonaggression Pact of 1939. In 1988, at the Twenty-Ninth Party Conference of the CPSU, as the chairman of the commission for the preparation of the project concerning the conference's resolution "On Glasnost," he removed all references to the "limits" and "scope" of glasnost from the final text. Undertaking the publication of the documents on Soviet-German relations in 1939-1940, on the forceful inclusion of the Baltic states in the USSR in 1940, and the Katyn shooting of Polish officers, he facilitated the enlightenment of many people.

Literary critics, economists, and publicists (N. Shmelev, O. Latsis, G. Popov, V. Seliunin, Yu. Chernichenko, I. Kliamkina, Yu. Kariakin, and others) made a significant contribution to the "revolution of minds." Their efforts helped the masses move from criticism of the specific "deformities" of socialism, Stalinism, and the "mechanistic limitations," which were first discovered in the economic management system in the 1970s, to recognition of the culpability of the social organization system itself (accurately defined by Popov as the administrative-command system). The system's roots did not lie in Stalinism but in Marxist-Leninist doctrine itself which was, in the opinion of A. Tsipko, "no more than a utopia, but a utopia suitable for tearing up life."[35]

But this situation provoked a sharp rebuttal from the adherents of the communist ideology. In March 1988, an open letter from a Leningrad chemistry teacher, N. Andreeva, was published in the newspaper *Soviet Russia* under the pretentious title "I Cannot Abandon My Principles." It openly condemned the "borrowing from the West" of the essentially antisocialist policy of glasnost and "perestroika," which in the author's opinion was leading to the falsification of the "history of socialist construction" and the open revision of Marxism-Leninism. Andreeva called for the defense of Stalin and Stalinism against the intelligentsia—"the intellectual heirs of Dan and Martov" and the "students of Trotsky and Yagoda." On the day after the article's publication Ligachev (Gorbachev was abroad at the time) declared her an "example of the socialist's adherence to principles" in a conference with the leaders of the mass communications media. That was enough for the local press to begin to reprint Andreeva's article. The regional party committees accepted this as a signal to stop the criticism of Stalinism and the negation of all of Gorbachev's perestroika.

Before the answer intended to reflect the Central Committee's official view was published in *Pravda* a month later, there was almost no criticism in the newspapers of N. Andreeva, Stalin, or his system. The article in *Pravda* contained a sharp and subjective criticism of Stalinism and characterized Stalin's apologists as opponents of the party's policy on "perestroika." This was enough to resurrect the issue in print and give even more strength to the wave of criticism of the totalitarian system. It was impossible to restrain the wave. And the attempts to "orchestrate" the press by holding regular meetings between party leaders and newspaper and magazine editors, television producers, and representatives of artists' unions had little effect.

The "Nina Andreeva Affair" marked the boundary between the conservatives and reformers in the party leadership as far as glasnost and perestroika were concerned. Ligachev was removed from his post as ideological leader and named supervisor of agriculture. In his place Yakovlev became the chief ideologue of the CPSU (the "number two" position in the party hierarchy).

But the actions of Andreeva and the other defenders of Stalinism had their own social base. Some were far from ready for a radical reexamination of values. Democracy and glasnost exposed the inconsistencies in society and accelerated a sharp collision between different courses and interests: the liberals and orthodox communists; the "westernizers" and "Slavophiles"; the privileged layer of the party-state nomenklatura and the broad masses; workers in state enterprises and the so-called "cooperatives"; a number of nations and nationalities, religious faiths, and so forth. The deterioration of the economic situation, the radicalization of the masses, and the weakening of the CPSU's authority over society caused these contradictions to become conflicts over time. The most serious and frequently bloody conflicts were between the nationalities. The armed conflict in Nagorno-Karabakh between the Armenians living there and Azerbaijan, in which this autonomous area was included, began in 1988. Between 1989 and 1991, mass conflicts and slaughter occurred in Central Asia. Hostilities between the residents of South Osetia and Georgia date from 1990. Dissatisfaction with and the deterioration of the state of affairs in society finally destroyed confidence in Gorbachev and the system for which he had acted as a reformer and at the same time a defender.

Therefore, glasnost showed the internal problems of society and exposed people to humanistic values; until then the West, its way of life, and democratic traditions were unknown. This was for many the real opening up of the world. It is well known that under Gorbachev the world was "physically" revealed. As a result of some relaxation in the rules for traveling abroad in 1989, the number of Soviet citizens traveling abroad (8.2 million) exceeded the number of foreigners visiting the USSR (7.8 million) for the first time. Probably glasnost was the most important factor in determining the irreversible nature of the changes in society and the emancipation of the consciousness of tens of millions of people. That, in the final analysis, led to the defeat of the conservatives in August 1991.

New Political Thinking

The Soviet leadership's new foreign policy created favorable conditions for internal reforms. It was based on the philosophical and political concept called "new political thinking." This concept proceeded from the thesis of a diverse, but mutually dependent and integral world and, therefore, the impossibility of resolving international problems by force. Instead of a balance of power, a balance of interests founded on the basis of common human values over class ones was proclaimed as the universal method for resolving international questions. Essentially there was nothing new in Gorbachev's ideas, which in one form or another had been proposed by the great thinkers, beginning with I. Kant and ending with M. Gandhi, A. Einstein, and B. Russell. The Soviet leadership's service consisted in the attempt to give to these ideas the appearance of a philosophical basis for a new foreign policy. Consciousness of the real threat of nuclear self-annihilation, and also the economy's inability to support the colossal burden of the cold war, permitted and simultaneously induced them to do this. The thesis on the impossibility of victory in a nuclear war, first expressed at the beginning of the 1950s by Malenkov, would be the cornerstone of the new political thinking.

The change in the Soviet leadership's foreign policy began, as happened earlier, with a change in the head of the foreign policy establishment. In June 1985 instead of A.A. Gromyko, who had headed the Ministry of Foreign Affairs for thirty years, the former first secretary of the Central Committee of the Georgian Communist Party, E.A. Shevardnadze, was named minister. A significant renewal in the ministry's leadership followed with the replacement of 10 of the 12 deputy ministers, the majority of the leaders of the administration. Since they retained the system of having a party leader represent all foreign and domestic policy viewpoints, Yakovlev who had earlier served as ambassador to Canada, continued to be directly responsible for foreign affairs in the Central Committee of the CPSU. But all key decisions were personally made by Gorbachev.

Three basic foreign policy directions were determined by the group of reformers: the normalization of East-West relations through disarmament; the defusion of religious conflicts; and the establishment of firm economic and mutually advantageous political contacts with various countries.

Regular Soviet-American meetings on a high level began. Gorbachev and Ronald Reagan met with one another in Geneva (November 1985), Reijkavick (October 1986), Washington (December 1986), and Moscow (July 1988). The signing on December 8, 1987, of the historic agreement on the elimination of a whole class of nuclear weapons—medium and short range missiles—was the result of those complex negotiations. For the first time the superpowers advanced from negotiating a reduction in the numbers of a specific weapon to their elimination. Agreements on the development of humanitarian cooperation and economic relations between the USSR and the United States and also with other western countries were obtained.

The very climate of East-West relations radically changed. The immediate threat of a thermonuclear conflict disappeared. In the West good feelings toward the USSR and Gorbachev emerged.

In February 1988, Gorbachev decided on the withdrawal of the troops from Afghanistan. On February 15, 1989, the last Soviet soldier left the Afghan land. Due to the efforts of Soviet and western diplomats success was achieved in controlling the conflicts in Ethiopia, Angola, Mozambique, Nicaragua, and southeast Asia. The USSR withdrew her support from the regimes in Libya and Iraq. And during the Persian Gulf crisis in the summer of 1990, Moscow was the first to take a position of support for the West in curbing the aggression of Iraq against Kuwait.

The change of leadership in the Chinese People's Republic and later in the USSR and also the termination of the conflicts in southeast Asia and the end of the war in Afghanistan made the normalization of relations between the USSR and China possible. Gorbachev's visit to Beijing in May 1989 gave an important stimulus to this.

The democratic movement in Eastern Europe acquired strength under the influence of the changes in the USSR. The pressure of the opposition caused the Communist regimes in Albania, Bulgaria, Hungary, the German Democratic Republic, Poland, Rumania, Czechoslovakia, and Mongolia to fall during massive demonstrations in 1989 and 1990. Vietnam set out upon the path of market reforms. The unification movement began to acquire strength in Germany. In July 1990, the USSR unexpectedly agreed to the union of the two German states and the recreation of a single Germany. The Warsaw Treaty organization and the Council of Mutual Economic Assistance (Comecon) were terminated. For two or three years radical changes occurred in Eastern Europe which surprised the Soviet reformers and in many respects defined the processes which had been moving forward in the USSR. These changes, on the one hand, required more consistent steps in the reformation of society and showed the path of these reforms. Yet, on the other hand, the changes consolidated the conservative forces in the country who demanded judgment against the "traitors" Gorbachev, Yakovlev, and Shevardnadze who had ostensibly produced a "pro-American" policy and ruined "the socialist system." But, despite the turn from confrontation to cooperation with states having different social systems and the denial of a world revolution (which in a transformed way had been held in the country for seventy years), the new political thinking gradually gave rise to an opposition. In the foreign policy actions of the Soviet leadership between 1985 and 1988 the former tactic of trying somehow to oppose and separate the United States from her allies and the countries of the "third world" was retraced for a time. Despite the announcement on the need to de-ideologize international relations, the USSR even more faithfully followed the principles of "socialist internationalism," to the detriment of its own interests at the time. From 1986 to 1989, the volume of free assistance to foreign countries comprised almost 56 billion rubles in foreign currency, more than one percent of gross national product. 67% of this aid (22 billion rubles) went to Cuba.[36] Some initiatives, such as the proposition for the liquidation of nuclear weapons by 2000, clearly had a propaganda purpose. Nonetheless, on the whole, there was a new policy. Ideological principles exercised less and less influence on the USSR's foreign policy after 1989. Moreover, the deterioration of the internal economic situation of the USSR forced its leadership to yield more, not infrequently one-sided, concessions to the West in the hope of obtaining economic assistance and political support. The country felt some of the negative consequences of such a policy for many years as in, for example, the failure to build housing for the soldiers returning from Europe.

Nevertheless by a series of bold initiatives the USSR broke the ice of international confrontation and acted as the leader of a radical reform of international relations, which meant the end of the Cold War.

The August Coup and the End of Perestroika

A crisis situation had taken shape in the country toward the end of the summer of 1991. The center, headed by Gorbachev, continued to mark time while the liberals advocated the radical reform of society. The threat came from the conservative side of the Communists. But the maneuvers and compromises of Gorbachev had a definite result: at the last plenum of the Central Committee of the Communist Party of the RSFSR the odious figure of the leader of the republic's party organization, Polozkov, was replaced. Moreover, after sharp discussions, the leaders of 9 republics arrived at a draft union treaty, the signing of which was set for August 20, 1991. The USSR stood on the threshold of reform. On August 21, a session of the Council of the Federation was designated for the discussion of a plan for the radicalization of reform. The signing of the new Union Treaty meant, in principle, the transition to a genuinely federal state, the abolition of a number of state structures which had been formed in the USSR, and their replacement by new ones. The conservatives in the country's leadership, being unable to destroy the process at the stage of the formulation of the draft of the Union Treaty, decided not to allow its signing.

At the time Gorbachev was essentially without advisers. During the year preceding the coup the departure of Shevardnaze, Iakovlev, and other reformers was accompanied by the strengthening of the role of the President of the USSR and consolidation around him of those who would later actively participate in the August coup. In the General Secretary's absence on the very eve of the coup the Vice President of Russia, A.V. Rutskoi, and A. Yakovlev, Gorbachev's closest comrade-in-arms, were expelled from the party by the decision of a Central Committee commission. On August 16, in an open letter to the Communists, Iakovlev declared that despite the reformers' strength, the democratic renewal of the CPSU had not occurred. Moreover, this deliberate line was leading to the party's isolation from all democratic thought and a flirtation with chauvinist or Stalinist organizations. "As far as the president is concerned," he wrote, "these are obvious attempts to assign to him the role of a hostage to a shady structure...."[37]

On August 18, the President of the USSR, M.S. Gorbachev, during his vacation, was isolated at his dacha in the Crimea (although there are still missing pieces to this story). Vice President G.I. Yanaev published a decree on his accession to the office of President of the USSR. On the night of August 18/19 the State Committee for the State of Emergency (GKChP) in the USSR was created, including G.I. Yanaev, Premier V.S. Pavlov, USSR Minister of Defense Marshal D.T. Yazov, USSR KGB chairman V.A. Kriuchkov, deputy chairman of the Defense Council O.D. Baklanov, the Minister of Internal Affairs of the USSR, B.K. Pugo, the chairman of the Peasants' Union, V.A. Starodubtsev, and the president of the Association of State Enterprises, A.I. Tiziakov. The GKChP declared a state of emergency in several regions; they announced the dissolution of those organs of power acting against the Brezhnev Constitution of 1977; the activity of opposition parties and movements was stopped; meetings and demonstrations were forbidden; firm control was established over the mass media; and troops were introduced into Moscow. The Chairman of the Supreme Soviet of the USSR (from March 1990), A.I. Lukianov, who had not been included in the GKChP, actually supported the conspirators.

B. Eltsin and Russia's leadership led the opposition to the participants in the coup. On the morning of August 19, their appeal to the citizens of Russia was broadcast, in which the actions of the GKChP were characterized as a reactionary unconstitutional revolt, and the coup itself and its decisions were declared illegal. The country seemed to calmly accept the rebels in the beginning. There were no massive strikes or demonstrations. But of the 2,000 Muscovites asked on August 20, "Do you consider the activity of the GKChP legal?" only 13% answered "yes" while 73% answered "no."[38] Toward the evening of August 19 thousands of Muscovites occupied a defensive position around the Russian White House on the Krasnopresnenskaia embankment of Moscow, and toward the evening of August 20, according to some estimates, more than 50,000 people formed a barrier on the square in front of the Russian Supreme Soviet building.[39] Three young people died in an attempt to stop the advance of the troops. Several of the country's regions and some military units refused to carry out the decisions of the GKChP. The rebels had lost. D. Yazov did not decide to send the order to storm the Russian Parliament building and accepted the decision for the withdrawal of the troops from Moscow. On August 21 an extraordinary session was called of the Supreme Soviet of Russia which had supported the republic's leadership. On August 22 the conspirators were arrested.

The cause of the coup's failure was the conspirators' ignorance of the changes in the consciousness of the masses, the new role of the republic, and the official center of the opposition—Russia had a president and democratically elected organs of power. The conspirators' calculations that Eltsin would not support Gorbachev were unjustified, even though he had done everything possible to prevent Eltsin's accession to power. The chief causes of the coup's collapse were poor organization and the GKChP members' fear of taking responsibility for decisionmaking.

After the August events the activity of the CPSU was banned; it had discredited itself: its organs had supported the GKChP, while all of the GKChP's members, with the exception of Tiziakov, were part of the Central Committee or the Central Committee Commission of the Communist party. The property of the CPSU was nationalized, its assets (those that could be found) were frozen, and the publication of some of its newspapers was temporarily suspended. The CPSU as a state structure ceased to exist. The fundamental levels of power passed to the "democrats." The majority of the republics after this refused to sign the union treaty, and The President of the USSR, M.S. Gorbachev, more and more began to play a decorative role. The question of the further existence of the USSR was called.

To withdraw from the center, which had discredited itself, and to preserve some of the connections between the republics, the leaders of Russia, Ukraine, and Belorussia (the founding countries of the USSR) renounced the union treaty of 1922 and created the Commonwealth of Independent States (*Sodruzhestvo Nezavisimykh Gosudarstv*) in Minsk on December 8, 1991. The last empire in the world, joined together for more than 7 decades by the Communists' ideology, social system, and coercion, collapsed like a house of cards. The amorphous SNG(CIS), which included eleven of the former union republics (without Georgia, Estonia, Latvia, and Lithuania) seemed then the only means for a civilized divorce. Perestroika ended in a way entirely unforeseen by its creator. The President of a country which no longer existed went into retirement.

The New Russia

After the August coup the state posts both in the center and in local areas passed not as much to the representatives of the democratic forces as to the workers in yesterday's nomenklatura. At the beginning of perestroika many of them presumed that active and honorable work in the party structures guaranteed the improvement of the people's lives. Observing the ineffectiveness of their own efforts, they advocated reform of the CPSU. Some of the them broke with the party. But there was a definite "boundary" to the reforms, beyond which neither Gorbachev nor the apparatchiks who would come to power in 1991 wanted to, or could, go.

The new regime did not proceed to what would seem to be the useful and necessary step—new general elections for the central and local organs of governmental authority. They preserved the composition of the Congress of People's Deputies and the Supreme Soviet, but they lacked the potential to support the radical economic reforms proposed by Eltsin's government in October 1991. The "architect" of the reforms was E.T. Gaidar, who had been called by Eltsin to the post of vice-premier. The growing decline of industrial production, inflation, the almost complete lack of monetary reserves, the unprecedented—even by Soviet standards—deficit of consumer goods and provisions, including bread: considering the catastrophic economic situation at the end of 1991, the withdrawal of price controls became the key element of the reform program, as the massive privatization of state property did later. Financial stability was supposed to be reached within a year.

The reforms proceeded painfully. Prices, which were decontrolled on January 2, 1992, soared to unimaginable heights. They rose by 2400% in a year.[40] National income and industrial produc-

Boris Eltsin

tion were reduced by approximately 20%. The consumption of meat by the population fell to 81%, of milk and dairy products to 75%, of fish to 56% of previous levels.[41] In the majority of families spending on food climbed to 60% to 70% of the budget.[42] The birth rate fell. As a result, in 1992, for the first time in the postwar years an absolute drop in the population of Russia by 70,000 persons occurred. At the beginning of 1993 the country's population was 148.6 million people. Professionals' salaries were abnormally distorted; a professor's salary comprised 10% of a miner's salary. An academician of the Russian Academy of Sciences received less money than a Moscow janitor. This caused a significant part of the scientific and pedagogical community to shift to commercial and other occupations. During 1992 the rate of departure of professionals from the Russian Academy of Sciences was 18% higher than 1991 while the rate of departure in institutions of higher education was 22% higher. The situation was only ameliorated somewhat by Eltsin's introduction of a tariff system of payments in December 1992.

The removal of the immediate threat of economic and financial collapse was the chief result of the first year of reform. The collapsed consumption market was finally stabilized, it seemed. The remarkable Soviet shortages in the towns disappeared, and along with them, the long lines. The extensive privatization of state property began by voucher. Of the 250,000 enterprises around 47,000 passed into private ownership. The revenues of the state from privatization comprised more than 150 billion rubles. In this way, in terms of economic reform along market lines the Eltsin-Gaidar government in a year was able to achieve more than all its predecessors.

But the main task—the attainment of macroeconomic stabilization—was unrealized. The reformers underestimated the degree of inertia and monopolistic power in the Russian economy, but the chief problem was still political opposition to the reforms. Under existing conditions at the end of 1991 there was hardly any other route to reform. It was soon apparent that the republics of the Commonwealth of Independent States who had not ventured on radical reform were in a much worse position than Russia. Some of them also had to decontrol prices, but years had been lost. Gaidar's problem was his inability to follow his own policy of shock therapy for more than a few months. He assumed the executive duties of the premier's office in June 1992, and the growing political opposition forced him to compromise by agreeing to reciprocal credit for the debts of the enterprises, which undermined the prospects for economic stabilization.

The failure of the August coup led to the swift collapse of the totalitarian system, beginning with its core—the Communist Party of the Soviet Union. But during the transition to apathy and confusion during the first months after the coup efforts to consolidate the Communist and pro-Communist forces went forward. On the base formed earlier in the core of the CPSU platform and movement, the rise of new political parties began in November and December 1991: the Socialist Workers' Party, the Russian Communists' Party, the All-Union Communist Party of the Bolsheviks, the Communists' Union, and the Russian Communist Worker's party.

In January 1992 the representatives of the former leadership of the Communist Party of the RSFSR turned to the Constitutional Court of Russia with an appeal to determine the constitutionality of President Eltsin's decrees on the ban of the CPSU and the fate of its property. In May a group of people's deputies of the RSFSR entered a countersuit, questioning the constitutionality of the CPSU's very existence. After many months of debate which evaded the question of the CPSU's constitutionality, the court adopted a compromise decision on the President's decrees forbidding the activity of the CPSU and the Communist Party of the RSFSR. The courts affirmed the right of the citizens of Russia, who adhered to Communist ideology, to unify on the basis of their territorial character. The recreation of the party organization was completed in February 1993 with the realizing of the Second (unification-restoration) Congress of the Communist Party of the Russian Federation in which a half-million people joined the party (i.e., more than in all the other political parties of Russia taken together). The parties and movements of a national-patriotic direction (the All-National Russian Union, the Russian National Assembly and others) acted with growing strength. The Congress of National-Patriotic Parties which occurred at the beginning of 1992 demonstrated the remarkable strengthening of their position after August 1991.

Several leaders of the radical opposition called the Gaidar government an "occupation" government of "national treason" and so forth. In all the structures of power, most of all in the Supreme Soviet, forces who intended to remove the Gaidar government from power began to unify.

One of these was the Civic Union, created on July 21, 1992, joining the representatives of the People's party of Free Russia (the leader was Vice President Rutskoy), the Democratic Party of Russia (the leader was Travkin), the Renewal of the All-Russian Union (the leader was A. Volsky), the parliamentary faction Change and the Russian Union of Youth. The task of the bloc was the "formation of a way for an active centrist opposition . . . suitable to propose its own nominations for every level of executive power."[43] The Civil Union represented, essentially, the interests of the managerial corps and the regional nomenklatura who modestly called themselves the "scientific-technological elite" of society. At the Second Congress of the Renewal of the Union the managers pointed out that with the beginning of privatization they could lose the key positions in industry and proposed to change the government before the end of the year and implement an "acceptable" version of privatization. The later confession of A. Dolgolaptev (vice-governor of the Moscow region) was characteristic: "Gaidar has failed to reach an agreement with the managers. If he had promised the managers a legal share of the property, had made them important property-owners, everything could have turned out differently."[44]

The coalition of national-patriots and the Communists either rejected the market in principle or advocated strong government regulation. But a political bloc of democrats with a promarket orientation was not created from the structuring of the democratic movement that had begun (before 1991 it had joined the opposition against the Communist leadership of the USSR).

The pay crisis of the spring and summer of 1992 threatened the Gaidar government when the size of the unpaid bills at the end of the second quarter reached 3.1 trillion rubles, raising prices for energy carriers, and others. After the crisis over nonpayments, the President had to make personnel changes in the government, including several representatives of the military-industrial complex and former leaders of its branches. At the same time the Gaidar cabinet, failing to endure the pressure of parliament, the managerial corps, and trade unions, reduced its efforts to stabilize finances and, together with the Central Bank, extended significant credits to unprofitable enterprises incapable of making payments. As a result, according to the estimates of western specialists, between July 1992 and January 1993, the number of rubles printed was four times greater than the number in existence up to that time.[45] This led to the second (post-January) wave of inflation, which spread over the country in September 1992 and was a turning point in the course of reform. The chances for the opposition rose.

At the Seventh Congress of the People's Deputies of Russia in December 1992 the tense fear reached its apogee. A sharp political crisis erupted. President Eltsin on December 10 made an appeal to the people in which he spoke of the obstacles to reform placed by the Supreme Soviet and the Congress of People's Deputies and demanded a referendum on confidence in the executive and constitutional authority. The political crisis was surmounted by a compromise on holding an all-national referendum on April 11, 1993, under the basic rules of the new Constitution of the Russian Federation.

The activity of the Gaidar government was characterized as unsatisfactory at the congress, and the acting premier himself did not collect the necessary number of votes for election as head of government. The former leader of the oil and gas industry of the USSR, V.S. Chernomydrin, was chosen as Chairman of the Council of Ministers of the Russian Federation. The correction of the government's course on the side of moderate reform began after his arrival. But the economic situation deteriorated in early 1993. In January the inflation level was 25%.[46] The inconsistent, at times mutually exclusive decisions of the government testified not only to the intensity of the political struggle over the basic direction of its work, but also to its lack of a clear, well-conceived program.

Under the influence of these circumstances the attitudes of the various groups in the population began to change both with regard to the reforms and to the very idea of the democratic reconstruction of society and the possibility of its successful realization.

The opposition to the governmental and executive authority reached the highest mark in March 1993, when the proposition on the impeachment of the President was placed before an extraordinary session of the Congress of People's Deputies. But it did not obtain the necessary number of votes. On April 25, 1993, a referendum was held during the course of which 62% of the participants declared their confidence in President Eltsin, but they did not advocate the reelection of the Congress of People's Deputies.

The results of the referendum were unexpected by the leaders of the opposition. But they were only worried for a time. On May 1, 1993, street disorders were provoked after they had announced the beginning of a campaign of civil disobedience.

During this period the President accelerated work on a new Constitution for the country which would be approved by a Constitutional Convention at the end of June. In one of the final stages of the convention the official representatives of the Supreme Soviet refused to participate in its work. The regime's opposition was reinforced during the summer by mutual blame over attempts to establish a dictatorship and the embezzlement of state property. Besides, the leadership of the Supreme Soviet occupied an even more outspoken national-Communist position: on the question of the restoration of the USSR, on the overthrow of economic reform, on the replacement of the presidential authority by the omnicompetence of the Soviets, and so forth. The open expulsion of the proponents of social reform from parliamentary committees and commissions also began. The Vice-President of Russia openly passed over to the opposition.

The political crisis broke out on September 21, 1993, when the President signed a decree announcing the dissolution of the Congress of People's Deputies and the Supreme Soviet and December elections for the new organs of state power—the Council of the Federation and the State Duma, and also a referendum on the country's new Constitution.

The leadership of the Supreme Soviet and also a majority of the members of the Constitutional Court, who called the President's actions unconstitutional, reacted harshly against the presidential decree. On the night of September 21 and 22, Vice-President Rutskoy, who began to form a parallel government, took on himself the executive duties of the President. An attempt was made to call an extraordinary Congress of People's Deputies. But it was not constituted because of the absence of a majority of the deputies.

The Front of National Salvation, Working Moscow, the Officers' Union, Russian National Unity, and a number of nationalist organizations announced their support for the Supreme Soviet. On the decision of the Supreme Soviet's leadership weapons were distributed to those in the White House.

On September 23 a group of guerrillas tried to occupy the staff of the Combined Armed Forces of the Commonwealth of Independent States, which resulted in the first casualties. On September 29 the President issued an ultimatum to those remaining in the Supreme Soviet building—to leave the building by October 4.

Patriarch Aleksei II's attempt to mediate between the sides was unsuccessful. On October 2 the Front for National Salvation and the leaders of Working Moscow organized major demonstrations which led to massive disorders. The first barricades were constructed. This inspired the defenders of the White House to active operations.

On October 3 at 4:00 p.m. Rutskoy and Khasbulatov called for those gathered at the White House "to storm" city hall, the television center, and then the Kremlin. At 6:00 p.m. city hall and the "Peace" hotel were seized. Appearing on television Gaidar asked Muscovites to go out into the streets "in defense of democracy." The attempt to seize "Ostankino" led to bloodshed, but was unsuccessful. In response to these actions the President declared a state of emergency in Moscow and introduced troops into the capital. On October 4 the bombardment of the White House with tanks began. As a result the White House building was taken by troops, and the leaders of the opposition surrendered. By the President's decrees the operations of the Front for National Salvation were stopped, some mass communications media were forbidden, and censorship was temporarily introduced.

The stabilization of political conditions in Moscow and in the country after the October events was relative. The elections to the new organs of state power were imminent, and some members of the opposition called for their boycott. But the majority of political forces participated in the preelection struggle. The elections were held on December 12 and were conducted not only by electoral districts, but also for the first time according to party rolls. The results were unexpected: the LDPR leader V. Zhirinovsky received almost a fourth of the votes of the electors. Gaidar's "Russia's Choice," which was in second place, won (without counting the single-seat districts, where he had a majority) around 15% of the votes. The Communists also won a convincing victory. A. Lukianov and V. Starodubtsev, who had been members of the GKChP, were among the deputies. The new Constitution of Russia was accepted by a majority of the electors' votes.

The new organs of authority began their work on January 11, 1994. Former Vice-Premier V.F. Sumeiko was elected Chairman of the Federation Council. The former secretary of the Volgograd regional committee of the CPSU, I.P. Rybkin, was chosen Chairman of the State Duma.

The new government, headed by V. Chernomydrin again, this time did not include those figures who personified the policy of continued reform and financial reorganization: E. Gaidar, B. Fedorov, and E. Pamphilov. The Prime Minister announced the need to correct the course of reform by the renunciation of monetary measures. Many trillions of rubles were promised to the budgets of enterprises of the military-industrial and agro-industrial complexes.

As a result controlling inflation in 1994 was unsuccessful. Despite the large-scale privatization (at the beginning of 1995 up to 60% of the gross domestic product was being produced in nonstate enterprises), a genuine market economy had not developed. In the village private land was still unrealized. Inflation and relative political instability prevented an extensive influx of private investment in industry. The volume of industrial production in 1994 in comparison to 1990 had been reduced by more than 50%.

And so, Russia again faces a choice. Either to continue the extremely painful movement to a full-fledged market economy, resolving such difficult problems as the structure of the reform of industry and mass unemployment, the further reduction of state spending in the military-industrial complex VPK, the actual reform of the army and the agrarian sector, or to escape with an imitation of reform and again, as already has happened more than once in our history, to become lost in a "semimodern" state from which it is so easy to return to the past. With the second, extremely undesirable choice, pregnant with colossal shocks, the country would return to the problems which it has not yet succeeded in resolving. But that would occur many years, and possibly, even decades later.

Notes

[1]*Na poroge krizisa [On the Threshold of the Crisis]*, Moscow 1990, pp. 217-218.
[2]See *Planovaia ekonomika [The Planned Economy]*, 1981, No. 10, pp. 8-9.
[3]E.K. Ligachev, *Djilas and Others*. Moscow, 1991, p.16.
[4]N.I. Ryzhkov, *Perestroika, Istoriia Predatelstv [Perestroika: A History of Betrayals]*. Moscow, 1992. p. 232.
[5]E. Shevardnadze, *Moi Vybor [My Choice]*. Moscow, 1992. p.107.
[6]*The USSR Economy in 1985: Annual Statistics*. Moscow,1986. p.38.
[7]The quotation is from V. Bakatin, *Abolishing the KGB*. Moscow, 1992, p.160.
[8]Ryzhkov, p. 33.
[9]A.N. Yakovlev, *Predislovie, Obval, Posleslovie [Prologue, Collapse, Epilogue]*. Moscow, 1992, p.102.
[10]D.A. Kunaev, *About My Time*. Alma-Ata, 1992, p. 201.
[11]G.A. Arbatov, *Zatianuvsheesia vyzdorovlenie [The Protracted Recovery]*. Moscow, 1991, p. 338.
[12]A.J. Toynbee, *Perceiving History*. Moscow,1991, p. 450.
[13]Yakovlev, p. 102.
[14]Ryzhkov, p. 74.
[15]Arbatov, p. 338.
[16]M.S. Gorbachev, *Socialist Idea and Revolutionary Perestroika*. Moscow, 1989, p. 3.
[17]*Materials of CPSU Central Committee Plenum, 25-26 June, 1987. Moscow, 1987*, p. 9.
[18]Privatization is a process of giving or selling state owned enterprises, transport, buildings, to people as their private property.

[19] *Party Work Restructuring Is the Most Important Task of the Day:* CPSU Central Committee Meeting of the First Party Secretaries from the Union Republics, Area and Provincial Party Organizations. 18 July, 1989. Moscow, 1989, p. 109.
[20] Ryzhkov, p. 345.
[21] L. Abalkin, *Neispolzovanny Shans [Missed Opportunity]*. Moscow, 1991, p. 91.
[22] *Materials of Joint CPSU Central Committee and Central Control Committee Plenum, 31 January, 1991*. Moscow, 1991, pp. 10-11.
[23] *Materials*, p. 17.
[24] *Moscow News*. 11 November, 1990.
[25] *Materials of the XXVIII CPSU Congress*. Moscow, 1990, p. 86.
[26] *Materials*, 24-25 April, 1991. pp. 39-40,45.
[27] M.S. Gorbachev. *The August Coup*. Moscow, 1991, p. 7.
[28] V.I. Dal. *Defining Dictionary of Usable Russian*. Vol.1, p. 355.
[29] M.S. Gorbachev. *Selected Speeches and Articles*. Vol. 3. Moscow, 1987, p. 241.
[30] Gorbachev, Vol. 6. Moscow, 1989, p. 210.
[31] See *Party Work Perestroika Is Today's Most Important Key Task*. Moscow, 1989, p. 69.
[32] See *Materials,* 31 January,1991, p. 32.
[33] Gorbachev, Vol. 4, p. 369.
[34] Gorbachev, Vol.7, p. 229.
[35] A. Tsipko. *The Violence of Lies or How a Ghost Has Gotten Lost*. Moscow, 1990, p. 257.
[36] Ryzhkov, p. 267.
[37] A.N. Yakovlev. *Sufferings While Reading Reality*. Moscow, 1991, p.334.
[38] V. Stepankov and E Lisov. *The Kremlin Plot. The Inspector's Version*. Moscow, 1992, p.168.
[39] Op cit., p.172.
[40] *Izvestiia*, 3 February, 1993.
[41] *Argumenty i fakty [Arguments and Facts]*. 1993, No. 5, p.3.
[42] *Izvestiia*, 29 January, 1993.
[43] *Materials of All-Russia Alliance "Unification" Constituent Conference*. Moscow, 1992, p.4.
[44] *Moskovskii Komsomolets,* 25 February, 1993.
[45] *Argumenty i fakty*. 1993, No. 5, p.4.
[46] *Izvestiia*, 3 February, 1993.

CHAPTER 10

RUSSIA AND THE WEST

In looking at the very difficult and winding path traveled by Russia one must consider the sources of her originality and the development of the motherland's history. Inevitably one is tempted to make historical and cultural comparisons with other, mostly European, peoples.

Probably Europe—the cradle of Western civilization—had the greatest influence on Russia, but the relative "well-being" of European history produced an enormous, although not always favorable, impression on Russian minds. It is not accidental that the formation of original philosophic ideas in Russia was connected mostly with attempts to compare Russia and Europe. This in turn channeled philosophical currents into two basic directions: Westernization and Slavophilism. Russian historical thinkers have either recognized the country's commonalty with Europe or, on the contrary, the exceptional uniqueness of Russia's historical path, in one or another state. But whether these views were reflected in a clear or concealed form in all of the later social doctrines, they have all turned into fundamental, painful, self-examinations of Russian consciousness.

S.M. Soloviev and other historians of the "state school" affirmed that the originality of the motherland's history was determined by the special geographic features native to the country: its vast expanse and intermediate position between Europe and Asia. This transformed Russia into a kind of mutagenic body, a "cauldron" of civilization which digested, in various ways, the divergent influences of the West and East. The geography of the country and the contradictory influence of two different streams of civilization left its mark on the Russian national character. "In the soul of the Russian people there is as much immensity, boundlessness, a tendency toward the infinite, as on the Russian plain," N.A. Berdiaev wrote. "It was therefore difficult for the Russian people to take possession of these vast spaces and put them into shape." The Russian national character has within itself an eternal striving for the absolute ideal, "truth and justice," with a disregard for everyday life; goodness and patience, with terrible fits of rage (the *Pugachevshchina*);* majesty with a inclination toward anarchy and civil disobedience; and finally, great talent and energy with indolence, *Oblomoshchina*. Having become accustomed to working intensely for a short period of time each year, the Russian peasant rested "during the course of the autumn and winter idleness," wrote V.O. Kliuchevsky. It is possible, therefore that "no other people in Europe is as accustomed to such intense labor over a brief time . . . and nowhere in Europe, it seems, can we find such a lack of being used to regular, measured, and continual labor as in Great Russia." The fluctuations and the unpredictability of the Russian national character stem from this. Having become accustomed to the "capriciousness of the climate and soil have deceived our modest expectations of it . . . the prudent Great Russian loves sometimes, thoughtlessly, to make a decision for himself whether or not it is hopeless or imprudent, opposing the caprice of his own valor to the caprice of nature. This tendency to tease fortune, to toy with success is perhaps Great Russian." Reading these lines, you may understand that the fantastic troubles along Russia's historical path reflect the contradictions of the national character. At the same time, Russia herself and the Russian national character were the product not only of native climatic conditions, but mostly, of real history.

The position of the medieval Russian land on the periphery of Europe, the dangerous neighborhood of the steppe, and the absence of traditions of antiquity which served as a nourishing environment for the new "barbarian" states in western Europe complicated the development of the old Russian society. Statehood in Rus' arose in the 9th and 10th centuries, 3 to 4 centuries later than in the West. But despite the delay and some developmental characteristics which were mostly connected with the slower development of private or patrimonial propertyholding, pre-Mongol Rus' was far from being in a "god-forsaken corner" of Europe. It successfully cultivated and enjoyed extensive international recognition, which the numerous dynastic marriages of medieval Russian princes with representatives of the royal houses of Europe vividly shows.

From the beginning two influences collided in Rus'—the Western European and the Byzantine. The very origin of medieval Russian statehood was connected with the invitation in the 9th century to the Varangians to assume the princely throne. The summons to the Varangians, who formed the Rurikide ruling dynasty, accelerated the process of crystallizing the state structure of the eastern Slavs. The acceptance of the Byzantine version of Christianity, which promoted the development of culture and literacy (vernacular literature became the most outstanding branch of culture), further accelerated a certain cultural and political isolation from Catholic, Latin-speaking Europe. It is no accident that many historians consider Rus' and Orthodox countries as a special civilization that is not identical to the West. At the same time, despite a whole series of unique features, the development of Old Rus' in its principal form was similar to Europe. From the 12th century, the influence of Byzantium faded while the connections with the Western countries became stronger.

But under the influence of the East, embodied in the Mongol-Tatar yoke, the specific features of the country's development increased immensely, forming a special Russian type of feudalism which was intermediate between the western and eastern versions, if, indeed, we can use such a term as "Asiatic feudalism."[1] Russia was cut-off from Europe and started on her own path of development, which was significantly different from Western Europe and which left a strong impression on all of the country's later history. The formation of serfdom and the tsar's autocratic authority, which extended to the entire society, was the cost of the creation of a state in which the essential social and economic prerequisites were lacking and the external political factor had priority; that is, the need to fight the Horde and the grand principality of Lithuania. From this sprang the idealization of the state as the sole bulwark at the time of the Orthodox faith. Although the oprichnina of Ivan the Terrible did not lead to the creation of a new type of political regime (it was possibly close to eastern despotism), it facilitated the formation of a series of specific Russian traditions, which retained a significant part of the *Asiatchina* (Asiatic despotism.) Henceforth two major and mutually connected features appear: the hypertropic role of the state and the failure of private ownership to develop fully and to be protected. These characteristics drew Russia together with the countries of the East, but the struggle between the original Russian traditions and the influence of the West became one of the themes of the motherland's history.

At the end of the 16th and 17th centuries European influence in Russia gradually began to grow. Boris Godunov, recognizing the cultural gap between the country and the West, tried somehow to surmount it. However, these attempts failed because of the profound socioeconomic and political crisis at the beginning of the 17th century caused by exhaustion of the country's strength as a result of the oprichnina terror, the failure of the Livonian War, the famine of 1601-1603, and the instability of the supreme power caused by the dynastic crisis. Russia emerged from the Time of Troubles by strengthening serfdom and the autocracy while gradually liquidating the Assemblies of the Land (*Zemsky sobory*) and other innovations, such as the idea of electing the tsar, of placing some restrictions on his rights, of sending young men to study abroad, and so forth. But the lag behind the West and the gradual penetration of European culture led to decisive measures.

Peter the Great undertook the first large-scale modernization of the country, actively using western experience. With the assistance of harsh, radical measures, he led the country into the ranks of the great powers in an unusually brief time and gave a strong stimulus to its Europeanization. "This was the first example of voluntary self-westernization by a nonwestern country," A. Toynbee observed.

The process of "assimilating" the Petrine reforms stretched over many decades, serving as the basis for the further strengthening of the power of Russia to the end of the 18th century.

But the Petrine reforms did not touch the country's particular kind of feudalism and they changed the way of life of the peasants very little. In contrast to the gradually Europeanized gentry, they still adhered to their traditional ways and system of values. This gave rise to a major sociocultural schism between the "lower" and "upper" layers of society.

The state acted as the major initiator and mover of Europeanization almost up to the French Revolution. But the Revolution, the Jacobean terror, and also the society's lack of readiness for radical reform caused a reevaluation of the western experience and transformed the Russian autocrats into ardent advocates of the country's original socioeconomic system. Alexander I was the only exception in the series. But, despite his progressive views, he too did not risk introducing the principles of a constitutional order or abolishing serfdom.

Meanwhile, toward the end of the 18th century, in Russia the first relatively free people who were not subject to military service (*neporotye liudi*) appeared since Ivan the Terrible, who had enslaved not only the peasants but even the ruling gentry (*dvoriane*). Some of them, familiar with the ideas of the French philosophes, tried to take the function of the "Europeanizers" on themselves. But the failure of the Decembrists' coup only strengthened the resolve of the state authority to preserve the traditional ways.

The second principal step toward the Europeanization of Russia, which was, like the Petrine reforms, a reaction to the growing gap with the West, was connected with Alexander II and the Great Reforms of the 1860s and 1870s. They altered the socioeconomic base of the country and its direction of development. An industrial society exactly like the West rapidly took shape in Russia. But the Russian reforms were not carried to their logical conclusion—the introduction of a constitutional order. The reform process was terminated in the 1880s: because of (1) the unfortunate assassination of Alexander II by revolutionaries on the day he had, apparently, agreed to the introduction of representative government, (2) the limited nature of the society's potential for reform before the end of serfdom, which had not reached the stage of total crisis, and (3) the country's political and moral shock from the stunning defeat in the Crimean War. The counterreform period added new conflicts to the earlier contradictions between the developing industrial society and the remnants of the traditional society, causing the first symptoms of the crisis of the empire.

The delayed reforms were introduced under the extreme conditions of a polarized society where the leadership suffered from the vacillation of the supreme authority. They were literally rushed into being because of the revolutionary events and were connected with the Manifesto of October 17 and the Stolypin reforms. However, they did not permit the completion of the modernization of the country before the beginning of the world war. Neither a system of complete private property nor a constitutional regime had been completed. The historic gap between Russia and the West remained, although to a smaller extent than in the 19th century. Moreover, the failure to complete the reforms did not facilitate the stabilization of authority and provided "combustible material" for the revolution (1861-1905, 1861 and 1906-1917). These revolts were a unique reaction to the inconsistency and intermittency of the reform process as well as to the "painfulness" of Western influence that had arisen from this protracted conflict with some of the ossified social institutions and original traditions. All this put the country on an endless cycle: the problems of overcoming the gap with the West, the sociocultural schism in society, the periodic internal crises, and the problem of guaranteeing an effective administration and stable authority. But there were no successful attempts to resolve them which, ultimately, threatened Russia's sovereignty. Thus, despite the firm and large-scale Europeanization of society between the 18th and 20th centuries, Russia still had failed to enter the western path of development. In 1917 under the influence of the world war, the chronic contradictions within society, and the unprecedented pressure of the Bolsheviks, Russia completed the transition to another social model.

On Some of the Roots of the Originality of the Motherland's History

The Great Reforms of the 18th and 19th centuries clearly demonstrated one of the characteristic features of Russian history. The country as a rule did not assimilate Western influence organically but filled the European forms with its own original content. This led to a sociocultural schism in society and gave rise to the coexistence of structures, social groups, and peoples from different historical periods. "Russia combines several historical and cultural ages, from the early middle ages to the twentieth century, from the very first stages, preceding the cultured state, to the very apex of world culture, . . ." Berdiaev asserted. "Here therefore is why it is so difficult to organize Russia." Thus the state played the major system-forming role, which compensated for the insufficiency of the social and cultural interdependence of the huge country. Both Russian and Soviet statehood, despite a difference of more than five hundred years in time, were formed at times when socioeconomic prerequisites were inadequate to clearly define the role of the political and governmental functions. The Russian state did not so much "grow" from the estates as form them by means of raising taxes, a political and administrative requirement. After 1917 the new Soviet "party-state," as Lenin intended, also created an inadequate economic, social, and cultural base "under itself." But the enormous role of the state in Russian society also assigned a major role to force in the motherland's history. The powerful intervention of the state in all spheres of the activity of social life created a schism between the authorities and the people. The long centuries of antagonism not only complicated the melting down of the diverse social structures and the formation of a civil society, but it aroused mass protests and revolts which, however, could not lead to positive results. The country's life depended on the stability of the state power.

These specific Russian features, and most of all the failure of a civil society to emerge, prohibited a "natural" kind of social evolution. On the contrary, the characteristic feature of Russian history for many centuries was its special painfulness, the crises-and-catastrophic nature of its development, in which the social contradictions were resolved more often than not by a harsh struggle and every step forward was accompanied by the destruction of society by force and by enormous material and human losses. Speaking figuratively, the wagon of the Russian state traveled forward on four wheels and their every turn not only shook all of the passengers to the core but also led to an inspection of the durability of the wagon itself, and twice—at the beginning of the 17th and the beginning of the 20th centuries—it did not withstand the inspection.

Everything discussed above also explains the uneven pace of Russian history and the repetition of its cycles. For a long time the country seemed to be in a stupor, when its social clock slowed; the ruling elite paid no attention to "western clocks" but, then, having received an immediate and painful lesson against "conceit," they raced, in hectic attempts, to catch up with the West by means of the overexertion of all of the country's strength and resources. This, in due course, deepened the contradictions within society without resolving them and instead obtained, in the best case, only limited successes; then society rolled back, again, into a state of relative social "stagnation." The possibility of long periods of development in breadth, without the intensive evolution of social mechanisms, was conditioned by the vast expanse of the country and its native wealth. It is not accidental that many of the leading Russian historians considered the distinguishing feature of Russian history to be colonization.

Kliuchevsky observed: "During the course of two hundred years, from the time when we began to draw near to Western Europe, the class of Russian society brought up under its influence more than once experienced severe crises. In general the class conducted itself peacefully, not thinking of itself very highly, and taught itself, reading European books, and grieved over its own backwardness. . . . But from time to time there was some sort of unrest in it: suddenly . . . it would begin to think that we are not entirely backward, but are traveling our own road, that Russia herself should suit herself and that Europe should suit itself, and that we are able to do without her science and art by our own homegrown means. This surge of patriotism and anguish for originality so strongly seizes our society that we . . . are beginning to feel some kind of animosity against everything European and are placing an unaccountable faith in the boundless energies of our own people." This observation of Kliuchevsky is with some modification applicable not only to the entire history of tsarist Russia, but to 1917 and succeeding years.

The October Revolution

Then, it seems, the strange prophecy of P. Ya. Chaadaev materialized: "One may say concerning us, that we comprise as it were an exception among the nations. We belong to one of those who have not become a component part of humanity, but exist only to give a great lesson to the world." Chaadaev wrote in 1829, "We grow, but do not mature, we move forward, but in an indirect direction, that is in a line without driving toward a goal."

But after the passage of time it is possible to see another historic aspect of the events that have occurred in Russia. The most important Western historian, Toynbee, saw in the October Revolution a historic reaction to the insufficiency of the reforms conducted in the 18th century to oppose the rapidly industrialized world, on the strength of which attempts were made to search for a special, actually, antiwestern path of social development. The conditions of the First World War, the sharpness of the contradictions within society, and the paradigm of Russia's "individuality" (*osobost*), which became deeply rooted in the Russian national consciousness and took on a socialist appearance in the 20th century, also accelerated this quest for an antiwestern path. The prevalence of socialist ideologies in Russia at the beginning of our century was explained not only by the growth of social and political tension but also by the beginning of the crisis in Orthodoxy. For some of the masses socialism seemed close to their own radicalism and their collectivist spirit: it was the merciless critic of capitalism and austere, like Evangelical Christianity. As a result the pressure of the diverse remnants of Russian feudalism in the socioeconomic, political, and spiritual realms not only worsened the situation in the country, but also created the preconditions for another, noncapitalist version of industrial society. This version—socialism—reproduced in a new form many of the traditional features of Russian feudalism: the hypertrophic role of the state (which became totalitarian), the autocracy (which became the *gensekderzhavie*, the absolute rule of the party General Secretary), serfdom (the Stalinist collective farms, the institutions for residence registration, universal military registration, and so forth), and the ideology of the Russian state, the struggle with the heresies (now with party deviants) reached its logical completion under the Bolsheviks.

It is worth remembering that the builders of the new society, who mostly came from the intelligentsia, were guided by a "western" ideology—Marxism. Its roots went back to western tradition and, especially, to the ideas of the Enlightenment, with their unswerving faith in the strength of man's intelligence which seemed suited to construct an ideal, utopian society (communism) on earth rather than in the heavens as Christianity promised. But despite the calculations of the "founders," only Russia embarked on this path, because of the major burdens of the world war, her incomplete transition to an industrial society, and the extensive and bloody use of coercion, "the subjective factor."[2]

The internationalist movement—"Western" Marxism—as it relates to Russia became filled with a Slavic content. On the whole, despite its "scientific" foundation, socialism was in reality not "the highway of humanity," but a specific and extremely wasteful variant of industrial society. Socialism in the USSR was able to resolve individual national problems, but at great expense: (1) hypercentralization of the strength and resources of society, (2) widespread ideological and moral compulsion, (3) exploitation of the "less valuable" peasants by the regime, and (4) the artificial reduction of the population's standard of living. But industrialization was completed, a strong military and industrial complex was created, illiteracy was eliminated, and the external political strength of the country rose sharply. As post-Petrine Russia in the 18th century was able to outstrip other countries in military strength and several areas of industrial production on the foundation of serfdom, the USSR also was able to become a military superpower and the second country in terms of the total size of industrial production on a socialist base. For this leap the Soviet people made an exorbitant, unprecedented payment: Tens of millions of dead and innocently condemned (15 million died in the civil war, 21.5 million were purged between 1929 and 1953 alone), a dysfunctional economic structure, a low standard of living, the absence of civil rights and freedom, and the country's self-imposed isolation.

But despite the expenses and ineradicable effort to "outstrip" and "leave behind," socialism was a new type of scientific-technological revolution. Moreover, after the exposure of Stalin's crimes and Khrushchev's removal, socialism began to lose its chief stimuli for labor—the all-encompassing fear and Communist enthusiasm. During the period of "stagnation," according to the evidence of sociological studies, only every third worker actually worked at full speed.

Like serf-owning Russia in the middle of the 19th century, the socialist Soviet Union at the end of the 20th century experienced ruin. But the second attempt to follow its own unique path of development, which was significantly different from the Western (or Asian and Latin American) paths was, although much shorter,[3] also much more difficult for Russia. The dramatic fall of socialism in the USSR was conditioned by the fact that the artificially constructed system, which had succeeded by violence and ideological manipulation in adapting society to its rule, experienced total failure. Moreover, the fall of socialism involved the final destruction of the Russian Empire, the overwhelming part of which the Bolsheviks were able to restore under a different social and political cover after its ruin in 1917-1918.

Thus, the Marxist ideology, which assimilated several Russian traditions (the prevalence of the collective principle over the private, the aspirations of the masses for the justice of leveling, their dislike of the higher educated layer of society, the fixed messianic attitudes[4]) for a long time kept the country on a specific, original path of development. The ruin of socialism therefore dealt a strong blow not only to the Marxist ideology, but once more demonstrated the hopelessness of any kind of special path that denies the experience of mankind, embodied at least in the last millennium in the countries of the West. Nevertheless, the "Marxist-Slavophile" heritage from the past is still strong. The current dramatic attempts to get onto the well-trodden path of world civilization from the virgin soil through which we have worked our way with all our might returns us again to the mechanisms and special features of the Russian reforms.

Russian Reform: Characteristics and Landmarks

By virtue of the characteristics of Russian history and, in particular, the presence in society of socioeconomic structures and sociocultural levels which are significantly different from one another, the recognition of the need to reform does not come easily. Kliuchevsky confirmed that the special character of the country, which lagged behind the progressive powers, was the fact that "the need for reform became imminent earlier than the people were ready for reforms." In Russia the need for reform was first understood by the intelligentsia or some representatives of the ruling elite who had experienced some influence of Western culture. But because of the inertia of the overwhelming part of society and the estrangement of the state power, the ideas of reform spread extremely slowly. This often provoked radical proponents of reform into antigovernmental actions or, as a lesser measure, propaganda. The suppression of these movements (for example, the Decembrists and the populists of the 19th century and the dissidents of recent decades) only caused more oppression and delayed reform.

When the necessity of reform gradually crept into the minds of state officials, it was precisely the state who began the reforms. Hence the position of the supreme authority—the tsars, emperors, general secretaries, and now the presidents—have had the opportunity to design the reform. This included Peter the Great and, to some extent, Alexander I. But the latter, like his grandmother Catherine II, did not risk everything like Peter I by undertaking radical reforms and by breaking the opposition and the apathy of the ruling elite, and to a significant degree, by winning the people.[5] The stimuli to reform in Russia were mostly triggered by external factors, namely the lag behind the West which often manifested itself in the form of a defeat in war. In the terminology of Toynbee, reforms in Russia began as a "response to Western suppression, which assumed the painful form of military blows." At the same time, foreign political successes, as the experience of the two fatherland wars eloquently demonstrates, leads to the opposite result. Territorial expansion also accelerates the preservation of antiquated social structures or even their regression.

It goes without saying, each reform had its own unique features, which did not conform completely to any kind of pattern. Moreover, the reforms introduced in the Soviet period had a definite character. For example, in contrast to the reforms of Peter I and Alexander II, which were stimulated by the defeats at Narva and in the Crimean War, the danger of the regime's military and political defeat rather than lost battles pushed reform in the Soviet period. The most important Soviet reforms—the transitions to NEP and perestroika—were initiated by threats to the Communist regime which were immediate in the first instance (resulting from the severe internal crisis and the recession of the revolutionary waves in the West) and in the second case indirect (the view of having lost the "cold war" and the clear symptoms of the social organism's decay).

Since reforms in Russia were implemented wholly by the supreme power and the bureaucratic apparatus (the reforms of the 1860s and 1870s were hardly less bureaucratized) and subject to the special influence of a multitude of "accidental" environmental factors, none of them were carried to their logical conclusion and did not fully resolve the contradictions within society which had summoned them to life. Moreover, many reforms because of their own inconsistencies and only made the situation worse later on. This also occurred with perestroika. In contrast with the leaders of the KNR (Chinese People's Republic), Gorbachev did not decide on radical market reforms. The political reforms which destroyed the monopoly of the Communist Party of the Soviet Union—the major force that held Soviet society together—led to the ruin of the Soviet Union. In this unfolding of events, the "subjective factor" has not been cited as much as historical tradition and especially the fact that the period of socialism's growth in the USSR was twice as long as in North Korea. The latter provided assistance for a rather deeper uprooting as it were of not very strong market traditions. In Russia, we remember the villages were turned over to the peasants (the Chinese reforms proceeded from here), the deep-seated contempt in society for "hucksters" and commerce, the almost complete absence in the country of trained market economists (they only appeared during perestroika), and finally the magical admiration for the word, the theory of Marxism. Unlike China where there was a strong Confuscist tradition, Marxism fully dominated the social consciousness of the Soviet people—with the exception of a small group of dissidents. But perestroika, in contrast to the great reforms of the 19th century and the Khrushchevite "thaw," did not cause the "open" or "creeping" counterreform, which provoked revolutionary excesses and mass actions or changes in the international situation. Moreover, as a result of the fall of the conservative pro-Communist forces in August 1991, major changes occurred: the fall of the USSR and the change of the political regime. The process of social reforms took on a new quality.

Will these reforms have a positive result? The historical experience of the Russian reforms suggests that success will depend, in the first instance, on a stable government, and in the second, on whether radical reforms will succeed in being implemented in a relatively short time, allowing the nation to pass between the Scylla of the reformers' impatience and the Charybdis of a social explosion "from below." Reforms in Russia, as a rule, do not fail because of their radicalism. Even the ultraradical Stalinist collectivization attained its intended goals, creating a firm channel for transferring provisions from the countryside to the city and securing the hoped-for political and administrative control over the peasantry. A complex, gradual reformation, despite the seeming advantages of such a type of reform, has no chance of successful completion in Russia. The cause of this is the specific character of the country, the main feature of which is the lack of a civil society with clear structured interests and mechanisms for their expression, which would have had a constant influence on the government and the policy it forms. The fate of reform for us depends on the changing relationship of the forces in the governing elite, the unforeseen events in internal and foreign policy, and the personal position of the leader. And although each major reform has had its own stabilizing factors (the need to industrialize, strengthening the military, strengthening the country), the "variable" factors have always led to the curtailment of the reform after the attainment of the first partial results. After the passage of many years or decades the cycle of reform begins anew.

What are the reference points of the Russian reforms? Do we in general try to travel the Western path of development again, without regard to the inevitable painfulness, even "trauma" of the perception of this experience, or, as earlier, search for some type of our own—a unique path? The best minds of Russia answered this question in the 19th century, advocating the Western experience. The 70 year tragic attempt to find our own path of development in the 20th century imposed innumerable burdens on the people of Russia and seems to confirm the impracticability of this alternative. The rapid economic and social development of Japan and some other Asiatic countries—also "non-Western" and no less original than Russia—is still the one serious argument for the universality of the Western experience. And as long as the world experiences the "Western era," as long as the "principles" for the effective social organization of society approved over the centuries (a market economy, a civil society, individual rights and freedoms, the rule of law, parliamentarism) are common human values—a necessary condition for economic prosperity and the freedom of peoples—the earlier words of Kliuchevsky will remain valid:

> In the West more of us is known and they are able to do better for us than we can for ourselves. Therefore, the West for us is a school and a shop of useful goods, and a course of its own type in the lessons of history.

All this should not in any degree gloss over the question of the specific national character, without which no serious reforms are possible. One cannot ignore the destructive influence of the indiscriminate copying of all Western forms on the national identity. One cannot ignore a feeling of patriotism which the great Russian historian and man of foresight, V.O. Kliuchevsky, had anticipated: "What sort of person was the Russian Westernizer? Usually a very agitated and bewildered man, . . ." he wrote. "Having divided the world into humanity and Russia, he considered the Motherland as a disagreeable apparition, from which people strove to alienate themselves through the forces of civilization." Essentially, the task involves the realization of an organic synthesis between "westernization" and "slavophilism." Japan, for example, shows how productive such a synthesis between the Western experience and some national traditions can be. "Every patriot should become a Westernizer but Westernization should only be one of the manifestations of patriotism," Kliuchevsky wrote in the 1890s. If now, after a century, we finally are able to follow this advice, then the indisputable talent and remarkable zest for life of the Russian people (who have passed through the most difficult crises and ordeals more than once in history) will permit the synchronization of our social clock with the West and astound the world not only by our heroism, self-sacrifice, and military strength, but also by our intellectual culture and the rapid growth of our commonwealth.

Notes

[1] In Russia the response to the Mongol-Tatar oppression "was the evolution of a new form of life and new social organization, which permitted for the first time in the history of civilization a settled society not merely to fight the Asiatic nomads . . . but to win a real victory . . . transforming at long last the nomadic pastures into peasant fields and the nomad's camp into a settled village," Arnold Toynbee wrote.

[2] All of the remaining socialist countries were created for the most part through the influence of the USSR.

[3] Recall that the special, Russian type of feudalism prevailed in the country from the sixteenth century to the middle of the nineteenth century, while socialism only lasted from 1917 to 1991.

[4] "Moscow is the third Rome," "the USSR is the vanguard of progressive humanity."

[5] In Catherine II's time the relative "apathy" of the people was interrupted by the Pugachev revolt.

Editor/Translator's Note

*The *Pugachevshchina* refers to the peasant revolt (1773-74) of Emelian Pugachev, who falsely claimed to be Emperor Peter III, the tsar overthrown by his wife Catherine II. *Oblomovshchina* refers to Oblomov, the central character of the Ivan Goncharov novel of the same name noted for his laziness and apathy.

BIBLIOGRAPHY

The October Revolution

Dumova, N.G. *Konchilos vashe vremia . . . [Our Time is Finished]*. Moscow, 1990.

Galili, Z. *Lidery menshevikov v russkoi revoliutsii [Menshikov Leaders in the Russian Revolution]*. Moscow, 1993.

Joffe, G.Z. *Beloe delo: General Kornilov [The White Affair: General Kornilov]*. Moscow, 1988.

Joffe, G.Z. *Revoliutsiia i sudba Romanovykh [The Revolution and the Fate of the Romanovs]*. Moscow, 1993.

Kerensky, A.F. *Rossiia na istoricheskom povorote: Memuary [Russia at the Historical Crossroads. Memoires]*. Moscow, 1991. (Available in English as Kerensky, A., *Russian and History's Turning Point*. New York, 1965.)

Oktiabr 1917: Velichaishee sobytie veka ili sotsialnaia katastrofa? [1917: The Greatest Event of the Century or a Social Catastrophe?] Moscow, 1991.

Rabinovich, A. *Bolsheviki prikhodiat k vlasti [The Bolsheviks Come to Power]*. Moscow, 1989. (Russian translation of Rabinowitch, A. *The Bolsheviks Come to Power: The Revolution of 1917 in Petrograd*. New York, 1976.)

Rabinovich, A. *Krovavye dni: Iiulskoe vosstanie 1917 goda v Petrograde [The Days of Blood: The July 1917 Uprising in Petrograd]*. Moscow, 1992. (Russian translation of Rabinowitch, A. *Prelude to Revolution: The Petrograd Bolsheviks and the July 1917 Uprising*. Bloomington, Ind., 1968.)

Sukhanov, N.N. *Zapiski o revoliutsii [Memoires of the Revolution]* 3 vol. Moscow, 1991. (Available in English as Sukhanov, N.N., *The Russian Revolution: A Personal Record,* 2 vols. New York, 1960.)

Znamensky, O.N. *Intelligentsiia nakanune Velikogo Oktiabria* [*The intelligentsia on the Eve of Great October*]. Leningrad, 1988.

The Civil War and the Formation of the Bolshevik Regime

Denikin, A.I. *Ocherki russkoi smuty* [*Essays on the Russian Troubles*]. Moscow, 1991. T. 1-2; Berlin, 1924-1926. T. 3-5.
Gimpelson, E.G. *Voennyi kommunizm* [*War Communism*]. Moscow, 1973.
Grazhdanskaia voina v SSSR [*The Civil War in the USSR*]. Moscow, 1986. T. 1-2.
Kabanov, V.V. *Krestianskoe khoziaistvo v usloviakh voennogo kommunizma* [*The Peasant Economy under the Conditions of War Communism*]. Moscow, 1988.
Kavtoradze, A.G. *Voennye spetsialisty na sluzhbe Respubliki Sovetov* [*Military Experts in the Service of the Soviet Republic*]. Moscow, 1988.
Kakurin, N.E. *Kak srazhalas revoliutsiia* [*How the Revolution Was Fought*]. Moscow, 1990. T. 1-2.
Kiselev, A.F. *Profsoiuzy i sovetskoe gosudarstvo* [*Trade Unions and the Soviet State*]. Moscow, 1991.
Pipes, R. *Sozdanie odnopartiinogo gosudarstva v Sovetskoi Rossii // Minuvshee: Istoricheskii almanakh.* [*The Creation of the One Party State in Soviet Russia in The Past: An Historical Almanac*]. Moscow, 1991. No. 3-4.
Revvoensovet respubliki, 6 septiabria 1918 — 28 avgusta 1923 [*The Revolutionary Military Council of the Republic, September 6, 1918 to August 28, 1923*]. Moscow, 1991.
Volkovinsky, V.N. *Makhno i ego krakh* [*Makhno and His Ruin*]. Moscow, 1991.

Russia during NEP

Arkhiv Trotskogo. *Kommunisticheskaia oppositsiia v SSSR, 1923-1927 / Red.-sost. Yu. Felshtinskii.* [*The Trotsky Arkhiv. Communist Opposition in the USSR, 1923-1927.* Edited by Yu. Felshtinsky.] Moscow, 1990. T. 1-4.

Bordiugov, G.A., Kozlov, V.A. *Istoriia i konyunktura: subiektivnye zametki ob istorii sovetkogo obshchestva* [*History and Conjecture: Subjective Observations on the History of Soviet Society.*] Moscow, 1992.

Goland, Yu. Politika i ekonomika: (Ocherki obshchestvennoi borby 20-kh godov), *Znamia*. ["Policy and Economics: Essays on the Social Struggle in the 1920s," *Banner*.] 1990. No. 3.

Gorinov, M.M. *NEP: Poiski putei razvitiia* [*NEP; The Search for a Development Path*]. Moscow, 1990.

Koen, S. Bukharin: *Politicheskaia biografiia* [*Political Biography*], 1888-1938. Moscow, 1988. (Translation of Cohen, Stephen, *Bukharin and the Bolshevik Revolution: A Political Biography, 1888-1938*. New York, 1973.)

Medvedev, R.A. *O Staline i stalinizme* [*On Stalin and Stalinism*]. Moscow, 1990.

Nashe otechestvo: Opyt politicheskoi istorii [*Our Motherland: The Experience of Political History*]. Moscow, 1991, T. 2.

NEP: vzliad so storony [*NEP: The View from the Side*]. Moscow, 1991.

Taker, R. *Stalin: Put k vlasti, 1879-1929: Istoriia i lichnost* [*Stalin: The Road to Power, 1879-1929: His History and Personality*]. Moscow, 1990. (Russian translation of Tucker, Robert, *Stalin as Revolutionary, 1879-1929*. New York, 1973.)

Tsakunov, S.V. *V labirinte doktriny: Iz opyta razrabotki ekonomicheskogo kursa strany v 1920-3 gody* [*In the Labyrinth of Doctrine: From the Experiences of Working Out the Country's Economic Policy from 1920 to 1923*]. Moscow, 1994. (Seria "Pervaia monografiia")["The First Monograph" Series].

Volkogonov, D.A. *Lenin. Politicheskii portret* [*Lenin. A Political Portrait*]. In two books. Book 2.] Moscow, 1994.

The USSR on the Road to the Construction of Socialism by Coercion

Bukharin, N.I. *Put k sotsializmu: Izbrannye proizvedeniia.* [*The Road to Socialism: Selected Works*]. Novosibirsk, 1990.

Doicher, I. *Trotskii v izgnanii* [*Trotsky in Exile*]. Moscow, 1991. (Translation of Deutscher, I., *The Prophet Outcast: Trotsky, 1929-1940*. New York, 1963.)

Dokumenty svidetelstvuiut: Iz istorii derevni nakanune i v khode kollektivizatsii 1927-1932 gg /Pod red. V.P. Danilov i N.A. Ivnitskogo. [*The Documents Testify: From the History of the Village on the Eve of and During Collectivization, 1927-1932*. Edited by V.P. Danilov and N.A. Ivnitsky.] Moscow, 1989.

Gordon, L.A., Klopov, E.V. *Chto eto bylo: Razmyshleniia o predposylkakh i ob itogakh togo chto sluchilos s nami v 30—40-e gody* [*What It Was: Reflections on the Causes and Results of What Happened to Us in the 1930s and 1940s*]. Moscow, 1939.

Khlevniuk, O.V. *Stalin i Ordzhonikidze. Konflikty v Politbiuro v 30-e gody* [*Stalin and Ordzhonikidze. Intrapolitburo Conflict in the 1930s*]. Moscow, 1993. (Available in English as Khlevniuk, Oleg. *In Stalin's Shadow: The Career of "Sergo" Ordzhonikidze*. New York, 1995.)

Koen, S. *Bukharin: Politicheskaia biografiia* [*Political Biography*]. Moscow, 1988. (Translation of Cohen, S., *Bukharin and the Bolshevik Revolution: A Political Biography, 1888-1938.* New York, 1973.)

Latsis, O. *Perelom: Opyt prochteniia nesekretnykh dokumentov* [*The Crisis: The Experience of Reading the Declassified Documents*]. Moscow, 1990.

Medvedev, R.A. *O Staline i stalinisme* [*On Stalin and Stalinism*]. Moscow, 1990.

Osokina, E.A. *Ierarkhiia potrebleniia: O zhizni liudei v usloviakh stalinskogo snabzheniia, 1928-1935* gg. [*The Hierarchy of Consumption: On the Lives of the People during Stalinist Supply Conditions, 1928-1935*]. Moscow, 1993.

Teptsov, N.V. *Agrarnaia politika: na krutykh povorotakh 20—30-kh godov* [*Agrarian Policy: At the Critical Turning Points of the 1920s and 1930s*]. Moscow, 1990.

Volkogonov, D.A. *Triumf i tragediia: Politicheskii portret J.V. Stalina* [*Triumph and Tragedy: A Political Portrait of J.V. Stalin*]. In two books. Book I. Moscow, 1989. (Available in English as Volkogonov, Dmitry, *Stalin: Triumph and Tragedy*. Mew York, 1991.)

The Soviet Union in the Second World War

Cherchill, U. *Vtoraia mirovaia voina*. [*The Second World War.*] V 3 t. [In three volumes.] Moscow, 1991. (Russian translation of Churchill, Winston. *The Second World War.* 6 vols., Boston, 1948-1953.)

Evropa mezhdu mirom i voinoi, 1918-1939 [*Europe between Peace and War, 1918-1939*].

Grif sekretnosti sniat: Poteri Vooruzhennykh sil SSSR v voinakh, boevykh deistviiakh i voennykh konfliktakh: Sta. issledovaniia. [The Stamp of Secrecy is Taken Away: The Losses of the Armed Forces of the USSR in the Wars, Military Operations and Military Conflicts: Research Articles.] Moscow, 1993.

Istoriia vtoroi mirovoi voiny [*The History of the Second World War.*] In 12 vols. Moscow, 1973-1982.

Kanun i nachalo voiny: Dokumenty i materialy [*The Eve and Beginning of the War: Documents and Materials*]. Leningrad, 1991.

Niurnbergskii protsess: Sbornik materialov [*The Nuremberg Process: A Collection of Materials*]. Moscow, 1987-1990. T. 1-4.

Proektor, D.M. *Put agressii i gibeli* [*The Path of Agression and Death*]. Moscow, 1989.

Rozanov, G.L. *Stalin — Gitler: Dokumentalnyi ocherk sovetsko-germanskikh diplomaticheskikh otnoshenii, 1939-1941.* [*Stalin ñ Hitler: Documentary Survey of Soviet-German Diplomatic Relations, 1939-1941.*] Moscow, 1991.

Samsonov, A.M. *Vtoraia mirovaia voina.* [*The Second World War.*] Moscow, 1989.

Shirer, U. *Vzlet i padenie tretiego reikha* [Shirer, W. *The Rise and Fall of the Third Reich.* In 2 vols.] Moscow, 1991. (Russian translation of Shirer, William, *The Rise and Fall of the Third Reich,* New York, 1959.

Volkogonov, D. *Triumf i tragediia: Politicheskii portret J.V. Stalina* [*Triumph and Tragedy: A Political Portrait of J.V. Stalin*]. Book II, Part 1. Moscow, 1989. (Available in English as Volkogonov, Dmitry, *Stalin: Triumph and Tragedy.* Mew York, 1991.)

Zhukhov, G.K. *Vospominaniia i razmyshleniia* [*Memories and Reflections*]. In 3 vols., 11th ed. Moscow, 1992.

The Climax of Totalitarianism: The Soviet Union (1945-1953)

Chuev, F. *Sto sorok besed s Molotovym* [*A Hundred Forty Conversations with Molotov*]. Moscow, 1991.

Istoricheskii opyt i perestroika: Chelovecheskii faktor v sotsialno-

ekonomicheskom razvitii SSSR. [*The Historical Experience and Reconstruction: The Human Factor in the Social and Economic Development of the USSR.*] Moscow, 1989.

Istoriia SSSR s drevneishikh vremen do nashikh dnei. [*The History of the USSR from Ancient Times to Our Days.*] Moscow, 1980. T. XI.

Medvedev, R. *Oni okruzhali Stalina* [*They Were Stalin's Circle*]. Moscow, 1990.

Shapiro, L. *Kommunisticheskaia partiia Sovetskogo Soiuza.* [*The Communist Party of the Soviet Union*]. Rome, 1975. (Translation of Schapiro, Leonard. *The Communist Party of the Soviet Union.* New York, 1970.)

Vert, N. *Istoriia sovetskogo gosudarstva* [*The History of the Soviet State*], 1900-1991. Moscow, 1992.

Volkogonov, D. *Triumf i tragediia: Politicheskii portret J.V. Stalina* [*Triumph and Tragedy: A Political Portrait of J.V. Stalin*]. Book II, Part 2. Moscow, 1989. (Available in English as Volkogonov, Dmitry, *Stalin: Triumph and Tragedy.* Mew York, 1991.)

Zubkova, E. Yu. *Obshchestvo i reformy* [*Society and Reform*], 1945-1964. Moscow, 1993.

The "Thaw"

Aksiutin, Yu.V., Volobuev, O.B., XX syezd KPSS: novatsii i dogmy. [The XX Congress of the Communist Party of the Soviet Union: Innovations and Dogmas.] Moscow, 1991.

Alekseeva, L. *Istoriia inakomysliia v SSSR* [*The History of Dissident Thought in the USSR*]. Moscow, 1992.

Beriia: Konets kariery [*Beria: The End of a Career*]. Moscow, 1991.

Burlatsky, F. *Vozhdi i sovetniki* [*The Leaders and Counsellors*]. Moscow, 1990.

Chuev, F. *Sto sorok besed s Molotovym* [*A Hundred Forty Conversations with Molotov*]. Moscow, 1991.

Khanin, G.I. *Dinamika ekonomicheskogo razvitiia SSSR* [*The Dymanics of the Economic Development of the USSR*]. Novosibirsk, 1991.

Medvedev, R.A. *N.S. Khrushchev: Politicheskii biografiia* [*Khrushchev: A Political Biography*]. Moscow, 1990.

Zubkova, E. Yu. *Obshchestvo i reformy* [*Society and Reform*], 1945-1964. Moscow, 1993.

On the Road to Global Crisis (1964-1985)

Alekseeva, L. *Istoriia inakomysliia v SSSR* [*The History of Dissident Thought in the USSR*]. Moscow, 1992.

Arbatov, G.A. *Zatianuvsheesia vyzdorovlenie* [*The Protracted Recovery.*] (1953-1985). Moscow, 1991.

Brezhnev, L.I.: *Materialy k biografii* [*Materials for a Biography*]. Moscow, 1991.

Chazov, E. *Zdorovie i vlast* [*Health and Power*]. Moscow, 1992.

Na poroge krizisa: Narastanie zastoinykh iavlenii v partii i obshchestve [*On the Threshhold of the Crisis: The Emergence of Stagnation in the Party and Society*]. Moscow, 1990.

Nashe Otechestvo: Opyt politicheskoi istorii [*Our Motherland: The Experience of Political History*]. Moscow, 1991. Ch. 2.

Vert, N. *Istoriia sovetskogo gosudarstva* [*The History of the Soviet State*], 1900-1991. Moscow, 1992

Zakharov, A.D. *Trevoga i nadezhda* [*Anxiety and Hope*]. Moscow, 1990.

A SHORT CHRONOLOGY

IV-VIII cc.	—	The Great Migration of the Peoples
V-VII cc.	—	The formation of the barbarian kingdoms
V-VIII cc.	—	The Dispersion of the Slavs
IX-X cc.	—	The formation of the state of Rus'
2nd half IX c.	—	The beginning of the Rurikide dynasty
c. 882	—	The reign of Oleg in Kiev
912-945	—	The reign of Igor
945-972	—	The reign of Sviatoslav
980-1015	—	The reign of Vladimir Sviatoslavich
c. 988	—	The Baptism of Rus'
1019-1054	—	The reign of Iaroslav the Wise
X-XII cc.	—	The transition to feudal disorder in Europe
2nd third XII c.	—	The separation of Rus' into independent lands
c. 1200	—	The founding of the University of Paris
1223	—	The battle on the Kalka
1237-1241	—	The Mongol-Tatar invasion of Rus'
1242	—	The battle on Lake Chud
1265	—	The beginning of the English Parliament
1270s	—	The formation of the principality of Moscow, the beginning of the reign of Daniel Aleksandrovich
1303-1325	—	The reign in Moscow of Iury Danielovich
1327	—	The uprising in Tver against the Tatars
1325-1340	—	The reign in Moscow of Ivan Danilovich Kalita (Grand Prince of Vladimir after 1328)
1340-1353	—	The reign of Semen Ivanovich as Grand Prince
1353-1359	—	The reign of Ivan Ivanovich as Grand Prince
1360-1389	—	The reign of Dmitrii Ivanovich Donskoi (Grand Prince from 1362)
1380, Sept 8	—	Battle of Kulikovo
1382	—	The attack on Moscow by Khan Tokhtamysh
1389-1425	—	The reign of Vasilii I Dmitrievich as Grand Prince

CHRONOLOGY

1425-1462	—	The reign of Vasilii II Vasil'evich as Grand Prince
2nd half XV c.	—	The creation of centralized states in France and Spain
XV c.- XVI c.	—	The Renaissance (in Italy from the XIV c.)
1462-1505	—	The reign of Ivan III Vasil'evich as Grand Prince
1480	—	The final collapse of the Horde's yoke
XV-XVI c.	—	The formation of the Russian state. The great geographic discoveries, the birth of capitalism in Western Europe
1505-1533	—	The Reign of Vasilii III Ivanovich as Grand Prince
1533-1584	—	The reign of Ivan IV Vasil'evich as Grand Prince (from 1547 — as Tsar)
2nd half XVI c.	—	The completion of the formation of the Russian form of feudalism
1549-1560	—	The reforms of the Chosen Council
1558-1583	—	The Livonian War
1565-1572	—	The oprichnina
1566-1572	—	The bourgeois revolution in the Netherlands
1598-1605	—	The reign of Boris Godunov as Tsar
1605-1606	—	The reign of False Dmitrii I
1606-1610	—	The reign of Vasilii Shuiskii
1606-1607	—	The uprising of I. Bolotnikov
1610-1612	—	The Semiboiarshchina
1612	—	The liberation of Moscow from the interventionists
1613-1645	—	The reign of Michael Romanov as Tsar
1640-1653	—	The English revolution
1645-1676	—	The reign of Alexis Mikhailovich as Tsar
1654	—	The Pereislavl Rada; the beginning of Nikon's clerical reforms
1670-1671	—	The uprising under the leadership of S. Razin
1676-1682	—	The reign of Fedor Alekseevich as Tsar
1682-1725	—	The reign of Peter the Great
1700-1721	—	The Northern War
1725	—	The founding of the Academy of Sciences in St. Petersburg
1725-1727	—	The reign of Catherine I

CHRONOLOGY

1727-1730	—	The reign of Peter II
1730-1740	—	The reign of Anna Ivanovna
1741-1761	—	The reign of Elizabeth Petrovna
2nd half XVIII	—	The birth of capitalism in Russia
1755	—	The founding of the first university in Russia
1761-1762	—	The reign of Peter III
1762	—	The manifesto on the emancipation of the nobility
1762-1796	—	The reign of Catherine II
1768-74, 87-91	—	The wars of Russia with the Ottoman Empire
1772, 93, 95	—	The partitions of Poland
1773-1775	—	The peasant uprising led by E. Pugachev
1784	—	J. Watt patents a steam engine
1789-1794	—	The Great French Revolution
1796-1801	—	The reign of Paul I
1801-1825	—	The reign of Alexander I
1812	—	The Fatherland War
1825	—	The Decembrist uprising
1825-1855	—	The reign of Nicholas I
1848	—	Revolution in Europe
1853-1856	—	The Crimean War
1850s-90s	—	The industrial revolution in Russia
1855-1881	—	The reign of Alexander II
1861	—	The abolition of serfdom in Russia
1864	—	The zemstvo and judicial reforms
1874	—	The military reform
1876-1879	—	The populist organization "Land and Liberty"
1877-1878	—	The Russo-Turkish War
1879-1882	—	The "People's Will" organization
1881, Mar 1	—	The assassination of Alexander II
1881-1894	—	The reign of Alexander III
1892	—	The signing of the Russo-French Military Convention
1894-1917	—	The reign of Nicholas II
1898-1903	—	The formation of the Russian Social Democratic Workers' Party (RSDRP)
1901	—	Formation of the Socialist Revolutionaries party
1904	—	The forming of the Assembly of Plant and

		Factory Workers of St. Petersburg
1904-1905	—	The Russo-Japanese War
1905, Jan 9	—	Bloody Sunday, the beginning of revolution in Russia
1905, Oct.	—	All-Russian political strike, creation of the St. Petersburg Soviet, the Cadets' party, the Black Hundreds' pogroms
1905, Dec 9-19	—	The Moscow uprising
1906, 4/27-7/8	—	First State Duma
1906, Nov 9	—	The beginning of the Stolypin agrarian reform
1907, 2/ 20-6/3	—	Second State Duma
1907, Jun 3	—	Dissolution of the Duma and the alteration of the Electoral Law
1907, Aug 18	—	Russo-English Agreement, formation of the Entente
1907-1912	—	Third State Duma
1911, Sep 1	—	The assassination of P.A. Stolypin
1912-1917	—	Fourth State Duma
1914, July 19	—	Germany's declaration of war on Russa. Beginning of the First World War
1915	—	The formation of the military-industrial committees, Zemgor and the Progressive Bloc
1917, Feb 23	—	The beginning of the February Revolution
1917, Mar 2	—	The abdication of Nicholas II, the creation of the Provisional Government
1917, 4/20-21	—	Anti-government demonstrations in Petrograd
1917, May 5	—	The inclusion of the socialists in the Provisional Government
1917, Jul 3-4	—	The Petrograd uprising
1917, 8/25-9/1	—	The Kornilov mutiny
1917,10/24-25	—	The Bolshevik Revolution in Petrograd, the beginning of the civil war in Russia,the openning of the II Congress of Soviets
1917, Dec 9	—	The entry of the Left SRs into the Bolshevik Council of People's Commissars(*Sovnarkom*)
1918, Jan 5-6	—	The activity of the Constituent Assembly and its dispersion

CHRONOLOGY

1918, Mar 3 —	The conclusion of the Peace of Brest
1918, May —	The introduction of food rationing
1918, Jul 6 —	The revolt of the Left SRs in Moscow
1918, Jul 17 —	The assassination of the Imperial Family in Ekaterinburg
1918, Sep 5 —	The introduction of the "Red Terror"
1919, Jan 11 —	The introduction of the surplus-appropriation system
1919, Mar 2-6 —	The founding congress of the Cominterm
1920, 4/25-10/12—	The war of the RSFSR with Poland
1920, Nov —	The end of the civil war in European Russia
1921, 2/28-3/18—	The Kronstadt uprising
1921, Mar 6-8 —	X Congress of the Russian Communist Party (The Bolsheviks) [RKP(B)]
1922, Apr 3 —	The election of J.V. Stalin as General Secretary (Gensek) of the Central Committee of the RKP(B)
1922, Dec 30 —	The formation of the USSR
1923 —	The first NEP crisis, the beginning of the struggle against "Trotskyism"
1925 —	The second NEP crisis, the struggle with the "New Opposition"
1927 —	The defeat of the "Combined Opposition"
1928-1929 —	The grain requisition crisis, the struggle with the "right deviation"
1929-1930 —	The beginning of mass collectivization and "dekulakization"
1929—32 —	The world economic crisis
1934, Dec 1 —	The assassination of S.M. Kirov, the unfolding of the mass terror
1939, Aug 23 —	The conclusion of the Soviet-German Non aggression Pact
1939—45 —	The Second World War
1939, Sep-Nov—	The introduction of Soviet troops into Poland
1939—1940 —	The war between the USSR and Finland
1940, Jun-Jul —	The Soviet occupation of Estonia, Latvia, and Lithuania

1941, Jun 22	The beginning of the Great Patriotic War
1942, Jan 1	The signing of the Declaration of the United Nations
1945, May 8	The signing of the document on Germany's unconditional surrender
1945, Aug 6,9	The atomic bombardment of Nagasaki and Hiroshima
1949	The creation of the Council for Mutual Economic Aid (SEV) (January 5-8) and NATO (April 4)
1950-53	The Korean War
1953, Mar 5	The death of Stalin, the beginning of "collective leadership"
1953, Jun 26	Beria's arrest at a session of the Presidium of the Central Committee of the KPSS (CPSU)
Mid-1950s	The beginning of the scientific-technological revolution
1954, Jun 27	The opening of the world's first atomic power station (AES) at Obninsk
1955, May 14	The creation of the Warsaw Treaty Organization (OVD)
1956, Feb14-25	XX Congress of the KPSS (CPSU)
1957, Oct 4	The launching of the first Soviet satellite into space
1961, Apr 12	The flight of Yu.A. Gagarin into space
1962, Oct-Nov	The Caribbean crisis
1963, Aug 5	The signing of the treaty prohibiting the testing of nuclear weapons in the environment
1964, Oct 14	The dismissal of Khrushchev, the election of L.I. Brezhnev as First Secretary of the Central Committee of the KPSS (CPSU) (from 1966—Gensek)
1965, Mar, Sep	The beginning of economic reform in the USSR
1968, Aug 21	The intervention of the countries of the Warsaw Pact in Czechoslovakia
1969, Jul 16-24	The first flight to the moon by American as-

CHRONOLOGY

	tronauts
1972, May 22-30—	The visit of R. Nixon to Moscow, the signing of the "Principles of Mutual Relations between the USSR and the USA," and the ABM (PRO) and Strategic Arms Limitation (OSV-1 or SALT-1) treaties
Mid-1970s —	The beginning of the second stage of the scientific-technological revolution
1975, Aug 1 —	The signing in Helsinki of the Final Act of the Agreement on Security and Cooperation in Europe
1977, Oct 7 —	The ratification of the Brezhnev Constitution
1979, Jun 18 —	The signing of the SALT-II Treaty in Vienna
1979-89 —	The Soviet intervention in Afghanistan
1982, Nov 10,19—	The death of Brezhnev and election of Iu.V. Andropov as Gensek of the Central Committee of the CPSU
1984, Feb 13 —	The election of K.U. Chernenko as Gensek of the Central Committee of the CPSU
1985, Mar 10,11—	The death of Chernenko and election of M.S. Gorbachev as Gensek of the Central Committee of the CPSU
1985, Apr 23 —	Plenum of the Central Committee of the CPSU, the policy of accelerating the USSR's social and economic development
1986, Apr 26 —	The Chernobyl disaster
1988, 6/ 28-7/1 —	XIX Conference of the CPSU, the policy of political reform in the USSR
1989, 5/25-6/9—	The I Congress of People's Deputies of the USSR
1990, Jun 12 —	Russia's declaration of state sovereignty
1991, Jun 12 —	The election of B.N. Eltsin as President of Russia
1991, Aug 19-21—	The attempted coup in the USSR
1991, Dec 8 —	The dissolution of the USSR, the signing of the treaty on the creation of the Commonwealth of Independent States (SNG)(CIS)

CHRONOLOGY

1992, Jan 2 — The decontrol of prices, beginning of Gaidar's reforms
1993, Apr 25 — All-Russian referendum on confidence in the President's policies
1993, Sep 21 — Elstin's decree on the dissolution of the Supreme Soviet of the RSFSR
1993, Oct 3-4 — The demosntrations and insurrection of the Opposition, the itnroduction of troops into Moscow and the siege of the "White House"
1993, Dec 12 — Elections to the State Duma and Federation Council. The ratification of the Russian Constitution in a referendum
1994, Jan 11 — The beginning of the work of the State Duma and Federation Council

---

1The dates before February 1918 are given according to the Old Style, after February 1, 1918 according to the New Style.

INDEX

A
A-bomb, 245
Abakumov, V. S., 270
Abilkhozhin, Zh. B., 188
Abuladze, T., 315
Academy of Sciences, 291, 350
Administrative-Command System, 166, 171, 176, 188-189, 304, 327-328, 334, 340
Administrative-Managerial Apparatus, 189
Aduev, N., 137
Afanasiev, Yu. N., 329
Afghanistan, 108, 319, 343-344
Afrika Corps, 225
Agrarian Artel, 191, 246
Akhmatova, A. A., 184, 250
AKhR, 138-139
Akselrod, P. B., 31
Aksenov, A., 338
Aksionov, V., 315
Alaska, 240
Albania, 152, 196, 235, 293, 320, 344
Aleksandrov, G., 184
Alekseev, General M. V., 96
Alexander I, 363, 370-371
Alexander II, 363, 371
All-Russian Central Executive Committee, 40, 49-50, 61-62, 80, 84-86, 88, 94
All-Russian Central Trade Union, 40
All-Russian Congress of Soviets, 37, 42, 54, 59, 109
All-Russian Congress of Workers, 59, 65, 100
All-Russian Democratic Council, 52
All-Russian Democratic Conference, 51
All-Russian Executive Committee, 49-51, 57, 61-62, 80, 84-86, 88, 94
All-Russian Revolutionary Committee, 81
All-Russian Soviet of Peasants, 44, 61
All-Russian Trade Union Conference, 40
All-Russian Union, 40, 352
All-Union Academy of Agronomic Science, 182
All-Union Central Council of Trade, 279
All-Union Communist Party, 143, 151, 179, 253-254, 351
All-Union Communist Party Central Committee, 151, 254
All-Union Population Census, 322
Alsace-Lorraine, 193
American Communist Party, 237
Anarchists, 41-42, 95, 110, 330
Anarcho-Communist Revolutionary Union, 330
Anarcho-Communists, 86
Anarcho-Syndicalist Confederation, 330
Andreev, A. A., 94, 162
Andreev, N. A., 94
Andreev, V., 185
Andreeva, N., 340-341
Andropov, Yury V., 307, 314-315, 325-326
Angarsky, I. S., 47
Anglo-Soviet General Treaty, 108
Angola, 319, 344
Anschluss, 151, 195

Anticomintern Pact, 151
Antonov, A. S., 109
Antonov, V. A., 61
Antonov-Ovseenko, V. A., 55, 131
Archangel, 211
Ardennes, 203, 227
Armenia, 79, 123, 234
Artsimovich, L. A., 291
Asafiev, V., 185
Aseev, N., 137
Association of New Architects, 139
Association of State Enterprises, 346
Atlantic Charter, 215
August Coup, 345-346, 348, 351, 357
Aurora, 59
Australia, 216
Austria, 71, 73, 142, 151, 195
Austria-Hungary, 182, 194
Austrian State Treaty, 293
Avilov, N. P., 61
Avksentiev, N. D., 30, 62
Azerbaijan, 79, 122-123, 234, 336, 341

B
Babel, I., 184
Babitsky, K., 313
Baikal-Amur Railway, 248
Bakatin, V., 336, 356
Baklanov, O. D., 346
Balkans, 194, 226
Baltic Fleet, 57
Barbarossa, 204, 211
Barvenky, 217
Batalov, N. P., 140
Bavaria, 71
Bebutov, E., 139
Beijing, 108, 196, 344
Belgium, 182, 203
Belgorod, 220
Beloborodov, A. G., 131
Belorussia, 73, 79, 89, 122-123, 202, 211, 218, 221, 226, 244, 254, 265, 314, 336, 348
Belostok-Minsk, 211
Bely, A., 137-138
Berdiaev, N. A., 126, 192, 338, 360, 365
Bergelson, D., 253
Bergholts, O., 276
Beria, L. P., 218, 245, 255, 257-258, 262-267, 269-270, 272, 282, 299-300
Beria Plot, 262
Berlin, 27, 71, 151, 200, 218, 227-228, 237, 294, 318
Berlin Wall, 294
Berlin-Rome Axis, 151
Bessarabia, 200, 205, 219
Big Three, 226-227
Bill of Rights, 237
Black Hundreds, 111, 126
Black Sea, 98, 107, 234
Bleikhman, I. S., 41
Blitzkrieg, 208
Bliukher, V. K., 108
Bliumkin, Ya. G., 94

392 INDEX

Blucher, V. K., 150
Bogdanov, N., 138
Bogolubov, N. N., 291
Bogoraz, L., 313
Bohemia, 196
Bolshevik Central Committee, 38, 42, 44-45, 53-56, 58, 62, 88, 95, 125, 183
Bolshevik Party, 32, 44, 47, 56, 82, 89, 91, 109, 124, 127-128, 141
Bordiugov, G. A., 189
Borodin, M. M., 108
Bovikin, V. I., 187
Brest Peace, 66, 73-74, 83, 89-90, 94-95, 97, 100, 339
Brezhnev, L. I., 276, 296, 298, 302, 304-305, 307-310, 315-321, 324, 338, 347
Britain, 27, 69, 71, 74-75, 98, 102-109, 145-146, 153, 164, 183, 194, 196-206, 209, 215-216, 227, 232, 237, 242, 293, 318
British Miners Federation, 108
Brodsky, I., 139
Brodsky, N., 338
Bronshtein, 61
Brusilov, A. A., 46
Brussels International Conference, 106
Brutskus, B., 126
Bubnov, A. S., 131
Budapest, 227
Bukharin, N. I., 88, 142, 187, 21-22
Bulgakov, M. A., 140, 184
Bulganin, Nikolai A., 272
Bulgaria, 106, 227, 235, 237, 344
Bunin, I. A., 40, 65
Burlatski, F. M., 299
Burlatsky, S. M., 300
Burma, 232, 294
Byzantium, 361

C

Cambodia, 294
Canada, 343
Caporetto, 25
Catherine II, 370, 374-375
Catholic, 361
Central Bank, 353
Central Committee Commission, 134, 154, 156, 174, 346, 348
Central Committee Presidium, 263-264, 266, 268, 272, 276-277, 282, 298-299
Central Control Commission, 134, 154, 156, 174
Central Executive Committee, 37, 40, 44-45, 49-50, 59, 61-62, 80, 84-86, 88, 94, 99, 111, 122, 172
Central Political Education, 135
Central Powers, 25, 165
Central Rada, 43, 79, 89
Central Turkmen Canal, 265
Ceylon, 232
Chaadaev, P. Ya., 367
Chaianov, A. V., 167
Chamberlain, Neville, 152
Chapaev, 138, 184

Chechen-Ingush Autonomous Republic, 280
Cheka, 81-82, 94-95, 110, 124
Cheliabinsk, 254
Chemcoal, 117
Cherkes, 280
Chernenko, K. U., 325-326
Chernichenko, Yu., 340
Chernobyl, 328
Chernomyrdin, V. S., 353
Chernov, SR V. M., 39
Chevengur, 338
Chicherin, G. V., 74, 98
Chief Economic Committee, 35
Chinese Communist Party, 278
Chinese Eastern Railway, 150
Christian Democratic Union of Russia, 330
Christian-Democratic Party of Russia, 330
Christianity, 361, 367-368
Christianity, Evangelical, 367
Chubarov, Viacheslav V., 142
Chudnovsky, G. I., 59
Chuev, From F., 260
Chukotka, 240
Chukovsky, K., 310
Chum-Salekhard-Igarka Polar Railway, 265
Church, Russian Orthodox, 126-127, 223
Churchill, Winston, 204, 225, 233
CIA, 314
Circassian, 280
CIS, 348
Cohen, S., 339
Cold War, 179, 231, 244, 271, 292, 339, 342, 345, 371
Collective Leadership, 262-264, 266, 268, 281, 285, 298
Collectivization, 155, 157, 160, 162-164, 167, 169-170, 181, 186-189, 273, 372
Comecon, 235, 320, 344
Cominform, 235
Comintern, 72, 106, 108, 149-150, 173, 231, 235
Commisariat of Agriculture, 99
Commissar of Heavy Industry, 159
Commissariat of Defense, 208
Commissariat of Food, 93, 114
Commissariat of Internal Affairs, 124
Commissariat of Justice, 82
Commissars, Ten Iron, 188
Committee of State Security, 270
Committee of Youth Organizations, 279
Commonwealth of Independent States, 348, 350, 355
Communist Party Central Committee, 154, 156, 254, 283
Conference of February, 191
Congress of National-Patriotic Parties, 351
Congress of Peoples Deputies, 339
Congress of Soviets, 37, 42, 51, 54-56, 59-62, 82-83, 86, 89, 95, 99, 109, 123, 159, 4-6
Conservative Party, 330
Constitution, 123, 175, 177, 249, 308, 333, 347, 353-354, 356
Constitution of Russia, 356

Constitutional Court of Russia, 351
Cossacks, 58-59, 84, 96, 101
Cotton, 163-164, 206, 323
Council of Economic Assistance, 235, 344
Council of Five, 50
Council of Mutual Economic Assistance, 344
CPSU, 64, 191, 266-267, 269, 273, 276-277, 279, 297-298, 304-305, 310, 315, 321-322, 325-329, 333-339, 341, 343, 346, 348-349, 351, 356-357
CPSU Agrarian Policy, 321
CPSU Central Committee, 304, 325, 327-328, 357
Crimea, 73, 75, 153, 217, 221, 226, 313, 346
Crimean War, 364, 371
Croats, 71
Cuba, 295, 345
Cuban Missile Crisis, 294
Curzon, 107
Czechoslovak Legion, 74
Czechoslovak National Council, 74
Czechoslovakia, 71, 103, 151-152, 196-198, 227, 235-236, 305, 313, 318-319, 344

D
Dan, 57, 59, 340
Dan, F. I., 31
Daniel, Yu., 313
Danilov, V. P., 188
Danzig, 152, 196
Dawes, 104-105
Dawes Plan, 104
Decembrists, 363, 370
Declaration of July, 46
Declaration of Principles, 319
de Gaulle, 203
Deinika, A., 139
Dekanazov, V. G., 270
Deladier, Eduard, 152
Delone, V., 313
Democratic Council, 52
Democratic Party, 27, 33, 65, 7-8, 16-17, 330, 352
Democratic Party of Russia, 330, 352
Democratic Socialism, 266, 334
Demsoiuz, 330
Denikin, General Anton I., 75, 96-97
Denmark, 203
Dennis, Eugene, 277
Derbyshev, 62
Dibenko, P. E., 57
Djilas, Milovan, 227, 238
Dnieper, 221, 248
Doenitz, Admiral, 227
Dolgolaptev, A., 352
Don Army, 73, 96
Don Basin, 122
Donbas, 122, 296
Doncoal, 117
Donets Basin, 217
Donugol, 117
Doumenc, General J., 201
Dovzhenko, A., 184

Drabkina, E., 338
Drax, Admiral R. A., 200
Dremliuga, V., 313
Druzhinin, V. G., 184
Dudintsov, B.
Dudintsov, V., 292
Dudintsov, V., 292
Dugin, N. K., 188
Dunkirk, 203
Durnovo, P. N., 41
Dybenko, P. E., 61
Dzerzhinsky, F. E., 81
Dzhugashvili, 61
Dzigan, E., 184

E
Economic Council, 35, 78, 117, 159, 162, 166, 235, 4-5, 285-286, 344
Efremov, O., 310
Efros, A., 315
Eggert, Z. K., 64
Egorychev, N., 310
Egypt, 294
Eighteenth Party Conference, 177
Eighteenth Party Congress, 198
Eighth All-Russian Congress of Soviets, 109
Einstein, A., 342
Eisenhower, Dwight, 216
Eismont, N. B., 172
Eizenstein, S., 250
Ekaterinburg, 37, 251, 294, 314
Ekk, H., 184
El Alamein, 224
Elanskaia, K. N., 140
Eleventh Communist Party Congress, 109
Eltsin, Boris, 329, 333, 335-337, 347, 349-351, 353-354
Engels, 185
England, 71, 151, 182, 203
Entente, 25, 69, 71-75, 87-89, 111
Erenburg, E., 137
Erenburg, Ilia, 274
Erendorf Island, 138
Ermolov, M. N., 140
Esenin, S. A., 137, 140
Estonia, 71, 75, 79, 107, 200, 205, 314, 348
Estonian Popular Front, 329
Ethiopia, 150, 196, 319, 344
Evdokimov, G. E., 172
EVM, 307
Extraordinary Commission, 34, 81

F
Fadeev, A., 138, 184
Fainberg, V., 313
Falk, R., 139
Fascism, 72, 151, 187, 195-196, 198, 225-226, 231, 233, 241, 339
Favorsky, V., 139
February Revolution, 27-29, 31-33, 36-37, 39-41, 83, 97, 99
Federal Reserve System, 146
Fedin, K., 136, 138

394 INDEX

Fedorov, B., 356
Feichtwanger, L., 178, 192
Felshtinsky, Iu., 66
Fifteenth Congress of All Union Communist Party, 187
Fifth Congress of Soviets, 95, 159
Fifth Supreme Soviet, 279
Filonov, P., 139
Finance Commissariat, 93, 118
Finnish War, 206
First Cavalry, 101
First Congress of Soviets, 37, 42, 123
First Legal Petersburg Committee of Bolsheviks, 65
First Machine Gun Regiment, 44
First World War, 52, 64, 69, 71, 102, 144, 146, 149, 156, 164-165, 193-195, 204, 230, 367
Five Year Plan, 152, 158-159, 166, 177-178, 187, 190, 246, 305, 327
Five Year Plans, 159, 247, 258
Fomin, I. A., 140
Foreign Trade Bank, 117
Four Party Pact, 198
Fourteen Points, 69, 71
Fourteenth Party Congress, 133
Fourth Congress of People, 334
Fourth Duma, 32
Fourth Extraordinary Congress of Soviets, 89
Fourth Supreme Soviet, 279
Franco, General Francisco, 150
Frank, S., 126, 326
Freedom Party, 43, 46-47, 282, 309
French Revolution, 363
Friends of Radio Society, 128
Front of National Salvation, 355
Furmanov, Dm., 138
FZU, 135

G

Gabai, I., 313
Gagarin, Yury, 291
Gaidar, E. T., 349
Galanskov, Yu., 313
Galich, A., 315, 338
Galkin, S. Z., 253
Gandhi, Mahatma, 198
Gatchina, 61
Gdansk, 152, 196
Gefter, M., 315
General Staff, 33, 45, 50, 212, 215, 217, 219
Geneva, 293, 343
Genoa, 107
George, David Lloyd, 103
Georgia, 79, 123, 132, 341, 348
Georgian Communist Party, 343
Georgian Soviet Socialist Republics, 122
Gerasimenko, G. A., 65
German Army, 150, 196, 203, 212, 215, 220, 226
German Democratic Republic, 236-237, 266, 319, 344
German Federal Republic, 294, 313
German General Staff, 45, 50

German Labor Front, 148
German National Socialism, 195
German Social Democratic Party, 27
Germany, Federal Republic of, 237, 266
GINKhUK, 139
Ginsburg, A., 313
GKChP, 346-348, 356
Gladkov, F., 137-138
Glasnost, 328, 331, 337-342
Glazunov, I., 315
Glier, R., 185
Godunov, Boris, 362
Gogolova, E. N., 140
Gomulka, Wladyslaw, 235
Goncharov, Ivan, 375
Gorbachev, Mikhail, 230, 321, 325-326, 328-329, 331-332, 334-337, 339-340, 342-349, 357, 371
Gorbanevskaya, N., 313
Gordon, L. A., 187
Gorky, Maksim, 40
Gosplan, 117, 245, 254, 299, 301
GPU, 124-125
Grabar, I., 139
Granin, D., 292, 338
Granovsky, 280
Great Patriotic War, 165, 177, 239, 273, 282, 290-291
Great Reconstruction, 187
Great Reforms, 60, 363, 365, 372
Greece, 64, 237
Green Guard, 57
Grekov, M., 185
Grigorenko, P., 313
Gromyko, A. A., 343
Grossman, V., 338
Grozny, Ivan, 173
Guchkov, 38
Guderian, Hans, 208
GULAG, 162-163, 180, 188, 248, 251-252, 264, 268-269, 338
Gulf of Finland, 110, 113
Gumelev, M., 338

H

Haas, H., 27
Halder, F., 212
Harvard Plan, 336
Helsinki, 42, 313, 319
Helsinki Accords, 313
Henderson, Laborite Minister, 28
Higher Economic Council, 286
Hippius, Z., 81, 99
Hiroshima, 229
Hitler, Adolf, 72-73, 147-149, 151-152, 195-204, 206, 209-211, 215, 217-220, 226-227, 230, 250, 275
Hoffman, E. T. A., 143
Hofstein, D., 253
Holland, 145
House of Representatives, 237
Huguenots, 173
Hungarian Soviet Republic, 71

Hungary, 71, 73, 211, 235, 276, 294, 344

I
Iakovlev, 346
Ianshin, M. M., 140
Iavlinsky, 336
Iazkov, E. F., 261
Ignatiev, S., 254-255
Ignatov, N. G., 307
IKP, 136
IL-2, 207
Ilf, I., 184
Illiteracy, 28, 128, 135, 182, 368
Inber, V., 137
Independent Social Democratic Party, 27
India, 232, 294
Indonesia, 232, 294
Industry Bank, 117
Industry Party, 167, 191
Information Bureau of Communist, 235
INKhUK, 139
Institute of Red Professors, 136
International Proletarian Solidarity Day, 37
Iran, 108, 293
Iraq, 294, 344
Israel, 313
Italy, 27, 71-72, 98, 107, 149-151, 196, 198, 211, 216, 225, 230, 232
Iuon, K., 139
Iuzhin, A. I., 140
Ivan, 173, 7-8, 362-363, 375
Ivanenko, D. D., 182
Ivanov, Vs., 136, 138
Ivanovo-Voznesensk, 42, 45

J
Joffe, A. F., 182
Joint CPSU Central Committee, 357
Joint Plenum, 156
July Conference of Russian Anarchists, 41
Jurenito, Julio, 137

K
Kaaev, V., 138
Kabanov, V. V., 66, 99
Kabardine-Balkar Autonomous Republic, 280
Kachalov, V. I., 140
Kadar, Janush, 235
Kadet, 38, 43, 46-47, 84, 97
Kadet Central Committee, 38, 46
Kaganovich, L. M., 253, 262, 299
Kaledin, M., 96
Kalinin, M. I., 135, 8-9
Kamenev, L. B., 32-33, 61, 172, 9
Kamkov, B. D., 31, 9
Kandinsky, V., 139, 9
Kanev, S. N., 65, 9
Kant, I., 342
Kapitsa, P., 310
Kara-Kum, 248
Karbardino-Cherkes, 280
Kareev, N. A., 184
Kariakin, Yu., 340

Kasatkin, H., 139
Kataev, V., 136, 310
Kautsky, Karl, 149
Kaverin, V., 136
Kazakhstan, 162, 188, 224, 244, 270, 285, 296, 314, 336
Kazin, V., 137
Keitel, 221
Keldish, M. V., 291
Kennan, George, 260
Kerensky, A. F., 38, 46
Kermont, L. E., 192
KGB, 188, 253, 270, 282, 307, 314-315, 331, 346, 356
Khalkhin-Gol River, 150
Khanin, G. I., 189, 261, 288, 301
Kharkov, 65, 91, 217, 220
Khlevniuk, O. V., 188, 191
Khmelev, N. P., 140
Khmelnitsky, Bogdan, 292
Khodasevich, V., 338
Khrushchev, Nikita, 254, 258, 262-263, 266-274, 277, 279-285, 287, 289-290, 292, 295-301, 308-310, 316, 369
Khrushchevas, 287
Kiel, 71
Kiev, 117, 211, 213, 221
Kim, Yu., 315
Kirichenko, A. I., 265
Kirov, S. M., 172, 177
Kirsanov, S., 137, 292
Kiselev, A. F., 100
Kizevetter, A., 126
Klementis, Jan, 235
Kliamkin, I. M., 190
Kliamkina, I., 340
Kliuchevsky, V. O., 360, 373
Kliuev, N., 184
Klopov, A. V., 187
Knipovich, B., 99
Knipper-Chekov, O. L., 140
KNR, 371
Kobulov, B. Z., 270
Kolegaev, A. L., 82
Kolontay, A. M., 45, 88
Komitete, V, 188
Konchalovsky, P., 185
Kondratiev, M. D., 155
Kondratiev, N. D., 167, 190
Konovalov, A. I., 52
Korea, North, 229, 233, 238-239, 371
Korean War, 237, 240
Korin, P., 185
Kornilov, General L. G., 38, 46, 49-50, 96, 101
Kornilovshchina, 49-50, 52
Korolenko, V., 137
Korolev, S. P., 183
Kostov, Traicho, 235
Kosygin, Aleksei N., 223, 298, 304, 307
Kovalev, S., 313
Kozibaev, M. K., 188
Kozintsev, G., 184

INDEX

Kozlov, V. A., 189, 191
KPSS, 64, 98, 191, 299, 301, 321-322
KPSS, Plenum TsK, 301
Krasnov, General P. G.
Kremlin, 112, 232, 259, 294, 309, 355, 358
Kremlin Plot, 358
Krestinsky, N. M., 173
Krimov, General, 49-50
Kriuchkov, V. A., 346
Kronstadt, 109-114, 184
Krovavye, A. Rabinovich, 65
Krupskaia, N. K., 100
Krylenko, N. V., 61
Kulaks, 94, 121, 154, 157, 160-163, 180, 189
Kulik, G. I., 207
Kurbas, L., 185
Kurds, 223
Kurile Islands, 229, 233
Kursk Bulge, 220-221
Kutepov, General A. P., 167
Kuusinen, O. V., 205
Kuwait, 344
Kuznetsov, A. A., 223, 254
Kuznetsov, P., 139
Kvitko, L., 253

L
Labas, A., 139
Labour Party, 108
Ladvosky, N., 139
Lake Baikal, 248
Lake Khasan, 150, 198
Landau, L. D., 291
Lansing, Robert, 102
Larin, Yu., 31
Larina, A., 338
Latin American, 369
Latsis, M. I., 44
Latsis, O., 340
Latvia, 71, 75, 79, 87, 107, 200, 205, 314, 348
Latvian Popular Front, 329
Lausanne Conference, 107
Lavrentiev, M. A., 291
Lazimir, SR P., 55
LDPR, 356
League of Nations, 98, 104, 150-151, 195, 198
Lebanon, 232
Lebedev, S. V., 182
Lebedinsky, Yu., 138
Lebvedev Physics Institute, 182
LEF, 137
Left Communists, 88-89
Left Social Revolutionaries, 95
LeMans, 203, 226
Lend Lease Act, 215
Lenin, Vladimir Ilich, 28, 32-34, 43-47, 51, 53-56, 58-62, 64-66, 75-79, 81, 83-85, 87-89, 92-93, 98-100, 112-116, 122-123, 125-126, 129-130, 132-134, 141-142, 149, 157, 173, 180, 183, 185-186, 218, 263, 267, 282, 309, 314, 333, 365
Leningrad, 64, 99, 101, 139-140, 172, 187, 205, 211, 214-215, 217, 220, 226, 244, 251, 253-254, 269, 272, 276-277, 299, 340
Lenulov, A., 139
Leonov, L., 137-138
Leonov, S. V., 98
Leontovich, M. A., 291
Liberal Democratic Party, 330
Libya, 234, 344
Ligachev, E. K., 325, 338-341, 356
Lisov, E, 358
Literary Center of Constructivists, 137
Lithuania, 71, 75, 79, 87, 205, 314, 348, 362
Litso, 261
Litvinov, M. M., 199
Liubimov, Yu., 315
Liudi, 300, 363
Livanov, B. N., 140
Locarno, 104, 150, 195
Locarno Pact, 150, 195
Loktionov, A. D., 218
Lominadze, V. V., 171
Londau, L. D., 183
Losev, A., 338
Lossky, V., 338
Lozovsky, S. A., 253
Lukianov, A. I., 347
Lukin, N. M., 184
Lunocharsky, A. V., 61
Luppo, I. L., 184
Lutsk-Brody-Rovno, 212
Lvov, Prince, 36, 46
Lysenko, V., 330

M
MacArthur, General Douglas
Machine Tractor Stations, 163, 171, 175, 289
Maginot, 202-203
Maiakovsky, V., 137
Makashov, A., 336
Makhno, N., 110
Maksimillionovich, Georgi, 300
Malenkov, G. M., 191, 254, 258, 262-264, 266-273, 281-282, 287, 289, 299-300, 342
Malevich, K., 139
Maliutin, S., 139
Malyshkin, A., 136
Manchuria, 150, 196, 228
Mandelshtam, N., 338
Mandelshtam, O. E., 184
Manifesto of October, 364
Mannerheim, 205
Mao Tse-tung, 239
Marder, Stephen, 230
Marinsky Palace, 38, 58
Markish, P., 253
Marne, 71
Marshal Plan, 235, 242
Martov, L., 115
Martov, Yu. O., 31, 81
Marx, 185
Marxism, 43, 53, 181, 183, 368, 372
Marxist-Slavophile, 369
Mashkov, I., 139

INDEX 397

Maximalists, 86
Mayakovsky, Vladimir, 181
McCarthy, Senator, 237
Medvedev, R. A., 299, 301
Meierkhold, V. E., 140
Meiji, 105
Melnikov, K., 139
Melnikov, L. G., 265
Menshevik, 31-32, 38-39, 43, 48, 50, 53, 55, 115, 125, 18-19
Menshevik-Defenders, 31
Menshevik-Internationalists, 31, 52, 54, 57, 60-61
Meshkov, V., 139
Mexico, 173
MGB, 253, 255-257, 313
Miasishchev, V. M., 183
Mikhoels, S. M., 140
Mikoyan, Anastas I.
Military Revolutionary Committee, 55, 57-59
Miliukov, Foreign Minister, 37-38, 46-47, 97
Miliutin, V. P., 61
Miller, V. I., 64
Minister of Defense, 253, 282, 299, 346
Minister of Electric Power Stations, 272
Minister of Internal Affairs, 299, 346
Ministry of Economics, 148
Ministry of Foreign Affairs, 343
Ministry of Internal Security, 315
Ministry of Labor, 35
Ministry of Provisions, 35
Ministry of Justice
Minsk, 40, 211, 252, 348
MKhAT, 140
Moldavia, 226, 314
Molotov, V. M., 199, 234, 253, 262, 299
Mongol-Tatar, 361, 374
Mongolia, 150, 344
Montgomery, Field Marshal Bernard, 233
Moonshining, 327
Moonzund Islands, 25, 57
Moravia, 196
Moscow Assn of Proletarian Writers, 137
Moscow City Party, 333
Moscow Conference of September, 215
Moscow Soviet of Workers, 51
Moscow University, 136
Moshkov, Yu. A., 187
Moskalenko, K. S., 266
Moskvin, I. M., 140
Mozambique, 319, 344
MTS, 166, 177
Muchyrin, I. V., 183
Mukhin, V., 185
Munich, 152, 196, 198, 202
Muralov, N. I., 173
Muranov, M. K., 32
Murmansk, 74, 206
Mussolini, Benito, 72, 152, 197
MVD, 264-266, 269, 315, 331
MVD-MGB, 267

N
Nabokov, V., 338
Nagasaki, 229
Nagorno-Karabakh, 341
Narodnoe, 321
Narva, 371
Nashe, 189, 261, 299
National Socialist German Workers Party, 73, 147
NATO, 236, 240, 292
Nazism, 150
Nekrasov, N. V., 46
Nekrasov, V., 46, 188, 315, 338
Nekrasov V. F., 188
Nekrosov, B.
Nemirovich-Danchenko, V. I., 140
NEP, 102, 109, 114-121, 125, 127-129, 131, 134, 138, 140-141, 144, 152, 154, 156, 164, 170-171, 371
NEP Social Model, 116, 140
Nepal, 294
Nepmen, 120, 136, 141
Nesterov, M., 185
Netherlands, 203
Nevsky, Aleksandr, 184, 223
Nevsky, V. I., 45
Nevzerov, 138
New Deal, 146-147
Nicaragua, 319, 344
Nicholas II, 34-35
Nina Andreeva Affair, 341
Ninteenth All-Union CPSU Conference,
Ninth All-Russian Conference
Nixon, Richard, 318
NKVD, 124, 162, 173, 175, 224
NKVD-MGB-MVD, 269-270
NKVD-OGPU, 171
Nogin, V. P., 33, 51, 61
North Atlantic Treaty, 236, 292
Norway, 72, 203, 206, 227
November Revolution, 73
Novgorod, Nizhni, 117, 313
Novikov, Air Marshal, 253
Novo-Ogarevo, 336
Novocherkassk, 96, 296
Novodvorskaya, V., 329
Novorossiisk, 75
Novosibirsk, 189, 261, 291, 301
NSDAP, 147
Nuclear Test Ban Treaty, 295
Nuremberg, 231
NYWT, 35, 265

O
Oblomoshchina, 360
Oblomov, 375
Oblomovshchina, 375
Obradovich, S., 137
Ocherki, 99, 101, 189
October Coup, 58, 76-77, 96, 298
October Plenum, 132, 298
October Revolution, 25, 53, 69, 71, 78-79, 82-83, 89, 100, 118, 120, 136, 149, 221, 234,

398 INDEX

294, 309, 367
Octobrists, 29
Oder River, 227
Odessa, 98, 213, 253
ODN, 128
ODR, 128
ODVF, 128
OGPU, 124-126, 128, 133, 156, 160-162, 167, 172, 175, 269
OGPU-NKVD, 312
Okudzhava, B., 315
Old Guard, 131, 134, 172, 174
Oppokov, G. I., 61
Order Number One, 34, 37
Order of Victory, 309
Ordzhonikidze, G. K., 159
Orekhovo-Zuevo, 45
Orlov, Yu., 313
Orwell, G., 339
OSA, 139
Oshchepkov, P. K., 183
Oshepkov, P. I., 183
Osinsky, N., 78, 88, 91, 131
OST, 139
Ostroumova-Lebedeva, A., 139
Ostrovsky, N. A., 184

P
Pakistan, 294
Pamphilov, E., 356
Party Control Commission, 174, 257
Pasternak, Boris, 292
Patolichev, N. S., 265
Patriarch Aleksei II, 355
Pauker, Anna, 235
Paulus, 219
Paustovsky, K., 276, 310
Pavlov, D. G., 218
Pavlov, I. P., 183
Pavlov, P. A., 108
Pavlov, V. S., 335, 346
Pearl Harbor, 216
Peasants Red Army, 258
Peking, 196
Penal Colonists, 128
Perestroika, 191, 323, 326, 328-329, 334, 337, 339-341, 345, 348, 356-357, 371-372
Pereverzev, P. N., 38
Persian Gulf, 344
Personality Cult, 258, 264, 268, 273-275, 277, 300
Persov, S. D., 253
Pervukhin, M. G., 299
Petain, Marshal, 203
Peter I, 370-371
Peter III, 375
Petliakov, V. M., 183
Petrichenko, S. M., 111
Petrograd, 30-32, 34, 37-38, 40-45, 47, 49-51, 53, 55-58, 61-62, 64-66, 76, 82, 84-85, 91, 96, 99-100, 110-111, 113
Petrograd Bolshevik Committee, 65
Petrograd Military District, 38

Petrov, E., 184
Petrov, V., 184
Petrov-Vodkin, K., 139
Piatakov, G. L., 131
Piatakov, Iu. L., 173
Pilniak, B., 137, 338
Pimenov, Yu., 185
Piontlovsky, S. A., 184
Pipes, R., 66
Piterskie, 64
Platonov, A., 138
Platonov, S. F., 184
Plekhanov, G. V., 33
Plushch, L., 313
Podgorny, N. V., 304, 307, 309
Podvoisky, N. I., 45, 55
Poletaev, N., 137
Poliakov, Yu. A., 142
Polozkov, I. K., 338
Ponomarenko, P., 254
Popov, G. H., 190, 329
Popov, Left SR D. I., 95
Popper, K., 339
Port Arthur, 293
Portnov, V. P., 65
Portugal, 149
Poshekhonov, A. V., 39
Potemkin, The Battleship, 184
Potresov, A. N., 31
Potsdam, 228, 233-234
Potsdam Conference, 228
Pravda, 45, 187-188, 190, 264, 341
Preobrazhensky, E. A., 47, 88, 115, 131, 189
Preparliament, 52, 54-55, 57-58
Prishvin, M., 136
Pristavkin, A., 338
Prokofiev, S., 250
Prokopovich, S. N., 119
Proletariat, 33, 38, 54, 56, 59, 65, 83, 93, 109, 116, 124, 136, 142, 149, 170, 179, 185, 284
Proshyan, P. P., 31
Protasov, L. G., 100
Provisional Revolutionary Committee, 41, 111
Pugachev, Emelian, 375
Pugachevshchina, 360, 375
Pugo, B. K., 346
Pusan, 239

Q
Quadruple Alliance, 73, 87, 98
Quadruple Treaty, 102

R
Rabinowitch, A., 339
Radek, K. V., 173
Raik, Laslo, 235
Railway Commissariat, 93
Rakovsky, Kh. G., 173
Rakozi, M., 266
Rapallo, 107
RAPP, 137-139
Raskolnikov, F. F., 45
Rasputin, Valentin, 181

Razgon, L., 338
RCP, 190
Reagan, Ronald, 343
Red Crescent Societies, 128
Red Cross, 97, 128
Red Guard, 57, 78, 80
Red Square, 313
Reichstag, 27, 147
Reisner, L., 122
Remizov, A., 137
Republican Party, 330
Revolution of Minds, 337, 340
Revolutionary Military Council, 131
Revolutionary Staff, 55
Rhineland, 150, 195
Riazanov, D. B., 127
Ribbentrop-Molotov Pact, 200
Riga, 25, 42
Riutin, M. N., 171
RKP, 100
Rodionov, M. I., 243
Rokossovsky, K. K., 222
Romania, 320
Romm, M., 310
Roosevelt, Franklin D., 146
Rozanov, V., 338
RSDRP, 33, 65-66
RSFSR, 75, 106-107, 243, 280, 285, 292, 335-337, 345, 351
RSFSR Artists, 292
RSFSR Communist Party, 336
RSFSR Writers, 292
RTsKhIDNI, 101
Rumania, 103, 205, 211, 227, 235, 344
Rus, Old, 361
Russell, B., 342
Russia, Vice-President of, 354
Russian Assn of Proletarian Writers, 137
Russian Central Committee Bureau, 32
Russian Christian Democratic Movement, 330
Russian Communist Party, 89, 94, 100, 112, 114, 123, 138, 142, 253, 351
Russian Communist Party of Bolsheviks, 89, 94, 100, 112, 114, 123, 138, 142
Russian Extraordinary Commission, 81
Russian Federation, 122-123, 244, 253, 330, 351, 353
Russian Federation Council of Ministers, 244, 253
Russian National Assembly, 351
Russian National Democratic Party, 330
Russian Revolution of October, 71, 149
Russian Social Democratic Workers, 33, 65
Russian Soviet Federated Socialist Republic, 106, 153
Russian Supreme Soviet, 347
Russian White House, 347
Russo-Japanese War, 194
Rutskoy, A. V.
Ruzhkov, N., 336
RVS, 131
Rybach, 205
Rybakov, A., 315, 338

Rybkin, I. P., 356
Rychagov, P. V., 218
Rykov, A. I., 33, 61, 78
Rykov, A. M., 173
Ryzhkov, N. I., 325

S
Saarland, 195
Sablin, V. M., 314
Saburov, M. V., 299
Sadovsky, A. D., 55
Sakharov, Andrei Dmitrievitch, 313
SALT-1, 318
Sarian, M., 139
Sats, N., 185
SBSE, 318
Schellenburg, V., 224
Schulenburg, F., 209
Sebastopol, 98
Second All-Russian Congress of Peasants, 82
Second All-Russian Congress of Soviets, 54, 59
Second Congress, 51, 54, 59-62, 82-83, 351-352
Second Five Year Plan, 177-178
Second Petrograd Party Conference, 47
Second World War, 149, 165, 179, 193, 200-202, 204, 210, 215, 220, 229-231, 233, 255
Seliunin, V., 340
Selvinsky, A., 137
Semenov, N. N., 182
Semenov, S., 138
Serafimovich, A., 138
Serapion Brothers, 136, 143
Serb, 75
Serebriakov, L. P., 132
Sergeeva-Tsensky, S., 137
Seven Year Plan, 283, 290
Seventeenth Party Congress, 172, 177
Seventh All-Russian Conference, 33, 65
Seventh Army, 112
Seventh Extraordinary Congress, 89, 100
Seventh Party Congress, 29
Shadr, I., 185
Shakhurin, Minister, 253
Shalamov, Varlam, 251
Shanghai, 196
Shaporin, Yu., 185, 250
Shatalin, S., 335
Shatrov, M., 339
Shchukin, B. V., 140
Shchusev, A. V., 140
Shelepin, A. N., 307
Shepilov, 281-282
Shevardnadze, Eduard A., 335, 343-344, 356
Shilov, A., 315
Shkiriatov, M., 257
ShKM, 135
Shliapnikov, A. G., 61, 65
Shmelev, N., 338, 340
Sholokov, Mikhail, 184
Shostakovich, D., 185, 250

400   INDEX

Shostakovsky, V., 330
Shreider, G. I., 61
Shteinberg, I. Z., 82
Shterenberg, D., 139
Sibachev, N. V., 261
Siberia, 74, 110, 222, 224, 251-252, 259, 270
Simonov, Konstantin, 260
Siniavsky, A., 313
Sixteenth Party Conference, 156, 159
Sixth Bolshevik Party Congress, 47
Sixth Party Congress, 32, 47
Skobeltsyn, D. V., 182
Skvortsov, I. I., 61
Skvortsov-Stepanov, I. I., 136
Slansky, Rudolph, 235
Slavin, M. M., 65
Slavophilism, 359, 374
Smilga, I. T., 42
Smirnov, D. P., 172
Smirnov, I. N., 132
Smoktunovsky, I., 310
SNG, 348
SNK, 78
SNKh, 286
Sobchak, 328
Social Democratic Association, 330
Social Democratic Party of Russia, 330
Social Democrats, 31, 149
Social Revolutionary Party, 30
Socialist Revolutionaries, 125
Society of Contemporary Architects, 139
Society of Easel Artists, 139
Society of Muscovite Artists, 139, 17-18
Society of Political Convicts, 128
Sokolnikov, G. Ia., 173
Sokolov, A. K., 188
Solidarity, 37, 72, 179, 320
Soloviev, S. M., 359
Soloviev, V., 338
Solzhenitsyn, A. I., 338
Somme River, 64
Sorokin, P., 126, 338
Southeast Asia, 216, 344
Soviet Army, 150, 215, 227, 250, 252, 258
Soviet Bloc, 235-238
Soviet Communist Party, 267, 278
Soviet Control Commission, 174
Soviet of All-Russian Peasants, 44, 61
Soviet of Peasants, 44, 51, 61
Soviet Open Public Association, 313
Soviet Peasantry, 190, 290
Soviet-Finnish War, 208
Soviet-German Nonaggression Pact, 339
Sovnarkom, 61, 78, 80-82, 89-90, 171, 173-174
Spain, 149-150, 179, 196
Special Far Eastern Army, 150
Spiridonova, M. A., 31, 95
Sputnik, 291
SR, 30-32, 38-39, 43, 50, 53, 55-56, 95, 100, 125
SR Central Committee, 50
SR-Menshevik Central Executive Committee, 45
SRs, Left, 48, 51-52, 54, 56-57, 59-62, 81-86, 89, 91, 94-95

SRs, Right, 59
Sri Lanka, 232
SS, 148, 221
SShA, 187, 261
SSSR, 66, 142, 188-191, 261, 301, 321-322
Stalin, Joseph Vissarionovich, 32-33, 42, 47, 61, 79, 99, 124, 128-134, 149-150, 154-156, 158-159, 161, 163, 167, 170-174, 176, 179-180, 183-188, 190, 192, 198-201, 203-207, 209-215, 217-219, 221-227, 234-235, 238-242, 244-245, 247, 249-251, 253-260, 262-269, 273-275, 277-278, 280-281, 283-285, 292-293, 299-300, 302-303, 307-308, 310, 316, 333, 339-341, 369
Stalingrad, 216-217, 219-221, 230
Stanislavsky, K. S., 140
Starodubtsev, V. A., 346, 356
State Bank, 78, 117-118
State Control Commissariat, 93
State Labor Camp Administration, 162
State Machine-Building Plant Trust, 117
State Planning Commission, 117, 158, 244, 285, 301
State Scientific-Economic Council, 301
Sten, Ya. E., 184
Stepankov, 358
Stern, L. S., 253
Stimson, G., 228
Studebaker, 215
Sukhanov, Menshevik N. N., 55
Sulakhshin, S., 330
Sumeiko, Former Vice-Premier V. F., 356
Supreme Economic Council, 78, 117, 159, 162, 166
Supreme War Council, 218
Suslov, M. A., 307
Sverdlov, Constituent Assembly Ia. M.
Sverdlova, K. T., 99
Sweden, 73, 182
Switzerland, 32, 182
Syria, 232, 294
Syrtsov, S. N., 171

T

Tadzhikistan, 336
Taft-Hartly Act, 237
Tairov, A. Ya., 140
Tamm, I. E., 291
Tarasov, A. K., 140
Tarasov-Rodionov, 138
Tarkovsky, A., 315
Tarnovsky, K., 315
Tarpova, Natalia, 138
TASS, 209
Tatars, 223, 280
Tatimov, M. B., 188
Tauride Palace, 44, 85, 99
Teheran Conference, 225-226
Tenth Party Congress, 57, 112-113, 129-130
Teodorovich, I. A., 61
The Agrarian Revolution, 66, 99, 170
The All-Russian Constituent Assembly, 100

INDEX   401

The Great Terror, 174, 177, 218, 231, 251, 260, 339
The USSR National Economy, 321
Third Cavalry, 49
Third Communist International, 72
Third Congress of Peasants, 86
Third Congress of People's Deputies, 332
Third Corps, 49, 61
Third World War, 165, 240, 272, 295
Thirteenth Congress, 132
Tikhon, Patriarch, 126
Timoshenko, S. K., 208
Titkov, A. E., 142
Tito, Joseph Broz, 235
Tiziakov, A. I., 346
Tokyo Bay, 229
Tolmachev, V. M., 172
Tolstoy, A. N., 184
Tomsky, M. P., 127
Tovstonogov, G., 310
Toynbee, Arnold, 357, 374
Trade Union Council of December, 191
Transcaucasia, 122
Transcaucasian Democratic Federal Rep, 79
Transcaucasian Federation, 123
Transcaucasian Republic, 79, 123
Trauberg, L., 184
Travkin, N., 330
Treaty of Brest-Litovsk, 86
Treaty of Rappalo, 104
Treaty of Versailles, 71,102-103, 107, 150-151,195
Tretiakov, S., 184
Trifonov, Yu., 338
Tripartite Pact, 198
Triple Alliance, 230
Triumf, D., 188
Trotsky, L. D., 32-33, 44-45, 51, 54-55, 60-62, 64, 87-88, 100, 115, 130-134, 143, 173, 183, 340
Trotsky-Zinovievite, 173
Trotskyites, 180, 278
Truman, President Harry S., 234
Trutovsky, V. E., 82
Tsereteli, Menshevik I. G., 39
Tsevaeva, A., 338
TsGAIPD, 65, 101
Tsiolkovsky, K. E., 182
Tsipko, A., 340
TsK, 66, 301
Tsvetaeva, M. I, 184
TU-104, 291
Tucker, R., 339
Tukhachevky, M. N., 109
Tuleev, O., 336
Tupolev, A. N., 183, 291
Turkey, 108, 293, 295
Turkistan, 110
Turkmenistan, 336
Twentieth Party Congress, 273, 278, 280, 288, 294
Twenty-First CPSU Congress, 310
Twenty-First Party Congress, 283

Twenty-Fourth Party Congress, 308
Twenty-Ninth All-Union Conference, 328
Twenty-Ninth Party Conference, 339
Twenty-Ninth Party Congress, 258
Twenty-Second Congress, 282-283
Twenty-Second Party Congress, 283
Twenty-Seventh Congress, 327, 337
Twenty-Third Party Congress, 308

U
U-2, 294
Udenich, 75
Udunian, A. A., 142
Ukraine, 35, 43, 73, 75, 79, 89-90, 98, 110, 122-123, 153-154, 162, 202, 211, 218, 221, 226, 241, 244, 251, 254, 265, 285, 314, 336, 348
Ukrainian Communist Party, 307
Unified Nuclear Research Institute, 291
Union of Soviet Socialist Republics, 123
Union of Soviet Writers, 184
Union Treaty, 123, 335-336, 345-346, 348
Unions of Jurists, 148
United Nations, 216, 230-231, 233, 237, 239,293
United Nations Declaration, 216
United Nations Security Council, 233
United States of America, 255
USSR Academy of Sciences, 291
USSR Council of Ministers, 254, 301
USSR Council of People, 159, 162
USSR Supreme Soviet Presidium, 304, 325
USSR Union of Cinematographers, 292
Ustinov, Marshal Dmitry
Utkin, A. E., 98
Uzbekistan, 222, 285, 323, 336

V
Vakhtangov, E. B., 140
Vanag, H. H., 184
Varangians, 361
Vasilevsky, A. M., 219
Vasiliev, G., 184
Vasiliev, P., 184
VASKhNIL, 182
Vasnetsov, V. M., 140
Vavilov, N. I., 183
VChK, 81
VCP, XV, 190
Venice, 197
Verberov, N. B., 338
Verdun, 64
Veresaev, V., 137
Victory Day, 228
Vietnam, 316-318, 344
Vinogradov, Professor V., 259
VKhUTEMAS, 139
Voinovich, V., 315, 338
Volchek, G., 315
Volga River, 162
Volga-Ural Canal, 265
Volgograd, 216, 356
Volkogonov, D. A., 161
Volobuev, P. V., 65

Voloshin, M., 338
Volsky, A., 352
Voronsky, A., 136
Voroshilov, Defense Commissar K. E., 207
Voznesensky, N. A., 223, 244
VPK, 152, 243
VRK, 55, 58, 81
VSNKh, 117
VTSIK, 61-62, 80
VTsSPS, 279
VVS, 218
Vyborg, 41-42, 184
Vysotsky, V., 315

W
Walesa, Lec, 320
Warsaw Pact, 320
Warsaw Treaty, 292, 318, 320, 344
Washington, 145, 216, 343
Wehrmacht, 212-213, 220-221
West Berlin, 318
White Army, 73, 96, 101
White Guard, 138
Wilhelm, Count, 94
Wilson, President Woodrow, 102
Winter Palace, 59-60
World War I, 105
World War II, 290

Y
Yagoda, H., 173
Yakir, P., 313
Yakovlev, A., 346
Yakovlev, A. N., 325, 339
Yakovlev, N., 357-358
Yalta, 227, 233-234
Yanaev, Vice President G. I., 346
Yanshin, A., 292
Yasensky, B., 184
Yat-sen, Sun, 108
Yavlinsky, G., 335
Yazov, Marshal D. T., 346
Yemen, 108
Yezhov, N. I., 173
Young, Owen D., 105
Young Communist League, 175
Young Plans, 105
Ypres, 26
Yugoslavia, 71, 103, 235, 237-238, 266, 293, 320
Yugov, A., 119
Yurenev, 62

Z
Zabolotsky, N., 184
Zacharov, M., 315
Zalezhsky, V. N., 65
Zametki, Bukharin N. I., 187, 21-22
Zamiatin, E., 137, 338
Zaslavskaya, Academician T., 306
Zelenin, I. E., 188
Zemskov, V. N., 261
Zemskovym, V., 188

Zemsky, 362
Zernovaia, 187
Zhatva, 188
Zhelev, Zh., 339
Zhemchuzhina, P., 253
Zhid, A., 192
Zhigulin, A., 338
Zhirinovsky, V., 336, 356
Zhiromsky, V. B., 189
Zholtovsky, I. V., 140
Zhukov, General Georgy K., 214
Zimianin, M. V., 265
Zinoviev, G. E., 33
Zinoviev, G. V., 72, 172
Zinoviev, Grigory, 108
Zolotarev, V. A., 142
Zorg, Richard, 209
Zoshchenko, M., 136, 138
Zvenia, 99